IS PIGUET · LUDMILA KLEPIKOW · LUDWIG ZOBRIST-KRÜSI · LUIGI MARCHESIN · LUIGI SCUOTTO · LUKAS KEEL
ZIA KASPER · MANFRED REICHMUTH · MANUELA MARTY · MANUELA SALM · MA...
RC FISCHER · MARC HUBER · MARC SULJIC · MARCEL DUBACHER · MARCELL...
RCO VOTTA · MARCO ZEMP · MARGRIT KOLLER · MARGRIT LANG-VON BERGEN...
LEMENTE-PANOA · MARIA DA SILVA-FERRADAS · MARIA GRECO-LAPERGOLA · M...
RINIELLO · MARIA ROBLEDO-ROMAN · MARIA SUOZZI · MARIA ANTONIA MARE-M...
NAL · MARIE-LUISE BERGMANN · MARINE CHAVANIS · MARK FREEBORN · MARK...
RKUS JAEGGI · MARKUS KAUFMANN · MARKUS KIENLE · MARKUS SAGER · MARKUS SCHMID · MARTIN BEERLI
RTINA BINZ · MARTINA DIRR · MASAKAZU HARUYAMA · MATTHIAS BRUN · MATTHIAS HOLZINGER · MATTHIAS WEBER
TTHIAS ZIMMERMANN · MAXIME REVILLOUD · MEHMET LIMANI · MEIKE ALLSTAEDT · MELANIE SCHÖTZ · MEN
AUCH · MICHAEL GERBER · MICHAEL GYSSLER MICHAEL KLARIN · MICHAEL KOLLER · MICHAEL
RKWALDER · MICHAEL MEYENBERG · MICHAEL SCHWAB · MICHAEL THIEL · MICHAEL TOBLER
CHAEL VOGEL · MICHAEL WEHRMEYER MICHAEL WELCH · MICHAEL JUFER · MICHAELA
MMERLADE · MICHAELA WERNLE · MICHELE COSCIA · MICHÈLE UEBELHART · MICK

ARNWORTH · MILENA MEIER · MIRIAM EGGER · MIRJAM KNOPP · MITSUJI KUMADA
ITSUTOSHI NOZAKI · MONICA TIZZONE- FUCHS · MONIKA GULER · MONIKA KUHN
ORITZ MAIER · MUSTAFA OSMA · MUSTAFI FJORIME · NADINE BURRI · NADJA VON ROHR
ATALIA DÄTWYLER · NERMIN TÜRKEKUL NICOLE BUSSLINGER · NICOLE LÜSCHER-
RCARI · NIKOLAJ AJAGANOV · NORBERT STEINLE · NORBERT WIRSCHUN · OLIVER HENKEL
LIVER WALKER · OLIVIER BENOIT ORIANA SCHMID · PASCAL BRÖNNIMANN
ASCAL SPIESS · PATRIC BÜRGE · PATRICK BORER · PATRICK MÜLLER · PATRIK
RBACH · PATRIZIA ROTHENBERGER PATRIZIA SALERNO · PATRIZIA STRÖBEL
AUL ALLEMANN · PAUL GEHRIG · PAUL RHYNER · PAULINE PERKS · PEPO KISSLING
ETER MENDE · PETER MÜLLER · PETRA MAIR · PHILIPP BRUN · PHILIPP HAURI · PIA ZIMMERMANN · PIERRE DUBOIS
AHEL SCHMID-ISELI · RAINER BUSSMANN · RAINER HAAS · RALF W. JASCHEK · RAPHAEL JAQUET · RAPHAEL
OSETTI · RAPHAEL SCHALLER · REBECCA BLUM · REBECCA BURGER · REBECCA GLAISEN · REINER TAGLINGER
NÉ MEISTER · RENÉ MEULI · RENÉ NIETLISPACH · RENÉ SCHLUMPF · RETO KRÄHENBÜHL · RETO RÜEGGER
ICHARD BOLT · RITA MARCHESIN-BERNARDO · ROB VAN DINTER · ROBERT FREI · ROBERTO DA SILVA · ROGER
CHWANDER · ROLF HEHL · ROLF SCHMID · ROMAN ETTERLIN · ROMAN SUTER · ROSA IVELI MEJIA ROA · RUDOLF
UNZIKER · RUDOLF KARRER · RUDOLF WYSS · RUEDI SCHÄRER · RUNE GULBRANSEN · RUNE STOKKEBEKK · RUTH
AUROUX-WACKER · RUTH WYSS-RIEDER · SABINE BUSSLEHNER · SABRINA ASCHWANDEN · SABRINA HUSCHECK
AMIR KONJALIC · SAMUEL MAIER · SANDRA BACHMANN · SANDRA SCHNEIDER · SANDRO AMATUCCI · SANDRO
ÖRTSCHER · SARAH DUBACH · SARAH NEUHAUS · SARAH PFLÜGL · SARAH TREICHLER · SARAH URECH · SASCHA
AMPMANN · SASCHA SALZMANN · SAVERIO PRESTIA · SEIETSU TOMIMURO · SEM HEDIGER · SERAINA BÜHLER
EVDIJE SACIRI-AVDILJI · SHAHIN BAECHLER · SHINTARO NAKAOKA · SIMONA FÄS · SIMONE BRUN · SONJA ESPOSITO
ONJA GALLITZENDÖRFER · SONJA HENKEL · SONJA SPACCAROTELLA · STEFAN BAUER · STEFAN MERKT · STEFAN
INIGER · STEINAR MARTINSEN · STEPHAN BÜCHLI · STEPHAN BRAUN · STEPHANIE GRUNDER · STEVE MC
AUGHLIN · STUART DUNCAN BROWN · SUE EDWARDS · SUSANA FIECHTER · SUSANNE BIETSCH · SUSANNE
OLLINGER · SUSANNE COLOMBO · SUSANNE FRÜH · SUSANNE KASPAR · SYLKE LAZAREWITZ · SYLVIA BEMMERL
YLVIA ZANKL · TAKAHISA HORIMATSU · TAMARA GRATWOHL · TANJA KÜHNIS · TATJANA RUOTOLO-ZILIOTTO
ESSA ANDERSON · THERESIA GRUBER-POELL · THOMAS BROCK · THOMAS HÖLZLE · THOMAS KNECHT · THOMAS
CHUMACHER · THOMAS WASER · THOMAS HODEL · THOMAS SCHETTY · THOMAS SENF · TOMAS DVORAK
ROY TRIMMER · UDO RAUNJAK · UELI WÜRGLER · ULF SÄNGER · ULRICH KLING · URS EGLI · URS KÜCHLER · UWE
OTTSCHALK · VALERIE BOSMAN · VEZIRA KONJALIC · VLORA IBRAHIMAJ · WALTER DIETIKER · WALTER LEHMANN
ALTER TELSER · WILL PENNEY · WILLIAM SUPPLE III · WOLFGANG IHL · WOLFGANG SCHUSTER · WOLFGANG
TICKLER · WOLFGANG WEBER · YLDIZ UENGÜDER · YUKITO ARIMA · YUMIKO NISHIKAWA · ZELINDA PAHL

www.as-verlag.ch

© AS Verlag & Buchkonzept AG, Zürich 2011
Editor: Mammut Sports Group AG
Layout: Urs Bolz, Heinz von Arx, www.vonarxgrafik.ch, Zürich
Translation: Nadja Stracey & James Heath, edited by Tim Carruthers
Proofreading: Adrian von Moos, Zürich
Printing: B & K Offsetdruck GmbH, Ottersweier
Cover: Grossbuchbinderei Josef Spinner GmbH, Ottersweier
ISBN 978-3-909111-88-6

150 YEARS STORIES

Editor: Mammut Sports Group AG

Lead Author: Karin Steinbach Tarnutzer

Editorial Team: Stephanie Grunder,
Karin Hörhager, Adrian Huber,
Kathrin Malzach, Jutta Römmelt

AS Verlag

CONTENTS

DANI ARNOLD, PROFESSIONAL ALPINIST, RECOMMENDS:

19

"Nowadays it is impossible to imagine living a life like Ulrich Inderbinen's – truly remarkable. Let's see how many ascents of the Matterhorn I manage to clock up in the course of my career as a mountain guide."

DAVID LAMA, PROFESSIONAL CLIMBER, RECOMMENDS:

26

"Those old school women climbers were just brilliant – hats off to them! Nowadays it's taken for granted that the girls climb like we do, but back then Loulou, Betty and Yvette were true pioneers."

ROBERT SUTER, GROUP CEO OF CONZZETA AG, RECOMMENDS:

48

"With the Mary Woodbridge campaign, Mammut took a new creative path. It was the starting signal for interactive communication through social media like blogs, forums, Facebook, Twitter and YouTube. Mammut now has a huge Internet community."

PETER BRABECK-LETMATHE, CHAIRMAN OF THE BOARD OF DIRECTORS OF NESTLÉ, RECOMMENDS:

60

"Mammut's journey from a niche alpine brand to an internationally active outdoor equipment manufacturer makes impressive reading. The correct assessment of what is achievable and the pleasure derived from this achievement are comprehensible."

REINHOLD MESSNER, EXTREME MOUNTAINEER, RECOMMENDS:

101

«Oswald Oelz gives an impressive description of the consequences of oxygen deprivation at altitude. In 1978, when Peter Habeler and I climbed Everest for the first time without supplementary oxygen, no one was able to estimate what that meant exactly, or indeed if it would be possible."

RAJA MUDA, CROWN PRINCE OF PERLIS, RECOMMENDS:

108

"It was a great honor for us to host the Mammut Team in the Malaysian state of Perlis when they came to climb some new routes on our cliffs. For this reason, the report about this Teamtrip is naturally very dear to our hearts."

ANNA STÖHR, BOULDERER,
RECOMMENDS:

116

"Reading Anke Hinrichs' account of the technical advances that have made it possible for her to enjoy mountain sports in spite of her limited mobility and, above all, the joy that this brings her, really inspired me."

BERNHARD RUSSI, SKI LEGEND,
RECOMMENDS:

120

"Ernst Kohler from the Swiss Air Rescue service gives a very balanced assessment of the fine line between risk appeal and irresponsible attitudes to danger. As a mountain sports enthusiast who likes to push his own personal boundaries, I enjoyed this differentiated way of looking at things."

@ Further information about contributions marked with this symbol can be found at
www.mammut.ch/150stories

A SMALL ROPEMAKER'S CLIMB TO SUCCESS
Benedikt Pfister | Aargau/Switzerland

Starting out is never easy. When he started out as a ropemaker in the 1860s, Kaspar Tanner was just about able to feed the seven members of his family. He set up his own business in 1862, following a three-year apprenticeship in Wohlen in the canton of Aargau in Switzerland and the then usual few years as a traveling craftsman, which he spent mainly in Germany. Aargau was different to other cantons in that it was no longer compulsory to be a member of a trade guild (the legislation was abolished in 1860). In other cantons, the practice continued until 1874.

Kaspar Tanner kept his materials in a small wooden shed in Dintikon, a municipality in the district of Lenzburg in the canton of Aargau. He worked in front of the shed, twisting and braiding his rope. There is a saying from the time: "Wenn Meister Seiler rückwärts geht, beweist, dass er sein Fach versteht" (A rope maker who walks backwards knows his trade). However, Kaspar Tanner soon decided that he wanted to move forwards, not backwards. In 1878, he moved his family and his business to Lenzburg, the next largest town, which had a population of 2,700. In return for a small fee to the local council, he was allowed to use the public right of way next to his home as a ropewalk to braid and coil his ropes. But he still had a long way to go before he could set up his own factory, as life was not easy for craftsmen in Lenzburg at that time.

The state of Illinois in the United States also has a town called Lenzburg, which lies next to New Athens. This is because in the 19th century, a large number of workers emigrated from Aargau to seek new opportunities in the United States. Many of them were craftsmen from the Lenzburg region. The town in Switzerland suffered from the fact that it had no major river – an important factor for industrial development. Besides, the newly established railway line from Zurich to Olten bypassed Lenzburg. At the same time, the industrial revolution put an end to the traditional work that many Swiss farmers carried out to supplement their incomes, especially in the winter months. The era of cottage industries and their involvement in the small-scale production of cotton, silk and straw goods was over. By the end of the 19th century, new companies such as Hero, a tinned food factory (founded in 1886), and the Wisa-Gloria toy company (founded in 1882) started to shape modern Lenzburg.

Oscar Tanner   Kaspar Tanner

Craftsmen suffered under this modernization and the increasingly expensive mechanization of their trades. At the same time, they found it difficult to compete with the new factories. In response to this serious situation, the *Aargauische Handwerks- und Gewerbeverein* (Aargau Crafts and Trades Association) was set up in 1863. One year later, a section was started in Lenzburg, specifically to promote the interests of small businesses.

Kaspar Tanner had been able to continue to feed his family – thanks also to his son Oscar, who by now was working alongside him. Oscar Tanner was interested in the newly emerging world of finance and originally intended to go into banking. He later decided to opt for ropemaking and took over the family business in 1897 when his father stopped taking an active role in the actual making of the ropes. "I went about building up my new business with great drive and tireless zeal," Oscar Tanner wrote in his memoirs.

Tanner Jr. also knew what he wanted – to continue to move the business forward. He got on his bike and went out to find new customers. In 1900, ropemakers mainly produced ropes for agricultural use, i.e. for wagons, for securing hay or for lead reins for horses and cows. So the young Tanner went out to visit the farms and companies of the surrounding area. At the same time, he invested in the company to modernize production facilities. New machines were used to produce new products, for example cords for rucksacks. This proved too much for Tanner Sr. As an "old school" craftsman with little love for "new-fangled" machinery, he withdrew from the business completely. Now his son could really move forward. Thanks to his willingness to embrace innovation, Oscar Tanner found a customer who was to prove very important to the development of the company: the Swiss governmental department for war material procurement.

From 1914, there was a shortage of hemp, the raw material required to make ropes. However, because Oscar Tanner was also supplying the military, he was still able to acquire hemp. At the end of the war in 1918, he was able to expand the business and buy in new machinery. In the years that followed, the small ropemaking business was transformed into a small company. In 1919, Oscar Tanner turned his sole trader company into a stock corporation. The new *Seilerwarenfabrik Lenzburg AG* now belonged to the *Schweizerische Bindfadenfabrik* (Swiss Rope and Cords Mill) in Flurlingen in the canton of Zurich in Switzerland. Oscar Tanner continued as director of the new company and led its commercial operations until he left in 1924.

In the first half of the 20th century, the production of ropes for agricultural use declined due to increasing mechanization. However, thanks to its own machinery, the company was able to enter new markets. It started producing high-quality ropes for mountaineering in the 1940s and 1950s. These ropes were difficult to make and were significantly more expensive. To demonstrate their superior quality, a red thread was included in the rope, with a lead seal of quality depicting a mammoth attached to one end. The animal giving the company its name was born.

CLIMBING – THE ANTIDOTE TO ACROPHOBIA?

Tanja Delfs | Climbing wall

Phobias come in all shapes and sizes: claustrophobia, arachnophobia, fear of flying – and fear of heights, or acrophobia. I experienced the latter for the first time when I was six years old, on the steps of the Kaprun cable car. Stepping out of the cable car in those days, you had a wonderful, unobstructed view through the metal grid of the steps down to the gulley and the stream way below. The view was rather lost on me, however. I threw my skis and poles down and clung to the railings, screaming. There was nothing in the world that was going to get me to let go and walk down those steps of my own free will.

In the years that followed, I managed to cleverly dodge similar situations: trees were left unclimbed, ladders avoided altogether, and in gym classes, I just specialized in floor exercises. With hiking trails in Northern Germany being on the whole relatively flat, that was not a problem for me. It was only when I moved to Switzerland and started to hike in the proper mountains and go on ski tours that I had to confront those old feelings of panic again, feelings that were triggered at the grand height of just one meter above ground level. Since hiking in the mountains and ski touring had become my passions, something had to change.

Just how do you overcome a fear of heights, though? With arachnophobia you use spiders, to combat a fear of flying, you fly – so with a fear of heights, it must be by getting up high. The stupid thing was that in the past, when I was in a 'hairy' situation, I used to just let go or jump off. On the bars in the gym, behavior like that is just painful, but on exposed hiking trails it can be tantamount to a death wish. So I decided that a rope was called for, to provide an element of security. It was clear that I had to start rock climbing.

On the climbing wall it took a while for the dizziness and mild nausea to go away, but I forced myself whilst climbing to take stock and look down every now and then. Once I had mastered this first step at the climbing wall, it was time to get out onto real rock. To begin with, it felt like I was back to square one. As soon as a route got a bit steeper, I just refused point blank to do it. But my climbing buddy's immense patience and encouraging words, plus some careful training on how to fall at the climbing wall, gave me the confidence to keep on trying. At first, I was only seconding of course. Just the thought of leading turned my legs to jelly and pressed the P for panic button. But I am now working diligently on that, too, and bit by bit, I am leading easier routes.

I have noticed a change in my attitude to heights in other areas apart from climbing now. When I am skiing or hiking, I can now tackle situations that I would have previously had a complete mental block with. It doesn't always work straight away, and there are still times when I freeze. What is important is to have good companions, who can talk me through things when I get to an exposed section, who let me take my time or, if needs be, will belay me on bits that others will have no need for a rope. One thing is clear as day though: I can only reduce my fear of heights if I keep on putting myself in those situations. And after all, what could be nicer than spending a sunny day climbing on warm rock, ski touring or hiking?

Oh yes, and I now count climbing amongst my passions just as much as skiing and hiking. The therapy must be working, I guess.

"I don't believe it's that important to reach
the summit. You can always come back
and have another go. It's not the summit that
you remember, but the things that happen along
the way. The nicest thing is to know that
you can rely on somebody else and that they
can rely on you."

Mo Anthoine

3

BREAKDOWN
Reto Rüegger | Frauenfeld/Switzerland

150 Pairs of Mamook GTX take the equivalent of three weeks' holiday in production.

If you take all the individual components of a pair of Mamook GTX and lay them out, they stretch 12.4 meters. Multiply that by all the Mamook sales since Mammut first started manufacturing footwear (spring 2009) and you get 124 kilometers, equivalent to the distance between Berne and Zurich.

A Mamook GTX boot is made up of 103 individual parts. Multiply this by all the Mamook sales since Mammut first started manufacturing footwear (spring 2009), and you could give every inhabitant of Geneva a part (= 206,000 individual parts).

The materials used to make a Mamook GTX have a total surface area of 0.6213 square meters, and therefore 1.2426 square meters a pair. If you multiply this figure by the number of Mamook boots manufactured up to summer 2012, the total surface area would be 12,426 square meters, equivalent to two football fields.

4

Foam
provides padding and individual
shape as well as a comfortable
fit and cushioning.

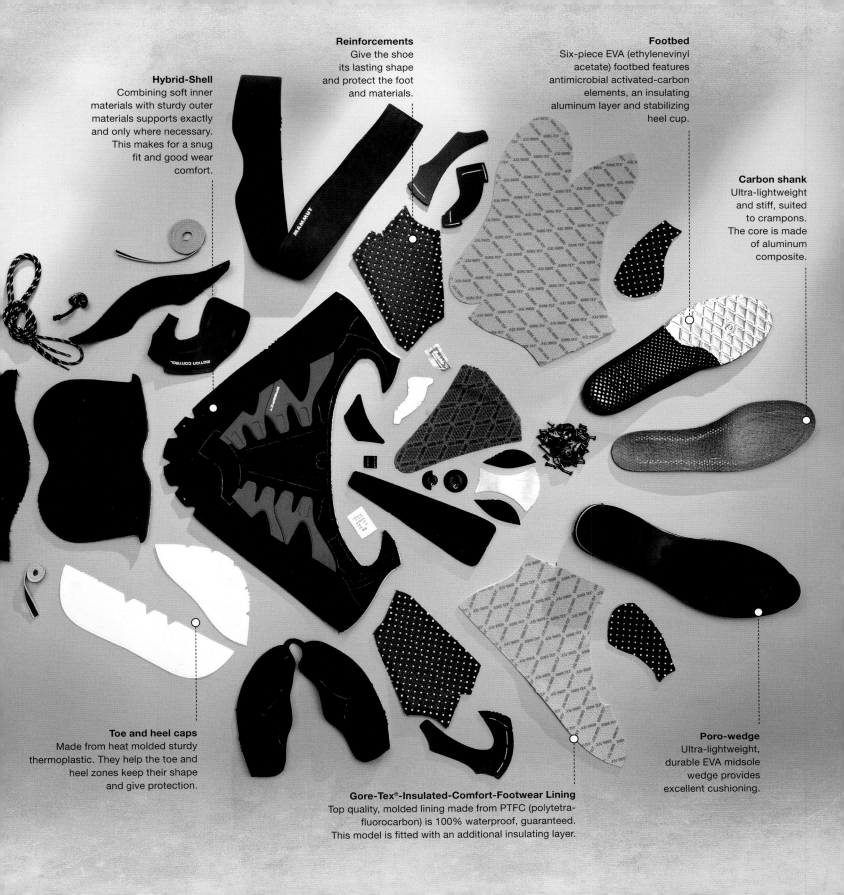

Hybrid-Shell
Combining soft inner materials with sturdy outer materials supports exactly and only where necessary. This makes for a snug fit and good wear comfort.

Reinforcements
Give the shoe its lasting shape and protect the foot and materials.

Footbed
Six-piece EVA (ethylenevinyl acetate) footbed features antimicrobial activated-carbon elements, an insulating aluminum layer and stabilizing heel cup.

Carbon shank
Ultra-lightweight and stiff, suited to crampons. The core is made of aluminum composite.

Toe and heel caps
Made from heat molded sturdy thermoplastic. They help the toe and heel zones keep their shape and give protection.

Gore-Tex®-Insulated-Comfort-Footwear Lining
Top quality, molded lining made from PTFC (polytetra-fluorocarbon) is 100% waterproof, guaranteed. This model is fitted with an additional insulating layer.

Poro-wedge
Ultra-lightweight, durable EVA midsole wedge provides excellent cushioning.

Yves and Claude Remy

MAKING A NAME FOR THEMSELVES IN CLIMBING HISTORY
Albert Wenk I Around the world

If you are a serious climber, then the name will be a familiar one. And if you've ever climbed one of their routes, then you are unlikely to forget the name in a hurry: Remy. Those who repeat their first ascents are constantly impressed by the boldness of the routes climbed by the Remy brothers, not to mention the fantastic lines. Gastlosen, Furka, Grimsel, Handegg, Sanetsch, Miroir d'Argentine, Schöllenen, Titlis, Tällistock, Wendenstöcke, Engstlenalp, Rothorn, Hintisberg, Schlossberg, Fieschertal, Salbitschijen, Graue Wand, Col du Pillon, Leysin, Petit Clocher du Portalet, Mont Blanc, Verdon and Presles – the traces of their extraordinary handiwork are still to be seen today as they continue to develop route after route. Their thirst for adventure has taken them to England, Italy, Sardinia, Kazakhstan, Yugoslavia, Jordan and the Greek island of Kalymnos.

At the start of the 1980s, news started to spread of the legendary climbing abilities of the brothers, Claude (born in 1953) and his younger brother Yves Remy (born in 1956). One of their milestone climbs was Yves's solo of a 7a route in 1981. The Mammut regional representative for West Switzerland suggested the idea of a partnership with the "wild boys". At that point, I was the Mammut Product Manager and was interested in partnerships based on competence, strength of character, cooperation and a longer term perspective, rather than big names to promote Mammut. This was the start of a win-win situation for Mammut, the Remy brothers and climbing in general. I went to visit them at their parents' house and came away impressed. They were genuine characters who were passionate about their climbing and were certainly not just looking to make a quick buck – we would be able to achieve great things together.

That was 30 years ago. Thirty years of collaborative material testing and the realization of many of their ideas and suggestions have followed, during the course of which a real friendship has developed. After some consideration, Mammut decided to supply the bolts for their first ascents in the Grimsel area, so that these fantastic routes could be made safer and, as a result, made available to a wider climbing public. Back in those days, there were no battery-powered drills. All the holes had to be chiseled into the rock by hand. This by no means held the brothers back in their quest for new routes. At the time, there were no real guidebooks like "Schweiz extrem" or "Schweiz plaisir" and no Internet, and the route cards that Mammut distributed with its annual mountain sports catalogue were an absolute "must" for all climbers. This is how Grimsel was established in 1982, followed by Sanetsch in 1985. Both areas soon became absolute classics. Grimsel is now home to more than 20 routes with 12 to 15 pitches; the crags at Sanetsch have over 4,000 bolts.

Sepp Gschwendtner, the former top climber, once asked me, "Is it true that Mammut pays the Remy brothers per bolt?" He was not the only climber to think this. In fact, Claude and Yves never received a penny from Mammut in all those years. They were given ropes, harnesses, slings, and a certain amount of bolts for their own personal use. In addition, they could purchase further equipment at a discounted rate; they were occasionally given a free T-shirt. You couldn't really call this sponsorship – anyway, it wasn't what the brothers wanted. They identified strongly with their climbing, they lived for it.

Just as they continue to do today, with incredible results. They have remained motivated over four decades of continually climbing new routes. At the end of the 1990s, they stopped counting their first ascents – at the time they had climbed more than 1,000, not including smaller crags. They have developed countless areas, whose routes continued to be maintained, re-bolted and extended to this day. The Remy brothers are still the same as they were in the 1980s, only 30 years older: modest, honest, competent, genuine, motivated and unique. They continue to be real partners.

AND BARRY CAME, TOO
Uwe Gottschalk | Seon/Switzerland

The days when avalanche probes and rescue dogs (in the ideal scenario, descendants of Barry, the famous Saint Bernard dog) were the only means of finding avalanche victims are thankfully long behind us. They are both still indispensible, of course, but the development of electronic avalanche transceivers has significantly increased the chances of survival in the event of avalanche. By emitting an electronic signal, the devices enable fast and precise location of buried victims so that rescue attempts can be started immediately.

In 1968, the Swiss Army commissioned the company Autophon AG to develop an avalanche transceiver. The resulting Barryvox VS 68 was a huge success. Up to 1994, more than 100,000 devices were produced. The VS 68 was superseded by the Barryvox VS 2000 in 1994 and then by the Opto 3000 in 1999. The Opto 3000 was the first transceiver to combine the classic analog and the new digital search modes. Mammut was its sole distributor. By the start of the 21st century, technical advances and new applications suggested it was time to completely redevelop the avalanche transceiver.

A team of 20 engineering and electronic experts set to work on the new prototype. From an engineering point of view, the transceiver needed a very robust waterproof housing that was neither bulky nor heavy. A major effort was made to combine these requirements with an engaging design. As a result, the Pulse Barryvox received the ISPO Outdoor Award and a Volvo Design Award. In terms of its electronic engineering, the Pulse Barryvox is based on a hardware platform which can be continually further developed, providing plenty of potential for the future. Software updates keep the device up to date, so that users don't have to buy a newer model.

The first Pulse Barryvox was released for the 2006/2007 winter season, after two years of research and development and several million Swiss Francs of investment. With its combination of digital and analog modes and full graphic display, the device is technically sophisticated but easy to operate. The transceiver has three antennas for fast and precise locating. It also provides a clear overview in situations involving multiple buried victims, saving valuable time, and its ability to detect vital data makes rescue operations more effective. Following its launch, a few minor updates were released that expanded the range and scope of usage for institutional users.

For winter 2009/2010, the introduction of Firmware 3.0 included additional updates for all users. The Firmware updates were available for a small fee at Mammut dealers. The main improvement was the introduction of two different user profiles. The "Basic" profile is aimed at less experienced users and uses the digital acoustic signal to quickly and easily locate avalanche victims. The "Advanced" profile for experts uses both digital and analog modes to provide more detailed information and options for multiple buried victims. This includes selecting victims according to their chances of survival. The Barryvox transceiver meets the requirements of a wide range of different users from novices to ambitious backcountry skiers and expert mountain guides and ski guides. Professional institutions such as mountaineering schools and international heli-skiing operators and several armies use the Pulse Barryvox, which also has the option to monitor a whole fleet of transceivers via computer. The Pulse Barryvox has been developed to the highest standards. However, Mammut's product development team is continually wracking their brains looking for areas which can be improved upon and new technological advances that could be applied to the transceiver. We've come a long way since Barry the Saint Bernard.

663: Fuji (3,776 m) The monk En-no-gyōja is said to be the first person to ever climb a mountain – this might just be a myth though. Miyakono Yoshika (834–879) climbs Mount Fuji and produces the first ever written report of a climb. In 1150, a Buddhist temple is built on the highest peak in Japan.

1289: Popocatepetl (5,462 m) The local priest Chalchiuhtzin climbs this volcano and its glaciers in central Mexico to pray for rainfall.

1400–1550: Llullaillaco (6,739 m) The Incas build a structure on the third-highest volcano in the world on the border between Argentina and Chile for cultic purposes. It is the world's highest archeological site. The first recorded ascent is in 1951 by the Chileans Bión González León and Juan Harseim.

1779: Entdeckungsfelsen/Roccia della Scoperta (4,178 m) The seven hunters Valentin and Joseph Beck, Etienne Lisgie (or Lisco), Joseph Zumstein (Delapierre), François Castel de Perlatoe, Nicolas Vincent and Sebastian Linty from Gressoney are the first to search for the fabled "Lost Valley". From a rocky prominence on the Lisjoch between Liskamm and the Monte Rosa, they look towards Zermatt and see only colossal ice masses instead of the lush, green valley they had hoped for. They are the first people in the Alps to reach the height of 4,000 meters. They repeat their expedition over the next two years, always heading for the Lisjoch.

1784: Dôme du Goûter (4,304 m) François Guidet and François Gervais climb the first 4,000 meter mountain in the Alps, one of the peaks in the Mont Blanc massif.

1786: Mont Blanc (4,807 m) On August 8, at 18:23, Jacques Balmat and Michel-Gabriel Paccard from Chamonix stand on the summit of Mont Blanc, the highest peak in the Alps.

1811: Jungfrau (4,158 m) The first 4,000 meter peak to be climbed in the Swiss Alps, by two chamois hunters from Wallis Alois Volken and Joseph Bortis and Johann Rudolf and Hieronymus Meyer, sons of the silk ribbon manufacturer Johann Rudolf Meyer from Aargau.

1855: Abi Gamin (6,780 m) During their research trip to the Himalayas, the German geographers Hermann, Adolph and Robert Schlagintweit reach 6,780 meters on the North Face of the Himalayan peak Abi Gamin (7,355 m) in the Kamet massif, after a bivouac at 5,890 meters. In 1950, the Swiss team Gabriel Chevalley, René Dittert and Alfred Tissières make the first ascent accompanied by the Sherpa Thondup Dawa via the same route used by the Schlagintweit brothers.

1883: Kabru (7,338 m) Kabru is a mountain in Sikkim in the southern Himalaya. On October 8, 1883, the English lawyer William Woodman Graham, hotel owner Emil Boss and mountain guide Ulrich Kaufmann from Grindelwald claim to reach the summit, which marks the beginning of a long controversy. The "Alpine Journal 2009" published new evidence which supports their claims. This meant that the world altitude record for mountaineering had to be revised. It had previously listed Pioneer Peak (6,893 m) in Baltoro (Karakorum), by William Martin Conway, Charles Granville Bruce and Matthias Zurbriggen 1892; Aconcagua (6,959 m), highest mountain in the Americas, by Zurbriggen 1897; Trisul (7,120 m) by Tom Longstaff, Alexis and Henri Brocherel with the gurkha Karbir Burakhoti 1907 (this was previously considered as the first 7,000 meter mountain to have been climbed); Pauhunri (7,128 m) by Alexander Kellas with the Sherpas Sonam and Ang Tharke 1910.

1909: Chogolisa (7,490 m) The attempt by Luigi Amedeo di Savoia-Aosta, Duca degli Abruzzi with Joseph Petigax, Alexis and Henri Brocherel fails just 200 meters from the summit (7,668 m) when bad weather forces them to return. In 1957, Hermann Buhl and Kurt Diemberger ascend by the same route (East Ridge). They too are unable to reach the summit of the mountain also known as Bride

Peak. Heavy fog forces them to retreat and Buhl falls through a cornice and dies.

1922: Everest (8,120 m) On May 21, 1922, during the second Everest expedition, George Leigh Mallory, Edward F. Norton and Howard Somervell gain a height of 8,120 meters on the North Ridge without using oxygen. They are the first men to pass the 8,000 meter barrier.

1922: Everest (8,380 m) On May 27, 1922, George Ingle Finch and Charles Granville Bruce get approximately 260 meters higher using bottled oxygen.

1924: Everest (8,570 m) On June 4, 1924, during the third Everest expedition, Edward F. Norton reaches a height of 8,570 meters without oxygen.

1924: Everest (8,500–8,850 m) On June 8, 1924, George Leigh Mallory and Andrew Comyn Irvine are last seen on Everest above 8,500 meters. How far did they climb on the North Ridge? Did they reach the summit? This remains one of the great mysteries of mountaineering.

1930: Jongsong Peak (7,457 m) 47 years on from the first ascent of Kabru, a higher peak is (finally) climbed as part of the international Himalaya Expedition to Kangchenjunga, led by the German mountaineer, who later chose Swiss citizenship – Günter Oskar Dyhrenfurth. The first ascent of the mountain on the borders of Nepal, Sikkim and Tibet is accomplished on June 3 by the German climber Hermann Hoerlin and Austrian climber Erwin Schneider. The second ascent follows only five days later as Günter Oskar Dyhrenfurth, the Swiss climber Marcel Kurz, English climber Frank Smythe and the German climber Ulrich Wieland reach the summit accompanied by Lewa Sherpa and Zirring Nurbu.

1931: Kamet (7,757 m) The first ascent is made by the English mountaineers R. L. Holdsworth, Eric Shipton, Frank Smythe with Lewa Sherpa. Since the Schlagintweit brother's first attempt, eight expeditions have tried to climb the mountain. Holdsworth skies up to Camp V (7,100 m) below the Col Meade – which also qualifies as a new world altitude record.

1933: Everest (8,750 m) During the fourth (British) Everest expedition, Lawrence R. Wager and Percy Wyn-Harris and later Frank Smythe equal Edward F. Norton's previous height record on the North Face.

1936: Nanda Devi (7,817 m) The British mountaineers Bill Tilman and Noel Odell are the first to reach the summit of the highest mountain in India by the South Ridge. The first recorded attempt was made by the English mountaineer W.W. Graham with his Grindelwald companions.

1950: Annapurna (8,091 m) Finally, the first 8,000 meter summit! It is a great success for the French expedition which could have easily ended in disaster. On June 3, 1950, Louis Lachenal and Maurice Herzog both stand on the summit. However, they pay for their success on the "premier 8,000er". Both climbers lose all of their toes and Herzog most of his fingers.

1952: Everest (8,595 m) First attempt from the south. The Swiss, Raymond Lambert and the Nepalese Sherpa Tenzing Norgay are able to reach a height of about 8,600 meters on the southeast ridge, setting a new climbing altitude record.

1953: Everest (8,751 m) On May 27, 1953, during the British expedition led by John Hunt; Tom Bourdillon and Charles Evans are forced to turn back on the South Col Route (8,751 m) – they come within 100 meters of the summit.

1953: Everest (8,850 m) On Friday, May 29, 1953 at 11.30, Edmund Hillary of New Zealand and Tenzing Norgay from Nepal reach the "Roof of the World". That's as high as it gets!

BREAKING MENTAL BARRIERS
Evelyne Binsack | Around the world

What happens after tiredness hits you? The question constantly nagged at me on my first alpine expeditions. I wanted to get to know myself a little better. Some people react to extreme physical exertion with aggression, while others become euphoric or break down in tears. Certain individuals inspire courage in others and demonstrate leadership skills they never knew they had. In my case, I noticed that I still had plenty left in the tank, even when my body was clearly exhausted.

Actually, I don't like talking about limits, as I don't really acknowledge them as such. Limits are not static; they are more of an abstract barrier in one's head that is continually shifting. Most important for me is the quality of concentration, mastering a task through mental power. When I operate at my limits, what drives me most is the desire to extend them, to learn from them and to develop myself further. I always begin by defining my objectives. I look for challenges where there are a series of problems to solve, where all my skills and potential are required, where I can learn from the experience. It is intensely satisfying to suddenly be able to achieve something you have never done before and which you would never have previously dared to attempt.

I have been an active mountaineer for over 25 years. The beauty of the mountains and the challenges they pose continue to fascinate me. I am continually amazed by the experiences that they allow me to enjoy, but I have not lost my respect for them either.

I don't think I could really describe this fascination in words, it remains something intangible. I actively submit myself to the process of being stimulated and challenged by the mountains, not giving up but continually searching. I see sunrises and sunsets, I marvel at rock formations and am inspired when I stand in places where, in some cases, no one has ever stood before, places that were previously inaccessible – and I am permitted to experience such moments.

I once spent a period working as a helicopter pilot in Andalusia, but I missed the mountains too much. Despite the beauty of the nature there, it was all rather lost on me. This sense of longing gave me the space to develop a new project. Having reached the highest point on the earth, I wanted to travel to its southernmost point. This meant leaving the mountains behind me and heading into the flatlands. For 484 days, I cycled from Switzerland to Southern Chile where I traveled to the South Pole by ski and sledge. All in all, I covered a total distance of 25,000 kilometers. Fortunately, my "Expedition Antarctica" was not entirely devoid of mountains; in the Andes, I climbed eleven summits ranging from 5,200 to 6,300 meters, mostly solo. Did I find what I was looking for? The expedition was both terrible and fantastic, it was heaven and hell. It was an enormous challenge and I don't just mean in the physical sense. Above all, it demanded considerable willpower and forced me to adopt the right attitude so as not to be defeated by the immensity of the task I had set myself.

Not all my mountain expeditions have been crowned with success. In 2010, I reached my limits during an expedition to Gasherbrum II (8,035 m) in Karakoram. After being sick and suffering from diarrhea for four days, I could feel how I had been drained of all my energy reserves. My whole body looked like some battered scarecrow and that was exactly how I felt. One fundamental question kept coming back: how important was the mountain to me? How far did I want to push my body? I decided to turn back and allow my body to recover. Willpower and achieving your objectives doesn't always mean having to bash your head against a wall. Strength of will should be applied wisely; knowing when to turn back can be a matter of life and death.

I have learnt by experience that there is no manual when it comes to borderline situations. It is more a question of successively getting to know oneself better, learning by doing, from experience, from emotions that take you further, the traces left by life itself. This is how limits get pushed. A climber forced to stop training for injury reasons will suddenly find it difficult to climb a straightforward route. In this ongoing and ever-changing perception of our limits, previous achievements do not continue to hold the same value. Instead, we are forced to analyze our personal situation, to search for our limits according to our momentary disposition or our actual state of mind. Not everyone finds this easy. Our limits have no real substance; as soon as they manifest themselves, they disappear again into nothingness.

ment, but also thanks to the airplane. Nowadays, you can get anywhere in the world in a day. You could argue that this is a good or a bad thing, but the fact is the world has become much smaller.

To date, most expeditions have tended to be group undertakings and have enjoyed increasing popularity as a result. I personally think this is a good thing; there is quite enough "going it alone" in our western society. But not every expedition is necessarily an incredible experience. Undertakings like these – as opposed to other all-inclusive holidays – take place in remote areas and are full of uncertainties. Success depends on a whole host of factors, and this makes the expedition one of the most demanding

There are many arguments for and against expeditions. For me, the positives outweigh the negatives. Contact with other people can be the most fulfilling experience of all. What would we be without other people? Then there is getting to know other cultures, other landscapes, and the great joy of being in places where others are unable to go. This exclusive aspect is often underplayed. And then, if you manage to climb that peak... For me, even after decades as a mountain guide, one of the most beautiful moments is when I see the beaming faces of the team members, people whose dreams I have been able to bring to life with a successful expedition.

I'M UP FOR IT AGAIN!
Claudia Laggai | Alps/Switzerland

It all started when I saw the Sleep Lab image in an outdoors magazine, I think it was "Alpin". It looked so cool, I immediately looked up the Mammut homepage to get some more info. That is when I found the link for the next Testevent, the Underwear Test, but I had missed the application deadline by two days so I had to hold out for the next Testevent. I waited in feverish anticipation for the new application date and, after a typically exhilarating Mammut-style selection process, was one of 200 lucky participants in the 2009 Safety Check Testevent at Melchsee-Frutt.

All the enthusiastic Mammut fan comments on the Basecamp Blog really got me in the mood for an unforgettable adventure with like-minded people. When I posted the offer for a lift share in my car, a girl got in touch from Munich, my home town. Our first phone conversation lasted so long that both our batteries ran out. Sonja had taken part in the Underwear Test and was really fired up by the event and the friendly Mammut fans who came from all over. Two participants whom she had kept in contact with were also amongst those selected for this event.

And so Rolli, Mike, Sonja and I made our way to Melchsee-Frutt in our pimped-up "I'm up for it" Mammut T-shirts, where the Mammut photographers immediately took a few shots of us. The event exceeded all my expectations and was a truly unique experience – potentially addictive. When I opened the long-awaited mailshot announcing the 2010 Testevent, I almost fell off my chair. The main image was of the four of us in our T-shirts, beaming happily, at the last event! I got to the office at an unearthly hour on the day the application opened, counted down the minutes and then got to it. On March 20, 2010, Rolli, Sonja and I (Mike was unfortunately not selected), in "I'm up for it again!" T-shirts this time and brimming with anticipation, went to the Acceleration Test in Engadin, where we met up with old and new Mammut friends and enjoyed an exhilarating and exceptional outdoor experience. My "early shift" to get my application in had been worth it. In Zuoz, I was given a golden PC mouse for being the very first applicant.

As seasoned Mammut fans, Sonja and I have naturally also entered Mammut's 150th anniversary Peak Project with our "Calvary Mountain" hoping to climb one of the 150 peaks in 2012.

ONE 15 METER LONG RACLETTE, COMIN' UP!
Harald Schreiber | Alps/Switzerland

behind every feat of technical catering, no matter how improbable it first seemed. Nothing is too much effort for this culinary genius. Whether overseeing ten cooking sites at once, or spending seven hours preparing five lamb carcasses over an open fire – in the end, it is the experience that counts. On occasion, he has even been known to set up a sausage and soup stall at the top of the Julier Pass!

Whether it is underwear, a safety check or acceleration testing, over the last few years, the Mammut brand image has increasingly been characterized by Testevents. Hundreds of participants from all over the world have gone to great lengths to make a pilgrimage to Switzerland for our popular test weekends and to model for the next billboard advertisements. In complete contrast to the cliché of the half-starved professional model, these guys were all super hungry. Whether it was an outdoor fondue for 130 people in Melchsee-Frutt or a 15 meter long grill for raclette and spit roasting in Zuoz, the man with the plan was always the one and only Stefan Winiger, or "Wini" as he is known. Wini has been the culinary mastermind

Top Secret Recipe:
Melt 250 grams of dark chocolate in a bain-marie and add 250 grams of butter cut into cubes. Make sure the butter stays creamy and does not melt too much. Whip 5 eggs together with 200 grams of sugar, add 50 grams of flour followed by the melted chocolate butter mix. Carefully fold it into the mixture and pour into aluminum molds. Once prepared, the molds can be taken along to the barbecue. Place the little cakes in the embers to cook for 15 minutes, keeping a close eye on them. (This is also of course possible at home in a preheated oven at 200 degrees . . .)

Caroline Fink talked to 1980s climbing celebrity Johnny Dawes about climbing on gritstone.

Johnny, as one of the best gritstone climbers of all time, you know every inch of gritstone in England's Peak District. Can you tell us what makes the rock between Manchester and Sheffield so special?

Well, you can't really compare routes in the Peak with other crags. Gritstone is much rougher, compacter and more rounded. This makes the routes really tricky and very technical. Some of them are difficult to protect, which makes them very dangerous. It also makes them a little bit crazy.

You were the first to climb some of these "slightly crazy" routes at the hardest grades in the 1980s. What does it take to be successful on gritstone?

The way you use your sense of gravity is more important on gritstone than on other rocks. You can't simply ensure that you can do the moves by being strong. The security comes from knowing what the move really is, not from being strong enough to do the move really easily. I also think that a dynamic style is very important for climbing on gritstone. You get to holds which you can just about hang on to, but where you can't pull any harder on them to get the next position. So sometimes, you've got to "unweight" the body to get some sort of movement . . . one move is used to do the next one. So I think we took dynoing a little bit further.

In descriptions of your climbing, it is often said that you invented the "dyno".

This is a bit of an exaggeration. But it is true that we really helped to push the boundaries of dynamic climbing in the Peak District in the 1980s.

Dynos on unbolted rock, sometimes with only marginal protection. Weren't you ever scared of taking a bad fall?

Fear . . . (pauses to consider) . . . it's not like "fear!" and completely losing it. It's more the case that you are completely aware of the situation . . . you work out what to do and then you do it. This doesn't make you afraid, it makes you concentrate. You are forced to concentrate on climbing your way out of trouble.

Even today, there are no bolts on gritstone anywhere in the Peak District. Why is this? The rock itself is capable of taking bolts.

That's true. It would be perfectly possible to bolt gritstone routes. But the rock doesn't give you a bolt, so it should be left alone. Let's be honest here: if you climb from the bottom of a cliff to the top, then this is "rock climbing". If you put bolts in, then its "bolted rock climbing". Personally, I think that calling it "sport climbing" is just sexing it up really. With the exception of the really dangerous routes, the ma-

jority of the easier routes on gritstone don't need bolts. They have wonderful cracks and holes and can be protected with friends, nuts and hexs. This is the way they have always been climbed.

There is a longstanding tradition of climbing on gritstone. Can you tell us a bit more about the history of the area?

Climbing first started here at the end of the 19th century. Things really kicked off after the Second World War. People still had old bits of equipment left over, for example ropes, which they used to climb the cliffs in the Peak District.

And this involved mainly working class men from Sheffield and Manchester?

Yes, exactly. This was the exact opposite of most mountaineers at the time, who were members of more elitist organisations, such as the Alpine Club. The 1980s were a further important stage in the development of the Peak District – it was a second heyday. My generation basically climbed everything left that was considered "unclimbable".

And you weren't exactly members of the upper class either . . .

No, that's true. We were students and workers. We didn't have any money. In actual fact, we should probably thank Margaret Thatcher for her neo-liberal, free-market policies of the time. Thanks to her, there were no jobs, which meant that we had more time to climb. It was an amazing time for young climbers in the Peak District; it was a really creative period that was full of energy.

What is there left to climb on gritstone today?

There's really not much left. There is one old quarry with some possibilities. It has around twelve routes that have never been climbed. They are all really desperate, even on top rope. But if there are climbers out there who are good enough – then they'll be more than welcome here. The routes are just waiting to be climbed.

FROM ROPEMAKER TO SPORTS BRAND
Benedikt Pfister | Aargau/Switzerland

13
@

"The mammoth is a symbol for power and strength. Guaranteeing and further improving this most important characteristic of our ropes and cordage has always been the aim of the company," wrote Robert Wobmann, the company director, in the 1940s. It was no idle promise. Mammut ropes were continually improved throughout the 1950s and 1960s and became famous for their high quality.

Up until the Second World War, ropes were made of natural products such as hemp, sisal and jute. After 1945, new synthetic fibers made innovations possible and the *Seilerwarenfabrik Lenzburg* (as Mammut used to be known) was heavily involved in their research and development. In the early 1950s, it launched the "Mammut-Argenta" – the first ever glacier rope by Mammut to be made of nylon yarn. A few years later, the rope manufacturer was able to clearly set itself apart from the competition. Its "Mammut-Everest" rope marked an important milestone in the development of ropes for mountaineering. It consisted of an internal core, made of one or more ropes, which was then protected by another rope braided around it. This "kernmantel" construction (from the German "Kern" meaning "core" + "Mantel" meaning "coat" or "sheath"; the term has now entered the English language) was a guarantee for quality and safety. As time went on, greater demands were placed on mountaineering ropes. The most important factor was that they were better able to absorb the impact force and thus cushion the climber in the event of a fall. In the 1960s, the *Seilerwarenfabrik Lenzburg* launched its new "Dynamic" stretch rope, which was the first single rope to achieve official UIAA certification.

Mammut went on to build on its reputation for producing high quality ropes to successfully establish itself as a sports equipment brand. Back in the 1960s and 1970s, no one would have thought this possible. At the time, things looked very different. While many similar companies were fighting to survive or had ceased produc-

tion, Mammut continued to demonstrate power and strength. The rope manufacturer continued to be successful because it diversified into the sports equipment market and later the outdoor and leisure sector. And because Mammut had the right investors with the right ideas at the right time. In 1968, Arova Management Services AG took over the company from its previous owners, the *Schweizerische Bindfadenfabrik* (Swiss Rope and Cords Mill). All the organization's companies bore the Arova name in their title. The rope manufacturer therefore changed its name to Arova Lenzburg AG. The product range was reorganized into "Sport & Leisure", "Industry & Trade" and "Ironmongers & Department Stores". But this new structure didn't last for long. Only one year later, the Arova Group was sold to the Heberlein Group.

Arova's textiles sector struggled to compete against cheap imports from Asia. In 1982, the Heberlein Group needed further liquidity and decided to sell Arova Lenzburg to the *Zürcher Ziegeleien* (a tile and brick works in Zurich, which has today become the Swiss holding company Conzzeta). Arova Lenzburg AG had continued to generate a profit, unlike other sections of the Arova Group, and was therefore interesting for a company's portfolio. Meanwhile, the company had outgrown its factory in Lenzburg and in 1992, it moved to the premises it still occupies today in Seon.

Conzzeta continued to strengthen the Mammut brand. This primarily involved a systematic diversification into mountaineering and outdoor products. Under Arova in Lenzburg, the company had started distributing high-quality products from foreign manufacturers in Switzerland. For example, the Mammut brand also featured mountain boots, mountain tents and rucksacks from the French brand Millet in its range of products. In 1981, the first ever "Mammut Collection" was launched. When Millet withdrew, a new partner was sought. As a result, Mammut acquired the Swiss company Fürst AG in 1989, originally a hat manufacturer that had diversified into rucksacks and travel bags. Mammut changed its strategy. Instead of marketing third-party products it started to sell its own products. In order to concentrate more on the mountaineering and outdoor sectors, it became necessary to separate off the industrial rope and hoisting technology division. During the first ten years of the 21st century, there were further company acquisitions, which strengthened Mammut's position as a leading mountaineering and outdoor brand.

The transformation from rope manufacturer to the successful Mammut sports brand represents an important chapter in the craft, industrial and financial history of Switzerland. In spite of huge changes and enormous growth, one thing has never changed: Mammut has continued to manufacture ropes – now only mountaineering ropes – in the heart of the Swiss canton of Aargau. Only a few kilometers from the location of the old shed where Kaspar Tanner started making his own ropes in 1862, 26 ropemakers now produce around 7,000 kilometers of climbing rope every year – ropes that are as strong as the mammoth on the label!

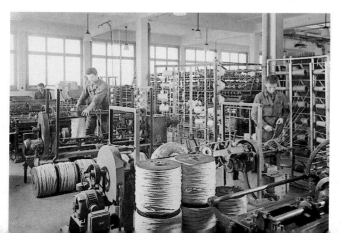

1953

MAMMUT SEILE

SEILERWARENFABRIK A.G. LENZBURG
CORDERIE S.A.

TEL. (064) 8 12 45

SWISS TECHNOLOGY MADE IN CHINA?
Adrian Huber | Seon/Switzerland

Mammut has manufactured ropes for 150 years. "Made in Switzerland" means we source our raw materials from a firm that is just 40 kilometers away from where we are based. The yarn is dyed by a traditional Swiss company, which has been run by the same family, now in its fifth generation, since 1845. The supply chain is simple and transparent, and transportation distances are short. We are fully aware of the social and economic working conditions that prevail because we have daily meetings with our production teams and because Swiss environmental regulations are very stringent.

Even our first Soft Shell pants, made from Schoeller stretch fabric, which is still woven and treated in the St. Gallen Rheintal region, are cut and sewn in Switzerland. Today, Mammut employs over 250 people in Switzerland. This includes the entire admin department were well as the design, development and quality assurance departments. This is the basis for our claim that our quality and technology are "Made in Switzerland".

The end of the 1980s saw textile and clothing manufacturers begin to relocate their manufacturing operations abroad in an attempt to save costs. This also proved a commercial necessity for Mammut. During this period, we also moved some of our manufacturing abroad, to begin with to neighboring countries like Italy and Portugal, then further east to Romania and finally all the way to China. This shift was largely down to the labor-intensive processes that the manufacture of highly functional clothing requires. Even these days, a deft hand is what is needed to stitch fabrics together, apply watertight laminates or to thread sewing machines. China in particular has a wealth of qualified seamstresses who work for comparatively reasonable wages.

The rapid progression of such relocation policies in various industries, but in particular in the textile industry, has had a series of ramifications. A once flourishing and highly regarded branch of industry steadily gave way to the service sector, declining in importance both in Switzerland and in other expensive European countries, becoming economically insignificant and in some cases disappearing altogether. With it went the knowledge and craftsmanship in textiles and clothing manufacture that had been acquired over decades.

There is no doubt that production in so-called 'low-wage countries' was economically advantageous. On the other hand, the enormous costs incurred were greatly underestimated, such as the multiple trips required to set up production, establish a working partnership, communicate work procedures and instructions in a foreign language and, last but not least, to ensure that quality requirements were complied with. Compared to the fashion industry, the manufacture of functional outdoor products places great technical demands on the skills of the seamstresses as well as the machinery. Some manufacturers in the fashion trade focused too one-dimensionally on the cost-saving aspects of shift production and ended up letting quality standards slip. And so the years of outsourced production led to items of questionable quality and fit working their way into the fashion houses. Many manufacturers ended up paying the price for low-cost production in the Far East. The situation was somewhat alleviated by the fashion styles of the 1980s, when cuts were boxy and shapeless, making everything appear slightly ill-fitting.

These teething troubles have long since been overcome. Our outdoor production facilities in China now have the most modern machinery at their disposal, together with highly trained seamstresses capable of mastering the most innovative of production technologies. Whereas financial calculations used to be the deciding factor and contractors were in a position of advantage, the situation has now developed in favor of the production plants. They have accumulated a great deal of knowledge over the years; they

plan their production capacity and have long since understood what we mean by "Swiss quality". However, items that are "Made in China" are still not well regarded in general. Although China is frequently associated with cheap mass-produced goods, often with good reason, our "Made in China" products are manufactured to the highest standards, at a cost that the customer is prepared to pay.

Twenty years of globalization later, it is becoming clear that it is not just rich Western countries that have benefited from international trade. It is increasingly the case that emerging markets are profiting from this development. Ultimately, this has led to a significant increase in average incomes in China and the emergence of an affluent middle class. It is quite conceivable that in years to come, these people will also want to go climbing and will want to buy Mammut ropes. This would mean that globalization has come full-circle. One thing is certain: China is discovering consumerism and starting to apply its purchasing power to its own domestic market, thereby absorbing production capacity that to date has been reserved for the export market. That capacity is necessary because the thirst for consumer goods is huge in China. The dimensions are unimaginable. For example, there are 700 cities with a population of over one million.

Furthermore, it seems clear that China is evolving and will shed its reputation as a low-wage, mass-production country. Since roughly half of our production is handled in Europe, we will not feel the direct effects as harshly. It is not yet possible to predict with

accuracy who will be the next country to follow in China's footsteps. However, it is vital that we judge this next phase in terms of corporate social responsibility, since globalization has also had some less than positive effects. During the 1990s in particular, there were scandalous reports of international fashion and sports labels manufacturing clothing in the most inhumane working conditions. Although we were never affected by such scandals, products like ours that bear a "Made in China" label are keenly monitored by concerned consumers and non-governmental organizations. We wanted to make sure that, in the case of our products, any such grievances were ruled out completely. So it was an important step for us when we joined the multi-stakeholder initiative 'Fair Wear Foundation' in 2008, an organization that stands for fair conditions throughout the supply chain. Even though we do not have the same full control over our suppliers' working conditions as we do here in our own rope works, we feel it is our duty to do everything in our power to ensure that even if workers are far away, they are given safe and fair working conditions.

As a discriminating non-governmental organization, the "Clean Clothes Campaign" appreciates our commitment and has classed us in their top category because we take our responsibilities seriously. We are nevertheless aware that we still have some way to go in such a complex globalized world, a world where it is no longer unusual to see "Swiss Technology" and "Made in China" side by side.

15

THE FIRST WOMAN SKI TOURER
ON THE HIGHEST PEAK IN THE ALPS
Karin Steinbach Tarnutzer | Mont Blanc/France

In February 1929, Marguette Bouvier of France (1908–2008) became the first woman to undertake a ski tour on Mont Blanc. Photos taken in the late 1920s and early 1930s show her as a smartly dressed, elegant telemark "skieuse". Like only a handful of women in her day, this talented sportswoman and daughter of a well-to-do family went out in search of exciting experiences and an adventurous lifestyle.

She was born on August 25, 1908 in Beni Saf, Algeria. Her family settled in Chamonix in 1913, where she and her sister Hélène had a bilingual upbringing, taught by two private tutors, one French, the other American. They were introduced to the alpinist and author Roger Frison-Roche in 1924, when he was a member of the Olympic Committee that organized the first ever Olympic Winter Games in Chamonix. Inspired by Roger, Marguette Bouvier worked at improving her skiing and tried her hand at skijoring and even ski jumping. In 1928, the two sisters took part in the World Ski Championships held in Chamonix. Marguette came second in the time trials and with it became French champion; Hélène won the style discipline ahead of Marguette. In 1929 and 1930, Marguette Bouvier competed together with her partner Charles Sabouret in ice dancing. In 1929, the pair came second behind the defending Olympic title winners. Marguette Bouvier ended her ski racing career in 1935.

She was not just passionate about winter sports but also went climbing in the Mont Blanc area, learnt to fly a glider and took her pilot's license in 1936. With her father's Farman 402, she made a solo flight from North Africa across to the Rhone Valley. To her, skiing down the highest peak in the Alps was not such a big deal.

She set off on February 4, 1929, accompanied by her guide Armand Charlet, the longstanding director of the École Nationale de Ski et d'Alpinisme (ENSA) and archetypical Chamonix mountain guide. One assumes they took the cable car from Chamonix up to the Gare des Glaciers (2,414 m). There had been a cable car running from Pélerins to La Para (1,685 m) since its completion for the first Olympic Winter Games in 1924. In 1927, it was extended to the Gare des Glaciers; the abandoned station building still stands, like a forlorn relic, to the west of the current Aiguille-du-Midi cable car's middle station. The cable car was further extended in 1937 to reach the Col du Midi at 3,600 meters, where some of the former buildings are still recognizable on the approach to the Cosmiques Ridge. Finally, in 1955, a new cable car was constructed further to the east that went straight up to the Aiguille du Midi.

Marguette Bouvier and Armand Charlet set off from the Gare des Glaciers to the 1853 Refuge des Grands Mulets (3,051 m), perched on a section of rock between the Bossons and Petit-Plateau glaciers. In the early morning of February 5, they left the hut and headed over the Petit Plateau to the Col du Dôme and the Vallot hut. A predecessor of today's emergency shelter has occupied the site since 1890, when Joseph Vallot built an observatory at 4,362 meters. They deposited their skis there and continued up to the summit at 4,810 meters using crampons, as is customary today – but at minus 40 degrees, conditions were not exactly favorable.

25 years earlier, on February 25, 1904, Hugo Mylius from Frankfurt, together with the Bernese Oberland guides Alexander Tännler, Kaspar Maurer and Heinrich Zurflüh, had become the first to do a ski tour on Mont Blanc via that same route. It was Elias Julen from Valais that first succeeded in skiing down from the true summit in 1930.

16

WITH ALI ON THE MIDI
Emil Zopfi I Aiguille du Midi/Frankreich

Aiguille du Midi, 3,842 meters above sea level. He stepped out onto the viewing platform of the cable car station and shielded his eyes from the glacier sun. I recognized him immediately. It was Muhammad Ali. He was clothed all in white and accompanied by two beautiful black women with bright red lips, white fur coats and red high heels. I was squatting on a ledge on the jagged cliff opposite him. It was just big enough to stand on and pretty exposed. I placed one of the cams I'd brought with me for our ascent of the South Face. We had five to six hours of climbing on vertical granite below us. To reach the cable car station, we still had to abseil down an arête and cross a pretty awkward snow ridge.

Muhammad Ali and his companions watched from the railings as we arranged the ropes, clipped in the carabiners, sorted out the pegs and untangled the etriers. This was back in the day when I was still a great climber and Muhammad Ali was a great boxer. What am I saying, he was the greatest. The whole world gathered to watch him float around the ring in his red gloves before knocking down his heavyweight opponents with that lightning-fast jab of his. And here he was, watching me as I abseiled down onto the snow ridge and cut steps into the ice underneath the treacherous snow covering the ridge. It must have looked pretty dangerous. It certainly was rather tricky and I was relieved when I was able to grab the railing and haul myself up onto the platform. The tourists, who were by now crowded around the rail like at a boxing match, clapped and cheered and then moved back to make room. And Muhammad Ali

– or Cassius Clay, as he was still called in those days – reached over and touched my arm in respect.

Mountaineers generally dislike being watched by cable car tourists in high heels from their safe viewpoints as they struggle up mountains, facing risk and danger. However, on that particular Sunday afternoon, I was more than prepared to make an exception. I stood there arm in arm with Muhammad Ali's two exotic, perfumed and glamorous companions in my wet trousers, with my scratched and bloodied hands, my lopsided helmet and my ice axe and allowed myself to be photographed like a dancing bear. The cameras flashed. My partner was still crouching on the ledge on the other side. He couldn't start climbing because in all the excitement I hadn't yet found time to belay him. By the time he made it onto dry land, everyone had gone.

"Who was that?"

"Cassius Clay," I said.

"You are mad," he said.

To be honest, I'm no longer sure if it really was him. But apart from that, every word of this story is true. I shall never forget that moment, standing there between those two gorgeous black girls on the Aiguille du Midi, 3,842 meters above sea level, while their heavyweight companion photographed us and then clapped me on the shoulder again in admiration. It might have been him. After all, in 1998, Hillary Clinton took the cable car to the top of the Säntis in the Appenzell Alps and described the whole experience as "great". Anyway, I like to think of the aging Muhammad Ali leafing through his photo album and pausing at the photo of the exhausted climber standing between two beautiful women to mumble: "Was a tough guy, this one, wasn't he?"

DRAMA ON THE MATTERHORN
Daniel Anker | Matterhorn/Switzerland

On July 14, 1865, the British mountaineer Edward Whymper and his fellow countrymen Francis Douglas, Douglas Robert Hadow and Charles Hudson, together with the guides Michel-Auguste Croz from Chamonix and Peter Taugwalder and his son from Zermatt climbed the Hörnli ridge to the summit of the 4,477.5 meter Matterhorn. "The slope eased off, at length we could be detached, and Croz and I, dashing away, ran a neck-and-neck race. At 1.40 P.M., the world was at our feet, and the Matterhorn was conquered. Hurrah! Not a footstep (from the Italian party, which had started out from the other side of the mountain) could be seen." This was Whymper's ninth attempt to ascend the seemingly impossible peak, located between the Matter Valley (Mattertal) in Switzerland and Valtournanche in Italy. His former guide and climbing companion Jean-Antoine Carrel had become his bitter rival.

Carrel was beaten to the summit; he reached the top of the "Cervino", as the Italians call the Matterhorn, with Jean-Baptiste Bich via the so-called Italian Ridge three days later. By this time, the catastrophe, which was to make the mountain instantly famous, had already occurred. Hadow, who had planned to crown his first summer of mountaineering in the Alps with the first ascent of the Matterhorn, slipped during the descent, possibly because his shoes were worn out, but more likely due to a moment of inatten-

tiveness. Hudson was not keeping the rope tight and Hadow fell and knocked Croz over, pulling him down with him. The rope between Taugwalder and Lord Douglas was unable to take the strain and broke. This proved fortunate; had it held, it would probably have cost the remaining members of the party their lives. Whymper's triumph turned into a dramatic tragedy.

The first descent of the Matterhorn with its four fatal casualties, three of whom were English (including a vicar and a Lord!) and the fourth, the best-known mountain guide in the whole of France, received considerably more media attention than the ascent itself. The London Times asked: "Is mountaineering criminal?" The hotel owners were not unduly worried as tourists flocked to see the ill-fated mountain at first hand. Zermatt and Breuil-Cervinia went on to become well-known tourist resorts. Nowadays, the summit of the Matterhorn is reached 1,000 to 1,500 times every summer (there are approximately 2,500 attempts) with somewhere between 100 to 140 ascents per day during the high season. Whymper's first ascent also marked the beginning of the international marketing of "Mont Cervin" (as the French call it). It has since been used to advertise all manner of likely and unlikely products. Thankfully, plans to provide access to the summit by road (1859) and then by rail (1892) were both scrapped.

The ascent of the Matterhorn also marked the end of the so-called Golden Age of Mountaineering, during which the summits of many of the highest Alps were reached for the first time. Edward Whymper (1840–1911) wrote his account and described his other first ascents in "Scrambles amongst the Alps in the Years 1860–69" (first edition 1871), which is also illustrated with his own excellent woodcuts.

The book, which was translated into German in 1872, has become one of the great classics of mountaineering literature. Whymper describes the moment that the rope broke in "Scrambles Amongst The Alps" with the following words: "I asked for the rope that had given way, and found, to my surprise – indeed to my horror – that it was the weakest of the three ropes. It was not brought, and should not have been employed, for the purpose for which it was used. It was an old rope, and, compared with the others, was feeble."

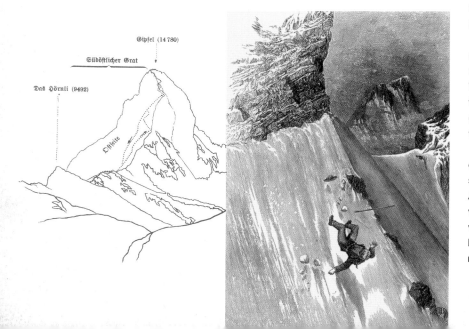

Gipfel (14780)

Südöstlicher Grat

Das Hörnli (9492)

Ostseite

18

"NO COMPARISON WITH TODAY'S EQUIPMENT"
Reinhold Messner | Eiger North Face/Switzerland

Reinhold Messner was the first man to reach all the 8,000 meter summits. In August 1974, together with Peter Habeler, he climbed the North Face of the Eiger in the record time of 10 hours. Karin Steinbach Tarnutzer asked him to describe the equipment that he used on this climb.

You climbed the North Face of the Eiger in what was an incredibly quick time for that period. How did you manage to do it so quickly?
Peter and I set out up the Eiger in 1974 with the standard equipment of the time: rucksacks, bivouac equipment and ice axes. By then, the North Face was no longer the ultimate in mountaineering, this era ended in the mid-1960s. The introduction of helicopter rescues had diminished its appeal. However, the North Face of the Eiger was still a route to treat with respect. In the 1960s, you only belonged to the "good mountaineers" if you had climbed the three great north faces of the Alps: the Eiger, the Matterhorn and the Grandes Jorasses. This was later superseded by the seven summits and the 14 eight-thousanders. In 1960, everyone knew exactly who had climbed the three great north faces. We set out in 1974 to climb the Eiger at a decent speed. We weren't planning to break any records. We did take bivouac equipment and each of us carried a rucksack, although they were relatively small. In theory, we would have been able to spend two nights up on the face. We made good time as the first party on the route that year, having overtaken another group on the Ramp. We were pretty amazed when we realized that we had climbed it in just 10 hours.

What did you find most difficult about the ascent?
The exit cracks! They were completely iced over; it was like climbing on glass. In places, we had to melt the ice with our fingers to find handholds, as the ice axes we had in those days couldn't be used. Dry tooling hadn't even been thought of back then. The exit cracks are vertical and in parts slightly overhanging: no easy task. This was the crux for me.

What kind of ice axes did you have?
We were using basic axes with a straight shaft. On my solo ascent of the North Face of Les Droites in 1969, I also climbed with a standard ice axe and an ice dagger – no comparison with today's equipment. There was some good gear about, even in the early years – if you were prepared to make it yourself. For example, Rudl Peters made his own ice axe for the first ascent of the North Face of the Grandes Jorasses (in 1935!). His widow donated it to the Messner Mountain Museum. Peters was clever. He designed an ice axe with a pick that could almost have been used for dry tooling and then welded a hammer to the back of the head. It is carefully made and is a good ice axe. Respect. It was better than most of the axes we were using in the 1970s. Of course, it is a far cry from modern technical ice tools. Today, it's possible to climb much more extreme terrain than in 1969. The equipment is better and techniques using the ice axe shaft are employed. Together with greater expertise and better training at climbing walls, modern equipment has helped fuel the explosive development of climbing. It's worth noting that most people today use far superior equipment just to climb Mont Blanc than Hermann Buhl had with him on Nanga Parbat in 1953.

THE OLD MAN OF THE MATTERHORN
Hermann Biner I Zermatt/Switzerland

19

He stood on the summit of the Matterhorn about 370 times, and in 1990, on the last occasion, he was almost 90 years old. The oldest mountain guide in the world was exceptionally proficient, modest and quick-witted – and also very fit. He lived to be 104 years old.

Ulrich Inderbinen was born on December 13, 1900 in Zermatt. It was not the Zermatt we know today but a small mountain village, where despite the emergence of mountain tourism, most of the locals were self-sufficient and lived from the land. This was also the case with Inderbinen's parents. The family lived in a small traditional Valais-style house. Their many children all slept in the same room and in the same bed. Water had to be fetched from the village well. The dinner table would usually only have a small selection of homegrown produce and sometimes they left the table hungry. As a reward for fasting during the 40 days of Lent, the children were given a slice of sausage. Their mother used to hide the little bit of sugar they possessed at the very top of the cupboard. There was no medical assistance. They were all born at home and any illness or pain just had to be suffered. This meant that flu could often be fatal. They were unaware of the existence of medicines and Inderbinen's father could not afford the contribution for the newly established health insurance scheme which cost 2 or 3 Francs per person for the year.

They addressed their parents with the formal German "Sie". Each child had to take responsibility from an early age and perform chores to help the whole family survive. At the age of five, Ulrich Inderbinen looked after the cows and sheep on which the family depended for its welfare. In those days, a cow was worth a small fortune. He was also responsible for looking after his sister Martha, two years his junior, for whom he had a real soft spot. At a later date, to illustrate how overbearing his sisters were, he said of his siblings: "There were three of us boys and each one of us had six sisters." In the autumn after his eighth birthday, he started to walk

to and from Zmutt to go to school. At the age of 13, he worked as a shepherd, earning 20 Rappen a day, which was paid to his father. Until he started a family of his own, he put all of his energies into helping his parents and siblings, as was normal practice in those days, and necessary for the family unit to survive.

Their life was deeply religious and permeated by strong traditions. They prayed together every day. Before leaving the house they would apply holy water, grace was said before and after every meal and on Sundays, they naturally went to High Mass. Religion was a source of solace and strength in their hard lives. You could find Ulrich Inderbinen at early mass every single day of his life – just as reliably as the priest. Despite the fact that he had a tough childhood, he viewed those years as the best in his life: "Back then, life was hard and beautiful. Nobody had anything, and everyone helped each other out. People were happier back then than they are today. Now they have everything, yet think only of themselves."

He left Zermatt when he was 18 years old for a job in a mine in St. Maurice, working 10 hours a day, 6 days a week for a wage of 90 Rappen per hour. The work was dangerous. There were no unions and little if any attention was paid to the workers' health. This meant Inderbinen missed Zermatt and his family all the more. In the years that followed, he had to regularly spend winters working away, too. Non-stop work in those days was a blessing rather than a curse. One lived to work and the words 'leisure time' and 'holiday' simply did not feature in the vocabulary of Zermatt in those days. Inderbinen never even had time to start a family of his own. In 1928, he met his future wife Anna, though they initially did not have enough money to get married, and later not enough time. In 1933, they finally exchanged vows at 6 A.M. at early morning mass, so that they could still make it to work on time. As for a honeymoon, the thought never even crossed their minds.

At the time, being a mountain guide was one of the very few ways of earning a living in Zermatt. And so Inderbinen decided to become a mountain guide. His first assignment was as a porter, "to carry the backpack of a lady who had enough to deal with herself". Their training had included standards of "etiquette". By 1925, he had passed his exams. To him, the mountains around Zermatt were not just a source of income, he loved them, and there are countless photos of a happy Ulrich Inderbinen standing on various summits. As a passionate climber – at the age of 70, he climbed the East Face of the Watzmann – he favored the climbing on the excellent rock of the Zinalrothorn or the Obergabelhorn. There were fewer people on these routes and he preferred this calm to the Matterhorn. It was important to him that he not only got his clients to the top and back safely, but that he also taught them his love of the mountains.

Up until the 1960s, finding work as a mountain guide was not easy. The two world wars had virtually brought tourism to a standstill. The situation only improved in 1962 when the Office of Mountain Guides opened and mountain tourism experienced a surge in popularity. At last, the demand for mountain guides was great. A telephone would have been useful for organization purposes but the 60+ year old decided there was no point in an old mountain guide getting a new phone just for the couple of years he still had left. He was still active throughout the 1980s though, so it might have paid to have a telephone after all. Eventually the media found out that there was an octogenarian mountain guide around, who showed no signs of tiring. In 1982, when he entered the international Mountain Guide ski race for the first time, Inderbinen, with his charisma and amazing ability for his age, generated such a media storm that it led to international fame for him.

He once said to one of his clients, who had voiced concerns over his age, only to become quite exhausted himself: "If you want to go slower, you will have to find yourself an older mountain guide in future." And when, on his 100th birthday, he was asked if he was afraid of dying, he said: "No, when I look at the papers, there is hardly anyone from my age group in the obituaries section." At 96 years of age, he hung up his ice axe and crampons and, 8 years later, he died peacefully at home. Although he never made any extreme first ascents or took part in any big expeditions, he was an exceptional mountain guide. He was characteristic of the century and left his mark on it. His clients viewed him as a friend. He showed the younger generations how to be a good mountain guide and what was really important to him: not the individual, but God, nature and his fellow man.

SPEED RUSH
Karin Steinbach Tarnutzer | Around the world

The highest mountain in the world was climbed in 1953; the last of the 14 8,000ers was climbed in 1964. In 1978, Mount Everest was climbed for the first time without bottled oxygen. Mountaineers in search of new records climb difficult new routes on the 8,000ers or look for new lines on the 7000ers. Or they race against the clock. The Austrian alpinist Christian Stangl established a new discipline, "skyrunning", which involves climbing the world's highest mountains as quickly as possible. "The challenge of beating the clock" is his credo, "Everest in a day" is his program.

In 2006, he reached the summit of Everest in 16 hours and 42 minutes. He made the round trip to the summit and back to the base camp in a total of 22 hours. After climbing the Seven Summits, the highest mountains on each of the seven continents, mostly in record times, he set himself a new objective: to climb the seven second-highest – and more challenging – peaks on each continent. There have been accusations that his record times were only possible because he used tracks made by other mountaineers. In 2010, Stangl claimed to have reached the summit of K2, but later admitted that he had lied about this feat. All his previous achievements are now under scrutiny. The inglorious result of record hunting?

Speed ascents in the Himalayas have their precursors in the Alps. In 1974, Reinhold Messner and Peter Habeler gained widespread recognition when they climbed the North Face of the Eiger together in under 10 hours. Solo ascents have continually reduced the record time. In 1983, Thomas Bubendorfer needed just 4 hours and 50 minutes. In 2003, Christoph Hainz took 4 hours and 30 minutes.

Yosemite Valley in America also has a tradition of speed climbing using time-saving belay and protection techniques. The hunt to set new records – or the "vertical speed rush" as Alexander Huber calls it – has brought enormous media attention to the "Nose" on El Capitan. In fall 2007, the Huber Brothers Alex and Thomas climbed El Cap in a new record time of 2 hours and 45 minutes. In 2008, this was beaten by 8 minutes by Yuji Hirayama and Hans Florine. The current record was set in November 2010 by Dean Potter and Sean Leary, who were 1 minute faster.

Between 2008 and 2009, "The Swiss Machine" Ueli Steck climbed the three great North Faces of the Alps in record time. He climbed the North Face of the Eiger in 2 hours and 47 minutes, the North Face of the Grandes Jorasses on a route he had never climbed before in 2 hours and 21 minutes and the North Face of the Matterhorn, again on a route he had no previous experience of, in 1 hour and 56 minutes. He views these speed ascents primarily as training for the Himalayas – being able to climb quicker means spending less time at extreme altitude, and thus reduces the amount of exposure to risk. Nevertheless, the rest of the world knows him as "the speed climber".

In summer 2010, Dani Arnold, a young mountaineer from the Urner Alps, literally ran over the 6 towers and 36 pitches of the West Ridge of the Salbitschijen in 1 hour and 35 minutes. "Climbing quickly is great fun," he commented modestly. It is obviously so much fun that, on April 20, 2011, he climbed the North Face of the Eiger in 2 hours and 28 minutes, taking 19 minutes off Ueli Steck's record.

"Are they all mad?", I hear you asking. Maybe. Or maybe not, if you put it into perspective. Just think back to the last time you climbed a long alpine route and each pitch flowed smoothly into the next; the changeovers at the belays were effortless; you were able to focus completely on the climbing. Remember how it felt when you opened the guide to read that you were an hour quicker than the recommended time? I rest my case.

The boss was unable to come to the phone. I explained to his assistant that he used to be one of the most well-known climbers in Switzerland and that he'd even done a new route on the North Face of the Eiger. "How fascinating," was her response. When I phoned back later, it transpired that the top manager of a major computing company did remember me after all. We once climbed together on the Salbit towers. It was a cold day and the conditions made things difficult. The granite face was battered by hailstones. He used to be a highly talented climber, but now he was scaling other heights. Such is life.

When I meet up with old climbing friends, it often strikes me that they have made a success of their lives. They've made it right to the top, as it were. Not only have they scaled North Faces and climbed 8,000 meter peaks, they have also reached the top of their respective professions. Take, for example, Heidi Schelbert, Emeritus Professor of Economics, who was the first woman to climb the West Face of the Scheienfluh in the Rätikon range of the Central Eastern Swiss Alps. Or the President of the board of directors and former CEO of Nestlé, Peter Brabeck, who still describes himself as a passionate mountaineer.

Why is it, I ask myself, that climbers often move up socially, too? Do their experiences give them so much courage and self-confidence that they are able to overcome social hurdles more easily than others? Or is it climbing itself that attracts the more competitive and motivated members of our society, like a bear to honey? One thing is for certain: mountaineers are motivated, whether it's to reach a summit or just the next hold, and this drive also gets translated into everyday life. "Passionate mountaineers are automatically assiduous followers of the achievement principle," writes Ulrich Aufmuth in his book "Zur Psychologie des Bergsteigens" (The Psychology of Mountaineering). The cliff face is therefore a reflection of our achievement-orientated society and not some refuge for drop-outs. According to Aufmuth, "the desire to always be better, faster, to achieve more – this imperative, which one describes as the achievement principle, applies as much to the mountains as it does to the executive floors of IBM or Toyota." Or, indeed, to political careers like those of the former General Secretary of the German Christian Democratic Union (CDU), Heiner Geissler, or José Luis Rodríguez Zapatero, the Prime Minister of Spain.

When I look around me on a Saturday afternoon in the fall at the local crag, amongst the freaks working their redpoint projects in shorts, I see computer technicians, engineers, doctors, biologists, physicists and philosophers. Unfortunately, climbing grade nine doesn't automatically qualify you for a position as managing director. The competitive world of performance climbing may even be a substitute for competition in everyday life. I have heard that a couple of the up-and-coming young talents spend so much of their time climbing that they have had no time to complete any vocational training, let alone an academic course of study. They apparently live in the hope that climbing competitions and free solos will bring them the recognition they seek and also allow them to earn a living. This might be so – but it's a narrow path to walk. However, those who don't make it on the World Cup circuit and survive their solo attempts often go on to pursue a successful entrepreneurial career in the outdoor clothing and equipment trade or the climbing wall business. Adolf Ogi, once the top climber in Switzerland, failed to complete his high school education. However, this didn't stop him from going on to become President of the Confederation and climbing the Matterhorn.

THE WAY TO THE TOP
Emil Zopfi | Around the world

José Luis Rodríguez Zapatero, General Secretary of the Spanish Socialist Workers' Party (PSOE) and Prime Minister of Spain since 2004, is the only Social Democrat leader of any of the larger member states of the European Union. The head of the Spanish government, who goes jogging every day and enjoys hiking and trekking in his free time, has announced that he will not seek a third term in office after the parliamentary elections in 2012. One reason for this might be that he wants to have more time for outdoor sports and trips to the mountains instead of politics and state visits.

Adolf Ogi, former Swiss Federal Councillor (1987–2000) and Special Adviser to the UN Secretary-General on Sport for Development and Peace (2001–2007), has his roots in Kandersteg and likes to refer to himself as a "mountain man". A passionate mountaineer, Ogi has hiked in the Swiss Alps with former UN Secretary-General Kofi Annan and in 2009, together with mountain guides, he led the two founders of the Swiss Economic Forum, Thun Stefan Linder and Peter Stähli, to the top of the Dufourspitze. In his opening address to the UN at the launch of the International Year of Mountains 2002, Ogi stressed that "mountains are not barriers, they unify and unite people throughout the world."

Peter Brabeck-Letmathe, CEO of the Nestlé Group from 1997 to 2008 and Chairman of the Board since 2005, has also demonstrated leadership qualities outside his management activities. Born and raised in the mountains of Carinthia, Austria, as a boy, he climbed mountains with his parents and, at 22, took part in an expedition to the 7,708 meter peak Tirich Mir in the Hindu Kush. Later successes included an ascent of the Matterhorn. One of his greatest role models is the British mountaineer Sir Chris Bonington, whose style of leadership places team performance above individual achievement on the mountain.

COMIC BOOK CLIMBING
Karin Steinbach Tarnutzer | Around the world

Man-sized, instable boulders obstruct the path – it's no easy matter to find a way through. Arriving at the foot of the cliff face, the essential items of equipment are of course buried somewhere at the bottom of the rucksack. Unpacking requires a certain amount of care to ensure they don't decide to roll off down the mountain side of their own accord . . .

The Zurich-based illustrator Esther Angst has captured experiences common to all mountaineers in picture form. Her drawings have plenty of stories to tell. There are diverging tracks in the snow, where partners fail to agree on which route to take. High winds on the summit blast not just the rope, but also pigtails horizontally up into the air or are so loud that hand signals are the only viable means of communication. Faces are shown strained with exertion or full of exhilaration. Her alpine adventures are observantly portrayed in the style of a modern graphic novel.

Climbing and mountaineering first really appeared in caricature and comic form in the 1980s, when Sebastian Schrank humorously documented the early days of sport climbing with the adventures of "Ron E. Bee from California". He was then followed by Georg Sojer and Hans Eberhard Köpf (aka Erbse), whose "Klettercomics" are now on their sixth edition. The Japanese manga series "Kamigami no Itadaki" (The Summit of the Gods) has been translated into French, German and English. The five-volume series by Jiro Taniguchi and Baku Yumemakura features mountaineering in the highest ranges in the world and was judged Japan's best manga by the country's Ministry of Education and the Arts in 2001.

However, the original ancestors of today's climbing comics are still household names to this day. As early as 1958/59, the Belgian author and illustrator Hergé sent Tintin and Snowy to the Himalayas ("Tintin in Tibet") to rescue Chang Chong-Chen, a Chinese boy Tintin had befriended. Captain Haddock was less than enthusiastic about the expedition: "Not on your life! I don't mind mountains as scenery but this passion for climbering about over piles of rock, that's what beats me! Beside, you've always got to come down again . . ." Fortunately for Tintin, Captain Haddock and Snowy they did have a rope with them. In fact, it was even one of the nylon ropes, which had just started to replace the old hemp versions. They put their rope to good use to rescue Tharkey, the Sherpa, from a glacier and climb a steep cliff. Captain Haddock: "And there are people who do this for fun!"

Over ten years later, René Goscinny (text) and Albert Uderzo (illustrations) published "Asterix in Switzerland" (the original French version was published in 1970). During their quest to find an Edelweiss flower, Asterix and Obelix find plenty of Romans to fight and climb a vertical wall into a world of eternal snow. They also make good use of a rope, too. Theirs appears to be made of traditional hemp, but it nevertheless has sufficient breaking strength to haul a drunken Obelix (who has passed out after draining a whole cask of plum wine) up and down a mountain. As a result, he draws the following conclusion: "So, Obelix, how did you find Helvetia?" His answer: "Rather flat".

DIGITAL NATIVES
ON VIRTUAL NORTH FACES?
Adrian Huber I Around the world

23

Many young climbers these days are themselves children of the digital revolution. Their decendents, however, are not part of that revolution any more but are Digital Natives – born after 1980 under the star signs of 'Internet' and 'Playstation'. If you look at how naturally children today get to grips with iPods, digital cameras and smartphones, it is clear that the digital technologies of their era are set to change them in ways we cannot yet comprehend. They navigate around the World Wide Web efficiently and with confidence, whilst their grandparents have only just realized that flicker.com is not some new high-tech lightbulb and Twitter is not a new comic strip, but the former is instead a virtual photo album and the latter a communications platform.

They nurture their friendships on social networking sites such as Twitter, Facebook and YouTube, they blog, chat and email. And more recently, they now keep fit by using a games console – something quite unimaginable before the Wii came onto the scene. The Wii Sports Resort and Wii Fit give you an insight into the extent to which computer games and physical sports can integrate and how they are transferred from real life to the virtual domain. Wii is a videogame console made by Nintendo and has been on the market since the end of 2006. It has new controls that look like a remote control but have inbuilt motion sensors. These mark the position and movement of the player and transpose them onto the screen. It is the motion itself, in other words, that makes it all happen on the screen. Virtual reality and real life have never been so closely interwoven.

To illustrate how the Wii console could potentially be a part of school sports, you just have to go to the German region of Lower Saxony. The news on the ground is that the Alfred Teves School, a primary and secondary school, has started using the Wii to support their school sports curriculum and to encourage students to get into sports. In a recent project called "Sports and New Media", for example, the Wii Fit Balance Board was successfully integrated into sports classes.

In March 2009, Satoru Iwata, CEO of Nintendo, announced the launch of the WiiWare game "Rock 'n' Roll Climber". The player has to climb up a virtual wall. As a reward, the player is then allowed to get rocking with his or her e-guitar on the summit. The game is on the Internet. It will certainly not replace real climbing, but then who would have thought 30 years ago, that there would be companies that made artificial climbing holds or installed artificial climbing walls in sports halls? 20 years ago, who would have imagined that it would ever be possible to climb the North Face of the Eiger in under 3 hours? Solo? Nobody.

We no longer have to wonder about virtual climbing, because it is already here. The question now is whether it will catch on. And if so, who with? Will climbing gear and climbing walls be a thing of the past? Will the crags and summits be abandoned? Will boulders be left to become overgrown with moss and lichen once again? After the heroic summit conquests of the war years, after the world's highest mountains have been conquered, after the limits of climbing grades have been pushed, after the latest trend of speed-climbing, will virtual climbing really take off? Will the digital natives conquer the north faces?

"It's where I'm going, not where I'm coming from, that carries me on the next mountain and beyond myself."

24   **Reinhold Messner**

A ROUTE THAT GETS YOU ADDICTED
Katharina Saurwein | Zillertal/Austria

Karin Steinbach Tarnutzer spoke to Mammut athlete Katharina Saurwein from Innsbruck about her successful ascent of the route "Ganja" in the Zillertal, Austria.

At the end of October 2010, you were able to complete the overhanging finger crack "Ganja", which is graded 8a+. How did you come across this project?

I tried to climb "Ganja" once three years ago. At that point, I wasn't so good at crack climbing and I didn't get very far. In recent years, I have gained a lot more experience of them and so I thought I'd give it another go. Martina Harnisch, my best friend and longstanding climbing and training partner, was really fired up by the idea and we both decided to work it together.

What is so special about the route?

It is one of the most amazing routes in the Zillertal! The valley is pretty much home turf for me; I'm often there at the weekends. "Ganja" is right at the end of the valley, past the sector known as the "Ewige Jagdgründe" (Eternal Hunting Grounds). Below the Klausenalm, there is a 10 meter high piece of rock, which is split by this perfect finger crack. It's not just the line that is really special. You have to place your own gear – friends in the crack – on the lead as you climb the wall which is gently overhanging.

Can you describe the technique needed to climb hard cracks like this?

Crack climbing means that there are no normal holds; instead you have to jam individual fingers into the crack. When we first started, I found that I often couldn't jam my fingers in. It can also be pretty painful. The route is 10 meters long, so you can appreciate that it requires quite a lot of jamming. The way you place your feet is really different, too. Since there are no footholds either, the only option is to get the tips of your shoes into the crack as far as you can. Martina and I slipped off a lot in the beginning, but slowly we got into the technique.

How long did you spend working the sequence before you led it?

It took about a month before we could do it. The hardest part is the start. After two weeks, we still hadn't managed the first two moves. The crack is so narrow that you can hardly get your fingers in it. Once we had managed the first two moves, it was only a matter of time – and the right weather of course.

Yours are the first ever ascents of "Ganja" by women. How did it feel after you'd sent it?

I could hardly believe it – I didn't think it would go. I was completely overwhelmed, really proud, delighted... I had a lot of fun working "Ganja", we were really addicted to the route. It's very satisfying to see the hard work and commitment pay off.

WITH EXUBERANCE, PASSION AND CHARM
Claude Remy | Around the world

There were three women from West Switzerland that became outstanding figures in alpine climbing in their time, causing a stir in what was then a male oriented domain. Loulou Boulaz climbed in an era where people who attempted extreme routes without a guide to lead them were viewed in a dim light. Betty Favre also led routes and had to remain as inconspicuous as possible when returning from her climbs with her husband and their friend Louis-Maurice Henchoz, so that nobody in the village found out about her unseemly endeavors, which took her to the mountains with not one but two men. Not a leader, but a perfect climbing partner together with her husband Michel, Yvette Vaucher was even accepted as a member of the elite French Alpine club "Groupe de Haute Montagne" in 1965.

Louise Boulaz (1908–1991) or 'Loulou' as she was known, was born in Avenches and learnt to climb in the Salève area near Geneva. She joined the Geneva group of alpinists led by Raymond Lambert in 1932. She was the first woman to dare to attempt the toughest faces in the Alps. This lively, slight woman was even at the forefront in the race for the Grandes Jorasses and the Eiger. Her medium was the big alpine faces, which demand absolute commitment and versatile alpine skills. Her achievements included the first ascent of the North Face of the Zinalrothorn and the second ascent of the North Face of the Dru, the Croz Spur of the Grandes Jorasses and the South Ridge of the Stockhorn. She also climbed the South Ridge of the Aiguille Noire de Peuterey, the Marmolada South Face, the Walker Spur and the Furggen Ridge on the Matterhorn.

As a member of the national ski team, Boulaz won a bronze medal for slalom in the 1937 World Championships. Modest as she was, she rarely uttered the word 'difficult'. For her, everything was 'lovely'. By 1939 expeditions took her to the Himalaya (to the 7,000 meter peak of Dunagiri), to the Caucasus, the Sahara and, in 1959, to Cho Oyu. Climbing mountains was not the only thing she did. Affected by the poverty and frequent periods of unemployment experienced by her parents, she spent her entire life involved in politics. "Loulou la Rouge" worked as a journalist and at the Bureau International du Travail. After she retired, she studied history and sociology, continued to partici-pate in leftist demonstrations and carried on climbing well into her old age.

Betty Favre (1918–1977), born Berthe Poschung in the town of Abländschen at the foot of the Gastlosen, grew up in modest circumstances in Château-d'Oex and was a bundle of energy even as a child. Betty's first big passion was her bicycle, which she rode on big tours together with her childhood sweetheart Ernest 'Jimmy' Favre. In 1937, for instan-ce, they rode from Chateau-d'Oex to Paris and back in just one week to visit the World Exhibition. As newlyweds they even spent their honeymoon in the saddle, cycling from Switzerland to Marseille, then by boat to Algeria, over the Atlas and Oran mountains in the summer heat, back to Algiers and back home again, all in one month. During the war, Betty did a Tour de Suisse on her own, spending nights sleeping outside for most of the way. The last stage gives you an idea of how strong this slightly built woman really was. In just one day, she rode from Airolo over the Nufenen Pass and Aigle to Chateau-d'Oex, 220 kilometers and 2,500 meters of height difference, on the types of roads and a pushbike of that age.

At the end of the 1930s, Louis-Maurice Henchoz was looking for climbing partners. His attention was drawn to Jimmy the plumber, who danced about on roofs whilst he worked and did handstands on chimneys to amuse children and passersby. When asked if he would be interested in climbing, down-to-earth Jimmy answered without hesitation: "Right away! Just let me go get Betty." When

he returned with his wife, Louis could barely hide his skepticism. Betty's delicate frame did not fit the profile he was looking for at all. But his doubts were soon allayed and the trio established a symbiotic relationship that lasted for decades. First they ticked off the limestone routes on their home turf. From Gummfluh to Gastlosen, existing routes were repeated and countless new ones put up. Then they took the Alps by storm, undeterred by the lengthy journeys, which they tackled on foot with heavy backpacks or by bike. Sometimes they took the car of Henchoz's unsuspecting father, if they could muster up enough gas.

Betty was practical, inquisitive, completely equal to her climbing partners and had great strength of character. On a par with her companions, she led routes just as frequently as the two men. What she lacked in strength and reach, she made up for in technique. She led the whole of the South Ridge of the Salbit and without realizing it or intending to, she made countless first female ascents. Of the three, she was also the photographer (she owned a Leica) and kept a record of all their ascents. Her alpine activities ranged from the South Ridge of the Peuterey to the North Ridge of the Dent Blanche. After climbing the South Ridge of the Stockhorn, Betty wanted to carry on over the as yet unclimbed ridge that linked it to the Bietschhorn, and it took considerable persuasion for her companions to hold her back.

The dream route of their climbing life, however, they owed to an encounter on the Piz Badile. Following their ascent of the ridge, they met the well-known climber from Geneva, Jean Juge, in the hut. He told them of a mysterious, almost surreal and unimaginably long ridge with countless pinnacles, on a mountain in the heart of Switzerland called Salbitschijen. Juge added: "It will never go." How wrong he was. In 1948, Betty and her two male companions were the first to climb the Salbit West Ridge – the most beautiful mountain ridge in Switzerland.

Yvette Vaucher, born Yvette Pilliard in 1929 in Vallorbe, grew up in the 1930s in Geneva. As a talented sportswoman, success in climbing and skiing came easily for her. Her first marriage took her away from the Alps to Neuchâtel, where she dabbled in parachuting for a while. She could not ignore the call of the mountains, however, and so in 1962, she returned to Geneva. An encounter with the then already famous Michel Vaucher was pivotal on her journey to extreme climbing, and after a few training routes in the Salève, he took her to the Mont Blanc Massif – and straight onto the East Face of the Grand Capucin.

Remembered in Alpine history as a unique husband and wife team, the pair tackled the North Faces of the Matterhorn, the Eiger and the Triolet, the Pilier d'Angle, the Freney Pillar, the Bonatti Pillar and the hardest routes in the Dolomites. In 1966, in just two days and in terrible weather conditions, they completed an impressive first ascent of the direct route on the North Face of the Dent Blanche.

In 1971, they both took part in the International Everest Expedition, which was sadly unsuccessful. Yvette – who by then had also climbed Denali – was the only woman to be invited to join the team of legends that included Don Whillans, Dougal Haston and Pierre Mazeaud. She did not climb exclusively with Michel Vaucher. Routes that she climbed with other partners include the Walker Spur, the Hemming/Robbins on the Dru, the Nose and Half Dome in Yosemite. Yvette was on the board of judges for the Piolet d'Or in 2005 and worked for many years as tour guide and as tour manager and president of the Geneva section of the Swiss Alpine Club.

RISKING DEATH TO LIVE LIFE TO THE FULL
Christine Kopp | Mount Blackburn/USA

It suddenly struck us with incredible clarity: we were alone. Two people on a remote mountain in the Alaskan wilderness, miles away from civilization. Our friend Paul had dropped us off in his plane and the roar of propellers was now a distant hum in the eternally light Alaskan summer sky. It was all down to us now for the next five days, where any kind of accident could turn into a disaster. Fear seized hold of me for a moment: what if one of us fell down one of the many crevasses in the icy labyrinth of Mount Blackburn? Or if either I or my partner got injured or suffered from altitude sickness on the way up to the 4,996 meter summit? Calling for help was out of the question. Our survival was now entirely up to fate – and we could only hope that ours was benign.

This was no time for getting scared. We immediately set off up to our first and only high camp at 2,800 meters. It was a real grind. With skis, heavy packs and expedition pulks, we made slow progress, swearing up the steep, crevassed slope. This led us up to a viewing platform, where we set up our tent and built a high windbreak out of snow. The view extended across the icy expanse of the Nabesna Glacier, stretching away for mile after mile below us. Somewhere at the other end of that glacier, a week's walk away, there were a few people living. Gradually, I was filled with a sense of peace. The words of Saint-Exupéry sprung to mind: "Only the unknown frightens men. But once a man has faced the unknown, that terror becomes the known."

After a stormy night and a windy morning, it was already afternoon by the time we broke camp the next day and headed for the summit. We were keen to make use of the daylight hours, still conditions and hard pack snow of this, the summer solstice. "It's a long, long way," Paul had warned as we left. He knew we were considering splitting a multi-day route into just two stages. His words rung in my ears for what seemed like an endless thirteen hours, as we climbed the 2,200 meters up to the summit and back with just a lightweight pack each, alpine style. Luck was on our side, though. By late evening, after the first steep and tiring 1,000 meters, we reached the wide ridge that, although peppered with crevasses, rose gently to the summit. The sun set at 11 P.M. but it never got dark. Beneath us, we could see the plume of smoke rising from Mount Wrangell, a glaciated volcano, the valleys dipped in shadowy light and the glistening spring snow of the glaciers – magical. We reached the summit at midnight on the dot, tired, thirsty and painfully aware that we still had a long descent ahead of us.

By 5 A.M., we were back at our tent. The sun had risen at 2 A.M. and was already high in the sky but there was also a storm brewing. A short rest and hot drinks were called for. Then, just in time, we packed up our tent and skied down to the flat glacier 1,000 meters below us, where Paul was due to pick us up again. Driving snow and hurricane-force winds then set in. We ended up tentbound for the next three days and nights until one beautiful morning, the familiar sound of our friend's little red plane heralded a return to warmth, greenery and people.

It was only then, in an atmosphere of safety and security again, that we finally felt happy, and just a little proud of our achievement – supposedly the quickest ascent of Mount Blackburn to date. Fear, tension, real and perceived dangers, all had vanished. What was left was a deep sense of the value of life, having just spent a couple of days teetering between it and deadly peril, treading the fine line between life and death and getting as close to that line as possible without crossing it. Life becomes condensed when you walk that line; your body, mind and soul are in complete harmony, concentrated on this one highly charged moment. Your every fiber is alive, as you experience the moment. The ascent of Mount Blackburn remains one of my most powerful mountain experiences.

Risking death to live life to the full is not just about the huge will to live, the feeling of living for the moment, of losing yourself in the action and sensing your own vulnerability. It is also about the images that we climbers take with us, that give us strength. With hindsight, even the toughest experiences turn into vivid images, images that you would never want to forget. Life is a rocky road sometimes, and it is then that you realize just how much your mountain experiences have enriched you. They are the embodiment of those moments in life when you cannot avoid something, and no matter how hard it is, you have to face it and find a solution.

It is rare to have those moments when you really feel fulfilled, at peace with the world. We climbers look for this in the mountains. Do we have a death wish? No, we have a thirst for life! We yearn for a life whose moments of fulfillment and clarity we carry back with us into the drudgery of everyday life. We are gripped by a deep longing for those seconds of harmony, because they are a symbol for a life well lived, for happiness and luck.

"Coping in hostile environments is in keeping with
our nature and our evolutionary challenge. It airs
the mind, and makes it free. To see that we are still
capable of coping in such environments gives us
such satisfaction that we return with fully
recharged batteries and fully able to function
in our unnatural civilization."

Oswald Oelz

28

FROM CRINOLINE SKIRTS TO SHOPPING QUEENS
Christine Kopp | Around the world

In the 19th century, climbing mountains was not viewed as seemly for women and the few female climbers that dared partake went into the mountains dressed in voluminous crinoline skirts. It was women like Félicité Carrel (the daughter of the mountain guide Josef Carrel, whose attempt on the Matterhorn in 1867 failed because the wind whipped up under her crinoline skirt and almost blew her off the ridge), Lucy Walker (the first woman to climb the Matterhorn in 1871) and Elizabeth Hawkins-Whitshed, who really shook things up in the male-dominated climbing world. Walker, for instance, usually climbed in a cotton dress and Hawkins-Whitshed, an upper class English 'lady', who appears in literature under five different names, used to leave her crinoline at the bottom of the route. They paid little attention to the conventions of the day and were pioneers when it came to mountain sports clothing.

During the course of the 20th century, women played an increasingly greater role in mountaineering but it was still a long time before equipment manufacturers recognized them as a customer group in their own right. It was only thanks to the sport climbing competitions of the 1980s that women were seen as a target market. Feminine looking climbers in tops and tights offered a whole new image of women in the mountains. It was time to have a rethink about clothing – and, of course, the vast increase in numbers of women taking up outdoors sports of all kinds was also a factor. All of a sudden, seeing a woman in the mountains was no longer a rare occurrence. Roughly 30 years ago, a few companies started to produce outdoor equipment for women. From 1995 onwards, things really took off. Within just a few years, the trade discovered that women represented by far the biggest growth sector. Today it is rare, if not unheard of, for a manufacturer not to run a special women-specific collection.

Having said that, marketing and fashion sometimes seem to play a more than prominent role. It is often the case that advertising is less geared towards the technical differences between men's and women's models and more about everything that the rather woolly term "lifestyle" encompasses. Directly linked to this are the designs, which can often be rather flowery or in pastel colors (girly-sweet?), or sometimes in bold colors like neon pink or fluorescent green (girly-dynamic?). All of these attempts have one thing in common: they are attempting to win over women as mature, independent consumers. The trade will go to great lengths, whether with genuinely, functional clothing that is designed to suit the female anatomy and physiology, or merely with fashion pieces.

From the woman who does two ski tours in the winter or two days of climbing in the summer, to the top freeriders or pro mountain guides, however varied their needs may be, women today will almost always select a woman's model as a matter of course. Moreover, the degree of self-awareness of many women has also changed. Outdoor equipment has also become a kind of status symbol for them. A woman will buy a complete set of products (as long as she can afford to) for each sport she takes part in, regardless of the frequency with which she uses it – to the great joy of the industry! According to industry insiders, women also shop differently to men. If men find a product that fits their functional requirements, they are willing to make compromises elsewhere. For women on the other hand, the aesthetics, color, texture and fit are deciding factors – and she will never buy a pair of pants that make her feel fat! According to the experts: "Women are more demanding than men. What makes women happy is good for men, too."

In the space of just a few years, women have become a serious, brand conscious target group with buying power and competence in the outdoor industry. The days of Félicité Carrel having to retreat on the Matterhorn because of her crinoline dress are well and truly over. Women have recognized the value of having good quality apparel for their chosen sport.

MAMMUT EXTREME – THE EVOLUTION OF A LEGEND

Harald Schreiber | Eiger North Face/Switzerland

Technical, innovative, award-winning and live from the North Face of the Eiger – the story behind Mammut Extreme is turbulent and full of spectacular highlights. Ever since its introduction in 1995, Mammut Extreme has been Mammut's flagship high-alpine collection. What is the secret behind these unique products?

Before 1995, Mammut was an established manufacturer of mountaineering hardware, and a brand with a worldwide reputation. Its brand profile was dominated and defined by ropes, harnesses, carabiners and slings. Mammut scored its first success on the textile front with its pioneering softshell apparel for high-alpine use and ski-touring made from Schoeller stretch fabrics. Its "Chamonix" pants became a best-seller and a symbol of the company's success. However, Mammut's wide range of jackets and rucksacks had yet to achieve the desired breakthrough. The launch of Mammut Extreme marked a turning point from hardware manufacturer to complete full-range supplier and established Mammut as a name to be reckoned with on the hardshell market.

The unconventional orange and blue color schemes helped the jackets and trousers to quickly set themselves apart both on the mountain and in the shops. Their extremely robust shell fabrics and flexible hood construction represented enormous technical breakthroughs and set new standards for alpine apparel. Conceived for extreme, high-alpine use, the range was aimed primarily at mountain guides and professional mountaineers.

Originally launched as the Mammut Sérac Extreme collection, the word Sérac was dropped for trademark reasons, which left the way clear for the more minimalist name Mammut Extreme, which soon gained cult status. In 1995, the *Deutsche Alpenverein* (German Alpine Club) expedition to the Nuptse East was the collection's first official outing. Jörn Heller, who today works as a mountain guide at the Mammut Alpine School was a member of that expedition. The recognition and acceptance of the core target group had been achieved.

The real breakthrough to a wider audience came four years later with the television production "Eiger live". On September 9 and 10, 1999, Swiss TV broadcast live from the Eiger as four professional mountaineers, Evelyne Binsack, Stephan Siegrist, Hansruedi Gertsch and Ralf Dujmovits, climbed its 1,800 meter North Face. They were followed by 13 cameras and were also equipped with mini cameras on their helmets, microphones and receivers. Evelyne Binsack and Stephan Siegrist both wore Mammut Extreme. The project, moderated by Röbi Koller, was a milestone for Swiss television and for Mammut. As a result, there was a huge increase in demand for the Mammut Extreme range, which at the time also included a rucksack. For a while, every product was sent out with an original stone from the Eiger.

The Mammut Extreme collection has remained inextricably linked with the historically significant mountain ever since. Images from the Eiger have accompanied the introduction of each new product in the Extreme collection. In addition, the line has also proved popular with professional mountaineering photographers across the world. Its strong colors provide a striking contrast with the high-alpine grey and white backdrop, making the climbers far more visible. Mammut had managed to achieve what only a select handful of other companies had done. Like Ferrari, the Swiss manufacturer had managed to set its own products apart by a distinctive use of color.

In 2006, ten years after the original success, the first revamped and expanded Mammut Extreme collection was launched. By combining the latest materials with contemporary designs, the legend was revitalized and carefully tailored to meet the demands of contemporary users. However, the emphasis on high-alpine functionality and innovative designs and fabrics remained unchanged. Brand presence had become an important factor in the meantime. In the late 1990s, Mammut customers welcomed the bold company logo and large lettering on their clothing, but by 2006, there was a definite trend towards understatement. The association with the Eiger still formed an important part of the collection's image. On the functionality front, especially the diametrically opposed developments affecting product weight and the robustness of the materials used were significant. It was now possible to make lighter and softer fabrics with equal, and in some cases, superior weather protection and durability. This provided greater wear comfort and enhanced freedom of movement for mountaineers.

In 2011, Mammut produced its second new Extreme collection, which again features completely new technical functions and color combinations. A new name – "Eiger Extreme" – was proudly introduced to put an end to any speculation about its intended use.

1995   1999   2006   2011

To demonstrate Mammut's longstanding connection with the Eiger, all the products in the collection are named after routes or places on or in the immediate vicinity of the mountain. For the first time, the range spans everything from headgear to rucksacks and apparel to mountain boots and covers nearly everything a mountaineer might need.

Tailored to the target group and incorporating the latest in technical advances, the products were developed in cooperation with selected partners (Gore, Polartec, YKK, Schoeller, Vibram), to guarantee outstanding quality and exceptional functionality. This was acknowledged at the ISPO 2011 in Munich, where the ultra-light "Felsturm" jacket was awarded the internationally recognized ISPO Outdoor Award. The Eiger Extreme is also the first range of its kind to react to the large number of female mountaineers on the hardest routes in the world by including products specifically tailored to women's physical characteristics. The Eiger Extreme range has retained its striking combination of oranges and blues, but also added new colors to widen the selection.

There was an enthusiastic response at the initial launch to dealers and journalists on the Jungfraujoch in November 2010. The event was also attended by three of the four climbers, who had climbed the North Face of the Eiger ten years previously live on Swiss television: Stephan Siegrist, Evelyne Binsack and Hansruedi

Gertsch. All the products in the collection have been subjected to rigorous testing. Under the professional supervision of Hansruedi Gertsch, selected items were even tested on the North Face of the Eiger itself. The results were conclusive: Eiger Extreme lives up to its name.

When compared to the previous Mammut Extreme collection from 1995, the Mammut Eiger Extreme 2011 range is significantly lighter and packs down much smaller. The "Extreme Nuptse" first-generation hardshell jacket weighed 1,062 grams in 1995, while its direct descendent, the "Extreme Logan" jacket tipped the scales at only 740 grams in 2006. The 2011 "Eiger Extreme Nordwand" jacket weighs a mere 550 grams and provides the same outstanding levels of weather protection at half the weight. The "Eiger Extreme Felsturm" jacket has literally blown the competition apart. At just 297 grams, it weighs barely more than a bar of chocolate. Huge advances in fabric technology have made improved breathability and considerable weight reduction possible without having to make sacrifices on weather protection. One thing has remained the same, however: Mammut Extreme continues to be tested, used and approved by top mountaineers on the most demanding routes in the world.

REALITY ALPINISM ON THE NORTH FACE OF THE EIGER

**Evelyne Binsack, Ralf Dujmovits, Hansruedi Gertsch,
Stephan Siegrist | Eiger North Face/Switzerland**

After four years of planning, two years of preparation and countless training climbs, the time had finally come. On September 9 and 10, 1999, over a million viewers tuned in to watch four mountaineers (three Swiss and one German) climb the classic route on the North Face of the Eiger live on television. For many mountaineering enthusiasts, it was a dream come true – authentic footage broadcast live from the infamous route, a route that many of them would probably never do themselves. Filming the ascent was an extraordinary experience for the four climbers involved, too. Here are their impressions as they look back on the "Eiger live" event:

"At the time, I didn't have much experience of dealing with the media. The thought of appearing on television made me feel pretty uncomfortable. For a long time, I was unsure about whether I wanted to be involved in the project at all. I also had strong reservations about some of the procedures, for example the proposal that all belay points were to be bolted. Once these issues had been settled and I'd discussed matters with an older colleague who was mentor to me at the time, I agreed to take part. Fortunately, the program was well-received, even by the harshest of critics – which was by no means a foregone conclusion. Looking back, I can see that the 'Eiger live' project marked an important point in my career, as it brought me widespread media exposure, which made working with sponsors easier.

The best thing about the whole event was working with the rest of the team. There was a really friendly atmosphere with everyone involved in the project. Even the producers had tears in their eyes when we completed the ascent. That was a very emotional moment. We all hugged each other spontaneously; including people whom you never suspected could be so emotional. It was an incredible experience. Everyone committed to the project and was proud about what we were able to achieve. The friendships made still exist to this day."

Stephan Siegrist

"The 'Eiger live' event was a fantastic project and not just from a mountaineering point of view. A huge team came together and co-operated in a superb manner. There were over 120 people involved, including film technicians and helicopter pilots, and it was great fun just getting the whole team into place and then achieving our objectives."

Ralf Dujmovits

"There's not much more to be said about the 'Eiger live' project that hasn't already been said, done or broadcast. The things that still stick in my mind are not the 'big scenes', such as reaching the summit, but the quiet moments off-camera, the final preparations and the days after the climb. For example, the camera placements had to be set up on the face. All four of us climbed numerous training routes before the live event, both individually and together. But these were all on other mountains; we didn't train on the North Face of the Eiger itself. Of course, I knew the Eiger from previous ascents. And I've climbed it several times since. Its status has changed somewhat over the years – it is no longer quite the definitive alpine route that it used to be. But to climb it, you still need the right conditions, to be very fit and to have the right people with you. Winter and spring 2011 saw excellent conditions – and several guides were up there on the face with their clients."

Hansruedi Gertsch

"Even today, the North Face of the Eiger is the yardstick for alpine superlatives. New routes are climbed, records are set, and films pull in big TV and cinema audiences, just like 'Eiger live'. The face, once known as the 'Wall of Death', has not lost its international reputation. Why has the Eiger not become just another climbing playground? Why is it still feared even today? Because it remains a monstrous ogre to anyone who approaches it without due respect. Any mountaineer standing at the foot of that face will feel their pulse racing before they even get started. The North Face of the Eiger gives, but it also takes. It makes huge demands of everyone who climbs it. Parties reaching its summit are rewarded with fame and honor; those less successful are robbed of their pride or even their lives. I decided that my third ascent of the North Face for the 'Eiger live' film was to be my last. Where emotions are so intense and happiness is so profound, friendships are made for life – such experiences should only be followed by new goals, new horizons and new challenges."

Evelyne Binsack

HANGING OUT WITH THE RUSSIANS
Robert Steiner | Tienschan/Kyrgyzstan

You hear all kinds of stories about Russian climbers. For example, that they are all total alcoholics and crazy risk-takers who don't know what fear is. When a route is too hard, too cold or too dangerous it often gets left to the "Russians". The climbers of Krasnoyarsk are to Russians what Russian climbers are to the rest of the world. "I wouldn't climb with them," one Moscow climber told me. "They're all crazy … Krasnoyarsk is in the middle of Siberia. It's cold for three seasons of the year, and when it finally warms up in summer, the Krasnoyarsk climbers head into the mountains, where it's still cold. Their winter training generally involves hacking holes in the ice on the Yenisei river and then jumping in. In January every year, they have their annual bouldering festival – at temperatures of minus 40° C!"

August 2004 found me sitting in a Russian pub, surrounded by empty glasses and a hoard of friendly Russian climbers. I was in good form, at least as far as drinking was concerned. I had recently climbed three 7,000 meter summits, lost 8 kilos in weight and was about to start a proper job. Somehow or other, I ended up agreeing to an expedition with the Krasnoyarsk climbers. The plan was an expedition for 2006 to climb the North Face of "Pik Pogrebetskij" in Tien Shan, a large mountain system in Central Asia. The face is virtually unknown, but then not every unknown face is bad, just as not every well-known face is good. It was almost 2 kilometers high; steep, cold, difficult and was the largest unclimbed face in the whole of the former Soviet Union. "The rock is crap, but the face is cool," was the inspiring comment from Sacharov, our trainer. "Get up there and show it what real men are made of."

Our team leader was Michalizin. It wasn't just his reputation that was big. As we boarded the helicopter, he weighed in at 114 kilos. We called him "Monster". He could walk ten hours through waist-high snow without food or drink. Apparently, all he needed was a sip from the bottle of cognac he carried inside his jacket to, I quote, "oil the voice and nourish the soul." He seemed to have all the energy he needed stored in his over-large stomach, which would decrease in size throughout an expedition. The other team mem-

bers said that he never did any sport at home and that instead just ate and drank. In 2006, he was apparently particularly overweight. "Michalizin was supposed to go to the West Face of K2 this year," they whispered, "as you can see, he's been doing some extra training!"

In Bishkek, we went out for what was to be a "quick drink". When I woke up the following morning my arms and legs ached so much it felt like I had already done the climb. We drove on to Karkara, a small village on the edge of the Tien Shan Mountains near the Kyrgyzstan-Kazakhstan border. Next to the wooden huts and the yurts, a helicopter stood surrounded by grazing cows and playing nomad kids. It looked as if someone had found it in a second-hand shop. The following day it flew us to the huge ice stream that forms the southern Inylchek glacier. Our mechanic was rarely sober and the helicopter flew badly. Reports that he had recently overhauled it did little to inspire confidence. The helicopter seemed to wobble and sway almost as much as he did.

Relieved to be back on solid ground, we set up camp near the other expeditions and immediately set about getting the food ready. When I saw what was on the menu, I started to worry that I was going to end up looking like Michalizin. "Tuck in boys – you're going to need it," Sacharov shouted grinning and quoting Einstein at us, "mass is energy!"

We set out under bright moonlight and reached the entry pitches at 4 A.M. High above us the blue-white walls of seracs towered against the night sky. We moved slowly, our ears straining to catch even the tiniest sound or indication of cracking, hoping that the seracs continued to slumber.

It took us a whole day to navigate the approximately 1,000 meter lower section of the face. That evening, we pitched the tents on a plateau below a stabile serac. We sat watching as the sun sank below the horizon and night fell. Looking in the direction of China, a mysterious group of mountains shone in the distant twilight as if made of white marble. We crawled into our tents to try and get some sleep.

We reached the actual start of the face the following day. Andrej and I climbed further to fix the ropes, while the others hacked out a platform for the tents on the bergschrund. Unfortunately, the spot wasn't completely protected from stonefall. You had to sit hugging your knees throughout the day and then repair the holes before you went to bed. According to a time-honored tradition, one tent was transformed into a casino. Here they would sit claustrophobically together to play a card game called "Preferanz", which could go on for days. During the first day our two-liter supply of cognac was reduced by 50%.

The climbing proved difficult and somewhat unusual. There weren't many cracks in the marble and falling stones threatened to knock us off as they plunged down the face. Stopping to place protection was particularly stressful. You had to be constantly on the look out for stones coming down. The next two days flew by. We were either climbing or resting, melting snow or trying to drive pitons into the rock or nervously shuffling up passages that couldn't be protected. At the end of each day, we collapsed exhausted into the bivouac tents.

On day three, we planned to move the bivouac up the face to the middle of the marble wall. But where in God's name are we going to put the tents? There was nothing but vertical rock and ice choked gullies. And so there we were, hanging like puppets on a string for hours on end, trying to chop out a ledge in an ice field. The ice we'd hacked away was dumped into a large hammock to extend our tiny balcony. Around midnight, we stopped, completely shattered. We had been able to hang one tent. "Sleeping bags outside, there's no room for them in here." All seven of us promptly squeezed into what was supposed to be a "two-man tent if you leave the rucksacks outside." Once inside, I planned to take off my inner boots but there were so many other legs and arms in the way I couldn't get to them.

The next four days was mainly spent getting up after not being able to sleep, scraping snow into a saucepan with freezing fingers, watching the stove for hours on end and forcing our tired heads

and bodies to concentrate so as not to make a mistake while abseiling, climbing, jumaring, etc. It snowed, the winds buffeted our tiny tent, we were constantly showered by spindrift. Even the card game got interrupted. The climbing, now at over 6,000 meters, remained strenuous. Each crack led to a new one, the limestone now gave way to marble. Our muscles were tired and aching; it took considerable effort to keep moving.

"How's it going?" Sacharov asked over the radio from base camp. "OK," we answered. It gradually dawned on me that "OK" actually meant "as expected" and that fear, danger, risk and setbacks all have their own predetermined order in this world.

The summit got nearer and nearer. We slept the sleep of the exhausted, hugging our knees to our chests. Constantly awoken by cramp and thirst, we kept asking the question we had no time or energy to deal with: why were we doing all this?

Day eight. Freezing winds chill us to the bone. Today, all seven of us are out climbing on the face. Late in the afternoon, Andrej climbs a band of black rock to reach the summit snowfield. Unable to find anything for protection, he digs himself into the snow to make a human belay and we jumar up to him. We walk the final few meters through the snow to the summit together.

GIVE THE ROCK A CHANCE
Martin Scheel | Alps/Switzerland

1978: On the cable car ride up to the Albigna Reservoir in the Bergell, the crack system of "Steinfresserweg" on Spazzacaldeira smiled at me. As luck would have it, the weather was not really conducive to alpine routes, so I was able to persuade my friend to climb this line instead. It turned out to be harder than I thought. On the fifth pitch, the crux section had to be climbed with only a marginal peg for protection. Not long afterwards, it was replaced by a bolt and Spazzacaldeira became an alpine sport climbing crag – which it was well suited to.

In the years that followed, I would spend days on end staring at cliffs through binoculars and learnt how to pick out lines that might go. With some lines, it took a lot of experience and imagination to be able to see them. "Supertramp" on Bockmattli was one such line. When we set off up this off-vertical face in 1980, the line was defined by a network of cracks between the smooth slabs, which ended up being very run-out. To climb a line like that free, not only do you need skill and courage but also a good measure of luck. If even the tiniest of holds were missing, you'd be left with just two options: use a chisel and bolts to force the route, or do it the fair way, admit defeat and retreat.

1988: Despite several attempts, the "Silbergeier" on the fourth Kirchlispitze in the Rätikon still eluded me. In the intervening years between "Steinfresserweg" and "Silbergeier", it had become clear to me that the crags had to be given a chance. In other words, you should either climb them free and only use bolts as protection, or do them trad style, without the use of bolts. Anyone using bolts or chisels to overcome seemingly impossible sections was robbing future generations of the opportunity. That kind of behavior is a dead end and was at its peak in the days of the "Superdirettissima". And so I left the "Silbergeier" to better climbers and I am proud to say that Beat Kammerlander made a clean first ascent of it in 1993.

"Modern" man has a tendency to want it all and have full control of everything. With safe cars, safe helmets, safe bolts, everything is possible and controlled. And so it is not surprising that a pleasure-seeking wave is sweeping the Alps and even classic crack systems and milestone climbs like "Supertramp" are being turned into bolted routes and spoiled. There are other people, however, who are looking for something different: challenge, nature, wilderness.

That is why it is important to maintain all types of climbing styles in the Alps. Let's not let the Alps be overrun by our consumer society! An ethics commission, made up of activists, regional representatives, the SAC and an association like Mountain Wilderness could suggest which routes should be cleaned and bolted and how, and which regions should be left "wild". That way, our children will also be able enjoy the variety of climbing the Alps have to offer.

DEAD SAFE
Emil Zopfi | Alps/Switzerland

Is climbing really still dangerous enough? A quick glance at the accident statistics is enough to confirm the worrying fact that the chances of slipping from a path (whilst wearing thick, red socks and sturdy boots) and falling into the void is far higher than breaking your neck on a route. Anyone with a death wish should forget those bolted overhangs and head for the next wet, grassy slope.

Of course, I don't wish to see anyone hurt. In my opinion, four climbing-related deaths per year is four too many. And I also welcome the fact that better equipment, bolts, training and technique have significantly reduced the number of accidents. However, we have now reached a point where sport climbers can hardly refer to their climbing as a risk sport, unless you include the race down the autobahn and over the alpine passes to get to the crag.

It wasn't always like this. On my second ever mountain route, at the age of 16, in the Glarus Alps in central Switzerland, a huge rock fell from the cliff above and cut my hemp rope, taking it down the mountain with it. Four years later, two friends were killed after falling 200 meters from the Bockmattli in the canton of Schwyz, Switzerland. Their packs remained on the cliff, attached to a peg. Death was a constant companion. The wobbly belay pegs were terrifying and we were always plagued by nightmares the night before an alpine route. No, I have no wish to go back to those days. On far too many occasions, the climbing community found itself assembled at a funeral on a Thursday, just in time to make arrangements for the weekend. The basic principle was: get out climbing again as quickly as possible! We were even straight back up on the Matterhorn the weekend following a terrible accident.

As an oldie, I'm pleased to see that sport climbing has become such a safe sport. It is encouraging to think that mothers no longer need to feel concerned about their children climbing or object to climbing as a school sport. On the other hand, with 40+ hiking deaths (2009), banning school hiking days might be justified. However, if it wasn't for the fear aspect, climbing would never have been invented. After all, it is only by overcoming our fears that we come to learn what courage is. We are haunted by a thousand repressed fears in our everyday lives, and yet, we seldom confront them. Up on a cliff face, we have no other choice. The sound of a quickdraw

clipping into a bolt after a hair-raising run-out delivers a sense of relief, which we are unlikely to experience in the office. If climbing did not involve fear, it would become as banal as everyday life, and there would be no reason to go and trash your fingers in a crack.

How many victims should be sacrificed to the mountain then? Four or forty? The question is obviously facetious. Climbing has become so safe precisely because most climbers are well aware of the dangers involved, because they constantly look danger in the face. We have a strong desire to live; it drives us up onto the cliffs, but also back down into the valley. Climbers are specialists at mastering dangerous situations or, as a psychologist might say, managing their limitations. We are driven by a lust for life, not a death wish. The saying: "He who exposes himself to danger will die thereby" is incorrect. The opposite is true. The forty hikers who die on average every year in the mountains have no intention of putting themselves in danger. They set out believing that their chosen activity is perfectly free from risk. And then they slip on a patch of wet grass. This is not that dissimilar to the hundreds of people who die on our roads every year; they don't stop to consider how dangerous it actually is.

Maybe the lesson learnt while climbing can be brought back into our daily lives; a risk consciously confronted is far less dangerous than a false sense of security. Life insurance has never prevented a catastrophe.

Fatal mountain accidents in the Swiss Alps			
Source: SAC			
	2008	**2009**	**2010**
Number of fatalities	104	112	124
Activity			
Hiking	39	42	54
Mountaineering	27	26	17
Climbing	6	4	7
Ski touring	8	12	27
Off-piste skiing	14	12	8
Other	10	16	11

Freezing cold

"I was reluctantly forced to make the acquaintance of Miss ......
after she introduced herself to me. She is the American mountaineer,
whom the newspapers reported climbed the Jungfrau last winter.
Apparently, she was accompanied by her dog Tschingel and nine
guides and porters with a sledge upon which she rode. She reached
the summit of the Bietschhorn before me and was hard work for her
guides." This is how Johann Jakob Weilenmann rather ungallantly
described Marguerite "Meta" Brevoort (1825–1876) from New
York. The maverick alpinist and first ascentionist of many summits
from St. Gallen wrote these words in the chapter "Auf Bellalp ein-
geschneit" (Snowed in on Bellalp) in the third volume of his collected writings "Aus der Firnenwelt" (Tales from the Mountains) (1877).
It is quite possible that he was disgruntled by the fact that the
American climber had beaten him to the Bietschhorn, in spite of the
poor conditions. The fact that she made the first winter ascent of
the Wetterhorn (3,692 m) on January 14, 1874 – eight days after her
successful first winter ascent of the Jungfrau (4,158 m) together with
her nephew W.A.B. Coolidge – two major achievements in the history of winter mountaineering – probably also did little to console
him. Maybe his contempt was due to the fact that he didn't like
dogs or at least dogs that could climb. He described Tschingel as
"vicious" and as a "fat and waddling pedigree lump".

Hot-blooded

"I just love him". This was Mary Isabella Straton's (1838–1918)
unauthorized reaction after making the first winter ascent of Mont
Blanc (4,810 m) on January 31, 1876. She reached the summit
accompanied by Jean-Estéril Charlet, the guide Sylvain Couttet
and the porter Michel Balmat. It was clear that the well-heeled English mountaineer really was passionate about the mountain, seeing
that she had already made three summer ascents. In the winter of
1875/76, she was the first to succeed where several other parties
had tried and failed. Isabella had to persevere though. She was
forced to stop for a rest day at the Grands Mulets refuge to nurse

two fingers that had lost all feeling. She treated them using snow
and schnapps. She recovered and the following day saw her out in
temperatures of -24 degrees. At 3 P.M., she sat together with Jean-
Estéril on the southern side under the summit out of the wind,
admiring the view. He had been the groom to her climbing partner
Emmeline Lewis-Lloyd in England, where the two had met. Shortly
afterward they traveled to the Alps together and made the first
ascent of the Aiguille du Moine in 1871 and the Pointe Isabelle
(3,761 m) – the peak to the southwest of the Aiguille de Triolet was
named in her honor five years later.

"I just love him." On November 29, 1876 Isabella Straton married
her guide in Argentière in the commune of Chamonix and changed
her name to Charlet-Straton. Together, they had two sons, who both
climbed Mont Blanc at the ages of 13 and 11 respectively.

Cold-blooded

"In the summer of 1881, I came to Chamonix for the first time. I
arrived there in bad health. As for mountaineering, I knew nothing
of it, and cared less." These are the opening lines of the first book
written by Elizabeth Main, née Hawkins-Whitshed (1861–1934), as
Mrs. Fred Burnaby, "membre Club Alpin Français, section du Mont-
Blanc" in 1883 in what was the first ever publication on the subject
of winter mountaineering: "The High Alps in Winter; or Mountaineering in Search of Health". During her first two years in the Alps,
Elizabeth Main – who was also known as Mrs. Aubrey Le Blond (her
second husband) – became a capable climber. However, the reception of her book in the British Alpine Club's "Alpine Journal" was
less than flattering. "The most frivolous and most insignificant publication ever to be presented to the mountaineering community,"
the editor W.A.B. Coolidge commented. Apparently, he had been
beaten to writing the first book on winter mountaineering.

Elizabeth Main's achievements were by no means only literary.
She made the first winter ascent of the Aiguille des Grands Mon-
tets, the Aiguille du Midi, the Piz Palü, Monte Sissone and Monte
Disgrazia, to name but a few. In March 1883, she was forced to turn

Meta Brevoort

back on the Dufourspitze at 4,200 meters due to the terrible cold: "Chicken, soup, champagne, in fact, everything except the cognac, was frozen as hard as a stone." Mrs. Main was in all likelihood the first woman to lead a man on a route in the Alps. In May 1883, she led a novice climber up the Col du Tour, which was covered in glaciers. They were forced to bivouac during the descent. The after effects of their expedition were the worse part. The two "tourists" were forced to remain in their hotel due to the severe sun burn they had received.

Bitter cold

"Croyez-vous que mes pieds soient gelés?"

"Non, je ne le crois pas. Ils sont devenus insensibles."

"C'est que, voyez-vous, s'ils étaient gelés, je préférerais mourir, car je ne voudrais pas vivre estropiée!"

"Et moi?"

"Vous … ce n'est pas la même chose, vous êtes un homme. Mais pour une femme, cela est horrible…"

This was the rather desperate dialogue that took place between Erica Stagni and Marcel Gallay, both from Geneva, as they were trapped in a crevasse below Mont Blanc du Tacul at around 4,000 meters on the afternoon or evening of February 13, 1938. The third member of their party, the Geneva mountain guide Raymond Lambert had left them to rush back down the mountain for help. He lost all his toes to frostbite in the process and had four of his fingers amputated. Marcel Gallay and several members of the rescue team also suffered a similar fate. It is therefore no wonder that Erica Stagni, a talented alpinist from a wealthy family, was worried about her feet. However, she and her companion were probably more concerned by the thought that Raymond Lambert might not make it down or be unable to describe their exact location.

The party of three had set off on February 7, 1938 to attempt the first crossing of the Aiguilles du Diable in winter. The difficult ridge on the Mont Blanc du Tacul includes five granite towers over 4,000 meters in height. After spending two nights in two different mountain huts, they set off and were caught in a vicious storm on February 10. They continued on to the final peak and then took refuge in a crevasse. This is where the rescuers found them, in arctic temperatures of -45 degrees. Erica Stagni was brought down safely and taken to the doctors on February 14; Marcel Gallay was forced to spend a night in the Refuge du Requin without medical assistance. Mlle. Stagni, as she was called by Gallay in his report on their expedition, did not suffer any frostbite, he presumed because the men made sure that she had the warmest position in the bivouac. They also concluded that trying to warm freezing arms and legs by hitting them with an ice axe was a poor idea.

Erica Stagni successfully continued her mountaineering career and went on in 1964 to be the first woman to climb the Hasse Brandler Route on the North Face of the Cima Grande. Raymond Lambert was involved in the first ascent of Mount Everest in 1952.

Ice cold

"It was perfectly clear to us that the first winter ascent would take a lot out of us. While this thought played on my mind yet again, Alena's call from about brought me back to my senses. 'Belay!' She led the next pitch, too. It had got so late that we were forced to look for a place to bivouac." This is how Zuzanna Hofmannová, née Charvátová, described the first winter ascent of the English Route on the East Face of the Piz Badile, which she climbed with Alena Cepelková, née Stehliková, from February 11–15, 1982, in the "Bergsteiger" magazine. The route had been attempted by numerous parties – and then along came these two Czech women climbers who freed it in alpine style. It marked a milestone in the history of both women's climbing and winter mountaineering. W.A.B. Coolidge and Johann Jakob Weilenmann probably wouldn't have thought it possible. Coolidge was the first man to climb the Piz Badile, accompanied by two guides in 1867. Weilenmann didn't know that the summit had already been reached when he made his attempt four years later. Due to his inaccurate map, he only made it to the pre-summit of the Petit Badile.

Zuzanna Hofmannová, Alena Stehliková

QUALITY IS NO COINCIDENCE
Josef Lingg | Seon/Switzerland

A sunny Saturday in March; it's late morning. The cliff faces south and has started to catch the sun; the rock is pleasantly warm to the touch. The climbing is tough but not impossible. The next belay is within sight. Suddenly, you've climbed yourself to a standstill. A foothold has broken off; the usual sequence is no longer possible. The next bolt is only a meter above you, and yet, it seems like a million miles away. Various scenarios flash through your mind: your partner is at the belay 20 meters below you, the ground is a further 30 meters below him, the last bolt is 4 meters away. A slip here would mean falling more than 8 meters. All of a sudden, the rock is too warm and your hands start to sweat. Will the rope hold?

When climbing, it is essential to be able to trust your equipment. Those who trust their lives to Mammut ropes justifiably expect the highest quality in return. Mammut has been committed to honouring this promise . . . for 150 years. Behind the scenes, a huge amount of hard work goes on in order to guarantee the legendary Swiss quality standards. At Mammut's production facilities in Seon, our ropes are subjected to a rigorous series of meticulous tests, meter by meter, to ensure that they fulfil the strictest requirements. This applies to both the inner core (kern) as well as the sheath (mantel). On modern climbing ropes, the sheath does more than simply protect the core; it forms an integral part of the load-bearing structure.

The smallest elements of a rope are the filaments. These fine polyamide yarns are used to make both the sheath and the core. Several yarns are spun together to make a twine. The twines are then combined to form a strand. A number of these strands form the core of the rope. The sheath twines are braided around the core strands. Mammut only uses yarns from certified suppliers. This guarantees that the materials are capable of meeting the technical requirements necessary for a Mammut rope and will continue to deliver the required strength in the future.

In the next stage, the twines are coated and thermally shrunk to around a third of their length. This provides greater dynamic elongation, which significantly reduces the impact force in the event of a fall. A sample is taken from every production batch (charge) and tested for elongation and strength before and after coating.

After this the sheath and the core are combined on the braiding machine. To do this, the sheath twines are rapidly braided around the core strands by numerous rotating spools. The machine's fine sensors monitor the process and interrupt the braiding immediately should the slightest inconsistency be detected. The rope is now nearly finished, but first, it has to go through another quality control. The surface and diameter of the rope are checked centimeter by centimeter using special sensors. At the smallest irregularity or deviation – even if it is just a protruding thread – the test is paused until a Mammut employee has removed the imperfection. All our ropes are fully inspected using this procedure.

Twenty meters of rope per charge are also removed for further testing. In order to do this, the ropes are first conditioned, i.e. subjected to a climate control test (temperature and humidity) according to statutory safety standards. In Mammut's test lab and drop tower, every single production batch is tested for all relevant specifications and to ensure that it fulfils the standards required. The most important test takes place on the drop tower. The drop test measures the impact force and determines how many standard falls a rope will withstand before breaking. Every rope must be capable of withstanding at least five standard falls. Depending on their construction, some Mammut ropes even achieve 20 standard falls. Only when the quality manager has signed the test report and approved the corresponding charge is the rope cut to the correct length, labelled and packed. A final inspection is carried out by machine, where electronic sensors again react to the slightest discrepancy. Every rope that leaves the Mammut factory is 100% manufactured and tested in Switzerland. For this reason, Mammut has been able to vouch for the quality of its ropes with a clear conscience for 150 years.

You stand there staring at the next handhold above you. There is no way to reach it statically. The rope is going to hold, you are confident of that fact. Even a fall of this length would be safely and dynamically cushioned. Knowledge creates trust; trust inspires courage. You push off and jump for it . . .

"THOSE WERE GOOD TIMES, DESPITE THE PRESSURE"
Susi Good | Around the world

Karin Steinbach Tarnutzer spoke with two-time climbing world champion and former Mammut athlete Susi Good about her time as the leading female competition climber in Switzerland.

You dominated the competition scene in Switzerland from 1990 to 1993. How did that come about?
Essentially, it was down to my husband Edwin. I started climbing with him when I was 17, and at some stage – we were already married by then – he suggested that we should enter some climbing competitions. The first of these competitions in Western Europe took place in July 1985, in Bardonecchia in the Piedmont region of Italy and soon after it was followed by the annual Rockmaster comp in Arco. At the start, these events took place on real rock, but in the interest of environmental protection and fairness – all climbers should ideally be subject to the same conditions – they soon shifted to indoor climbing walls. The Arco competition still takes place outside these days but it is held on an artificial wall. Italy and France were the driving forces on the competition scene. 1989 was the year that the first official Sport Climbing World Cup took place.

Did Edwin also take part in the competitions?
At the beginning, yes, when we first got started in 1990. But he soon stopped. For me, I was winning every Swiss competition I entered, so of course there was the impetus to keep at it. I was also pretty successful on the international circuit. We were on the road a lot in those days, in winter mostly in France and Italy. One winter, we spent three months in Australia.

"Pretty successful on the international circuit" is good – you were world champion twice and won practically everything there was to win!
Well yeah, it wasn't quite like that really. Winning the world championships was of course brilliant for me. October 1991 was my first Sport Climbing World Championship in Frankfurt, and, in 1993, at the second World Championships in Innsbruck, I also came first ahead of Robyn Erbesfield and Isabelle Patissier again. In 1992, I won the European Championships in Frankfurt. At Rockmaster in Arco, I came second in 1991, third in 1992, and then first in 1993. In the World Cup, I came first five times, second four times and third six times. At invitational competitions, I was first four times, second three times and third three times. I also won the Swiss Championships in Wengen in 1993.

And then in 1993 you just stopped?
Some time in the summer of 1993 I decided to take a break. But then I never started again because I wanted to retire from the competition circuit on a high note. Somehow, I just felt that it was all over for me.

Do you have fond memories of your time in competitions?
When I think about it, those were good times, despite the pressure and my nerves before the eliminators. We still have a box in the cellar with memorabilia from the competitions. The trophies were on display until the summer of 2010 in a glass cabinet at the Sargans climbing wall.

I take it you still climb though?
I still like to climb pretty hard but these days it's with the whole family. Indoors, I was climbing between 7c and 8a last year, depending on the route, outside I was still managing 8b. I imagine it will all be downhill from here on in though... Our four kids like to climb, the twins even compete. They all ski as well, better than me. We prefer to climb outdoors. But when the whole family wants to go climbing, the wall is easier because of the different levels of ability.

Were you able to make a living from climbing in your competition days?
I had a job with a firm of architects in Sargans up until the fall of 1991. The company always gave me time off for my competitions or for training, which really helped. Then I turned pro – but in those days pro climber status meant more expense rather than more income. The prize money was never very much. I was supported by Ruedi Eichenberger and his company Alpin Bergsport in Grabs from 1990 to 1993, before we became associates of Alpin Bergsport in 1994. In 1991, I approached Mammut, amongst other companies, to see if they were interested in sponsoring me. I got a positive reply back quite promptly and I was really pleased. Our partnership lasted until 1995.

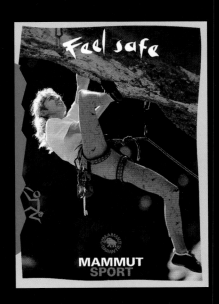

A GIFT FROM THE GODS
Ralf Gantzhorn | Cerro San Lorenzo/Patagonia

It's way too hot. We sit lethargically around the campfire swatting "tabanos" – the vicious, local horseflies. So engrossed are we with these annoying insects, we almost forget where we are: at the foot of Cerro San Lorenzo, the second highest mountain in Patagonia (3,706 m). If we were to turn around then we'd have a direct view of the huge ice mushrooms on the summit, the elegant, filigree rock towers on its ridge and the wild, crevassed glacier at its foot. The East Face of the Cerro San Lorenzo is over 2,000 meters high – but looking at it and given the height differences you could be forgiven for thinking that you were in the Himalayas rather than in front of "just" a 3,000 meter mountain. But we see nothing and say nothing as we sit and watch the fire, waiting for the meat to roast. It's too damn hot to do anything else.

It's been like this for over a week. Every day, the temperatures nearly reach the 30-degree mark and we have to remind ourselves that we really are in Patagonia, at the southernmost tip of the Americas, known for its never-ending storms and torrential rain. After seven days of good weather on the Northern Patagonian Ice Field, our allowance of sunshine and calm winds should actually be used up for the whole summer. Philippe and I have been climbing in Patagonia on numerous occasions, but we have never seen anything like this. We suspiciously greet every cirrus cloud on the horizon as the first sign of incoming bad weather. Heinrich sees things differently, referring to his good karma. We finally start out for base camp with differing expectations, our bellies full with half a Patagonian sheep.

The camp lies at the end of a wood, which the Chilean poet Pablo Neruda once described with the following words: "He who does not know the woods of Chile, does not know the world." The woods are scented, wild and serpentine. Methuselah beards of lichen hang from the trees around us. It looks like a fairytale forest, where you might almost expect to meet the seven dwarfs. We don't meet any dwarfs, but instead find a new wooden hut, which is also suitable for fully-sized humans. It was built to commemorate a

climber. In 2003, the Swiss climber Toni Rohrer fell during an attempt to climb the summit ice mushroom on the Cerro San Lorenzo. His estate paid for the hut, which would provide good shelter during a storm.

The next day, we again awake to sunshine and a perfect blue sky. By 6 A.M., we have packed the rucksacks and are ready to leave. We heave on our "torture boxes" as we have started calling our high-tech backpacks and make our way arduously up over the scree and glacial debris to the first pass, the Paso Comedor. We're planning to climb the Normal Route, which was first discovered and climbed in 1943 by the Italian Salesian priest Padre Alberto Maria de Agostini,

tance, we can see spectacular jagged black towers of the Torres Feruglio. They jut up from the ridge like the fingers on a hand; the amazing crenellations remind me of the Dolomites. On reaching the Brecha de la Cornisa, we drop down 300 meters before we can again head for the summit. We set up base camp at around 2,600 meters above sea level, in a level section of the Calluqueo Glacier on the West Face of the Cerro San Lorenzo. If you should get hit by bad weather up here, then one thing is clear – you have a big problem. There is no ridge or hill to absorb any of the force of a Patagonian storm. We decide to build a thick man-sized snow wall around our tent. As clouds gather in the west towards the end of the day, Phillip and I are pretty sure that there's a storm coming. I spend an uneasy night waiting for the brutal winds to be unleashed upon our little tent. Heinrich doesn't seem that bothered, he snores incessantly.

The following day, there is not even the slightest sign of a breeze. We set off for the summit feeling relaxed. The first challenge involves negotiating the 800 meter high ice slope, which has a gradient of 60 degrees at certain points. We cautiously circumnavigate crevasses big enough to drop a block of flats into. Then we have to negotiate the 20 meter high ice mushrooms, which can't help but make you feel uneasy given that these structures, typical to Patagonia, are known to be particularly fragile. At last, we reach the gap between the secondary summit and main summit and have only the final slope above us. We top out in our T-shirts; it's so hot up here. The view spans from the mountains at the edge of the Northern Patagonian Ice Field down to Fitz Roy, which dominates the seemingly endless horizon 200 kilometers to the south. Incredible! Only a few weeks ago, I failed to reach its summit because the usual Patagonian storm was unleashed and scattered all my mountaineering aspirations to the four winds. And now this: base camp to intermediate camp to summit in just two days. There's an old saying which says you just have to take things as they come. In Patagonia, it doesn't really matter who you are, how well you are prepared or what equipment you have. Either Nature will let you climb or she won't. We just have to be grateful for every chance we get.

who one might justifiably describe as one of the most important explorers of the last century. Patagonia and the Andes in particular, were still virtually unknown at the start of the 20th century. Agostini spent over 50 years exploring the southernmost tip of the Americas and his book the "Andes Patagoniche" is still considered the bible for anyone planning to explore Patagonia today. It was his attractive photos that brought great climbers such as Cesare Maestri, Carlo Mauri, Walter Bonatti and Gino Buscaini to Patagonia.

We reach the Paso Comedor, soaked in sweat. Then we head on up to the next pass, the Brecha de la Cornisa. Finally, it's time to get the crampons on, no more scree, it's ice from here on. In the dis-

WHY I CLIMB
Bernhard Russi | Around the world

In the area around Andermatt, where I come from, it would have been hard not to climb. My uncle was a mountain guide and hut warden at the Albert-Heim hut, and he would occasionally take me climbing with him, so I just fell into it automatically – in those days it was still traditional climbing with big boots. By the age of 13 or 14, we were mad for it, we just wanted to climb some routes. We had to nail our own boots back then – whether they held or not was another matter. When I was active on the ski racing circuit, I stopped mountaineering and rock climbing altogether. The main reason I took it up again was my son. I wanted to go climbing with him and sport climbing, which was just emerging at the time, offered the perfect way of doing that while minimizing the objective dangers. In the end, I got hooked again.

The most impressive routes I have done were certainly the ones I did with Röbi Bösch: the "Nose" on El Capitan, the Devil's Tower and "Chant de cygnet" on the North Face of the Eiger. I have a special relationship with that face. When I used to stand on the other side of the valley at the start line of the Lauberhorn Race, composing myself before my run, I would look across at the North Face and say to myself: well, going down here is nothing compared to that. That is how I used to calm my pre-race nerves. So climbing "Chant de cygnet" was special to me. I had always dreamt of laying hand to rock on that face one day. It was similar with the Matterhorn. It is only natural for a ski racer, who spends countless summers training on the Rosa Plateau looking at the Matterhorn, to say "I just have to climb that mountain!" But it was 30 years before I was able to climb the Matterhorn. There were always obstacles: time and time again, snow storms meant we had to turn back or could not even get started. Last summer, I finally stood on the summit. Of course you could say the Matterhorn is a heap of rubble and of course there are always too many people on it but for me, being able to climb it with my son was just an amazing experience, a fantastic big mountain route.

I am not so much into slabby friction climbing; I climb more with strength than technique. So I prefer limestone to granite, despite the fact that I started climbing on granite. I grew up with layback cracks; I can do laybacks better than precision footwork. Skiing and climbing both have an element of pushing limits, though I find skiing more dangerous than climbing. Climbing bolted routes, I am not taking such great risks, in the way I used to at Kitzbühel, for example. Success in both sports is measurable; with skiing it is all about your times and with climbing it is the grade of difficulty. This is probably the reason I became such a keen climber, because I was always results-driven throughout my skiing career; it defined me and was my source of satisfaction. Maybe climbing was even a way of getting out of skiing for me?

In the meantime, however, I also question my need to climb. Why is it that I climb past a piece of protection, when the next one is at least 4 meters further up and I am at my limit? Why do I do that? Then I realize I only do it for myself and nobody else. Climbing is a selfish sport. You only do it for yourself, for your own experience, to feel what it is like to push the limits and maybe even go one step further, and to enjoy that great feeling you get when you succeed. Unlike ski racing, which takes place in public, climbing – the way I do it – is private, anonymous. But the ambition, the urge to reach your limit, the focus on performance, all of these are the same as ski racing. As is the satisfaction afterwards. The memory of winning the youth Skiing Championships in Andermatt at the age of 14 is just as intense as my victory in the Olympics or when we topped out on the Nose on El Cap. The feeling of happiness was the same every time: the feeling that, at that moment, you had just succeeded on your highest objective.

TRIAL AND ERROR –
IN CLIMBING AND IN LIFE
Miss Kamikaze | Around the world

You have to be brave if you are going to learn to climb up stuff. But it takes even more courage to fall off. Jumping off and taking a proper fall right onto the rope – that is the royal discipline. For me, it is even more demanding than executing a really hard sequence of moves. I hope you enjoy this 'best-of-list' of my most spectacular falls.

1. On a beautiful spring day in Claro, Ticino
Trying to impress my new boyfriend, I selected a technically demanding route. On the crux I get to twist sideways and get myself really flat against the rock. Right at this crucial moment, I suddenly realized that my bra was caught in the crab on the quick-draw. I could not hold the move and fell off. When he lowered me off, I was virtually naked – my bra had ripped in two and even my T-shirt proved to be anything but 'tear-resistant'.

2. Birthday bouldering in Fontainebleau in October
I turned 30 that day and invited a few friends to come with me and celebrate my birthday and the beauty of the Fontainebleau boulders. Maybe that was why I felt particularly brave that day. After a short warm-up, I followed the burly boys up a wonderful arête that a few of them had already done. I wanted to see how I measured up to them. And it worked – almost. I got to the top and got stuck, with my upper body over the ledge and the rest of me dangling in the air, as is often the case in Font. There was no way out over the top, it was a case of going back down, in an uncontrolled manner. Although I hit the bouldering mat, all 60 kilograms of me landed right on my coccyx. My birthday party that night was a purely stand-up affair for me.

3. The Ceüse we all know and love
In Ceüse, the first three bolts are usually easy to clip and are moderately spaced. But the higher you get, the more bare rock there is between them, and there is always a horrible run-out waiting for you at the top. A band of bombproof blue-grey limestone looked like it had been made for me and so I summoned up all my courage to climb it. Ten meters up, I had to make a decision: traverse to the left or make a really hard move right. I opted for the traverse and kept going left. When the time came to get back on route, this difficult boulder problem seemed to appear from nowhere, a gruesome move off a sloper with tiny footholds. It looked scary yet manageable but turned out to be unmanageable. As we climbers

learn in our physics classes, a body at the end of a rope behaves much like a pendulum. And mine was no exception. However, because we humans are not made in a particularly compact shape, in a case like this, it is usually the head that makes contact with the rock first. When visiting Ceüse, I would highly recommend you take one of Mammut's new sport climbing helmets with you. Even though I lost a few brain cells in that fall, they still allowed me to work for Mammut.

4. My last weeks of freedom before embarking on a serious working career
During my last few days of freedom, I just wanted to climb, climb, climb. Having just got back from a short trip to Osp in Slovenia, I decided despite my lack of motivation to put in a small training session at the Flakturm in the center of Vienna. At the end of my session, I opted to have a go at one last boulder problem. The very last hold was worse than anticipated – a total sloper. I got to it with my arm fully extended and my body horizontal, with no footholds underneath (did hands-follow-feet bouldering really have to be invented?), and could not get my other arm across. I fell off and hit the ground with all my weight on my outstretched arm. I spent my subsequent first few days at work with a heavily bandaged arm in an oversized sling. It took two paramedics to wrench my ulna and radius bones back into my elbow. None of the doctors believed it was possible for those two bones to simply pop out of the joint without any serious damage – they were clearly not familiar with the powers of a good long warm-up session.

5. Topping out on El Cap
We had topped out the previous evening and that morning I rapped down the last pitch, collecting what gear was left, including our shit bag. I tried to rig things so that the incredibly smelly bag was hanging as far away from me as possible. Hanging on the wall, feeling the tiredness in my muscles from the exertions of the last three days, I was tying off the shit bag – and let it slip from my hands. The three day old stink bomb was now on a 1,000 meter free-fall and there was nothing I could do about it. To this day though, I am still glad it was the bag and not me.

   The life of a climber is not straightforward, especially when things don't turn out as they should – but hey, you just gotta keep trying!

WHY I LIKE MAMMUT
Kathrin Malzach | Seon/Switzerland

1 **Josef Lingg** – Chief Supply Chain Officer,
Mammut Sports Group AG, Switzerland
"Exciting tasks, challenging and progressive projects, super-motivated colleagues and the great trust of our superiors are the basis for an 18 year success story in the transition from Arova-Mammut to the Mammut Sports Group."

2 **Bettina Stähli-Wüst** – Supply Chain Assistant,
Mammut Sports Group AG, Switzerland
"The many exciting challenges that come from a constant process of change. Clear and transparent collaborative work."

3 **Bernd Wodarz** – Head of Sales,
Mammut Sports Group GmbH, Germany
"Opposites attract: a Rheinlander working for a Swiss company, a guy from the flatlands selling mountain sports equipment, breaking through cultural barriers. And: being part of a top international climbing team, with the summit always in your sights, combining mountain sports and occupation, being able to count colleagues and clients as your friends, always striving to attain new summits."

4 **Andres Lietha** – Head of Business Unit Hardware,
Mammut Sports Group AG, Switzerland
"Aside from the wonderful situation that I can combine my hobbies with my career, there is this: even after 150 years, Mammut is more dynamic than ever, open to new ideas and has the strength to see them through."

5 **Adrian Huber** – Head of Business and Brand Development,
Mammut Sports Group AG, Switzerland
"Mammut is a big animal. There is a lot of creative leeway. Working creatively for the future, initiating change, I get new inspiration every day."

6 **Ernst Schweble** – CEO, Mammut Sports Group GmbH, Germany
"I have loved mountain sports since I was a kid. I enjoy negotiating and selling, working and having fun with a highly motivated, excellent team."

7 **Bill Supple** – CEO, Mammut Sports Group, Inc.
"I have worked for 30 years in the outdoor business. As an avid climber, skier and trail runner, I like our dedication to developing innovative and technically highly developed, top quality products for core users and aspiring outdoor people."

8 **Christian Rohr** – Head of Accounting,
Mammut Sports Group AG, Switzerland
"The dynamic work environment at Mammut and a close connection with the products are daily motivators. The spirit of openness amongst the employees is unique."

9 **Oliver Henkel** – Head of Rope Production & Quality Management,
Mammut Sports Group AG, Switzerland
"Because my colleagues are open-minded and sporty, and because Mammut allows me to combine my profession (engineer) with my hobby (the outdoors)."

10 **Carmen Hafner** – Human Resources Manager,
Mammut Sports Group AG, Switzerland
"My work at Mammut is incredibly varied and I am lucky to work with a very strong team. The great potential for growth and exciting challenges in a dynamic setting makes Mammut an attractive employer for me."

11 **Michael Gyssler** – Chief Marketing Officer,
Mammut Sports Group AG, Switzerland
"Being able to drive and shape one of the strongest outdoor brands not only fills me with great pride, it is also pure fun. All the more so, because there is a super-motivated team behind the brand, who are fully committed to marketing the brand around the world."

12 **Stefan Merkt** – Head of Category Management,
Mammut Sports Group AG, Switzerland
"Mammut is one of the most appealing outdoor brands, competent and authentic. Category management is a new and very fascinating area of responsibility, with all kinds of exciting creative possibilities, such as the Eiger Extreme project."

13 **Agnes Häcki** – Secretary to CEO,
Mammut Sports Group AG, Switzerland
"Mammut is great! Really good, safe products for all altitudes, a lovely cheery team, a reliable employer and an amazing life expectancy for an animal that is already extinct!"

14 **Yukito Arima** – CEO, Mammut Sports Group Japan, Inc.
"I love Mammut because our global strategy as a premium alpine brand has been concrete and not just focused on short-term growth. And I like our Mammut logo. I always thought that Mammut would be more popular once our stylish Mammut logo was recognized; it's come true!"

15 **Markus Jaeggi** – Head of Purchasing,
Mammut Sports Group AG, Switzerland
"I was fortunate enough to be part of the team when Mammut was still a small company. I have watched Mammut grow every year since and it fills me with pride. I find it really motivating to be able to influence the company's future on a daily basis. I have never been bored at Mammut!"

16 **Antonietta Mare** – Group Leader (climbing harnesses, lifting and lashing straps), Mammut Sports Group AG, Switzerland
"A great interest in and identification with the brand (I've been here for 40 years!), the civilized and flexible work patterns for home workers."

17 **Bernhard Bolliger** – Country Manager Switzerland,
Mammut Sports Group AG, Switzerland
"I have witnessed the incredible success that Mammut has experienced for 30 years. No other company could offer me the opportunity to combine my hobby and my career in such a fulfilling way."

il negozio
Bramani
di antica
tradizione alpinistica ha fornito
l'equipaggiamento della spedizione
all'Huascaran (Perù), dedicata al
centenario del CAI di Milano

dal 1936 scarponi con suole da
montagna **vibram** marchio Oro
per la massima sicurezza.

Bramani

pinismo / sports / abbigliamento sportivo
a Visconti di Modrone, 29 - Milano

Vitale Bramani

THE FATHER OF THE RUBBER SOLE
Marco Volken | Bergell/Switzerland

We climb up the ridge in silence. Placing our feet on small footholds, our rubber soles grip without a sound, not even slipping one millimeter and preserving the rock. The scratch marks on the crux sections are evidence that in times past things were different – back then, they wore hobnailed boots. Because leather soles provided little if any grip on rock and compacted snow, until three generations ago it was normal practice to have 'nails' in the toe, heel and edges of your boot soles to provide better grip. Times have changed. Nowadays, we climb and hike on rubber – safely, soundlessly, without leaving a trace. The man behind all of this was Vitale Bramani. This is his story.

At the beginning of the 1930s, prominent mountain climbers experimented in the Dolomites using soles made from flexible India rubber, but just on climbing slippers. Soon afterwards, the Zurich climber Hans Frei (1910–1937) developed a light, stiff rubber sole with a slightly roughed up surface which he used to climb many first ascents in the Bergell. Count Aldo Bonacossa (1885–1975), who

was working on a climbing guide to the Bergell, heard about the sole and visited Hans Frei in Zurich in the winter of 1934, where Frei explained the reasoning behind it. Bonacossa immediately discussed the idea with the climber Vitale Bramani (1900–1970), who owned a sports shop in Milan. Bramani and his friend Ettore Castiglioni (1908–1944) came up with the idea of making a similar but somewhat heavier sole and equipping it with rubberized studs. With the help of tyre manufacturers Pirelli, the Frei boots were examined and a first prototype was made. Mrs Bramani was then allowed to test them out on the glacial slopes of Passo di Bondo. The rubber studs proved too soft and she slid all over the place. The next prototype was a success, and in 1937, Bramani and Castiglioni wore the boots on the North West Face of the Piz Badile, while Gervasutti and Devies climbed several other big routes in them. Within a very short time, these soles revolutionized the sport of mountaineering. Despite many attempts to copy them, the soles are still known by the name Vibram – the abbreviation of Vitale Bramani.

DOLOMITE DREAMS
Eugen E. Hüsler | Dolomites/Italy

43

is bitterly cold. It is February after all. Winter. In winter, one can be forgiven for having summer dreams. Of big mountain days in the kingdom of bleached mountains, in the Sexten range, on Sorapiss, the Tofana, Schiara, Rosengarten . . .

I went on my very first via ferrata in the Dolomites. It was a while back – Neil Armstrong was just stepping down onto completely new territory. Things have changed a bit since then, both in the world and in the Dolomites, and increasingly, I find myself looking back on my own "good ol' days". For a while now, experiences have counted more than climbing 1,000 meters in record time, and I now visit the mountains like old friends. Some of my dearest ones are between Eisack and Piave. I still get Dolomite fever; I can feel an expectant rumble in my stomach whenever I set out on a nice via ferrata again. And that is what is so fascinating about the vie ferrate delle Dolomiti, what makes them so special: the intense enjoyment of that magical landscape from the perspective of a wire cable. It is not about performing gymnastics on a rock face close to the valley base, nor pseudo-bouldering on some over-bolted overhang, but climbing mountains by way of their faces and ridges, up to their summits.

Ah, but I am dreaming again . . . It will be a couple of months until the last of the snow has retreated into the shadowy crevices of rock, even in the Southern Alps, a couple of months until the sun rises at four in the morning over the jagged horizon. Then, you can stand at the Torrani hut, with the Civetta behind you, wondering why you can feel a bit of a chill. Is it the cool morning air or the 3D display that Mother Nature has painted for you?

Click – click. I am standing on a small ledge and, holding the cable tight, I clip both karabiners across. To my left, a bottomless void, to my right, steep rock – dolomitic limestone, weathered by the Tethys Sea eons ago and, according to Le Corbusier, "the most beautiful construction in the world". I climb on. The safety cable cum guideline leads diagonally upwards to a steep vertical section. I'm on the tiniest of footholds, the grey asphalt ribbon of the Dolomites Highway lies 1,000 meters below, and in the wide, green valley basin, I can see the sea of roofs of the Olympic village of Cortina d'Ampezzo. I am on the via ferrata to Punta Anna and the Tofana di Mezzo: the supreme Dolomite experience. Basking in the sun is the monumental South Face of Tofana di Rozes with its rock spires. In contrast, the Marmolada Glacier left of stage is icy and cool. Even the Cinque Torri look like toys compared to the two giants of the Zoldano, Civetta and Pelmo. Pelmo? I can't quite see Pelmo, but it must be just . . .

I awake from my dream; a dream about the Dolomites, about via ferrata climbing in the Dolomites. It was beautiful. I daren't open my eyes, waiting until both the quiet disappointment and the heavenly mountain scene fade away. Outside, there is a blanket of snow covering the fields and meadows, and the roofs of houses and cars. It

HOW THE MAMMOTH LEARNED TO WALK
Beat Aerni | Seon/Switzerland

The mammoth image as a brand logo was introduced in 1943 by Robert Wobmann, whose intention was that it would become a symbol of quality. "The 'Mammut Ropes' brand arose from the customer's need to distinguish those products made by the Lenzburg rope works from all the other similar looking ones on offer. The mammoth represents power and strength. These are vital characteristics that this rope manufacturing firm has always aimed to guarantee and to improve upon." This is how an undated brochure from the 1940s reads. The new logo was to develop into an icon and a binding symbol for all the company's products.

Mammut's trademark logo – a distinctive image from then on – was retained over the coming years with only minor changes made to it. A rather insignificant rehash emerged in 1965, where the border was left out, the lettering slightly altered and the French word for ropes, 'cordes' added. The mammoth itself stayed the same.

It was in 1974 that the logo was first fully reworked. The lettering was changed to "Mammut Garantie". This indicated that the brand was not only committed to quality but would also guarantee that quality. The mammoth itself was given a fresh image, making it more abstract and a little bolder. It slowed its pace, lowered its trunk and became steadier and more consistent as a result. The overall impression was of a brand that was more serious, worldly-wise and technologically aware. One can assume that in the 1970s, this new logo was also considered more modern.

For the next 20 years, the logo only underwent the occasional small alteration. The company name changed to Arova-Mammut, and following the acquisition of Fürst, the lettering under the logo read "Mammut Fürst". From 1992, the two areas of the company were then referred to as "Mammut Sport" and "Mammut Tec". The image of the mammoth remained unchanged until 1994, when it was given a radical makeover. According to Hans-Ulrich Aerni, Marketing and Sales Manager at Arova-Mammut from 1973 and Director of Mammut Sport from 1985 to 1996, these changes were in part necessary because the Mammut Guarantee logo, as a kind of quality seal, was difficult to adapt to suit the growing, fashion conscious clothing sector, and was therefore replaced by various interim solutions. One of these was the addition of "Mountain Life", which was adapted for all mountain and outdoor products from 1990. In addition, Mammut had wooed its mountain sports customers since 1978 with the additional catalogue slogan "Peak Safety". This slogan was only replaced in 1992 by the words "Mountain Sports & Outdoor".

Today's Mammut logo dates from 1994. It correlates with the complete corporate identity overhaul and was created by the Zurich corporate identity company Nose. The "Mammut Garantie" was removed from the logo and replaced with the word "Mammut", which could be added to the logo if needed. The mammoth was more authentic and more concise and was instantly recognizable as a unique brand image. The mammoths new wooly coat and more substantial body suggested a certain warmth, which fitted in well with the key clothing sector. It was also more down-to-earth than its predecessors. In spite of this, the new mammoth was now attempting something the previous mammoths had been unable to achieve – to break out of the logo. The 1974 version only just touched the edge of the logo, and like its colleagues from 1943 and 1965, it seems to be walking in the wrong direction. The new logo on the other hand has broken through the logo's rim with its tusks, giving a sense of its immense power, a rebellious streak and the desire for innovation. The fact that it is able to do this is due in no small part to the solid foundations of the brand it stands for, enabling it to go out on new expeditions, with the "Absolute alpine" slogan to support it.

1943
The Mammut brand is launched, and represents a seal of quality for climbing ropes. The mammoth is a symbol for power and strength.

1965
Further minor changes are made. The border is left out, the lettering slightly altered and the French word for ropes, 'cordes', is added.

1974
The lettering is changed to "Mammut Garantie". This indicates that the brand is not only committed to quality but also guarantees that quality. The mammoth itself is given a fresh, more abstract image.

1994
A radical change is made to the logo: the mammoth changes direction. The new mammoth is more authentic and more concise and is instantly recognizable as a unique brand image.

450 YEARS OF MAMMUT?
Torbjørn C. Pedersen | Kathmandu/Nepal

I have just returned from a trip through India, Nepal, Iran and Turkey. Half way through the trip, I landed in Kathmandu and got ready for a fourteen day trek to Everest Base Camp. I treated myself to a nice long sleeved black shirt with a big Mammut logo right across the chest.

Whilst trekking through the mountains, my shirt attracted many comments, such as: "How many elephants do you have?" For fun I replied "Two." And then I explained about the Mammut thing.

During one such encounter, a man asked in amazement if it was true that the Mammut brand was founded in 1562, as the print under the logo read. It was then that I realized I had bought a fake, and that somebody in some backstreet factory must have thought the 8 was a 5 and printed these T-shirts like that. It must have happened that way – either that, or Mammut had a 300 year head start in the Himalayas!

"TIME AND AGAIN, I FOUND THAT I WAS UNDERESTIMATED"
Veronika Meyer | Around the world

Karin Steinbach Tarnutzer speaks to Veronika Meyer of Switzerland, the first woman from the German-speaking region of Europe to climb the Seven Summits.

Between 1991 and 2007 you climbed the highest peaks on every continent. How was it that you came to set yourself the goal of the Seven Summits?

I only started climbing seriously at the age of 30, and I then set about ticking off the 4,000 meter peaks. Once I had climbed half of the Swiss 4,000ers, I thought I may as well climb them all. That kept me busy through to 1995. At the end of the 1980s, I read an article about Dick Bass and his Seven Summits idea in a mountain magazine. I was fascinated – but it was not for me. It was far removed from my reality. In those days, 8,000 meter peaks were only tackled by very strong, very famous men.

But then you became hooked on the idea?

In 1991, I climbed Mount Kilimanjaro. I did my PhD quite late on and it was only after my doctorate that I got to know the mountains outside of Europe. It was then that I became aware that there is a lot more out there than the Alps. Then, in 1992, I stumbled upon an advert for Carstensz Pyramid and off I went. With that, I had taken one more step towards the Seven Summits, but Everest still seemed totally impossible to me. That kind of altitude was unthinkable, and with Mount Vinson also being so far away, it seemed out of the question. But I could not shake the idea. In 1995, I attempted to climb Aconcagua, but was defeated by storms. In 1998, I climbed Mount Elbrus, in 2000 Aconcagua and in 2001 Denali and Vinson.

You succeeded on the highest of the seven, Everest, on your fifth attempt.

I wanted to try it at least, and I was audacious enough to apply for Everest in 2002. I never had any issues with the altitude but I got sick with diarrhea and was too weak to continue. The following year, on my second attempt, I made it up to 8,550 meters. After the First Step, there was a strong wind blowing and there was such a queue of climbers just below the Second Step that I turned around. But I got the feeling that I would be able to do it – with oxygen of course. In 2005, it was extremely cold, the weather never really cleared and I turned back at 7,800 meters. In 2006, things went so badly that I did not even make it to Base Camp. But in 2007, everything went perfectly.

Had you decided you would keep trying until you succeeded?

No. In 2007, I told myself that if I failed this time, I would stop all this nonsense. Setting aside two months every year, missing spring every year, so much money every time . . . And then it was just so amazing. Of course I did suffer, too, especially on the way up the snow ridge. There was fresh snow and no wind. I almost died of sun radiation. The summit day itself was simply stunning. It was not even arriving at the summit that was so good – I was kind of expecting that, it was the reason we were there – but after fifteen minutes at the top, when we were heading back down and the day slowly broke, there was a magical moment where the clouds parted. It was incredible, standing on the ridge and watching the light show. Despite that, I still had the constant thought in my head: get down, get down – this is no place for humans to be.

At the age of 23, you were diagnosed with a heart valve defect. Was that never an obstacle to your climbing?

Having the experience of making good times and being able to do tough climbs gave me confidence. But there was always an underlying fear. Whenever I went for a check-up, they always said climbing is fine, but just don't go doing anything crazy. Of course, I didn't tell them what I was really up to. Sometimes I did wonder whether I should really be doing what I was doing. In 1997, when I started to feel that I had to conserve energy and my performance was suffering, I decided to have the operation. So now I'm living with an artificial heart valve. I just wanted to keep doing what I love most: climbing.

Would the fourteen 8,000 meter peaks be one of your goals if you were younger?

If I was in my prime, collecting the 8,000ers would probably be an enticing proposition. Of course, I am not comparing myself to women who climb professionally. I would never have thought I could make it up Everest at the age of 56; now I know it is possible. But I would not have made it without the fixed ropes. And above 7,800 meters, I was using oxygen, let's be clear about that. Nevertheless, Everest was still a huge achievement for me. Sometimes I even find myself talking about it! Time and again, throughout my whole life, I found that I was underestimated by people. So it is great when you can say that you have been up the highest mountain in the world. It gives me a real lift. One day, when I end up in an old people's home, I will hang a picture of Everest on the wall.

47

NIGHT ASCENT
Nives Meroi | Himalaya

We tell ourselves that the snow was white paper and that it would turn white again. At night, however, it is black, and with a headlamp only illuminating a small section, your surroundings become even blacker. But it is nice to set off for the summit in the dark, with your little beam of light shining from above your nose. The snow crunches softly beneath your crampons. The peace and the nighttime snow are one and the same, and your footsteps disturb both of them.

When the moon sits big and fat in the sky, it gives an impression of warmth. With a full moon, you can climb without a headlamp. The snow is the same pale color as the sky, and each step carries you further up to the expanse that links the earth to the moon. On full moon nights, you are simply climbing steps towards the moon. On the other nights, the moonless nights, the ascent is like stumbling across a scree slope of stars. There you are, right in the middle of this tremendous mass of stars, you can see swarms of them above the surrounding peaks, then below, the incessant twinkling of little lights everywhere, above you, next to you and below. You are walking on a scree slope of stars. It happens at about 7,000 meters; you notice then that you are walking on stars. When you stop to catch your breath, their light gasses permeate your lungs.

On new moon nights, you ascend like a thief, stealthily, to break into the top floor. We climb on the fresh plaster of the snow and try not to make a sound, so that we do not wake the owner of the house. We just want to pass through his yard. There are no guard dogs barking; it is the wind that can suddenly pounce on us, bite at our pants and make us beat a hasty retreat. When we climb at night we do not talk, nobody feels like it. We stop when we have to do something but we do so in silence, and then we set off again, silently crunching uphill.

Just like thieves, we have to laugh about it, and it does us good. A nighttime ascent is a happy affair.

UP EVEREST OR ANY OLD HILL
Karin Hörhager | Mount Everest/Himalaya

In December 2005, 85 year-old Mary Woodbridge announced that she and her dachshund Daisy intended to climb Mount Everest – without oxygen, without stopping between base camp and the summit and without any Sherpas (in her own words: "I can certainly carry my own food. I have prepared a solid Irish Stew and Power Crunchies! And the few cans of dog food for Daisy"). To help make this unusual plan a reality, the sprightly Brit wrote emails and adverts to gain support from sponsors and looked to the mountaineering community for advice.

The story of Granny Woodbridge's plan to climb Everest spread around the world in no time at all. The international press, bloggers and forums were all debating this crazy idea. Little did they realize that Mary Woodbridge was actually the product of a resourceful advertising agency and marked the start of a new campaign by Swiss mountain sports company Mammut. Mary Woodbridge's 'place of birth' was of course not the quaint village of Greenfield in the UK, but instead Mammut's headquarters in Seon, Switzerland.

At weekly meetings, a small group of employees who were in the know would convene under the auspices of CEO Rolf Schmid to further develop the idea and the adventures of their sprightly pensioner. And so they had Mary training hard (on Botley Hill – at just 5 meters, sure to be Britain's smallest mountain) and her grandson Phil creating a professional looking homepage which grandma could use to report on her project with videos and pictures. Though the initial "Task Force Mary" meetings were rather tentative – after all, this was new territory for them – as the campaign's success grew from week to week, so did the creativity. Should Mary make an appearance at the World Economic Forum WEF in Davos? Should one of Granny Woodbridge's rivals turn up on the scene with an even more insane project? Their imagination knew no bounds and ideas were discussed, outlined, acted upon or ditched.

The online community's reactions were keenly watched and served to fuel the Mammut team. A group of worried dog lovers expressed more concern over the safety of Mary's dachshund bitch Daisy – who, incidentally is a male dog called Ben in real life – than for Mary's own safety. The team was not only challenged by the online community but also by professional journalists. Prominent TV and radio stations asked for interviews and wanted to know more about this headstrong lady from Great Britain. For radio interviews, the team managed to find an English teacher in Zurich to give Mary a voice. Organizing television interviews was a whole different story. The shoot with Mary Woodbridge had long since been wrapped up and Mary, Daisy and their home was no longer available. Mary managed to put off the TV people, explaining she had no time with all the training she was doing.

There must be a few journalists who, with hindsight, are happy they did not secure an interview. As public interest peaked, it was time to come clean, leaving many media representatives at a loss for words. The fact that a couple of well-known editors had been taken in by a "mockumentary" (where fiction is presented in the style of a documentary) divided opinions in the media world. One thing they all agreed upon was that Mammut had pulled off an exceptional stunt with their Mary Woodbridge story.

Mary attained cult status and the subsequent campaign with the slogan "Warning: equipment this good can lead to loss of common sense" went down in advertising history. The "Task Force Mary" won't forget those exciting creative months they spent on it either. "It was risky, something completely different and incredibly exciting, a really special experience," enthuses Christian Gisi, now Mammut's Head of Marketing Communication, who was fresh from uni back then and was hired especially for the project. From apprentice to head of department – not all Mammut stories are fiction.

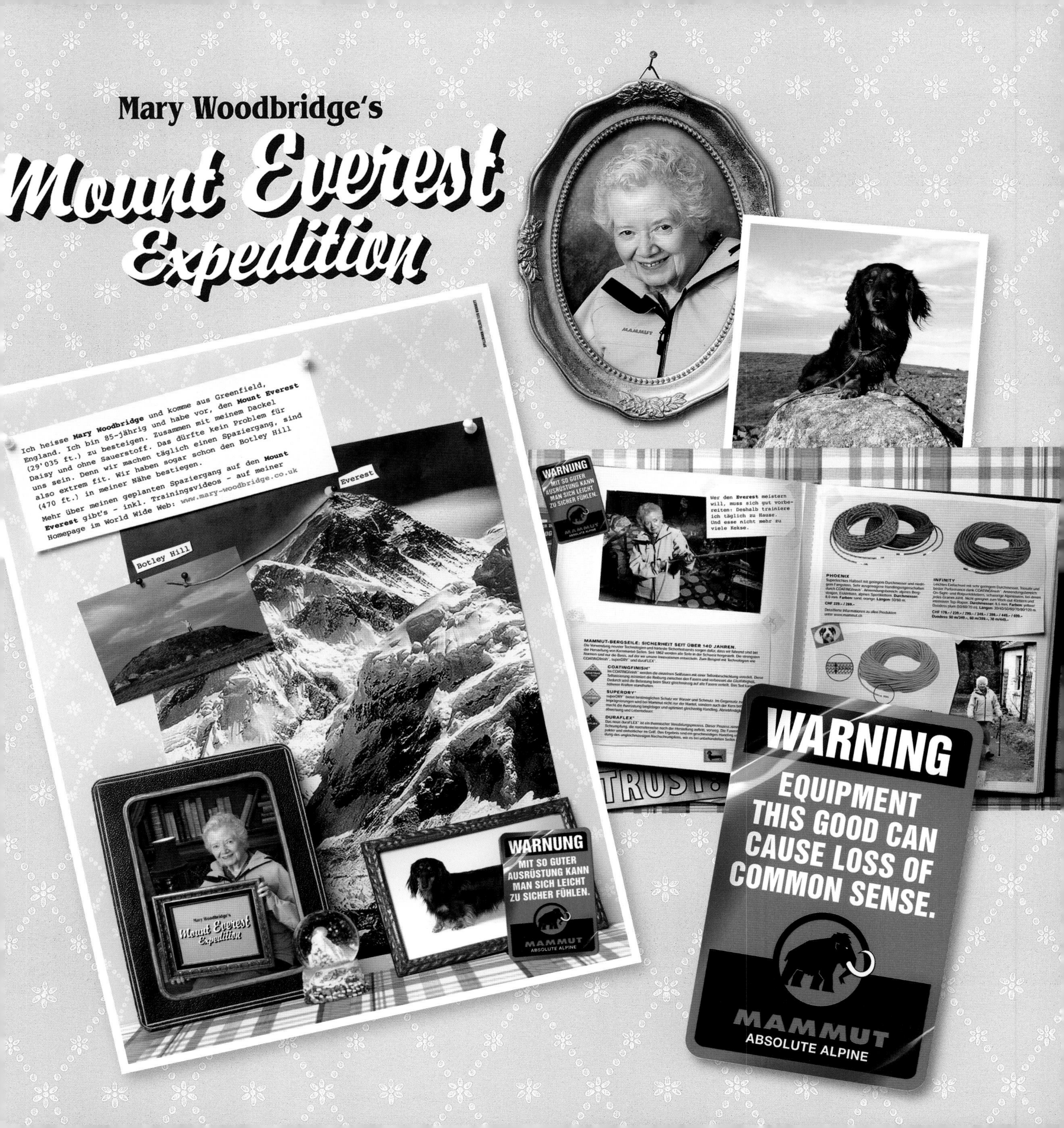

Mary Woodbridge's
Mount Everest Expedition
Ich heisse Mary Woodbridge und komme aus Greenfield, England. Ich bin 85-jährig und habe vor, den Mount Everest (29'035 ft.) zu besteigen. Zusammen mit meinem Dackel Daisy und ohne Sauerstoff. Das dürfte kein Problem für uns sein. Denn wir machen täglich einen Spaziergang, sind also extrem fit. Wir haben sogar schon den Botley Hill (470 ft.) in meiner Nähe bestiegen.
Mehr über meinen geplanten Spaziergang auf den Mount Everest gibt's – inkl. Trainingsvideos – auf meiner Homepage im World Wide Web: www.mary-woodbridge.co.uk
Everest
Botley Hill
Wer den Everest meistern will, muss sich gut vorbereiten: Deshalb trainiere ich täglich zu Hause. Und esse nicht mehr zu viele Kekse.
MAMMUT-BERGSEILE: SICHERHEIT SEIT ÜBER 140 JAHREN.
PHOENIX
INFINITY
COATINGFINISH
SUPERDRY
DURAFLEX
WARNUNG
MIT SO GUTER AUSRÜSTUNG KANN MAN SICH LEICHT ZU SICHER FÜHLEN.
MAMMUT
ABSOLUTE ALPINE
WARNING
EQUIPMENT THIS GOOD CAN CAUSE LOSS OF COMMON SENSE.
MAMMUT
ABSOLUTE ALPINE

TO THE DEEP BLUE WATERS OF TSOMORIRI

Karin Steinbach Tarnutzer | Ladakh/India

It was the light that took my breath away. Crossing the main Himalayan range on our flight from Delhi to Leh, the capital of Ladakh, the sharp outlines of one chain of mountains after another emerged through the rays of the rising sun. Several of the ridges still had the last traces of snow etched in fine lines on them, but the mountain slopes themselves were already clear. Over to the west, the two distinctive 7,000 meter peaks of Nun and Kun. The early hour afforded us amazing views over the Himalaya for hundreds of miles, across a sea of peaks that stretched as far as the eye could see. The contrast between the faces in the sun and those in the shade gave the effect of a solid wave of stone.

As a Buddhist region, the Indian province of Ladakh has little in common with its Hindu motherland. After the Chinese occupation of Tibet, many Tibetans fled to Ladakh. The suppression of their religious way of life there led to Ladakh being the only other region, aside from Bhutan, where Tibetan Buddhism still thrives. Throughout the province there are monasteries, chortens and long mani walls with carefully engraved stones. According to Buddhist philosophy, gods and demons live on the summits of mountains, in the rivers and in the earth. Spirituality is omnipresent and the sheer number of gods initially baffling.

Our trek took us from Leh up to the Changthang Plateau, a barren, uninhabited upland at 4,500 meters above sea level, which is largely on Tibetan territory but to the west reaches into Ladakh. It is the land of the nomads. For centuries, they have lived here with their animals: yaks as pack animals and to provide milk and meat, also horses, sheep and, because of their particularly soft, warm fleece, Pashmina goats. These self-sufficient nomads move from one grazing spot to another throughout the summer months. Every now and then, you come across stone corrals used to keep animals penned in or over which nomad tents are pitched – square and woven from dark yak wool.

This is an isolated region, and since there are no paths to speak of or any decent maps, we entrusted ourselves to a 'guide'. In his early twenties and from a nomadic family himself, Karma Namdak guided us for six days from Rumtse to Korzok, cooked for us and gave us many insights into his homeland. Since there would not be any settlements along the way, we had a lot of baggage with us, the transport of which was handled by Tsering and his five horses. We set off from Rumtse, at 4,095 meters, and after a relatively short four hour walking day, reached our first camp at Kyamar (4,383 meters). Dinner was served in the big mess tent and usually consisted of soup, rice with an assortment of vegetables and dessert. In the mornings, as is traditional, we were woken up with tea, followed by a breakfast fit for kings: from freshly baked flatbreads to scrambled eggs and porridge, everything you could wish for.

Throughout the following day, which took us over two passes, the Kyamar La (4,870 m) and Mandalchan La (4,996 m) to Tisaling, we were already able to marvel at the surprisingly varied fauna on the high plains: big herds of yaks, seemingly wandering free, picas, a type of marmot, Kyang wild asses, and a type of antelope the Ladakhis call Chiru. Full of impressions of this unfamiliar landscape and physically exhausted, we were glad to arrive at camp at 4,792 meters. The acclimatization process we had been through certainly paid off when sleeping at altitudes like this, but headaches still seemed par for the course. Luckily, the next day was a relatively short climb up to Shibuk La pass (5,015 m) before descending to the brackish lake of Tso Kar, where we spent the night at a pleasant 4,387 meters.

Next, there was a long stretch ahead of us over the 4,712 meter high Horlamkongka La pass to Rachungkaru, giving us lots of time to chat to Karma, whose good English meant communication was easy. Karma was a student in Delhi and spent his summers as a trekking guide to earn his keep. Compared to Europe, India's incredibly high unemployment levels and poor career prospects means guiding is a good option for regular work. That day, we met Karma's grandparents, who still live as nomads on the Changthang Plateau, and again we felt lucky to have a local guide with us, who not only gave us a real insight into nomadic living but by trans-

lating for us also made it possible to communicate with the local people. The old couple, with their expressive faces, warmly invited us into their tent where we were served bread, yoghurt and butter tea.

In the evening, we reached camp at Rachungkaru tired, and spent the night at 4,668 meters near some more nomads and with a herd of yaks all around us. The next morning, we were to ascend to the Kyamayur La pass, which at 5,125 meters was the highest point of our trek, and then over the Gyamaparma La pass (5,100 m) before reaching our highest campsite at Gyama Lhoma, at the respectable height of 4,895 meters. Getting there was another thing. Finding safe passage through the numerous tributaries of rivers was no easy task.

That night, we wore all the clothes we had with us and in the morning, the puddles in front of our tents were frozen over. It was the last day of our trek and in two hours, we reached Nyalangnyugu La pass (5,100 m), with fantastic views of our destination, the deep blue waters of the saltwater Tsomoriri Lake and the monastic settlement of Korzok. The mountains just on the other side of it were already in Tibet.

Up above the clouds, the silver plane slowly turns to head for Central Asia. Not too far to go now before we reach Atschik Tasch base camp at the foot of Lenin Peak (7,134 m). Hours spent on the plane, the flight bumpy with turbulence, quarrelling with inquisitive border guards, document and luggage inspections, loading and unloading, driving on dusty roads in vehicles which probably once belonged to the Soviet military.

At the camp, two proud, old veterans of Soviet mountaineering sit on a bench near the kitchen tent enjoying the warm mountain sun. The two comrades look as inseparable as the Klitschko brothers. Andrej and Oleg were good friends at university, where they both grappled with mathematical theories, statics, condensed matter physics and Marxism and Leninism. One day, Oleg found himself hanging around wondering about the point of academic life, not for the first time, when a strange, hand-made poster caught his eye. The university's mountaineering club suggested dropping mathematical formulae to opt instead for a life of adventure. On the poster, someone had drawn some climbers wearing huge backpacks working their way up a glacier to a summit. They seemed extremely happy, despite their heavy packs – maybe because they had statics the following morning? Across the horizon, you could see the snowy summit of the Caucasian and Tian Shan mountains. The ultimate goal of the difficult, rocky ascent was clearly communicated: mountains make a man!

This day was to mark a turning point in Oleg's life. 20 years later, sitting on a bench, drinking beer, the two friends watch a group of young climbers from Europe with a friendly smile. The group consists of five young climbers, all in their mid-twenties. Their equipment is arranged on a wooden pallet that also forms a base for the tents. A rather heated discussion is taking place. They disagree and argue, one of them is waving his hands in desperation. No grasp of language is necessary to understand what they are talking about. There is a fundamental disagreement over how the heavy and bulky kit is to be divided between their rucksacks.

"Can you still remember how it used to be with us?" asks Andrej nodding thoughtfully in the direction of the young men.

"It was pretty clear-cut," smiles Oleg. "What the captain said, went. If you disagreed, you had to do either all the cleaning up and cooking or 100 push-ups on the spot. The choice was yours!"

They reminisce about the days of the mountaineering club, training together and the first easy beginners' routes. Once you had climbed your first four-thousand-meter peak you were theatrically knighted as a "Mountaineer" by the club leader and received your log book – the "passport into adult life". According to the club tradition, you had to pledge allegiance to the "spirit of the mountain". In reality, the "spirit" was often quite drunk and despite his extravagant costume and make-up, bore a striking resemblance to the club leader. To show humility and devotion to the mountain spirit, the candidates had to kiss the holy mountain boot. The ancient item in question had its climbing days far behind it, but was quite by chance covered in the sacred dust of mountain paths and all sorts of other things – it normally stank of cow dung. Whosoever refused to kiss the boot was plunged without further ado into the holy mountain stream to help bring him to his senses.

However, these happy times came to an end and adult life caught up with them. But even the humdrum daily routine of work sometimes had a few surprises in store. Thanks to his position in the renowned Lenin factory, Oleg had access to the materials needed to make climbing equipment in secret – which was to become a real labour of love. Oleg and Andrei had long dreamed of a first ascent on the North Face of the Ak-Suu. They soon realized that climbing required not just skill and audacity, but that even the bold-

polished and filed pitons and carabiners – the equipment they needed to realise their dream to climb the North Face of Ak-Suu. During all this time, the guards dozed peacefully on the sofa in the office upstairs without any idea of what was happening on the floor below.

Once he had finished the carabiners and pitons, Oleg also went on to manufacture other new and equally important hardware. He produced his own nuts, wires, ascenders, crampons, buckles for backpacks and other useful items. Due to shortages in the 1970s, news of the new equipment spread like wildfire. Colleagues and friends eagerly adopted the idea of making their own free climbing hardware and within a few months, each section member was fully equipped. The secret production remained confidential and senior management were unable to explain the loss of materials or the lack of efficiency on the night shift. Instead, the unreliable accounting department got the blame.

Luck and good fortune had remained on their side. However, this was not always to be the case. Andrei, who was teaching at the university, once drove with Oleg to Khan Tengri. The mountain was anything but welcoming. Constant storms, avalanches, the conditions were extremely dangerous: at one point, Oleg fell 20 meters and had to be rescued. This prompted Andrei to write to his boss to get their vacation extended by a few days. No problem, they assumed his boss wouldn't have the faintest idea about climbing! He sent a telegram: "Belay device stuck during abseil down. Will be 1 week late." To his surprise, he received the following reply: "Cut the Prusik, idiot! You're fired! Signed: Head of Department, Master in Mountaineering, Professor Vladimir Ivanov."

The two veteran mountaineer goats continue to chuckle about their past in the Soviet Union, while in the meantime, the young Europeans have managed to sort out their luggage situation. In high spirits, they pack the equipment into their rucksacks. Enjoying yourself is the best way to ensure you have a good time on the mountain, laughs Andrej. The two Russians rise from the bench and swing their own ready-packed rucksacks into position. Together with the Europeans, they follow the route to camp 1 at the foot of the mountain – a passage they know so well, it almost feels like meeting up with an old friend.

est climber in the world wouldn't get far without decent equipment. At the end of the 1970s in the Soviet Union, climbing hardware was either non-existent or not commercially available. Suddenly Andrej came up with a brilliant idea.

Oleg had already been working for five years in his factory. He had been nominated several times as "worker of the month" and had even once won a trip to Bulgaria. The boss liked him and trusted him. More importantly, he had no understanding of mountaineering and never questioned Oleg's long holidays. Apparently, surveillance was not the factory's strong point and the guards generally spent the night shift sleeping in the factory manager's warm and comfortable office. Oleg worked for almost three weeks on his own project with machinery he knew so well. He designed, sawed,

Since 2007, Mammut Sports Group AG has been pursuing its commitment to training mountain guides in Kyrgyzstan in accordance with international standards. The project is run in cooperation with the International Federation of Mountain Guides Associations (IFMGA), the British Association of Mountain Guides, the Swiss Mountain Guides' Association and the expert mountain guides Adolf Schlunegger (Switzerland) and Terry Ralphs (United Kingdom). The local partner is the Kyrgyz Mountain Guides Association (KMGA). The second phase of the project started in 2010 to train aspirant guides and expert guides in accordance with IFMGA standards.

AVALANCHE RESCUE IN A COURSE OF HISTORY
Manuel Genswein | Around the world

During the last 20 years, the procedures and technologies applied in companion rescue and organized rescue have significantly changed. Besides the simplistic search technologies available at the time, particularly the fact that only a few formalized procedures existed, made it much more demanding to offer and teach interesting avalanche rescue courses. In the early 1990s, some countries had just stopped using 2.275 kHz transceivers, some applied the tangential search system with single antenna analog devices, others instructed the orthogonal grid search system. No systematic approach existed – neither for the problem of deep burials, nor for multiple burials – which would have been easy to teach, learn or apply. No formalized procedures were known even for elementary problems, like how to excavate the buried subject.

Hence evaluation criteria for working tools like probe, shovel or transceiver were only rudimentary. The quality rating of a transceiver was mostly focussed on its maximum range, while ease of use was hardly a topic. During my military service at recruit school in Andermatt, I was struck by how inconsistent our success was during deep burial searches, even though we always applied exactly the same search strategy. In numerous experiments the search strategy "fine searching in a circle", which allows for a very precise location of the buried subject independently of its antenna orientation was developed. The success of this practical application was only moderate, as at the time, I had not yet recognized that the probe always needs to be applied in a perpendicular angle to the snow surface when used in conjunction with a transceiver search.

The end of the probe therefore was always too low in the slope – retrospectively it is still not clear to me why it took me many years to recognize such an obvious mistake.

Inspired by a new transceiver development from the US, suddenly there was momentum: transceivers with two antennas allowed the display of distance and direction information. This meant that the rescuer no longer had to determine the direction of the search by himself, which lead to a great simplification in search and training. User friendliness has since then been the main focus of further transceiver development, which initially almost put important search and rescue techniques and functions on the back burner. Soon, consternation about the "new transceivers" arose: They were user-friendlier, but did not any more fulfil many practical requirements which never before needed to be worried about with traditional Barryvoxes. Nevertheless, it was clear to all involved at the time that the new path was the right one! It still took many years until the manufacturers were finally able to straighten out the teething problems of this new transceiver generation. As the performance and capabilities of the avalanche transceivers increased, so did user expectations. Whereas twenty years ago, people where happy to see one search target located within a reasonable time, today one is upset if the fourth search target is not hit by the probe within the same timeframe.

With the development of the first triple antenna avalanche rescue receiver, Barryvox was able to provide – before the turn of the millennium – the first operationally reliable solution for helicopter-based avalanche transceiver searches.

Organised rescue became increasingly faster and more efficient and by shortening the response and rescue times minute by minute they are now more and more able to save lives of buried subjects in the asphyxia (suffocation) phase. Modern search means not only reduced search times, but also shorter exposure time of rescuers, hence minimizing the residual risk of the rescue mission.

Triple antenna technology was soon implemented into normal avalanche rescue transceivers and allows for a precise search of the buried subject without misleading low-points in distance indication, which in the past could lead the rescuer to start probing or excavating the buried subject quite far away from its real location – fine search precision was henceforth increased.

After 1999 the "micro search strips" provided a search strategy which facilitated a systematic approach that led with high probability to a successful search in multiple burial scenarios. The development of the "mark" functions led to another big simplification of the search for multiple burials. Even though these "mark" functions can still only solve a part of the scenarios today, they nevertheless provide indispensable advantages to most rescuers and scenarios – for all other scenarios, the fundamental skill to interpret the analog tone in conjunction with the application of a search tactical approach remains a must. Closely associated with the problem of multiple burials is the topic of triage, since especially during companion rescue there are often too few rescuers available to rescue all victims simultaneously. The newly developed function to detect vital signs has re-invigorated the often suppressed discussion about triage. After a start with very emotional arguments, the discussion is now more realistic and objective. While there is no doubt about the ethical and moral correctness of triage as a measure to optimize the survival chances of a group of buried subjects, it was not easy to sacrifice the belief in the rescue of an individual for the sake of the increased survival chance of the group.

The last piece of the avalanche rescue puzzle was completely non-technical: after numerous optimizations of transceiver and probe search, the last and crucial step was tackled – the efficient excavation of the buried subject. After much deliberation and several weeks of practical tests, the V-shaped snow conveyor belt method was born. In the discipline of avalanche rescue, where every minute counts in saving a life, it is also of utmost importance to regularly train the excavation of the buried subject – and with a certain sense of urgency.

When teaching beginners and average users, it is today crucial to discipline oneself to limit the instructions to the bare necessities of a successful search and rescue. This includes the analogy between a transceiver search and the "airport approach", spiral probing and the elementary version of the V-shaped snow conveyor belt – while topics like "flux lines" and "grid searching in the fine search" are definitively out of date and only counterproductive.

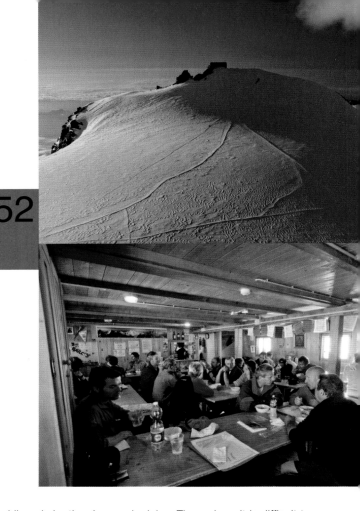

MARGHERITA, THE QUEEN OF HUTS
Marco Volken I Monte Rosa/Switzerland

What a view! Close by: Dufourspitze, Nordend, Liskamm. A little further away: Strahlhorn, Matterhorn, Dent Blanche, Zinalrothorn. The view goes on and on: Weissmies, Mischabel, Grand Combin, Mont Blanc, Aletschhorn, Gran Paradiso, Monviso, Piz Bernina; the Alpine foothills of northern Italy, the lakes of Lombardi, the Po Valley; a sea of clouds. It is utterly spectacular. And what do most alpinists do? They sit inside the hut, rubbing their temples because they have a headache. Or, exhausted from the climb and unaccustomed to the altitude, they sleep. Only a very few of them have eyes for the panorama. It is afternoon at the Capanna Margherita, the highest hut in the Alps. At 4,554 meters above sea level, the Margherita towers above tens of thousands of mountains. There are only four summits in the Alps which are higher than this hut: Mont Blanc, Dufourspitze, Nordend and Zumsteinspitze. The setting is also unique. Built right on the summit, it is exposed to winds and storms, attracts lightning and is frozen even when the freezing level rises to a summery 4,500 meters. It is without a doubt a milestone in hut construction – especially when one considers it has stood here since 1893. By comparison, the highest mountain hut in Switzerland, which opened in 2009 on the Klein Matterhorn, is at a 'mere' 3,820 meters. It is sheltered by the summit, connected to mains electricity and the cable car linking it to Zermatt runs no matter what the weather.

On February 19, 1889, Vittorio, Corradino, Gaudenzio and Erminio Sella – all cousins from a prominent family of alpine mountaineers – climbed the Dufourspitze via the southern spur. In the report they wrote for the Club Alpino Italiano (CAI), they added a lengthy observation. They suggested the CAI should support the construction of a high-altitude hut. "Anyone with a real love for the mountains will not be satisfied with reaching the summit and then rushing straight back down again. They want to linger up there for

a while, admire the view, and rejoice. These days, it is difficult to spend a long time on the summit; one arrives exhausted, one does not have a blanket, and the relentless howling wind makes your clothes freeze solid. [. . .] Apart from that, the most beautiful views and magical light effects occur at dawn and at dusk, in other words at times when one is seldom able to be on the summit. There is also the fact that one can only climb the mountain in good weather conditions, whereas the natural phenomena at high altitude only really achieve their incomparable glory when the weather is bad. In our opinion, the days and nights that we have spent in mountain huts, in the wind and snow storms, have been more vivacious, more gratifying and, we would like to say, provides more alpine memories for us than many ascents of the highest peaks. It is for these reasons that we believe our suggestion to construct this hut would be of great benefit. It was right and proper for earlier huts to be built half way up the mountain in order for ascents to be possible without too much effort and discomfort. But now that the most important mountains already have huts that halve the ascent, we must take a further step and build a hut at the highest altitude, in which one can spend a few days, perhaps even in the winter. Anyone who appreciates the beauty of the mountains, and who does not measure enjoyment in terms of kilowatt hours and difficulties conquered will surely share our views."

The Sella cousins also extolled the virtues of such a hut for meteorological research and for the examination of snow conditions. They were specific: the hut had to be easily accessible and provide an approach route that was safe from avalanches. Therefore, the locations of Mont Blanc, Matterhorn, Dufourspitze and Nordend had to be discounted. Two further summits on the Monte Rosa massif seemed to them to be ideal: the Zumsteinspitze and the Signalkuppe.

The CAI decided that same year to build a hut on the top of the Signalkuppe to accommodate mountaineers and to serve as a station for meteorological and geological research. Construction began in 1890. By mid-August 1893, the highest house in Europe was ready for business and was visited by the Italian Queen and mountaineer Margherita von Savoyen. And ever since, the hut has carried her name.

It has been in great demand. Over the years, the hut has been improved and extended several times. In 1908, it got the "highest telephone line in Europe", in 1937, radio equipment was installed, in 1970, a telephone-radio connection followed. In 1978, the hut

was demolished to create a bigger area. When it reopened in 1980, the new building provided 70 beds and great comfort. The rooms are heated, the kitchen offers a large selection of food and drink, and a comprehensive library helps to while away the days when the weather is bad. "Doing" the Margherita hut at least once in their life is almost a duty call for any Italian climber, which is why the Signalkuppe is perhaps the best loved 4,000 meter peak in Italy. Although the hut was built on the border, following an exchange of land in 1941, it stands entirely on Italian territory.

Today, the Margherita is a coveted summit for many climbers. For others, it is the experience of staying overnight at such a great height that attracts them. There are those, too, who use the hut as a base from which to explore the wide mountain expanse of the Monte Rosa massif or for acclimatization in preparation for even higher goals. For glaciologists and doctors, it serves as a research laboratory. Even in the 21st century, all who come here are fascinated by this intrepid house above the clouds. And although many visitors have to deal with headaches, spending a night at the Queen of Huts is not to be missed – the place where sunset and sunrise are so close together, where the night is shorter than in any other house in the whole of the Alps.

PASTA MAKES YOU HAPPY
Monica Wyss-Läubli | SAC hut/Switzerland

The windows are covered in condensation. Somebody uses their finger to draw a few symbols in it. There are skins, jackets, gloves and hats hanging up to dry over every available inch of space. A fire crackles in the hearth, tea water steams and cozy warmth radiates throughout the room. Outside, it is freezing cold and the sky is clear and sprinkled with stars.

A fascination with snow covered peaks attracts many people to the mountains in the winter, each of them comes with their own stories, dreams and desires, each with their backpacks packed and ready. Now, these lie unpacked in the corner. There is some food on the table, ready to be made into a good, filling evening meal. An extra bit of luxury has been brought in the form of a bottle of wine, and to the surprise of everyone, a few olives. A few leftover slices of salami from the daytime make for the perfect canapé. A simple dinner can be prepared with minimal effort even in the most basic of situations. An unforgettable mountain hut experience strengthens body and soul and enriches our lives with beautiful memories.

Ingredients (for 2 people):
20 grams dried porcini mushrooms
50 grams sundried tomatoes
1 onion
1 clove of garlic
80 grams cream cheese (e.g. 1 tub Philadelphia)
thyme if possible
250–300 grams pasta

Soak the mushrooms in approx. ½ liter of water for 30 minutes. Finely chop the onion and garlic and – if available – fry in a little oil, otherwise brown them in a dry pan. Add the mushrooms together with the water they were soaked in. Dice the tomatoes and add them to the mushrooms, leaving to simmer with the thyme for around 20 minutes. Season to taste with salt and pepper.

Bring a pot of water to the boil with a little salt for the pasta. Boil the pasta until it is al dente. Serve with the sauce adding the cream cheese on the top.

If you have space in your pack, you can enrich the sauce with ham or bacon. The red wine may be a bit too heavy to carry, however...

CHOP STICKS AND ICE AXES
Aljaž Anderle | Japan

If Japan is a fascinating mixture of tradition and technology served up in 15 delicately painted bowls on the floor, then Japanese ice climbing is like a Bonsai: small, varied and carefully packaged. Nevertheless, it's hard enough to pack a few surprises.

Hokkaido, Japan's northern-most island has the greatest potential for ice climbing and mixed routes. The most important areas are around the Sounkyo Canyon and on the coast north of Sapporo. Winter conditions are similar to those in Québec – damp, cold and windy. There is also plenty of snow. Most years, there is plenty of good, hard ice and the conditions are quick to produce the feelings well-known to all ice climbers, no matter how good their equipment – cold fingers and cold feet. In fact, the landscape reminds me of Québec, too. Even the architecture looks similar to buildings in Canada, and so do the ubiquitous 7-Eleven stores.

We were over for the Sounkyo Ice Climbing Festival, a colorful and interesting event. The organizers had everything so well planned, that they hardly needed our support, apart from to demonstrate the routes and give a slide show in the evening. The competition itself ran like clockwork. The routes were fluid and well set and the climbers gave their all. The weekend was dominated by a relaxed, happy and motivating atmosphere. The bitter cold weather dictated the daily rhythm. We climbed, got very cold and then sat in hot tubs to warm up, watching in bewilderment as the pretty Hong Kong tourist girls walked about in their mini skirts in temperatures around minus 20° Celsius (!).

The next day, our Japanese host took us to Chiyoshibetsu, a beautiful climbing area on the west coast of Hokkaido. We spent the day there and climbed the routes "Nezumiotoko" and "Nezumigaeshi". The steep ice and the cold, windy weather made it feel like we were climbing something much higher – but the roar of the crashing waves and spray constantly reminded us where we were.

The climbers taking part in the Ice Climbing Competition reflected Japanese society in general. Japanese people are modern traditionalists and ready to take on any challenge; they train hard and are quick to learn from others and improve. Honor and responsibility are important values, which are applied to everything they do. We saw an example of this out climbing with a local veteran. We wanted to give him the honor of leading a pitch, which was going to be filmed by Urban. He ran out of steam and fell, it was only then that we realized that the pitch was too hard for him. Battered and bruised as he was, he got back on the route and finally fought his way up it.

Tokyo. A city of superlatives. It's a city with a constant and fast-beating pulse. The main highways are busy from five in the morning and remain that way until ten in the evening. The subways run incessantly, and the streets and train lines crisscross each other on multiple levels. The city is like a giant vibrating organism. Nevertheless, the people are amazingly friendly and the place has a low crime rate, too.

Being in Japan means eating fish with chopsticks sitting barefoot on a heated toilet seat watching the countryside fly past at 300 km/h. Everyone you meet bows their head as a sign of respect. In the distance, the polite voice of the train attendant announces the connections from the next station. Stirred but not shaken, we really enjoyed being there.

We traveled to Nagano. Cveto Podlogar was our host for the remainder of our trip; he's a Slovenian mountain guide who lives in Tokyo. The weather had changed: it was much warmer and millions of trees had started to blossom. As a result, we headed into the mountains around Nagano to find the winter. We made several quick ascents of the most famous ice falls in the area. The Saganpeki Valley offers various styles of ice climbing, including a few multi-pitch mixed routes. However, it was getting near the end of the season and most of the ice had already melted. Instead we went on a ski tour through steep woods to a high plateau. It was quiet and really relaxing and we felt pretty sad – we were well aware that our trip was drawing to a close.

We said goodbye to Cveto and took a ride on the Shinkansen high speed bullet train from Uema back to Tokyo. Next stop: Europe.

WHEN A PROJECT BECOMES
A PART OF YOUR LIFE
Thomas Ulrich | Eiger North Face/Switzerland

I became a photographer by chance, more or less. My brother and I used to take a few snaps when we were out climbing and one of these ended up getting published. I did not, however, start out in mountain photography. Initially, I spent a few years taking photographs for hang gliding and paragliding magazines. I was working for a hang gliding company, organizing commercial tandem flights for a while and used the money that I earned to buy my first set of photographic equipment. It was a while, of course, until I was able to live from photography – but I was also a carpenter, a mountain guide, and a helicopter flight assistant; I've always liked a bit of variety.

My most significant photography assignments have largely been my own projects: the first winter ascent of the Ferrari Route on Cerro Torre, published in "National Geographic", also the traverse of Patagonia's ice-cap, which was the beginning of my passion for the horizontal arena, as it were – these days, I am mostly drawn to the Poles. Aside from the professional success these images brought, the projects themselves were incredible experiences. That was also true for the re-creation of the first ascent of the North Face of the Eiger, using equipment from that era, which I produced for Swiss television in 2002. I got it into my head that I wanted to shoot it in black and white and searched a long time for the right theme for this nostalgic look. I had discussed it with Stephan Siegrist and Michal Pitelka, to see if they thought my idea was feasible. When the TV station came on board, I then had the filming and photography to deal with, which was a challenge in itself. At the time, I had only ever worked on much smaller film projects.

The great thing with assignments like these is that they become a part of your life. The preparatory work for the North Face of the Eiger story was especially exciting and took up almost two years in the end. The equipment for the ascent had to be as authentic as possible, so we went in search of original pieces of kit from the era and visited one of the first men to climb it, 95 year-old Anderl Heckmair. We showed him the equipment we had collected and asked him questions about it, regarding the boots for example. He was the only man who could tell us how mountain boots were hobnailed in those days and we subsequently had the boots we used for filming modified according to his exact instructions. He was thrilled about our idea and explained precisely how his 1938 ice axe differed from the antique model we had found. He was no longer very talkative, but when we asked him for example how they roped up in those days, he patiently described it to us in detail.

Being able to visit this lean old man was very special for all of us. Heckmair's level of achievement in 1938 could probably be compared to that of Ueli Steck today. Back then, he was absolutely top league, with muscles trained right down to their core. I have climbed the classic route on the North Face of the Eiger five times now, and even as a relatively good climber, you still have to hang on. The face is exposed in places, it is really wild. Heckmair still had a dry sense of humor and true to his famous saying: "Alcohol enjoyed in moderation also does no harm in larger quantities" was not averse to a little schnapps, despite his advanced years.

Our antiquated equipment proved challenging for Michal and Stef at times. The soles on the boots were too soft and kept bending, making it difficult to climb with crampons. And the crampons were hinged, so that the front points, which Heckmair was one of the first to use, were not actually much use, as the sole would bend together with the crampons. The modern technique of torqueing the shaft of the axe was not possible with the kind of ice axes

they had then, and besides, Heckmair and Vörg only had one ice axe and one hammer each. To increase the hemp rope's safety, our rope manufacturers added a nylon core to the re-created version. However, when we tested it before the shoot on the Mammut test rig, it turned out that this was of no benefit. The stiff hemp mantel tore first, closely followed by the elastic core. Stef and Michal were very aware that they could not afford to take a lead fall on that rope.

During the ascent, Hanspeter Dubach and Michi Wärthl either belayed me or fixed ropes so that I was able to move independently and alternate between the stills camera and the film camera. That was quite a strain in itself, and I also felt responsible for the safety

of my friends Michal and Stef, without whom none of this would have been possible. The moment I savored the most was on day two, when I topped out on the summit of the Eiger and realized that my plan had worked. I felt relieved, liberated and happy. The book deal on the project, the articles, the pleasing viewing figures for the film – all that came much later. But it served as yet another reminder to me: When you have an idea and believe it to be a good one, you have to keep going and make it happen!

THEN AND NOW
Reto Rüegger | Alps/Switzerland

Product	Weight in gm	Year	Material
Climbing rope	2,400 (30 m)	1912	Hemp
Ice axe	1230	1920	Wood, forged steel
Piton	164	1929	Forged steel
Crampons	820 (pair)	1902	Forged steel, leather
Snowshoes	1,084 (pair)	1916	Wood, hemp, steel wire binding
Backpack	630	1928	Leather
Helmet	111	1930	Felt, leather
Headgear	26	1935	Silk
Goggles	37	1919	Glass, aluminum, elastic band
Jacket	760	1927	Cotton
Pants	900	1930	Wool
Pullover	1210	1925	Wool
Baselayer	1260	1947	Wool
Gloves	260	1928	Wool, leather
Leg warmers	294	1925	Wool
Mountain boots	2047	1920	Leather, steel, brass, aluminum
Carabiner	130	1910	Forged steel
Total	**13,363**		

Product	Weight in gm	Year	Material
Climbing rope	1,770 (30 m)	2012	High quality polyamide 6
Ice axe	320	2012	Steel, carbon, polyamide
Piton	120	2012	Carbon steel
Crampons	380 (pair)	2012	Aluminum alloy, polyamide
Snowshoes	1,720 (pair)	2012	Aluminum, neoprene, polyamide, rubber
Backpack	1290	2012	Polyamide, aluminum, EVA foam
Helmet	250	2012	Polystyrene foam, polyamide, polycarbonate
Headgear	20	2012	Microfiber, polyester
Goggles	50	2012	Glass, plastic, rubber, elastic band
Jacket	550	2012	Polyamide, elastane, polytetrafluorethylene
Pants	570	2012	Polyamide, elastane, polytetrafluorethylene
Pullover	480	2012	Polyamide, polyester, elastane
Baselayer	520	2012	Merino wool, polyester
Gloves	305	2012	Polyamide, polyester, elastane, polyurethane, goatskin
Gaiters	210	2012	Polyamide, polytetrafluorethylene
Mountain boots	1888	2012	Synthetic leather, polyamide, polyester, rubber, EVA, carbon
Carabiner	40	2012	Aluminum 7075-T6, aluminum-zink-magnesium-alloys
Total	**10,483**		

"FALLING WAS NOT AN OPTION"
Max Niedermann | Alps/Switzerland

Max Niedermann climbed 40 new routes in the 1950s and 1960s. He was active in his local area of Alpstein, as well as the Churfirsten massif, the Bockmattli and the Rätikon. Above all, however, he is known for his routes in the Urner Alps. Many of them are now considered classics, for example the "Zwillingsturm" on the South East Face of the Salbitschijen, the South West Face of the Gross Bielenhorn or the "Niedermann/Sieber" route on the Graue Wand. Karin Steinbach Tarnutzer spoke to the 83-year old mountaineer about the tactics he employed on his first ascents.

Mr. Niedermann, your routes are famous for their great lines. Can you explain to us how you found them?
You have to have an eye for it. We used to scour the cliffs with binoculars first. Unlike nowadays where you can bolt any section of rock you want, in my day we had to look for cracks, which we could protect with pitons or wooden chocks. We followed the natural fault lines in the rock, which provided logical routes to climb. You sometimes hear today that new routes are equipped from above. We climbed everything ground up.

And how did you select your cliffs?
In climbing circles, you often heard where there were new routes to be done. I visited the Rätikon a few times with my climbing partners from the Alpstein Climbing Club and stole a march on my fellow climbers from the Chur Climbing Club. At the Scheideggwetterhorn in the Bernese Alps, I remember seeing a photo of the North Face of the

Wetterhorn in "Der Familienfreund", a newspaper of the time. It had really good details of the rock structures; I knew I had to climb them! That was in 1954; at that point, I had been climbing for four years. The climb involved 69 pitches on a 1,300 meter cliff and was very probably one of my most difficult routes. But he who dares, wins.

Reinhold Messner has said that some of the crux sections of your 1950s are grade seven. This is a grade that was first introduced in 1978.
That may be so. It probably does apply to the West Face of the Scheienfluh. Until the 1970s, grade six was as high as the scale went, so most of my routes were graded five or six. Nowadays, they are often upgraded.

How did it feel climbing into unknown terrain?
During our first ascents, the rule was that the leader had to be capable of climbing back down to the belay, as we never knew how the climbing would be on the next section or above an overhang. I often practiced down-climbing, especially on the Brüggler, where I climbed the "Silvester" route unroped on several occasions. I didn't really have any problems finding the best line – if it wouldn't go any further then I would simply climb back down and try another way. In general, our routes were determined by the structure of the rock itself and at certain cliffs, you simply had to be ready for surprises. This was as it should be: you really had to be capable of climbing a route and given the not particularly reliable protection, we never climbed at our limits. Falling was not an option in those days.

How did you protect your routes?

First and foremost using slings and pitons. Where we could, we banged the pitons out and took them with us as they were heavy and we were only able to carry a limited number of them. There were no such things as nuts. We often used wooden chocks, but they were just too bulky. We also used knotted slings; I copied the idea from Peter Diener, whom I continued to climb with in later years. He came from Saxony, in East Germany, and had managed to escape to the West shortly before the building of the Berlin Wall. He learnt how to use knotted slings for protection on Saxony sandstone.

In the beginning you climbed with hemp ropes.

My first ever rope was a Mammut hemp rope. In 1952, I used it to climb the Karlspitze in the Wilder Kaiser in Austria where we got caught in a storm. We were forced to abseil back down, but couldn't pull the wet rope down after us. I had to climb back up it using prussik slings and arrange the rope differently. I abseiled down again, but the rope still refused to budge. It only came on the third attempt.

This used to happen a lot. In 1953, I purchased my first nylon rope. My climbing shoes were made in Austria: they had leather uppers and a so-called "Innsbruck climbing sole", which was much stiffer than today's climbing shoes and had a tread. We tied the rope around our waists, and there were no climbing helmets in the 1950s either. In 1964, I acquired my first harness, it was a chest harness; sit harnesses weren't invented until 1972.

Do you know that your routes are still held in high esteem by climbers today?

It makes me happy every time I hear that someone has enjoyed climbing one of my routes. I didn't climb them for other people, though. For me, climbing was all about finding a balance to my working life, to the everyday world of work as a mechanic and then later on as a manager. My main occupations were my work and my family. Climbing was just a . . . it was just an enjoyable hobby.

Do you still climb?

I don't climb as hard as I used to. I also have to keep the walk-ins and the descents short because of my hip arthrosis. Having said that, I still enjoy climbing grade four or five routes in Ticino in the south of Switzerland, in the Susten area in the Swiss Alps and in the Dolomites or the mountains around Lake Garda. You start to go rusty if you stop.

A TRUE RAICHLE MAN
Claudio Miozzari | Frauenfeld/Switzerland

"Raichle of Switzerland" – the company slogan of the Kreuzlingen based firm was everywhere in the 1960s and 1970s. While others in the footwear industry were disappearing overseas, Raichle became the symbol for quality Swiss workmanship. "All of Switzerland was proud of its quality brand that led the field in the manufacturing of plastic boots," Marcello Trianni, Footwear Developer at Mammut remembers. By the mid-1980s, the footwear firm was turning out over half a million pairs of boots worldwide.

Back then, Trianni had just completed his apprenticeship at Raichle as a boot modeler. He has fond memories of the days when "skiing greats like Maria Walliser and Vreni Schneider used to call in at the Raichle offices in Kreuzlingen." In addition to Walliser, Schneider, Bernhard Russi and Franz Heinzer, others such as the American Bill Johnson, the Olympic Gold medal winner in downhill

in Sarajevo 1984, also relied on Raichle boots. The slogan "Raichle for the best" was fully justified and had its own history. In the early 1960s, when Raichle's industrially manufactured boots replaced conventional hand-stitched models and ski racing success followed, the company advertised with the slogan "winners wear the latest buckle boots" in their 1963 catalogue.

The stars of the ski world benefited from the Kreuzlingen tech guys' knowledge. They ran their own research and test centers and played a key role in the development of the modern plastic ski boot. This showcase company for Swiss entrepreneurship employed mostly foreign workers. In 1964, around half of the workforce was from Italy, as the newspaper the "Thurgauer Zeitung" noted in its report on the move to the new factory premises. A further 20 percent commuted daily to Kreuzlingen from neighboring countries and 5 percent were Spanish or Turkish.

After the boom of the 1980s, the 1990s saw the downfall of Raichle. Trianni remembers how many longstanding employees cried when, in 1995, Raichle declared bankruptcy: "Raichle was a classic family business that often employed several generations of a family. For it to come to such an abrupt end was very traumatic for many in Kreuzlingen." Raichle was then taken over by the Aus-

Mammut's little brother
"Top Swiss brand ELEFANT is the result of decades of experience and continuous improvement. There is none better!" That is how footwear manufacturer Raichle praised its own product line of particularly robust, well made footwear in the 1940s and 1950s. The elephant, which looked like the Mammut brand logo's little brother, was the "seal of quality" adorning every pair of shoes, ensuring that Raichle footwear also had "a quality seal of approval on the outside", which showed they really were something special. The mammoth of the Lenzburg rope firm and Raichle's elephant were both created as labels of quality. While the prehistoric beast went on to become the namesake and symbol for an entire firm, the Raichle elephant was somewhat forgotten. When the firm became one of the world's leading ski boot manufacturers during the 1960s, 1970s and early 1980s, the little elephant was no longer deemed suitable for Raichle's winter sports image.

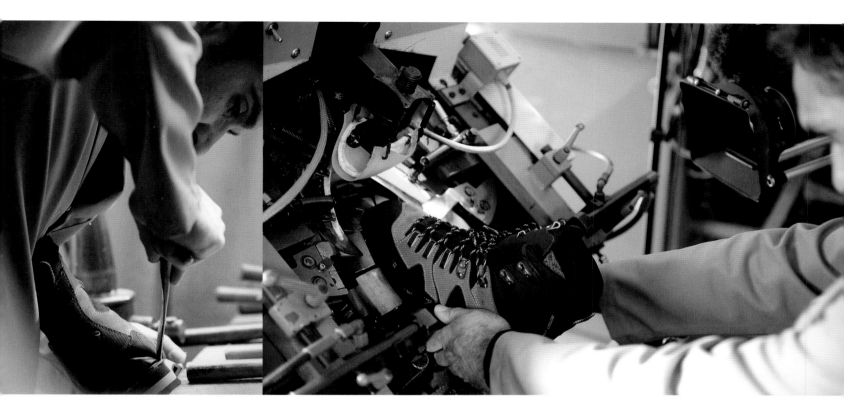

A century of Raichle

1909	Louis Raichle opens a footwear factory making slippers, work shoes and military footwear.
1924	Ski and mountain boot production begins
1936	Death of Louis Raichle, public company formed
1958	Specialization on ski, mountain and hiking footwear
1968	The Fiber-Jet, an "astounding plastic ski boot", dominates the market
1995	Raichle bankruptcy, Kneissl Dachstein takes on the brand
2003	Mammut buys Raichle
2009	Raichle technology continues under the Mammut brand

trian firm Kneissl Dachstein, before Mammut finally brought it back to Switzerland in 2003. Of the 470 jobs that were once there, only ten still remained in the development department. But according to Trianni, these jobs were important in saving some of Raichle's expertise and quality standards. He and his colleagues now work in Frauenfeld and liaise with production facilities in Eastern Europe and Asia.

Trianni is now one of the very few true 'Raichle men' left. He has put his heart and soul into it for the last 28 years, as he himself confirms: "The name Raichle is like a tattoo for me, it's not going away in a hurry." Initially, he struggled with the fact that the boots he and his colleagues were making were not called Raichle. In the meantime he has enjoyed the great success that the brand migration to Mammut has brought, and is pleased with the creative freedom he has been granted. "This change has actually made our work more interesting. Mammut footwear is more sporty, so we can really go for it."

1ST PITCH
1857 The Alpine Club AC
1862 *Oesterreichischer Alpenverein OeAV*
1863 **Schweizer Alpen-Club SAC**
1863 Club Alpino Italiano CAI
1869 *Österreichischer Touristenklub ÖTK*
1869 Deutscher Alpenverein DAV
1869 Alpenverein Südtirol AVS
1871 **Gyms-Montagnard de Genève**
1871 **Sezione Ticino del Club Alpino Svizzero,**
     1875 dissolved, 1887 reformed
1872 Società Alpinisti Tridentini SAT
1873 **Club des Grimpeurs** (Geneva)
1873 *Deutscher und Oesterreichischer Alpenverein*
     DuOeAV (OeAV and DAV merged together);
     dissolved 1945
1874 Club Alpin Français CAF
1874 Hrvatski planinarski savez HPS (Zagreb)
1875 Société des Touristes du Dauphiné STD

2ND PITCH
1876 Appalachian Mountain Club AMC (Boston)
1876 Centre Excursionista de Catalunya CEC/Club
     Alpí Català
1878 *Österreichischer Alpenklub ÖAK*
1879 Alpine Gesellschaft Krummholz (Vienna)
1881 **Union montagnarde ancienne** (Geneva)
1881 **Union montagnarde de Genève**
1883 Club Alpin Belge CAB
1885 *Alpine Gesellschaft Preintaler AGP*
1885 Svenska Turistföreningen STF

3RD PITCH
1885 *Touristenverein «Die Naturfreunde»* (Vienna)
1886 **Club Alpino Ticinese CAT**
1886 Den Norske Turistforening DNT
1887 Club Gimnástico Alemán in Valparaíso (Chile),
     together with Club Excursionista Concón, formed
     1909, which was renamed the Deutscher Ausflug-
     verein Valparaíso, this was the start of the Deutscher
     Andenverein/Club Alemán Andino
1889 Scottish Mountaineering Club SMC
1891 Mountain Club of South Africa MCSA
1891 New Zealand Alpine Club NZAC
1891 Skiclub Todtnau
1891 Krymskij gornyj klub KGK (Krim-Gebirgsclub,
     Odessa), from 1906 Krymsko-Kavkazskij gornyj
     klub KKGK
1892 Akademischer Alpenverein München AAVM
1892 Klub Pipa (Ljubljana)
1892 Planinarsky Savez Bosne i Hercegovine PSBH
1892 Sierra Club (San Francisco)
1893 *Akademischer Alpenklub Innsbruck AAKI*
1893 **Piolet-Club de Genève**
1893 **Ski-Club Glarus**
1893 Schneeschuhverein München
1893 Slovensko planinsko društvo, now Planinska
     zveza Slovenije PZS
1895 Skiclub Schwarzwald
1895 Dissatisfied members of the Munich Section
     of the DuOeAV form the Bayerland Section
     to "preserve purely alpine pursuits"
1896 **Akademischer Alpen-Club Zürich AACZ**
1897 Český Horolezecký Svaz ČHS
1897 Société des Excursionnistes Marseillais
1898 The Climbers' Club CC
1898 **Alpina** (Bellinzona), from 1904 **SAC-Sektion
     Leventina,** today **SAC-Sektion Bellinzona e Valli**
1900 **Bergsteigerverein Excelsior** (Bern)
1900 *Akademischer Alpiner Verein Innsbruck AAVI*
1901 **Skiclub Zürich**
1901 Russkoe gornoe obščestvo RGO (Russian
     Mountaineering Association, Moscow)

1902 Alpiner Ski-Club München ASC
1902 Koninklijke Nederlandsche Alpen-Vereeniging KNAV
1902 Polski Zwiazek Alpinizmu PZA
1902 Kavkazskoe gornoe obščestvo v gorode
     Pjatigorske KGOP (Caucasian Mountaineering
     Association in Pjatigorsk)
1902 The American Alpine Club AAC
1904 *Alpiner Klub Karwendler* (Innsbruck)
1905 **Akademischer Alpenclub Bern AACB**
1905 **Naturfreunde Schweiz NFS**
1905 Japanese Alpine Club JAC
1906 Fell & Rock Climbing Club (Lake District)
1906 The Alpine Club of Canada ACC
1907 The Ladies' Alpine Club LAC
1907 *Österreichische Bergsteigervereinigung ÖBV*
1908 *Österreichischer Touristenverein ÖTV*
1908 **Club montagnard du Grütli** (Geneva)
1908 The Alpine Ski Club (London)
1908 The Ladies' Scottish Climbing Club
1909 Association of British Members of the
     Swiss Alpine Club
1909 Liechtensteiner Alpenverein LAV
1909 **Alpine Vereinigung Bern AVB**
1909 Kosciusko Alpine Club KAC (Australia)
1910 Alpiner Club Hoch Empor ACHE (Munich)
1911 Sächsischer Bergsteigerbund SBB
1911 Club Alpin Monégasque CAM
1913 **Le Cervin. Club montagnard** (Geneva)

4TH PITCH
1918 **Akademischer Alpenclub Basel AACBS**
1918 **Schweizer Frauen-Alpenclub SFAC**
1919 Groupe de Haute Montagne GHM
1919 Vereinigung der Pfälzer Kletterer PK
1919 Unione Ticinese Operai Escursionisti UTOE
     (Bellinzona)
1920 **L'Ondine des Alpes,** from 1924 **Androsace** (Geneva)
1921 Slovenský horolezecký spolok James SHS
1921 The *Sektion Donauland des DuOeAV* was formed
     in Vienna by Jewish and liberal mountaineers, after
     they had been expelled by the fascist and anti-
     Semitic Eduard Pichldem who introduced a so-called
     "Aryan paragraph" that reserved membership solely
     for members of the Aryan race from "his" Sektion
     Austria. In 1924, the new Donauland section was
     banned from the Austrian Alpenverein altogether;
     its members then changed its name to *"Alpenverein
     Donauland"* and joined together with members of
     the Deutschen Alpenverein Berlin.
1922 Federación Española de Alpinismo, later changed
     its name to Federación de Montañismo, today
     known as the Federación Española de Deportes
     de Montaña y Escalada FEDME
1924 Club Alpino Accademico Italiano CAAI
1924 Euskal Mendizale Federazioa EMF (San Sebastián)
1927 **Groupe alpin académique de Genève,** since 1929
     Club Alpin Académique de Genève CAAG
1928 Türk Dağcılık cemiyeti (Turkish Mountaineering
     Association), the yürüyüşçülük, Dağcılık Kış sporları
     Kulübü (Turkish Mountaineering Winter Sports
     Club) was founded in 1933, today it is called the
     Turkiye Dagcilik Federasyonu
1929 Bulgarian Alpinist Club BAC/Българския
     планински клуб БПК
1932 Groupe Pyrénéiste de Haute Montagne GPHM
1932 Union Internationale des Associations d'Alpin-
     isme/International Mountaineering and Climbing
     Federation UIAA

5TH PITCH
1933 Federació d'Entitats Excursionistes de
     Catalunya FEEC
1934 **Groupe de Haute Montagne de Lausanne GHML**

1937 **Società Alpinistica Ticinese SAT**
1937 **West-Alpen-Club W.A.C.**
1939 Scoiattoli di Cortina
1940 Mountaineering and Skiing Club of Iraklion
1941 Federación Argentina de Ski y Andinismo FASA
1942 **Churer Kletter-Club CKC**
1942 Federación de Andinismo de Chile FEACH
1944 British Mountaineering Council BMC
1945 **Groupe Alpin Ouvrier GAO** (Geneva)
1945 Ragni di Pieve di Cadore (Provinz Belluno)
1945 Fédération Française de la Montagne et
     de l'Escalade FFME
1946 Ragni di Lecco
1948 **Kletterclub Alpstein KCA**

6TH PITCH
1949 *Verband alpiner Vereine Österreichs VAVÖ*
1949 *Sektion Holland des Oesterreichischen Alpen-
     vereins;* which then became the Nederlandse
     Bergsport Vereniging NBV
1951 *OeAV* reverts to its original name
1951 Sektion Touristik der BSG Lok Leipzig Mitte,
     renamed Bergsportverein Leipzig Mitte in 1990
1951 Dansk Bjerg- og Klatreklub
1952 Alpine Climbing Group ACG
1954 Himalayan Mountaineering Institute HMI (Darjeeling)
1955 Groupe Alpin Luxembourgeois GAL
1956 **Bergsteiger Gruppe Alpina BGA**
1957 Indian Mountaineering Foundation IMF
1957 Tuesday Hillwalking & Climbing Club TCC (London)
1962 Suomen Alppikerho
1964 **Scoiattoli dei Denti della Vecchia** (Lugano)
1965 **Federazione Alpinistica Ticinese FAT**
1967 Castle Mountaineering Club (Sheffield)
1968 **Rendez-vous Hautes Montagnes RHM**
1968 **Kletterclub Bergfalken KBF** (Frutigen)
1970 Club Pirinenc Andorrà CPA
1970 **Società Alpinistica Valmaggese SAV**
1971 Federation of Mountaineering Clubs of Ireland FMCI
1972 **Kletterclub Rätikon KCR**
1973 Nepal Mountaineering Association NMA

7TH PITCH
1978 **Kletterclub Üetliberg** (Zurich)
1978 **Associazione Strade Alte della Calanca ASAC;**
     today **Associazione Sentieri Alpini Calanca**
1979 Alaskan Alpine Club
1980 Red Rope Socialist Walkers and Climbers
     Club (London)
1980 Gay Outdoor Club GOC (London)
1983 **Fédération des Clubs Alpins Académiques
     de Suisse/Vereinigung der Akademischen Alpen-
     clubs der Schweiz FCAAS**
1983 **Società Escursionistica Verzaschese SEV**
1986 **Chlätterclub Steibisser** (Aargau)
1986 Gay Outdoor Club GOC (Munich), which in 2004
     became the Gay-Lesbian section of the DAV
1989 IG Klettern Deutschland
1994 Suomen Kiipeilyliitto SKIL/Finlands Klätter-
     förbund FKF
1995 **IG Klettern Basler Jura**
1995 Club Arc Alpin CAA
1998 Nederlandse Klim- en Bergsport Vereniging NKBV
     (Fusion of KNAV und NBV)
1997 Azerbaycan Alpinizm Federasiyazi AAF
2000 Mountaineering and Climbing Federation
     of Cyprus KOMOAA
2003 **Kletterclub Wil**
2003 Russian Mountaineering Federation RMF
2007 Klim- en Bergsportfederatie KBF (Berchem, Belgium)
2007 International Federation of Sport Climbing IFSC
2008 **Kletterclub Oberwallis**
2012 **Mammut Alpenclub MAC?**

GOING CLUBBING
Daniel Anker | Around the world

In 2012, the oldest German-speaking mountaineering company in the world celebrates its 150th anniversary. The oldest German-speaking alpine club, the Austrian Alpine Club (Oesterreichischer Alpenverein/ OeAV) also celebrates its 150th birthday in the same year. As the list below shows, this makes the OeAV the second oldest of the 150 alpine clubs in the rest of the world. Only the Alpine Club (British) is older. The list makes no claims to be definitive; some of the associations have merged or been disbanded over the years. (**Bold = Swiss Club**, *Italic = Austrian Club*)

1st pitch, 1857–1875: The first alpine clubs are formed. English mountaineers were the original pioneers and formed the Alpine Club in London in 1857. Mountaineering "tourists" from the Alpine countries decided to get organized so as not to leave all the (virgin) first ascents to Leslie Stephen, Edward Whymper & Co. (although British mountaineers used local guides). Austria was the first of the Alpine countries to form its own club in 1862 and France was the last with its Club Alpin Français in 1874. An alpine club was also founded in Zagreb (Croatia) in the same year, dedicated to the exploration and "conquest" of the Eastern Alps. During the same period, other national associations were formed, such as the Austrian Tourist Club (Österreichischer Touristenklub) and local organizations such as the Geneva Climbing Club. Their members mostly came from upper- and middle-class backgrounds.

2nd pitch, 1876–1885: Horizons are expanded. The Alps are not the only mountains in the world, of course. Mountaineers were also active in other ranges such as the Appalachians and the Pyrenees. Here too, new clubs sprang up. For example, the Appalachian Mountain Club was formed in 1876. This development was accompanied by new clubs in the Alpine countries at a national, regional and local level. Mountaineering's development remained more horizontal than vertical, though.

3rd pitch, 1885–1913: The boom years. The years before and after 1900 saw great upheaval and important changes in many areas of life, for example the rise of organized labor, new art movements, the popularization of sport (in particular football and cycling). These changes are also reflected in the newly formed alpine associations of the period. The working classes won the right to vote and Factory Acts were introduced to limit working hours (introducing weekends and even holidays). The older alpine clubs struggled to maintain their rather elitist hold on mountaineering. Skiing became an important new activity and increased access to snow-covered peaks, making mountaineering possible all year round, particularly in the Alpine countries. New Alpine countries formed their own organizations, amongst them Slovenia (which at the time was still part of the Austro-Hungarian Empire), Liechtenstein and Monaco (where the great sweep of the Alps rises up out of the Mediterranean Sea). Developments on new continents were followed by a further important development in a rather different area: the Ladies' Alpine Club was founded in 1907. A large number of male mountaineers were opposed to the idea of women using their mountain huts and climbing "their" mountains, let alone joining their clubs and organizations. Women became increasingly active in the world of mountaineering, on the summits and at club meetings. It's worth noting that more than a third of the clubs and associations listed here were formed 30 years either side of 1900. By 1914, Geneva alone had 42 climbing clubs. These were mountaineering's boom years. And then World War I broke out.

4th pitch, 1918–1932: Separate ways and shared paths. The climbing elite continued to distance itself from the masses. In Germany and Italy, this period saw climbing clubs and associations subscribe increasingly to fascist ideology and entrench and propagate its ideology through their own ranks. In countries new to mountaineering, new organizations were formed. In 1932, 18 leading national alpine associations came together to form the Union Internationale des Associations d'Alpinisme (UIAA) in Chamonix. 18 years later, the UIAA represented half a million alpinists around the world. Today, the UIAA has 80 member associations and represents 1.3 million members in 57 countries.

5th pitch, 1933–1948: The in-between years. During the second half of the period between the wars, mountaineering made huge gains in all directions. Mountaineering and skiing became fashionable activities; whole cities would literally empty on weekends as their inhabitants poured into the Alps in search of the winter sun. The last great problems of the Alps were all solved with the accompanying stonefall, casualties and newspaper headlines (The North Face of the Eiger was climbed in 1938). In the associations, things mostly remained as they had done before 1933. However, new climbing clubs continued to spring up and in Great Britain the British Mountaineering Council was formed to provide an umbrella organization to unite smaller clubs and associations.

6th pitch, 1949–1973: Renewed impetus. There was much work to be done after the Second World War to clean up and rebuild the climbing movement, especially in Germany and Austria where organized mountaineering was heavily involved in the Nazi establishment. From 1951, Germany also had two German Alpine Clubs, one in West Germany and one in East Germany. In 1947, India became independent and its mountaineering organizations followed suit. Mountaineering in Nepal, which was more or less governed by other nations, also developed its own organizational structures.

7th pitch, 1978–2012: Specialization and internationalization. Mountaineering continued to grow both vertically and horizontally. This was due in particular to free climbing and sport climbing from the end of the 1970s, which set new standards and introduced the sport to a wider audience. There were conflicts of interest and further organizations were formed by climbers as a result. At the same time, smaller clubs and organizations merged to form larger associations. The process, which began back in December 22, 1857 when the Alpine Club held its inaugural meeting at Ashley's Hotel in London, has come a long way since.

MAMMUT CONQUERS THE WORLD
Adrian Huber | Seon/Switzerland

"My new Mammut jacket is fantastic!" Thomas Feldmann posted on February 9, 2011 on Mammut's "Facebook wall". He had recently purchased an Ultimate Pro Jacket. He was convinced by the jacket because it protects him from the harsh northern winds – Thomas lives in Ireland. Mammut has long since outgrown Switzerland. It is now an internationally successful company. There are Mammut customers all over the world, many of whom, like Thomas Feldmann, go on to become fans of the brand.

The foundations for Mammut's international marketing strategy were laid in the mid-1990s. The mountaineering sector, which the company was primarily involved in, was never going to be a source of major profit. Mammut had been owned since 1982 by *Zürcher Ziegeleien* (the company that has today become Conzzeta Holding), which is in turn majority-owned by Tegula AG, i.e. the Schmidheiny, Auer and Spoerry families. The group expanded at an early stage with the acquisition of Kesel GmbH & Co. (1987) in Kempten, South Germany. The textile company was newly founded and made responsible for the distribution of Mammut products across Germany as Elite-Mammut Sportartikel GmbH. Further takeovers included the addition of the rucksack manufacturer Fürst AG (1989) and the ski wax company Toko (1993). The market grew rapidly in these years.

In 1992, Arova-Mammut AG moved to new premises in Seon, not far from its former home in Lenzburg. New buildings were purpose-built, including modern offices, a fully-automated high-bay warehouse, a logistics building and two buildings which house all the manufacturing. The planning and construction of these facilities absorbed a considerable amount of energy and attention. As a result, the company's market focus suffered to a certain extent. The new acquisitions did not prove as economically successful as

hoped and by the middle of the 1990s, a new strategy was required. In order to grow, new structures were needed. In 1996, a new management team was brought in to supervise the restructuring. Mammut's focus on mountaineering was broadened to encompass the outdoor and snowsports sectors. This significantly increased Mammut's customer base. In 1997, the company's first "Outdoor Collection" was launched, aimed at trekkers and outdoor types as well as mountaineers and climbers. This was followed two years later by a clothing collection for skiers and snowboarders.

Following the successful extension of its target group and its expanded collections, a further round of acquisitions took place. In the 1980s and 1990s, Mammut had started to take over companies whose products it used to distribute. From 2000 to 2003, the brand was further reinforced. In 2000, the North-American mountaineering and outdoor specialist Climb High came on board. This enabled Mammut to assert its market position in the United States, as Climb High was the largest distributor of European outdoor equipment in the USA. One year later, Mammut acquired the Norwegian sleeping bag specialist Ajungilak; this also enabled it to set up a distribution network in Norway. Two years after that, Mammut was able to capitalize on the Ajungilak technology to make jackets and gilets with down and synthetic fiber fills. In 2003, Mammut brought Raichle back into Swiss hands. The renowned mountain and trekking footwear manufacturer had been purchased by the Austrian group Kneissl & Friends in 1996. With the acquisition of Raichle, Mammut became the Mammut Sports Group AG.

Mammut was now ready to conquer international markets. This first meant that the necessary distribution channels needed to be established. In 2006, Mammut Sports Group Benelux BV was formed to concentrate on the Benelux countries of Belgium, Luxemburg and the Netherlands. In 2007, Mammut transformed its longstanding Japanese distributor into a subsidiary company. A further subsidiary was formed in the United Kingdom, which again strengthened the distribution network. Investment in important out-

door markets such as Austria and Korea also contributed to growth. This rapid expansion meant that Mammut grew quicker than the market. The development of the Mammut stores, which had been run on a franchising system since 2007, also contributed to its success. The first ever Mammut store was opened in Kempten, the largest city in Allgau, Southern Germany. Today there are Mammut stores in Switzerland, Germany, Austria, Italy, Japan and Korea.

Simultaneous to investing in an international distribution network, the Mammut Group began to concentrate on its most successful brand: Mammut. As part of this mono-brand strategy, the group hived off its rope and hoisting technology division and in 2009, the brand Raichle was renamed Mammut. Raichle's one hundred years of shoemaking expertise now lives on as an official technology label at Mammut. The Toko ski wax brand was also sold off in 2010 to the Norwegian company Swix Sport AG. As Mammut's CEO, Rolf G. Schmid, explained in a company press release on September 1, 2010, "Our rapid growth in recent years and the challenges of Mammut's future international expansion require our full concentration and is the prime motivation for this decision."

Mammut's international growth can also be expressed in figures: in 2009, Mammut generated 70 percent of its sales volume of CHF 215 million outside of Switzerland. The company sees three main reasons for this success. Firstly, its employees identify very strongly with the brand, as many of them are climbers and mountaineers themselves or choose to spend their leisure time outdoors. The good feelings that result as being part of trusted and popular brand are very motivating and mean that employees are prepared to work hard for the company. It also means that they are passionate and creative about what they do and are continually looking to further improve products and services for the customer. Secondly, the consistent focus on the brand's advertising slogan "Absolute alpine" has been very important. Mammut is one of only a few companies who started out with a high level of credibility as a manufacture of mountaineering equipment and were then able to come

down off the mountain to market less alpine-specific apparel and equipment. This is obviously much easier than trying to do it the other way around. Mammut has always remained true to itself. Everything that Mammut does is about mountains. This is what drives Mammut. Other sports, urban life and the world of fashion may sometimes be seductive. However, Mammut will remain in the mountains, where it belongs!

Thirdly, Mammut has launched its own range of innovative new products in recent years. Take for example, the new "Alpine Underwear" line, which was specifically designed to meet the requirements of mountaineers and now rounds off the apparel range. The incorporation of Raichle footwear into the Mammut brand also opened up a whole new world of possibilities, with huge potential for growth. Mammut is now successfully established as a leading manufacturer of rucksacks and climbing harnesses thanks to its targeted investment in research and development. The new flagship Mammut Extreme collection is also proof of the high degree of innovation in the company. Once again, Mammut has succeeded in making its presence felt in the industry.

The company's unique and creative marketing campaigns have also played an important role. Mammut's recent series of Testevents, spectacular seasonal highlight product campaigns and drive to getting customers involved and identifying with the brand have all significantly increased customer loyalty. Inspired by this success, Mammut plans to continue to evolve: "The Mammut brand has to be there for people to experience," commented Michael Gyssler, Chief Marketing Officer at Mammut since 2004. Mammut is consistently investing in new technologies. This includes iPhone Apps and social media applications such as Facebook. The company's Facebook profile had 55,000 friends at the end of July 2011. Thomas Feldmann with his Ultimate Pro Jacket is just one of them.

The Swiss Alpine Club SAC was founded in 1863. In 1907, women were excluded from the club.

These days, when women are leading a climb by head torch in the dawn light, they are more often than not greeted by other alpinists with a "good morning gentlemen!"

Today, 34 percent of the members of the SAC and 13 percent of all guides are women. In the German Alpine Association (DAV), 40 percent of the members and 6 percent of the chair people are women. In the Austrian Alpine Association (OeAV), 42 percent of the members and 17 percent of the guides are women.

When women lead a mixed sex group of climbers, some alpinists assume they must be mountain guides.

The Swiss Association of Mountain Guides (SBV) is made up of 1,527 male mountain guides and 25 female mountain guides. Over the last three years, the association certified 78 new mountain guides; not one of them was a woman.

When an all-female group of climbers reaches a summit, other alpinists sometimes question them in amazement. For instance, asking them where they have left their menfolk.

When the Institute for Snow and Avalanche Research (SLF) was founded in 1936, there were no female employees. Today, 30 percent of its employees are women. 185 observers record snow data throughout Switzerland. Fourteen of these are women.

If three women and a man are sitting round a table in a mountain hut after completing a climb and a male alpinist ap- proaches them to enquire about conditions on the mountain, he will address his questions to the man.

The SAC's Performance Mountaineering project currently has a team of 10 young climbers training for a junior expedition. There are 9 boys and 1 girl in the team.

Many top male climbers are able to rely on their wives to look after their children whilst they are away on expeditions and can also count on this happening should they fail to return from their at times very risky endeavors. Most top female climbers do not have children.

In 1918, the Swiss Women's Alpine Club (SFAC) was founded by women. In 1979, they joined forces with the SAC. Today, 40 percent of all new SAC members are female.

Looking back on the past 150 years of mountaineering, it is clear that much has changed. Many things which were a struggle for their predecessors are today achievable and taken for granted by women. But it is also clear that we are a long way from enjoying equal opportunities on the mountain. With this is mind, all you women out there who love the mountains, keep on packing your rucksacks, making your way across talus slopes and spring snow, climbing spurs and ridges, keep on searching in the sun, the rain and the wind. Plan your next summit attempt; leave the first tracks on that slope. Enjoy the rough rock, the crunch of scree underfoot, the powder snow. Seek it out and dare to do it – and do it your way.

WOMEN AND ALPINISM: FACTS **+ REALITY**
Caroline Fink I Alps

61

" Everyone must take the path that is right for him, and each of these paths is different. "

Reinhold Messner

62

IN CONFLICT
Andy Kirkpatrick | Sheffield/England

The taxi came at 6 A.M., beeping twice. It was a Sunday morning early in June 2001, the beginning of my journey to solo one of the hardest climbs in the world, certainly the hardest climb of my life.

And my life was falling apart. I was running away.

I'd lain awake on the settee most of the night waiting, my mind a mess; in part this was the usual jumble of worry and doubt about the climb, and in part, it was the presence of darker clouds, the worry of what it meant to be sleeping down in the living room alone while my wife slept upstairs.

Did she sleep?

All night, I'd tried to order my thoughts, put things in perspective, get my life straight in my head before I left. It was impossible. I thought about writing her a letter to try to explain why I was going, why I was so compelled to climb. But I just knew those words would be transparent and wouldn't come close to how I really felt. No words could explain why. Nothing I could say would make her understand. There was no sense to it, only the absurdity of traveling halfway round the world to climb a lump of rock.

You don't have to go.

A pendulum swung within my thoughts, its point rising and falling, one moment making me feel invulnerable, the next draining away all my self-belief, making me just want to stay here forever with my wife Mandy and my daughter Ella.

How can you leave them?

It would be easy to tell the taxi to go away, to creep up the stairs and slip into our bed. I could hug Mandy and whisper that I wanted to stay. For once she would know that I put her first. I could still be here when Ella woke up. See her smile.

But what about tomorrow?

You have to go.

I lay and imagined myself lying in a pool of my own blood, shattered bone sticking out of me at crazy angles, slowly dying on the climb, imagined the feeling of loss, knowing I would never see them again, their world shattered like my body.

What will you find there that will justify risking everything you have here?

The taxi beeped again.

I wished it was still dark. In the night I would often feel the most level-headed about climbing hard routes. Getting out of a warm bed to go to the toilet, I would stand naked in the dark, shivering with cold, knowing all I wanted to do was get back under the covers with the woman I loved. The thought of being anywhere else, sleeping in a snow hole, perched on the side of an icy north face, or forced to abseil through the night would seem ludicrous. Pointless.

You sound like her.

There is a point.

I could think of no rational reason for climbing anything. I just knew I had to do it.

The climb is the question.

I would be the answer.

I was about to leave, and travel halfway across the world to solo one of the longest routes on the planet, a climb only a handful of people had ever dared to attempt, one which had taken one of the greatest climbers in the world a staggering fourteen days to solo. I knew the route was out of my league. I knew I could die, or worse, yet I slept alone on the settee.

You might never come back.

The taxi beeped once more.

I stood up and, already dressed, began lifting the huge vinyl haul bags that held my climbing gear out of the house and to the taxi. [...]

"Only got one small one left," I said, as I nipped back down the alley to my house.

I walked through the back gate, past Ella's frog-shaped sand-pit and small red scooter, and in through the back door of our tiny Sheffield terraced house.

My last bag lay on its side surrounded by Ella's toys.

There was one more thing I had to do. I crept up the steep nar-row stairs and slipped into her bedroom. She lay on her side, her thumb in her mouth. Perfect. Nothing in my life seemed to fit to-gether properly any more, my marriage, work, climbing. Nothing but her. She was the only thing in my life that I didn't doubt.

But even she wasn't enough.

You have to go.

I wanted to kiss her, but knew if she woke up I wouldn't be able to leave.

I spent a lot of time wondering what she would think when she grew up, if I were to die climbing, and I thought about it again now: the selfishness of what I was about to do, risking my life once more, and in turn, risking her life and future. Many climbers, or peo-ple who do dangerous things, give it up once they have kids, but for me her birth had come at the start of it all.

At that time, people made judgements about me as a climber and a father, often asking me how I could do it. I didn't know, all I had was excuses. I'd said that you shouldn't sacrifice who you are for your kids, but I wasn't so sure. Wouldn't it be me sacrificing them for what I wanted? But I knew that if I didn't, I wouldn't be a person worth having as a father, and in a way that was why I was here now, about to set off on another climb. The more I tried to quit, the more the pressure built inside me.

What if you never see her again?

I told people I didn't want to die before she was born, just as much as after she was born. But the truth is dying is never in any climber's plan.

She made sense, but she also made what I loved even more senseless. Mountains don't care about love.

I wanted to stand there forever. I could. But I wouldn't.

I crept out of her bedroom, closed the door, and turned to see the stairs leading up to our bedroom, where Mandy probably lay awake. She would be angry with me, leaving her again to go climb-ing. She wanted so little: a normal life, a normal husband. I could-n't give her that, but we were both stubborn and we'd been together for ever. We didn't quit, so here we were. Still fighting. We also loved each other.

I knew she would be lying in bed hating me now, yet wanting me to climb the stairs and say goodbye, or even to say I'd stay – not because she was weak, but because she loved me.

I was about to solo a climb so hard only the best had attempt-ed it, a route I doubted I could do. Yet, in that moment the thing I most feared was climbing those stairs, climbing up to face her and say goodbye.

What if you never see the baby growing inside her?

I went out to the garden and tried to compose myself, not want-ing the taxi driver to see I was upset. I was everything I despised.

They will be better off without you.

As I'd done so many times before, I opened a box in my head and placed the feelings inside, closed the lid, and moved on.

TICINO SPECIALITIES
Pesche Wüthrich | Ticino/Switzerland

I've beaten him again. All it takes is the swift click of a carabiner as the rope is clipped in and he's gone. Ha! That's shown you – you won't get me again! I steady myself, concentrate and climb on. There's a pinch I can just about hold. I manage to get my feet up, move up for the next crimp. Damn it, he's back. Why won't he just leave me alone? He starts by pulling at my feet and then tries to prise my fingers off the holds. Get lost! My muscles fight back with all the energy they've got. Two moves on and he's got the better of me. I'm completely pumped. My head is in bits. My mind screams "use a skyhook!", but there's just nowhere to put my iron finger. Can I hold that crimp? Now he's standing in front of me, my inner scaredy-cat alter ego, laughing monstrously ... Every part of me tenses as I fall. Eight meters lower down, I come to an abrupt, jangling halt together with half the contents of a medium-sized climbing shop and a Hilti drill, as the "Soloist" auto-belay device stops me.

My nerves are in shreds, my mind a blank. Actually, the feeling was not that dissimilar to having to write a report about climbing in Ticino but failing to get started on it. The Word document on my laptop screen couldn't be blanker. But the editor is at least as persistent as my alter ego and I'm cajoled into coming up with a few tasty Ticinese recommendations for you to enjoy.

Let's start with the well-known Ponte Brolla Ost area, a classic sport climbing area near Locarno, which is easily accessible via a five minute walk past some old grottos, traditional restaurants in caves. In 1987, Susi and Edwin Good put up *Schattenjagd* (Chasing Shadows), probably the best 8a in the whole of Ticino. In fact, this is where it all started. In the early 1980s, three climbers from Solothurn, Martin Brunner, Markus Kissling and Stefan Kaltenbach,

came down and developed the first routes. For my part, I was able to make one of the first ascents with *Stärnstunde* (Moment of Glory) 6c. Christoph Hänggeli rebolted the route and unceremoniously renamed it *Pesches Frühschoppen* (Pesche's pre-lunch drink). A few years later, Ponte Brolla was to become my home. I brought my family to live in Ticino and got to work on the eastern side of Ponte Brolla. By the year 2000, just 2 years later, there were 64 routes from 5a to super-technical 8b+. Today, the east sector has over 70 routes.

Travel on into the Valle Maggia and you'll find routes up to 8c in Someo to stretch those arms and more steep stuff at Cevio, where you can still climb on rainy days. If you've had enough of the gneiss with its little edges and slopers, thirty minutes down the motorway is Lugano, where a not-short uphill walk brings you to the *Denti della Vecchia* (The Old Widow's Teeth) and the finest pocketed limestone you could ask for. *La Perles* (The Pearl) is the best 6a+ for miles around – 30 meters of perfect climbing. In 1964, the Gruppo Scoiattoli Denti della Vecchia climbing club started to systematically develop the area. In more recent years, Fausto Sonzogni and a couple of others were responsible for the introduction of modern sport climbing. The crags are north-facing, which makes it the perfect venue for summer training. The fantastic pocketed limestone has got a fair selection of long stamina routes. All in all, there are more than 100 routes from 4a to 8a to go at.

On the way home, make sure you check out Cresciano. Cresciano is the home of big mats, big boulders and big problems – a bouldering mecca. And if its bolted routes you're after, there are also over 100 sport climbs. Once Fred Nicole had repeated all the hard routes, he climbed a few projects (all graded 8b+), before moving on to the countless boulders. Hot on his heels followed such impressive names as Klem Loskot, Chris Sharma, Beat Kammerlander and many others, who made their own marks on Cresciano bouldering. Thanks to Dave Graham, we currently still have the world's hardest problem (Fb 8c+). However, let's get back to the routes. Giovanni Peduzzi and Bruno Bernasconi from the Scoiattoli (Squirrels) climbing club bolted the first routes. All the club's numerous active members were involved in the development of the area, which culminated in the 1990s with the development of the sectors "Beautiful" and "Federica". It's no easy job to name the top routes, after all there are 120 of them graded 5c to 8b+, and all of them on the finest gneiss.

Also not to be missed are the areas Prato, Sobrio, Russo, Caslano, Brontallo, Someo Panorama ... there's plenty to go at. For more information, visit www.picalciot.ch, a website produced by some of the guys responsible for the development of the area (Rolf and Dario, Egon, Eric, Gérard and myself). The drills continue to glow and there are sectors for trad routes being opened up, too. Get down to Ticino, it's got everything from boulders to big walls!

GOOD EQUIPMENT – NO LONGER A QUESTION OF LUCK

Adrian Huber | Cordillera Blanca/Peru

Finding good quality mountaineering equipment in Peru is tricky. When you do come across any good kit, it is so expensive that the average Peruvian could never afford to pay for it from his or her wages. On the other hand, finding an abundance of beautiful mountains and trekking routes is easy in Peru. The Cordillera Blanca has numerous 6,000 meter peaks just waiting to be climbed. Understandably, the local mountain and trekking guides need good equipment to be able to do their jobs. Up until now, getting their hands on good gear was a question of goodwill, skilled negotiation or sheer luck. Tourists were one source. They would often hand over their equipment after finishing their trip, either as part payment or as a tip. Now, thanks to Mammut, this uncertain dependency on hand-outs is over. From now on, getting good equipment is no longer a question of luck.

Their anniversary celebration year sees Mammut increasing their work with the International Federation of Mountain Guides Associations (IFMGA) with a long-term project called "Roped Together in Solidarity" supporting Peru's official mountain and trekking guides. Unlike Kirghizstan, where Mammut has helped fund the training of mountain guides since 2007, the main focus in Peru is on kitting out guides with modern mountain sports equipment.

On April 27, 2011, the official mountain and trekking guides of Peru came together to attend the launch event in Llaca, above the outdoor Mecca of Huaraz, in the Cordillera Blanca.

A BORN FIGHTER
Thomas Schmid | Grenoble/France

When Cédric Lachat walks into the arena for a World Cup final route, he looks like a warrior going into battle. His highly focused stare upon leaving the isolation zone is that of a fighter. Everyone there is clear about one thing: he wants to win more than anyone else. He has also proved time and again that he is capable of doing just that. As he climbs, Cédric is very expressive and lets off his pent-up energy freely. He shouts, swears and cheers and could not care less what the spectators or the other competitors think.

Cédric won his first Swiss Youth Cup in the city of Freiburg at the age of 12 and his will to win and fighting spirit were decisive elements in his success. "No matter what the situation, I will always fight to the bitter end, until I just can't do it anymore. That is my strength." Unlike other top climbers – David Lama for example – it was never Cédric's excellent technique or skill that shone through in his earlier years. He would often slam his feet clumsily against the wall and he struggled to read the routes. He made mistakes, had to correct them, got angry but still managed to fight his way, red-faced, to the top. But Cédric has long since ironed out his technical and tactical shortcomings. What remains today are the reserves of strength he acquired through hard training as a youth. Anyone who saw Lachat win the bouldering event in the last European Championships in Innsbruck will have seen how he left the other competitors far behind with his sheer energy and will to win.

Where does the kind of energy come from that enabled Cédric to train on his own for years, cranking circuits on a small bouldering wall in the garage? Who is this small, wiry sportsman whose fighting spirit is without rival? Cédric grew up in the small town of Porrentruy in the Swiss Jura, the youngest of three children. When asked about his background, Cédric says: "The Jura is a special spot on the Swiss map, secluded and very unique. There are no good facilities for performance sports in the Jura, though; you are left to your own devices. If you want to get anywhere with your sport, above all you have to be determined!" Cédric mostly received support from his personal circle, in particular his parents. "They always believed in me and supported me, even though things were sometimes tough in our family. That gave me strength." Cédric's father suffered a severe accident that left him unable to walk, and his mother has also been ill for some time now.

Cédric started climbing when he was ten years old. Playing in the vertical arena, Cédric immediately found his calling and put all his energy into it – quite the opposite to his approach to school, which he never found easy and did not enjoy. Cédric's biggest weakness has always been languages. "Even though I am a professional athlete and travel a lot, I still can't speak a foreign language. I have tried to learn another language a few times, but I just can't get with it. I am embarrassed about it but have now learnt to accept it."

Cédric's life changed completely when he started to take part in climbing competitions. From then on, he was constantly on the move, seeing the world at first through the European Youth Cups and later World Cups, until he finally became the pro athlete that he is today. When asked where he thinks he might be if he hadn't turned to climbing, Cédric (who trained as a plumber after leaving school) says: "I would probably still be in the Jura, working on some building site every day, and getting home from work exhausted every night. In other words, I would be leading a normal life. I am really grateful for the exciting life that I have thanks to climbing."

Cédric and his partner Nina Caprez have lived in Grenoble since 2009. The reason they chose to move to France was not only the ideal training facilities and active climbing scene in this Alpine town; Cédric also took training courses in Grenoble as a climbing guide, canyoning guide and caving guide. Although he is still rated as one of the best climbers in the world and manages to earn a crust from the sport, now, at the age of 26, he wants to slowly establish a livelihood for when he is out of the pro scene. "I wouldn't change the life I have now for anything, but the tough training schedule, the constant pressure for results and the continual demands to get by financially sometimes get to me." His dreams for the future? "After the competition circuit in France, finding a job in the climbing industry, building a small house together with my girlfriend and maybe later, starting a family – that wouldn't be bad!"

"It's true that climbing
on monos places extreme
strain on one finger.

WHICH WAY'S THE SUMMIT?
Karin Steinbach Tarnutzer | Alps/Japan

Here we were again. Ahead of us, there was a fork in the path and next to it was an artistically designed signpost with comprehensive directions. There was just one hitch – we could not read the beautiful curved lines of the Japanese script. And the only numbers on it, representing kilometers, were not helpful to us either. We got the map out and tried to get our bearings, not an easy task with a map that is also solely in Japanese, and just about managed to work it all out with the help of height indicators and the annotated walking times between huts. Finally, a friendly Japanese hiker assured us that the left fork was the one we should take to get to the Karasawa hut. Although his English was only as good as our Japanese, we had already had plenty of practice at making ourselves understood with the help of mime and gesticulation.

Lack of orientation is the lot of the solo traveler in Japan. Although you do come across quite a lot of English signage in the big cities and, in particular, people who at least have a passive understanding of English, once you are in the countryside, that soon disappears. Travel timetables or restaurant menus rapidly become a big challenge, not to mention making telephone reservations for mountain huts. You soon develop a strategy to overcome such difficulties, like letting the tourist information office make reservations and asking people who look like they might be able to speak

English for their help. One thing is for sure, the Japanese are always helpful.

Three hours later, we were sitting on the terrace of the Karasawa hut, evidently the only two Europeans amongst the 150 or so guests. Not all of them would be staying the night in the hut. Japanese mountain huts are comparatively expensive, which is why many stay in the campsites that belong to the huts. There is then just a fee to pay for the use of the sanitary facilities. Now, we understood why many Japanese mountaineers carry packs of almost backbreaking proportions and weight. They give the overall impression of taking the matter very seriously, as though they were on a Himalayan expedition rather than an average mountain tour. Even on hiking trails, they are kitted out from head to toe in Gore-Tex, wear heavy mountain boots, head protection and the customary white gloves for protection against the sun and the cold. Anyone who finds this amusing has not experienced the speed and frequency

with which the weather can change in the Japanese alps. On the backpack, there is always a tea mug and often a bell – it helps keep away the bears, which although present in some of Japan's national parks, are not in the Japanese alps. The Japanese also tend to wear a small towel round their necks for sweat.

Those who are not already fluent in the formal greetings "go-saimas" and "konnichiwa", will have mastered them after only a couple of hours spent on the trail up to a hut. The season is short, which is why you are seldom alone during the months of July and August. The fact that mountaineering is so popular in Japan is not surprising when you think about it. This 3,800 kilometer long chain of islands off the east coast of Asia was created by volcanic activity. It lies on a fault line, is regularly shaken by earthquakes and of the 240 volcanoes, a total of 40 of them are still active. 73 percent of the land is covered in mountains. The vast length of the country means there is a broad spectrum of climates and vegeta-

tion. The mountainous regions are mostly covered in dense woodland that is hard to access and the valleys are lush and green.

Where there are many mountains, people climb them, and in the summer, they also provide welcome respite from the humid heat of the low country. In Japan, hiking is part of the tradition of pilgrimage, so to have climbed Mount Fuji once in your lifetime is, for many, almost a national duty. Standing at 3,776 meters, the highest mountain in Japan is viewed as a holy mountain in Shintoism, which, aside from Buddhism, is the most popular religion. This means that in the summer, or more specifically in the months of July and August, up to 350,000 'pilgrims' climb Mount Fuji. Because we did not want to join the masses, we had already decided in advance that we would not climb Mount Fuji.

The alternative was the Japanese alps. In terms of structure, there is no comparison to the symmetrical volcanic cone of Fuji but they are home to the next highest mountains and are also on the main island of Honshu. The Southern Japanese alps are roughly 50 kilometers northwest of Fuji. At 3,194 meters, the highest of the peaks, Kita-dake, is Japan's second highest mountain. The Central Japanese alps are 100 kilometers northwest of Fuji and 50 kilometers further on are the Hida Mountains or Northern Japanese alps. The 3,190 meter high Hotaka-dake is the third highest mountain in Japan and that is the peak we had set our sights on.

In the dorm at the Karasawa hut, we rolled out our tatami mats and thin futons and lay down to sleep. The following day held more surprises for us. Breakfast was Japanese and substantial, and since we still had a few meters of ascent ahead of us and a big appetite, we ate our way through Miso soup, grilled fish, rice and pickled vegetables – although the fermented soy beans were one step too far. Packed lunch: you can order a Bento-Box the night before and enjoy rice, tiny fried fish and vegetables on the trail. The toilets: water is sparse and so there is not usually a flushing mechanism in Japanese hut toilets. However, the diesel generator that chugs away at the back of the hut must provide plenty of electricity because the toilet seats are heated. The same strict footwear rules that apply everywhere else in the country also apply in the huts:

there are outside slippers, indoors slippers and toilet slippers, and of course the odd untrained tourist regularly appears in the dining room wearing toilet slippers.

It took us three sweaty hours to hike up to the next hut, the Hotaka-dake Sanso, where we left our bags, and we were on the summit of Hotaka-dake an hour later. The route is peppered with short ladder sections that can potentially result in bottlenecks. Awaiting us at the summit, apart from a small Shinto shrine, was a thick blanket of clouds that meant we were unfortunately unable to see the amazing view that would have stretched all the way to Mount Fuji. Instead, we ourselves became the attraction; it seemed there were not too many European climbers passing this way. Anyone who spoke a bit of English asked where we were from and on hearing the answer "Switzerland", regularly responded with an enthusiastic "Ah!" and sometimes followed it up with the words "Matterhorn" or "Jungfraujoch". This did not just happen in the alps but also in one of the most expensive stores on Ginza, Tokyo's famous shopping street.

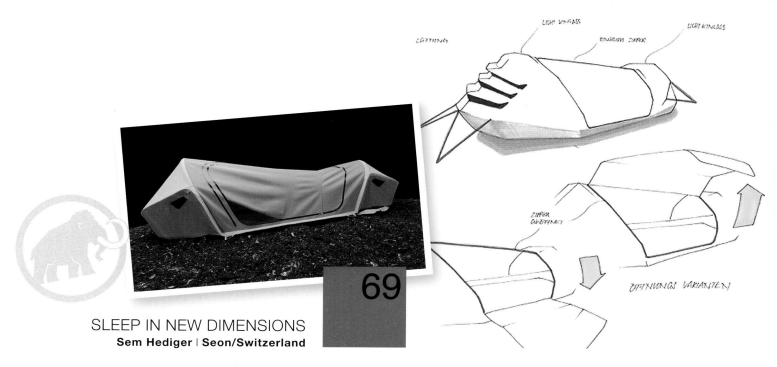

SLEEP IN NEW DIMENSIONS
Sem Hediger | Seon/Switzerland

Creating innovative equipment is one of the core functions of product development at Mammut. To make it happen, we nurture a close relationship with our athletes and customers, so that we are aware of their needs and can keep pace with developments in mountain sports. We then tailor our products accordingly. The use of new technology or the combination of various solutions enable us to continue to create innovative products.

In the case of the Mammut Lodge, it was new customer needs, as well as new technology, that spurred on the design and development of the product. From the customer's perspective, it was a desire to sleep out in the open in comfort on short trekking or hiking adventures. We were looking for a lightweight sleeping system that was quick and simple to set up. On the technology side, we had already considered extending our sleeping mats with a tent shell and using air-filled poles to create a space.

So this was the task we assigned to two industrial design students from the Polytechnic of North West Switzerland, Dominik Meier and Tobias Nüesch. The first step was to analyze all existing sleeping options and work out the pros and cons of tents versus

bivouac bags. The results encouraged us firstly to dispense with solid tent poles altogether to make handling simpler and secondly to create a space that, unlike a bivi bag, did not rest directly on the sleeping bag. In addition, the product's design and shape would have to be inviting and provide a sense of security.

Various ideas and concepts were then developed and paper models were made for testing and review. Using a model made from bicycle inner tubes, we were able to engineer a completely new structure made from inflatable poles which, with the help of just two short side sections of solid poles, produced a roofed inner space. Thanks to this innovative approach, we were able to create a comfortable shelter that only took up a small area. This idea was developed further and a whole product concept, complete with a model, was compiled.

The students' concept had convinced us. We started scaling the model to its actual dimensions and together, we produced the first 1:1 prototype. After six months of developmental work, we were finally able to field test the product and carried out a first endurance test on a snow bivouac in Andermatt with our pro athletes.

CLIMBING IN THE FREEZER
Stephan Siegrist | Torre Egger/Patagonia

We had set ourselves a real challenge: the first ever winter ascent of Torre Egger, the most demanding peak in the Patagonian Cerro Torre group, which is seldomly climbed even in summer. The plan was to go alpine style, light and fast, without fixing ropes in advance or stashing gear up on the face. Once started, we intended to climb all the way to the summit.

On July 27, 2010, Thomas Senf from the Bernese Oberland, Mario Walder from East Tyrol, Daniel Arnold from Central Switzerland and I reached base camp at El Chalten. This is the starting point for the various base camps in the Fitz Roy and Cerro Torre group. After hearing that a period of high pressure was coming in, we decided to pack up and get moving as quickly as possible. We reached Camp Bridwell, our base camp, the following day on skis with our heavy rucksacks and then skied back that same evening. It was snowing heavily. Mario was having problems with his knee. The pain was so bad that he was forced to pull out of the expedition before it had even properly started. We left the next day without him to transport the remaining equipment needed for a winter ascent on sledges to Camp Bridwell.

The fresh snow, cold conditions (temperatures down to minus 25 degrees) and short days (it got light at 09:30 and was dark by 18:30) made it hard work pulling the equipment. We spent the next night back under the East Face of Torre Egger (Camp Bridwell) and then moved our first load of equipment to the foot of the wall, wading through snow that was waist-high in places. We then marched back for three hours to spend a very cold night at Campo Niponino. And woke in the early hours of the next morning, as usual. We

were pretty tired from the efforts of the past few days and had not quite shaken off our jet lag. Nevertheless, we fought our way out of our tiny expedition tents to stand under a clear, star-lit sky. We had not decided yet whether to start climbing or to use the good weather to transport more equipment to the foot of the face. The weather report indicated that we would have only one chance to reach the summit, if everything went according to plan. From past expeditions to Patagonia, I knew that this might be our only good weather window.

We decided to go for it. No one spoke; we all knew what had to be done before we could start up the face. Using our footsteps from the previous day, we collected the remaining gear and reached the start of the climb on Swiss National Day at ten in the morning. The conditions were perfect. There was no wind, a low sun shone in an incredibly blue sky, just as Karl Gabl, our Austrian meteorologist and the Weather God of all Mountaineers had forecasted. The initial pitches led us in a straight line up the ice to where the glacier broke off between Cerro Standhardt and Torre Egger – an ideal place to set up camp, just as we had planned. "Ice Master" Dani climbed the next two pitches with me belaying him, while Thomas set up camp.

We had brought sleeping bags and bivouac tents with us to see us through the cold and windy winter nights. It took considerable will power to crawl out of them in the morning. We tried to ignore the fact that the summer in Switzerland would be something like 60 degrees warmer than it was in Patagonia! On August 2, we climbed two pitches of an unfinished route to the Col de los

Sueños between Torre Egger and Punta Herron. Two completely new pitches brought us on to the Titanic Route, which was first climbed in 1987. The face got the sun for just a couple of hours, which was enough to cheer us up and warmed our hands. This was especially welcome as the next section involved a long crack. As you might expect in full winter conditions, it was filled with ice. I was constantly forced to hammer the ice away to find a hold or place protection. The climbing was difficult but incredibly beautiful. Thomas, a highly-respected alpine photographer and a strong climber, provided some extra excitement when he tried to remove a 2 by 2 meter chunk of snow from a corner on the route. It promptly fell 7 meters, taking him with it. There was no damage done apart from breaking his sunglasses.

The sun was setting as we started the long traverse. The wind picked up and it turned bitter cold. There was nowhere for a good bivouac and spending a long, cold night hanging from the face was definitely not an option. We climbed on through the night. This put us ahead of schedule, which, given that the weather can rapidly deteriorate in Patagonia, could make all the difference. What would normally be easy climbing up the ramp proved extremely challenging. The narrow band of rock that led up through the vertical granite face was covered in ice and powder snow. This made climbing by the light of our head torches a rather delicate affair.

At 03:30 A.M., after 22 hours of climbing, we reached the foot of the summit ice mushroom. These ice formations, typical for the Cerro Torre group, are seldom encountered elsewhere in the world. Take a freezer which gets defrosted for the first time in years, mul-tiply the ice hundreds of times over, shape it like a giant mushroom and then stick it on top of a mountain where extreme winds freeze it to the rock. Now you have a Patagonian ice mushroom – it's like climbing in a giant freezer. The mushroom was the final barrier between us and the summit. They are generally a real nightmare as you basically have to tunnel up unprotected through vertical frozen powder snow. We needed daylight for this last pitch and anyway we were all exhausted. So we dug ourselves a seat in the steep snow and spent the next four hours in our sleeping bags with the bivouac tent pulled over our heads to protect us from the wind, which had picked up in the meantime. As we dozed uneasily, each of us was haunted by dreams of being caught by a full Patagonian storm just short of the summit.

Slowly, it started to get light. The wind did not let up, cirrus clouds scurried across the sky, a sign that the weather was about to change. We had no intention of turning back so close to the top and got moving as quickly as our cold and stiff fingers allowed. I knew from a previous expedition that there was supposed to be an ice corridor up through the mushroom somewhere on its southern side. If it was still there, it would allow us to reach the summit quickly and more easily. We were in luck, it was still there. At midday on August 3, 2010, all three of us stood on top Torre Egger, only a week after we had left Switzerland. I have spent a total of 12 months over the past 18 years climbing in Patagonia, but this was the first time I had been fortunate enough to reach a summit as quickly as this.

Mammut Teamtrip to Thailand in 2006 and was instantly hooked. There is something really free and relaxed about it. You are not wearing many clothes, no harness, no clipping in – you just step off the boat right onto the first move, it's totally cool. The only annoying part is the chalk – when you fall in the water, it takes ages to dry out, so you have to take several chalk bags with you. With your climbing shoes, it's not so bad. The rubber just has to dry and the Thai heat deals with that pretty quickly.

A LEAP INTO WARM WATER
David Lama | Tonsai/Thailand

71

@

We spent ten days happily ensconced on Tonsai Beach, staying in cozy little beach huts. Every morning, we would have breakfast on the beach and then head out in a longtail boat to the limestone towers that rise straight up out of the sea. There are sport routes on Tonsai Beach and some of the more accessible towers have seen some DWS activity but we wanted to hit uncharted territory so we ended up going right out with the boat to places half an hour away.

To start with, I was a bit wary of jumping into the water. But then, you just get on with it and climb. On grade 5s, you'll be 20 meters up in no time, since you assume that you are not going to fall and will down-climb the route. On the harder routes, I took my first fall from 5 meters, then I got brave and pushed it to 10 meters and by the end, one of our routes was 18 meters high – you get used to the big jumps and the splashdowns. On shorter jumps, you try to straighten up quickly but when you bale out from 18 meters, it spins you out of position so you have to try and get your balance by paddling with your arms until you are just above the water and can then tuck your arms in just before entry. It only gets dangerous when you fall off without warning and cannot prepare yourself. This one time, a hold broke off in my hand and I fell really close to the boat. I also fell twice from our 18 meter route. The last move was a dyno to the finishing hold. We all tried it a few times but we just couldn't stick the finishing hold. The solution was to climb round it using little pockets and edges. If you came off after the dyno, the fall was totally out of control and you had to paddle like mad to right yourself before splashdown. Once, I landed on my side and, boy did that hurt, I took a real hammering. I have even heard of people dislocating their shoulders by hitting the water wrong, there are some crazy stories.

In Tonsai, we would mostly spend all day concentrating on one cliff. We were keen to pick out radical looking lines. One after the other, we would try to work the route from the bottom, getting higher and higher each time, and pulled off a few really cool first ascents. What I loved most about it was that it was a real team effort.

Ever since my first Testevent, the "Underwear Test" up on the Eiger Glacier, I have become a keen climber. Before that, I only went to the wall occasionally, but now I prefer to climb outside on real rock. It is a good alternative when the weather is not right for flying (I am a competition pilot in the Swiss Paragliding League). Aside from that, I go mountaineering, ski touring and running, and ride a racing bike. I am a real mountain lover, which surprises me sometimes, considering I was born in Hamburg.

I read about the Testevent on Mammut's homepage and applied with a bunch of fun comments. That morning, I had a safety training session to attend, but then made my way straight to Grindelwald. I was lucky enough to be selected for all the events that followed. After a while, it is like you are part of a big family. I would be disappointed now not to be at one of the events. At the last one, the Acceleration Test on Piz Julier, I was awarded the Golden Loser

LIKE ONE BIG HAPPY FAMILY
Sandra Monse I Alps/Switzerland

72
@

Nightcap, because I was the last to get on the bus in the morning. I still wear it!

The Testevents have become like class reunions for me, just that every time you hope and pray that you will be selected. When you finally hear that you have been accepted, you just can't wait. It's all about the fun atmosphere, the feeling of anticipation at what new experiences might lie in store, the great people and the brilliant memories. Moments, people and friendships that connect you and that you never forget – that's something no other outdoor brand achieves, and for me that's what makes Mammut and the people who work there so very special.

I hope we'll see each other at the next event!

73
@

THE TINY RED DOT
Manuela Imboden I Alps/Switzerland

I took part in the "Underwear Test" in early summer 2008 and have attended every Testevent since. It's great when you find you've been selected from hundreds of applicants to take part in a really unusual event, together with a bunch of cool people – it's a really unforgettable experience. I formed friendships that have lasted from the very first Testevent. I feel a real connection with the Mammut brand. No Mammut jacket or pair of Mammut pants escapes my notice! But the best bits are the actual photo shoots. At the Underwear Test, we were divided up into groups, I was in group 1. Cool, I thought to myself, I am always in group 1 at running camp – I am a mountain and ultra-mountain marathon runner. But then, group 1 was sent up first, right to the very top, and Röbi Bösch was taking pictures from way down at the bottom. Every time I look at that picture now, I know that tiny little red dot way back at the end of the line, that's me!

"IN EUROPE, EVERYONE KNOWS WHAT CLIMBING IS"
Alex Johnson | Wisconsin/USA

Karin Steinbach Tarnutzer spoke with World Cup winner and Mammut athlete Alex Johnson at the International Mountain Summit 2010 in Brixen about the competition scene in America.

How do you feel about today's competition?
I'm curious to see what's going to happen. We've seen the wall already – it's going to be fun. Climbing is different to team sports, which are always very competitive. When I'm climbing I'm essentially competing against myself.

Why have you chosen to specialize in bouldering?
I enjoy lead climbing just as much as I do bouldering, but I'm not as good at it. This is why I enter bouldering competitions. I often climb sport routes outside.

What was your biggest win?
2008 in Vail, Colorado when I won the World Cup. It was my first ever World Cup and the first to be held in the USA. Winning came as a complete surprise, which is why it means so much to me.

How important is climbing to you?
I really love it – there is nothing I would rather be doing. If I had to stop climbing, I think I would find it difficult. I don't know what I would do.

At the moment you make your living from climbing. Where do you see yourself in five years time?
I'm sure that I will still be climbing in five years time. Whether I'll be doing it professionally is another matter. If I still enjoy it and can still make a living from it, then why not? However, it's not possible to live from climbing forever in the United States, so I will go back and finish studying at some point.

Does America have a national team, like Austria, Germany and Switzerland?
Officially, there is a national team, but we only meet twice a year – at the national championships and in Vail. The athletes are spread all over America. This is very different to Austria, for example, where just about everyone who is anyone lives and trains together in Innsbruck. I train for myself and with friends. I come from Wisconsin, where there are no cliffs to climb on, so I train at the indoor climbing wall.

What do American climbers think about the climbing scene in Europe?
The lifestyle is completely different. I think that most Americans have little idea of what is going on in Europe. You are much, much better organized than we are. Most American climbers don't even know who is in the national team or who the trainer is. It's chaos – but it's friendly chaos. At competitions, the public is often really surprised when somebody from Europe wins, whom they have never even heard of. It normally turns out that the climber is really well known in Europe, but the American climbers just haven't been following what is going on. There is a large ocean between us . . .

Climbing is slowly becoming a mass phenomenon in Europe. Does the same apply in America?
In Europe, everybody knows about climbing. In America, there are people in areas really famous for climbing who have no idea what all these people are actually doing on their cliffs. If you walk with a Crash pad through the Rocky Mountains, people stop and ask you what the hell you are carrying. I think Europe is cool. Everyone knows what climbing is, everyone knows how climbing competitions work.

"Nobody understood me, nobody loved me, nobody cared about me. I bought a bottle of water and packet of biscuits in Barbizon, headed for the Gorges d'Apremont and started climbing on the boulders. After a while, all my problems disappeared, nothing else mattered. I was completely focused on what I was doing. It felt like nothing could make me tired, each movement linked perfectly into the next – the magic of climbing."

75 **Catherine Destivelle**

A LONG HISTORY TOGETHER
Robert Bösch | Alps/Switzerland

Back in the late 1970s, Mammut was a one man band. Albert Wenk was Mammut. If you were looking for fixed ropes for an expedition, had faulty crampons or wanted to know anything about the soles on climbing shoes, Albert Wenk was your man. He knew everything and took the trouble to get involved in everything. I knew him back in the early days of my 'climbing career' so to say. I was servicing skis in a small workshop for the Zurich mountain equipment firm Eiselin, together with Walti Müller, the free climbing pioneer of Switzerland. If a client had an equipment problem that neither Walti Müller nor branch manager Emil Schär could solve, it was obvious who to call: Albert Wenk.

Several years later, I came across Albert Wenk again, whilst out climbing with Martin Scheel. Martin was one of the leading activists of the alpine rock climbing scene and was supplied with gear by Mammut, or rather by Albert Wenk. In 1986, when Martin and I made the first ascent of "Hannibals Alptraum" (Hannibal's Nightmare) in the Rätikon, neither of us would ever have thought of going back on the route to get photographs, even though it was an exceptional route back then and Mammut had given us the gear for it. We had taken a couple of photos during the first ascent – but you know the type, taken from a belay stance, looking up. There were no decent images of any of Martin's big climbing feats, such as 'Freetrip', 'Supertramp' and 'Amarcord'. Things were different back then. But they were set to change at breakneck speed over the coming years.

New sports were 'invented' – freeclimbing, paragliding, mountain biking, snowboarding – and breathed new life into the scene. Outdoor sport was born, and with it, the outdoor market. These so-called 'action', 'extreme' or 'adrenaline sports' were not only exciting and interesting for those taking part but also for the media. An effective symbiosis was evolving, with the outdoor trade, athletes and the media working together brilliantly. The demand for images of these new adventure sports was increasing. Those were exciting times for us photographers – to begin with there were perhaps only a handful of us in the German speaking countries – as we discovered there was a lot more to discover about photography. More and more top athletes obtained sponsorship and were therefore dependent on publicity. As the images improved, so did the expectations. Everyone had to go along with it, including Mammut.

At the end of the 1980s, together with Albert Wenk and top Australian climber Kim Carrigan, who worked for Mammut in Switzerland for a few years, I went up to the Susten Pass to photograph the latest Mammut jackets and packs. It was one of my first real photographic commissions, and I was suitably nervous. In those days, it was not about complex shoot scenarios. It was enough just to position the model, Kim, a few meters from the side of the road in the foreground with the Stein glacier in the background. It would soon become more costly: climbing shots with top British climber Martin Atkinson on the Tour d'Aï above Leysin (the photographer stayed on the ground to save time), then tent images on the edge of a Valais vineyard (cropped out) with snowy peaks in the background (in frame); or apparel photography with Yves Remy up above Grindelwald, below the North Face of the Scheideggwetterhorn (no distance from the road). Yves was actually one of Mammut's sponsored climbers, but he could hike a bit, too. We did not take the silent rumbling above us seriously straight away – a low layer of cloud blocked our view of the glacial break-off 1,000 meters further up – and it very nearly cost us dearly. As the avalanche of ice hit the foot of the face and a sea of snow and ice bore down on us, we broke off the shoot pretty fast and ran for the road, hurling ourselves into a water course at the last minute. The mass of snow shot over our heads, while our car, 500 meters away from the foot of the cliff, was totally plastered on the side closest to the slope. This would not be the last time there would be a near miss on a shoot.

The standards demanded for photographic material were increasing. Albert Wenk commissioned me to photograph two strong climbers from the Bernese Oberland on the Wendenstöcken. With equipment supplied by Mammut, Heinz and Ueli Bühler had just completed the first ascent of "Batman", which at the time was one of the hardest free climbs in this very demanding climbing area. We climbed the route, fixed ropes and the next day, I took pictures of the two of them. In those days, this was an extravagance not usually afforded for climbing images. Shoots were increasingly carried out abroad, in neighboring countries. My fondest memories are of two photo shoots with top French climber Alain Robert, at the time sponsored by Mammut, in the Verdon Gorge. The subject was ropes. A massive run-out and an epic fall were the order of the day. I had photographed Alain Robert several times before on radical solos and he was the craziest guy I had ever come across – just the man for the job. The whole thing was hair-raising and pretty hectic – but we got the shots we needed.

In the years that followed, I tried to transpose the arrangements used for rock climbing photos onto big mixed routes and north faces. The Lauper route and later the Heckmair route on the Eiger were milestones in this development. What counted as groundbreaking in those days is taken for granted today. In the interim, there is now no location that I have photographed or filmed more than the North Face of the Eiger. I have been on many different routes ('Spit verdonesque', 'Deep Blue Sea', 'Le Chant du Cygne', 'The Young Spider', 'Pilz', 'Paciencia'), and with a range of people (Hansi Kessler, Oswald Oelz, Kobi Reichen, Ueli Bühler, Robert and Daniela Jasper, Stephan Siegrist, Roger Schäli, Peter Schäffler, Marco Büchel, Röbi Koller, Chäppi Ochsner, Ralf Dujmovits, Evelyne Binsack, Hansruedi Gertsch, Thomas Kohler, Robi Marti, Bernhard Russi, Heinz Müller and Ueli Steck). And for different reasons, too. As a climber I've done a number of routes, in summer and in winter. As a photographer, I've used a range of 'tactics'. I was deposited from a longline by helicopter onto the Spider, climbed out of the Stollenloch onto the wall, and jugged up 800 meters of fixed lines to the Spider's legs. I've started at the bottom and climbed up to the First Ice Field, and climbed down from the summit to the Exit Cracks. Sometimes, I was belayed by a partner but mostly there were just two of us and we were largely unsecured. Some of the time, it was pretty relaxed, in good conditions and pleasant temperatures, but other times, there were 100 mile an hour winds, the thermometer read minus 20 degrees and it was more of a survival exercise.

Then, in November 2010, there was the "X" factor, a Mammut-X (for "X-treme") shoot on the summit ice field of the North Face of the Eiger. It wasn't the most dangerous North Face project but it was certainly the most expensive. The whole thing was the brainchild of one of the Erdmannpeisker agency's two founders, Gabriel Peisker, and this test campaign was the culmination of a long course of action. I was glad to be able to rely on my 20 years plus of experience; I needed every ounce of it to be able to meet the demands of the job. Photographic knowledge was just as essential as good knowledge of Alpine locations and of what would work in the Alps. Each individual subject required a huge outlay. The actual day of the shoot was just the tip of the iceberg – and for my part of course, quite a test of nerve; there was no room for error. I benefited not only from my experience as a photographer and climber but also from my extensive contacts, including top-class climbers, mountain guides and helicopter pilots. It was these people, with their knowledge and ability plus their willingness to take on considerable responsibility, that were pivotal factors in the campaign happening at all.

Twenty years back, when I started out with Albert Wenk and Kim Carrigan, the thought of investing so much money and effort in a mountain sport photography project was plainly unthinkable. But then again, who would have guessed back then what Mammut would become!

YOSEMITE IN THE 1970S – A VERTICAL PARADISE
Reinhard Karl | Yosemite/USA

I simply found myself there one day, at the end of the road, in Yosemite National Park, California, standing at the foot of El Capitan. It was hot, maybe 40 degrees Celsius. I felt a bit like a housecat seeing a tiger for the first time. This was the King; I felt tiny, like a little mouse. I could not imagine climbing it, such a massive wall, so hot, so featureless. The other tourists who stepped out of the bus with me were saying things like "great", "marvelous" or "beautiful" and then getting back on board after just a couple of minutes staring skywards.

Hermann and I arranged to meet at Camp IV, the legendary climbers' campsite. John Muir, the man who founded the national park, would turn in his grave if he could see it today. To him, the 'Valley' was the most splendid of all of nature's temples. But 100 years on, things have changed a lot. The 3 million visitors every year have to be catered for somehow. There are now banks, hair dressers, supermarkets, hotels and laundromats. The Indians

called Yosemite 'the valley without equal'. Shortly after they drove them out, the white men discovered this harmonious mountain wilderness with its waterfalls, an abundance of wildlife from eagles to brown bears, sequoia and redwood forests, the flood plains of the Merced River and the gigantic granite domes of the Royal Arches, Half Dome, Sentinel Rock and of course the 1,000 meter high monolith that guards the entrance to the valley – El Capitan. Then the hordes of tourists arrived in their cars, turning it into a Disneyland for nature lovers. And the natural world really was still there, alive and healthy. As a European accustomed to the Alps, nature this pure seemed unnatural. If ever there was a Garden of Eden, this had to be it. By contrast, the climber's camp, now called "Sunny Side Walk in Campground", was more like an offshoot of the Berkeley and Los Angeles sub-culture. Back then, I still believed that climbers were shining lights with a desire to achieve great things in high places. But all I found here was a bunch of crazy hippies and freaks. And these people were meant to be such good climbers? Better than us Alpine climbers? There were none of the swanky camper vans you would see on a normal camping site, those cheap mobile imitations of middle-class houses; climbers here hung out looking like tramps, living in tiny tents or under plastic sheets strung between two trees. The whole place was a little scruffy and flea-bitten. But the people here had none of those McDonalds rolls of fat around their waists. The climbers stood out immediately because of their muscular physiques. At night, there were mostly big parties round the campfire. Guitars, Budweiser and crazy conversations about one topic: climbing. Marijuana, peyote buttons and who knows what other kinds of drugs were flying round. Everyone was on some kind of high, marijuana at the very least. Most of them spent their whole summers like that.

Being lazy was a fundamental prerequisite to becoming a good climber in Yosemite. The five essential things they had to get done in a day, in order of importance, were: 1. Climb, 2. Sunbathe, 3. Eat, 4. Drugs, 5. Women. The word "work" did not feature in any way. Some lived as full-time "local residents" in the camp. Little attention was paid to what was in the daily newspapers. Even the issue of gathering enough "bucks" to live off seemed a non-issue. When I asked how they managed to get by without working, they just shrugged, saying "we don't talk about that". You didn't need much to live on here in any case. Every day was a beautiful day. The ever-blue skies and the ever-beautiful natural environment raised the spirits, but never the worry of what lay ahead. One thing was certain: "Tomorrow will be another beautiful day." So what was the point in wrecking your head by worrying?

THE NEWLY FOUND PARADISE – YOSEMITE TODAY
Steph Davis | Yosemite/USA

Before I even knew what a big wall was, the desire to climb long routes naturally pulled me to Yosemite Valley. Like every climber who comes to the valley, I soon discovered that it truly has everything – bouldering, cragging, easy free solos, long free climbs, aid routes, backcountry adventures. But with each visit, I found the Valley a more impossible place. I loved the climbing, but I was easily overwhelmed by the crowds and nonsensical rules. I couldn't deal with fast-food stands, tourists who stopped in the middle of the road to gawk at a squirrel, and most of all the endless talk about climbing. I didn't want to talk about climbing or other climbers, I just wanted to do it. I felt like a rat in a cage in Camp IV, and was always sleeping in the forest and getting harassed by rangers essentially for existing. Being a dog, my beloved companion Fletcher was even more guilty of existing and felt even more hunted than I did. I usually only lasted a few weeks in Yosemite before fleeing to the peace and normalcy of a place like Indian Creek, near Moab, or Pakistan. Yet, I was always drawn back, and after marrying Dean, a devout Valley climber, I understood that I needed to make Yosemite as much my home as Moab.

From the Valley locals I learned to cruise the solo routes and to maneuver the obstacles of the Yosemite lifestyles, and from Dean I learned to escape the artificial amusement-park chaos by staying on the big walls at the backcountry. Fletcher, the social one in the family, made plenty of friends of her own and enthusiastically joined the crew of Yosemite "derelicts" when we were up on the walls. Half Dome, Mount Watkins and El Capitan became my second, third, and fourth homes. Gradually, I learned how to live a simple, natural life in the Valley, and with it I gained the freedom to just climb. Finally, I was able to experience Yosemite as a true paradise.

"Appreciation of the moment is one of the best aspects of climbing, something that I find missing from normal life, with its countless worries. On a wall, there are no thoughts of savings, promotions or pensions. Your future only stretches as far as the next two shiny bolts at the belay above."

Andy Kirkpatrick

MOTÖRHEAD FOREVER
Claude Remy | Grimsel/Switzerland

Motörhead, the famous route on the Eldorado slab at Grimsel, is about more than just climbing. The name reflects the culmination of an extraordinary era in music. For my brother Yves and me, it started in the middle of the 1960s, listening to the Beatles and their songs such as "Revolution", "Back in the USSR", and "Helter Skelter"... We were sure we could hear the sound of an airplane in the background. A few years later, music got harder with bands such as The Who, Grand Funk Railroad, Led Zeppelin, Deep Purple, Black Sabbath and many others. Judas Priest introduced new force into music without compromising the melody.

However, it was Motörhead, the exceptional trio from London, who produced the most amazing sound of all. The group was formed by bassist, singer and songwriter Ian Fraser Kilmister. Known by his stage name Lemmy, he is a man who defies all norms. The fact that he plays bass and sings at the same time says a lot about his extraordinary talents. With his distinctive rough voice, he creates uncompromising music that explores the subtleties of infernal rhythms and generates a unique sound. Six years after they formed in 1975, Motörhead brought out their first live album in June 1981, "No sleep 'til Hammersmith", recorded in London. Time stood still and the world held its breath in amazement that such a pure sound could exist.

At the time, we often drove the two and a half hour stretch between Lausanne and the Grimsel Pass and played our Motörhead tape over and over again. Even the car seemed to enjoy the innovative and convulsive heavy metal. We used to keep the windows shut though, so as not to miss the slightest moment and to avoid traumatizing the wildlife.

Eldorado is the most beautiful granite slab in the Alps. It's nearly 500 meters high and completely mind-blowing. We had already put up a route on the left-hand section the day before, "La Genève". When we saw the slab, we immediately wanted to bring two art forms together, namely hard rock and hard rock climbing and to unite them in harmony. Motörhead is a climbing and musical expression on perfect rock and amazing holds that require fantastic movement. Every artist is in pursuit of perfection, whether the search for the perfect note or, as in our case, the search for the perfect route. On July 7, 1981 – a few days after the release of the "album of the century", "No sleep 'til Hammersmith" – we made the first ascent of "Motörhead", the ultimate expression of the unique symbiosis between hard rock and rock climbing.

This was our second route on Eldorado and we went on to make the first ascent of "Simple solution", the striking system of cracks in the central section of the slab and "Les pieds et les mains" on the Marée sector. In later years, numerous new routes were added. On September 15, 1982 Yves and I linked up six Grimsel routes, starting at the car park at the mountain hostel: "Septumania", "Motörhead", "Venon" and "Métal Hurlant" on Eldorado and then "Les larmes de rire" and "Uzumati" on the Oubli sector. During the 1982 season, around 1500 climbers were counted on Eldorado's routes – this is unique for the Alps.

Motörhead
- Bernese Alps, Grimsel, Eldorado
- first ascent by Claude and Yves Remy, July 7, 1981, using nuts and 10 pegs
- repeated on July 10, 1981 and equipped with bolts
- cleaned and re-bolted in 2003

Difficulty/lead climbing

Year	Grade	Climber	Route
1918	6a expo	Emanuel Strubisch	Wilder-Kopf Westkante, Saxony sandstone, DE
1930	6a+ expo	Frank Elliot, Harry Dover, Gilbert Ellis	Wall End Slab Direct, Stanage, Peak District, GB
1936	6b/6b+ expo	Willy Häntzschel	Schrammtorwächter North Face, Elbsandsteingebirge, DE
1949	6c expo	Peter Harding	Demon Rib, Black Rocks, Peak District, GB
1958	7a solo OS	Don Whillans	Goliath, Burbage, Peak District, GB
1960	6c solo	John Gill	Final Exam, Castle Rock, Colorado, USA
1961	7b+ solo	John Gill	The Thimble, Needles, Dakota, USA (12 meters high)
1973	6c solo OS	Jim Erickson	Cassandre, USA
1974	7c	Steve Wunsch	Supercrack, Gunks, USA
1977	8a	Peter Cleveland	Phlogiston, Devil's Lake, USA
	7b f	Lynn Hill	Shawangunk Ridge, Gunks, USA
1979	7c f	Lynn Hill	Ophir Broke, Telluride, Colorado, USA
	7b+ expo	Bernd Arnold	Direkte Superlative, Elbsandsteingebirge, DE
	8a	Toni Yaniro	Grand Illusion, Sugar Loaf, California, USA
1980	7b+ OS	Patrick Edlinger	La polka des ringards, Buoux, FR
1981	7c+ expo	Maurizio Zanolla (Manolo)	Il mattino dei maghi, Totoga, Dolomites, IT
1983	8a+	Jerry Moffatt	The Face, Altmühltal, DE
1984	8b	Wolfgang Güllich	Kanal im Rücken, Altmühltal, DE
	7c+ OS	Jerry Moffat	Pol Pot, Verdon, FR
	7c+ f	Lynn Hill	Vandals, Gunks, USA
1985	8b+	Wolfgang Güllich	Punks in the gym, Mount Arapiles, Australia
	8a solo	Antoine Le Menestrel	Revelations, Raven Tor, Peak District, GB
1986	8b+/c	Antoine Le Menestrel	Ravage, Chuenisberg, Basler Jura, CH
	7c solo	Wolfgang Güllich	Weed Killer, Raven Tor, Peak District, GB
	8a f	Luisa Iovane	Come Back, Val San Nicolò, IT
1987	8c	Wolfgang Güllich	Wallstreet, Krottenseer Turm, Frankenjura, DE
	8a+ solo	Jean-Christophe Lafaille	Rêve de gosse, Les Arnauds, FR
	8a f	Christine Gambert, Lynn Hill	Rêve de papillon, Buoux, FR
	8a OS	Antoine Le Menestrel	Samizdat, Cimaï, FR
	7b f OS	Lynn Hill	Numerous routes in the USA
1988	8a+ f	Catherine Destivelle	Choucas, Buoux, FR
	8b f	Isabelle Patissier	Sortilèges, Cimaï, FR
1990	8c+	Ben Moon	Hubble, Raven Tor, Peak District, GB
	8b+ f	Lynn Hill	Masse critique, Cimaï, FR
1991	9a	Wolfgang Güllich	Action Directe, Frankenjura, DE
	8b solo	Alain Robert	Compilation, Omblèze, FR
1992	8a f OS	Lynn Hill	Simon, Frankenjura, DE
	9a	Alexander Huber	Om, Triangel, Endstal, DE (9a+)
1993	8b OS	Elie Chevieux	Les liaisons dangereuses, Calanques, FR
1994	8a+ f OS	Lynn Hill	Overdose, Lourmarin, FR
1995	9b	Fred Rouhling	Akira, Grotte de Vilhonneur, Les Eaux Claires, FR (NC)
	8b+ OS	Elie Chevieux	Massey Fergusson, Calanques, FR
1996	9a+	Alexander Huber	Open Air, Schleierwasserfall, Tirol, AT
1998	8c f	Josune Bereziartu	Honky Tonky, Onate, ES
1999	8b f OS	Katie Brown	Omaha Beach, Red River Gorge, USA
2000	8c+ f	Josune Bereziartu	Honky Mix, Onate, ES
	9a+	Eric Talmadge	Im Reich des Shogun, Tüfleten, CH
2001	9a+	Chris Sharma	Realization, Céüse, FR
2002	9a f	Josune Bereziartu	Bain de sang, St-Loup, CH
2003	8b solo	Alexander Huber	Opportunist, Schleierwasserfall, Tirol, AT
	8b+ solo	Alexander Huber	Kommunist, Schleierwasserfall, Tirol, AT
	9b	Bernabé Fernandez	Chilam Balam, Archidona, ES (80 meters)
2004	8c OS	Yuji Hirayama	White Zombie, Baltzola, ES
2005	9a+ f	Josune Bereziartu	Bimba luna, St-Loup, CH
2006	8b+ f OS	Josune Bereziartu	Hydrofobia, Montsant, ES
2007	8c+ OS	Patxi Usobiaga	Bizi Euskaraz, Etxauri, ES
2008	9b	Chris Sharma	Jumbo Love, Clark Mountain, USA (75 meters)
2010	8c f OS	Charlotte Durif	Les rois du pétrole, Pic St-Loup, FR
2011	8c+ OS	Adam Ondra	5 routes within short time, ES
	9b	Adam Ondra	Several routes throughout the world

THE DEVELOPMENT OF FREE CLIMBING STANDARDS
Claude Remy | Around the world

Collecting information about the development of free climbing is no easy task, but that's nothing compared to trying to rank climbs in order of difficulty. The huge variations in ascent styles, protection and grading systems particular to different countries and different periods make it a very tall order. How do the achievements of the early pioneers compare to those of modern climbers? Mountaineering with heavy and unreliable equipment was a very different matter to climbing cleaned and bolted routes in lightweight rock shoes with tried and trusted protection. How do you compare short, well protected climbs where moves are rehearsed over and over again with long, exposed routes, climbed on sight? And that's not to mention free-solo ascents ... Nevertheless; here is my (incomplete) attempt to collect and collate the most outstanding climbing achievements of all time, together with names and dates. It is broken down into two categories: difficulty/lead climbing and multi-pitch alpine routes. Of course, some of the climbs could be included on more than one list. I have used the

following abbreviations: solo without a rope (solo), on-sight (OS), long, exposed run-outs (expo), obligatory difficulties which have to be climbed free (obl.), ascents by women (f), non-confirmed grades, as the route is still to be repeated (NC). I would like to thank the following people for their help in compiling this information: Josune Bereziartu, Stephan Denys, Nicolas Favresse, Lynn Hill, Andreas Kubin, Fred Labreveux, Bernard Newman, Fred Nicole, Rikardo Ortegui, Maurizio Oviglia and Maurizio Zanolla.

Grading climbs is not an exact science. Certain grades have yet to be confirmed; others have changed over the years as handholds or footholds break, get polished (or chipped). These two lists are based on the French numerical grading system and should be regarded as suggestions. They could equally be complemented with boulder, boulder traverses, trad routes climbed exclusively with natural protection and hybrid routes (routes that start as boulder problems and finish with roped protection).

Multi-pitch routes			
1492		Antoine de Ville	Mont Aiguille, Vercors, FR (early mountaineering, with ladders)
1881	4c	Benedikt Venetz	Mummeryriss, Grépon, Chamonix, FR
1911	5a solo	Paul Preuss	Campanile Basso East Face, Brenta, Dolomites, IT
1913	5c solo	Hans Dülfer	Dülferriss, Fleischbank, Wilder Kaiser, Tirol, AT
1954	6b OS	Paulet Girardin	Face de la Heutte, Jura, CH
1978	7a+ OS	Maurizio Zanolla (Manolo)	Carlesso, Torre Trieste, Dolomites, IT
1979	7c OS	Maurizio Zanolla	Biasin/Scalet, Sass Maor, Dolomites, IT
1981	7b+ solo	Maurizio Zanolla	Sorvegliate i Bugiardi, Monte Totoga, Dolomites, IT
1985	7b+ f	Catherine Destivelle	Pichenibule, Escalès, Verdon, FR
1988	8a OS	Maurizio Zanolla	Bonvecchio, Pala di San Martino, Dolomites, IT
	8a+	Todd Skinner, Paul Piana	Salathé, El Cap, Yosemite, USA
1991	8b+	Beat Kammerlander	Unendliche Geschichte, Rätikon, CH (7c obl.)
1993	8b+ f	Lynn Hill	Nose, El Cap, Yosemite, USA
1994	8a, f OS	Lynn Hill	Mingus, L'Escales, Verdon, FR
	8b+	Beat Kammerlander	Silbergeier, Vierte Kirchlispitze, Rätikon, CH (7c obl.)
	8b+	Stefan Glowacz	Des Kaisers neue Kleider, Wilder Kaiser, Tirol, AT
	8b+	Thomas Huber	End of Silence, Feuerhorn, Berchtesgaden, DE
1998	8b	Alexander + Thomas Huber	El Niño, El Cap, Yosemite, USA
2001	8c	Alexander Huber	Bellavista, Westliche Zinne, Dolomites, IT
	8b+	Stefan Glowacz	Trilogie: Silbergeier, Des Kaisers neue Kleider, End of Silence
2002	7c OS	Denis Burdet	Divine providence, Pilier d'Angle, Mont Blanc, FR (at 4,000 meters)
2004	8b+	Maurizio Zanolla	Cani morti, Campanile Basso, Pale di San Martino, IT (8a obl.)
2006	8c	Maurizio Zanolla	Solo per vecchi guerrieri, Pale di San Martino, IT (8a obl.)
2007	7b solo	Hansjörg Auer	Weg durch den Fisch, Marmolada South Face, Dolomites, IT
	8c	Alexander Huber	Pan Aroma, Westliche Zinne, Dolomites, IT
2008	8c	Adam Ondra	WoGü, Siebte Kirchlispitze, Rätikon, CH (8a+ obl.)
	8a+ OS	Adam Ondra	Hotel Supramonte, Gola di Gorroppu, Sardinia, IT (7c obl.)
2010	8b+/c	Adam Ondra	Tough enough, Karambony, Madagascar

Mammut ropes have been the equipment of choice for climbers for more than 50 years, especially those with their sights set on the big mountains. In 1956, a Swiss expedition set out to make the first ascent of the fourth-highest mountain in the world, Lhotse, after Swiss mountaineers had narrowly failed to become the first to reach the summit of Mount Everest in 1952. They came close: Raymond Lambert and Tenzing Norgay reached a height of 8,600 meters. Their attempt pioneered a new route from the south and as such paved the way for the successful 1953 expedition.

The 1956 Lhotse expedition was financed by the Swiss Foundation for Alpine Research (founded in 1939) and in autumn 1955, it requested an offer from the *Seilerwarenfabrik A.G. Lenzburg* to supply ropes, webbing, belay slings and avalanche cords. The company's offer (their logo already included the Mammut) was sent to the foundation on October 20, 1955. An order was placed on December 1, 1955 and the bill was sent out on January 3, 1956. The final bill came to 2,082.85 Swiss francs. This included a sales tax of 3.6 percent and a 2 percent discount. In January 1956, the equipment was delivered to the central warehouse of the *Neuen Warenhaus AG*, which was the name that EPA, a Swiss chain of department stores, traded under in the 1950s. The Foundation was based at the same address.

The ropes, slings and webbing didn't stay there for long. By February, the expedition was on its way to Kathmandu, from where it set out in March for base camp on the Nepalese side of Mount Everest. On May 18, 1956, Ernst Reiss and Fritz Luchsinger became the first men ever to stand on the 8,516 meter summit of Lhotse. They were tied together with a "Mammut-Argenta" glacier rope. A few days later, Jürg Marmet and Ernst Schmied made the second ascent of Mount Everest, and on May 24, 1956, Hansrudolf von Gunten and Adolf Reist made the third.

82

"EXTRA SPECIAL PRICES" FOR THE HIMALAYAS
Karin Steinbach Tarnutzer | Mount Everest/Himalaya

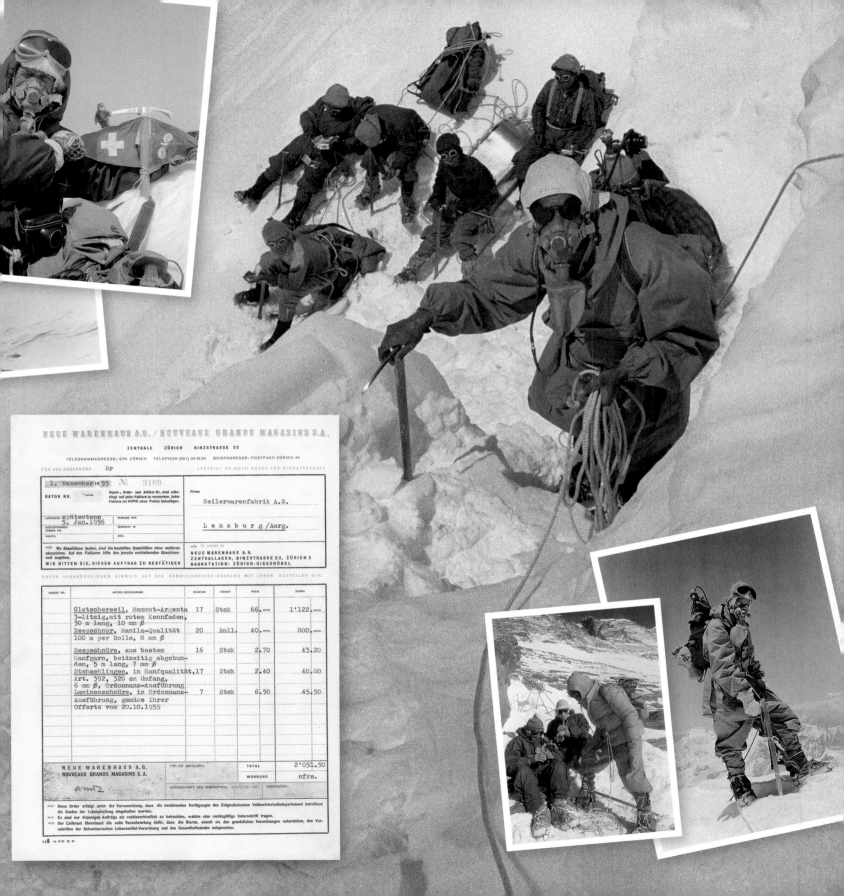

THE EIGER NORTH FACE IS HIS SOFA
Robert Steiner | Eiger/Switzerland

83

@

The German writer and alpinist Robert Steiner wrote this portrait of Stephan Siegrist after meeting him on a Mammut Teamtrip in South West Kyrgyzstan. The team's objective was to make the first free ascent of the Timofeev route on 4,230 meter Mount Asan.

Pulling the Velcro straps tight on his shoes, he checks the gear at the belay and starts climbing. Normally, you would dip your hands in the chalk bag before a difficult pitch. There's not much point in that here – the steep crack has water running down it and its sides are covered with a slippery coating of slimy moss and lichen. Dry conditions will have to wait for another day. "This will be learning by doing," Stef smiles and starts moving. Sometimes you have no other choice. This applies in particular up in the greater mountain ranges, where nature sets the tone, not man.

Like so many experienced mountaineers, he has that special combination of calmness and incredible energy. Stef presses his feet against the wall; his hands disappear into the dark maw of the crack. If it were dry, it would probably be graded 7a. These are the hands that wielded his ice axes as he hung from the overhanging ice mushroom on the summit of Cerro Torre in 1999 during the first winter ascent of the Ferrari Route. They also saw him through the icicles hanging from the horizontal roof of "Flying Circus" (M 10) at Breitwangfluh, Bernese Oberland, Switzerland, one of the world's most difficult ice climbs. These are the hands with an intimate knowledge of the rough limestone of the Wendenstöcke in the Urner Alps in Switzerland, big walls in India, and the deathly cold of Antartica, where he joined the Huber brothers to climb the mountains on Queen Maud Land, which emerge like sailing ships from the inland ice. These hands probably also dug into the snows of Gasherbrum East, before he decided that it was too dangerous to continue. The continual "voom" noises made it feel as if the whole slope could collapse at any minute, so he climbed back down.

I remember my first encounter with Stephan well. We shook hands; he clapped me on the shoulder, smiling that big grin of his. It felt like meeting an old friend. There was no vanity and no show.

He is very down to earth. People. Everyday life. He enjoys chatting, no matter whom he might be talking to. On the Mammut Team trip expedition, David Lama was with us, along with Nina Caprez and Giovanni Quirici. It took us three days by train to travel the 3,700 kilometers from Moscow to Kyrgyzstan. At one point, on a scorching hot day somewhere at the Aral Sea, Stephan reached into his rucksack and pulled out a menu from his favourite ice-cream parlour in Interlaken; he said that helped him to cool down. He constantly amused us with his funny stories and antics. For example, how friends in the Middle East invited him to an "Aerobic Lesson". Stef duly pulled on his stretch clothing, draped a towel around his shoulders and was looking forward to a bit of dancing when he arrived at the meeting point. His friends were dressed normally, carrying books, and the women wore veils – ready for the "Arabic Lesson".

He started climbing at an early age. Hiking was never really his thing. He says he found the "tramping through cowpats" boring. Ski tours were more interesting, but still involved too much "hobbling about". "Steep is best" – that was his motto. Instead of taking over the family carpentry business, he became a mountain guide and then turned professional at the age of 26. Probably no easy decision, but one that he has never regretted. He chose to "live the dream". Project followed project. He was already strong and he got even stronger. Hard alpine routes followed, including the four Torres in Patagonia, first ascents all over the world, film projects, articles, interviews and sponsors. In spite of his success as an internationally acclaimed mountaineer, he is pretty much the same as he always was: the friendly guy from next door, who is always a pleasure to bump into. And a passionate alpinist, who sees people and mountains as more important than success itself.

He's worked with Mammut for a long time. The company philosophy suits him; he likes the people there. He saw sponsorship

as a partnership and was always there, when he was needed. Product development, testing, giving talks, photo shoots, advice. He became the face of the brand. He says that it's important to keep your feet on the ground and that the world of mountaineering stars is sometimes too selfish and narcissistic for him. This is why he continues to work as a mountain guide. Every year he is out in the mountains with longstanding clients – he prefers to use the word "friend" – for example with Marwan Shakarchi, who was born in Lebanon and runs a successful gold business, "Pamp Swiss Made Solid Gold", based on Lake Geneva. Whenever he can, he loves to be up in the mountains – preferably with Stephan.

The 38 year old mountain guide is not away on expeditions quite as much as he used to be. He has built a house at Ringgenberg near Interlaken, where he lives with his charming Canadian partner. Together they lead a half-Swiss German, half-English life and have two children. When he's not on a lecture tour, an expedition or simply out climbing, this is where you'll find him. The Eiger is not far from Ringgenberg and he's spent countless days climbing there. One of his friends joked, "The Eiger is his sofa, it's where he goes to chill out." He's climbed it 27 times, via all manner of routes. Together with his friend Ueli Steck, he made the first ascent of the "The Young Spider", a to date never completely repeated route in the slope line of the peak. With "La Paciencia" and "La vida es silbar" he added two extremely difficult free routes. For "Eiger live", a live television broadcast, he climbed the North Face of the Eiger with Evelyne Binsack, setting off on 09.09.1999 at 09:09. He also doubled for Benno Fürman on location in the movie "Nordwand".

In one rather special project, he made the first successful redpoint ascent of the "Magic Mushroom", a rock pillar on the North Face of the Eiger. After several days freeing the route, he reached the summit and then BASE jumped back down into the valley. He had prepared carefully for the project, completing his parachute training, and practising on ever more complicated BASE jumps. "For me, it was a coming together of two contrasting things. When you climb, you hold onto the rock with everything you can to avoid falling. Then you reach the summit and voluntarily jump off it. It's earth meets the sky – with a bit of fire under your backside!" His most memorable experience was repeating the original route on the North Face of the Eiger with the same equipment that was originally used. He went to see Anderl Heckmair, persuaded Mr. Grivel in Courmayeur to forge him some classic-style crampons and found a shoemaker who could still make boots with Tricouni nails. More or less unprotected, with only a marginally reliable hemp rope, a handful of pitons, and bendy nailed boots, he climbed the route of the first ascent with Michal Pitelka. He was left full of respect for the first ascensionists.

There is a lot of cursing and swearing going on above me. Stef is apparently in good spirits, but his choice of vocabulary on this wet and slimy pitch is not particularly family friendly. He opens with "Hure" and ends with "Schiessdräck". Even if I had a dictionary of Bernese Swiss-German slang and swear words, I doubt I could understand the rest of his tirade. We'll be on the summit soon. I have rarely climbed with someone where I have felt so calm and so safe. My thoughts turn to the letter in my pocket, which Stef's partner Nicki passed to me in secret. It's a wanted notice. Of a rather special kind:

WANTED!!!
This man travels under different names: Stephan, Stef, Rubi … Distinguishing characteristics: attractive man with blond hair and big smile on face. APPROACH WITH CAUTION: his deep blue eyes are used to getting want they want. DANGER, RISK OF FATAL INJURY: the suspect has a deadly instinct for humorous antics. Likely whereabouts: difficult big walls, above 8a, M7 and 4,000 meters. If found, please return missing and wanted man back to Ringgenberg, Interlaken, Switzerland!

May you always return home safe! Ahoi, Stef!

PACKS EXPERT CIRCLE ON THE SHEER ROCK FACE
Jutta Römmelt I Alps/Switzerland

How ideas take shape

Every marketing campaign starts with a big idea. Creative sketches from the agency are discussed by Mammut and the photographer before the best one is chosen. Then it's a matter of finding the right location. This normally proves to be more complicated than one might think. The Backpack Testevent was no exception to the rule.

The project team needed to know their way around the Swiss Alps to find the perfect rock face. Should it be the Bernese Oberland, Valais, the Urner Alps or Ticino? Switzerland has no shortage of cliffs to choose from, as we know. But which one could be easily reached by 100 Mammut dealers from all over the world? Where would the quality of the rock be good enough? Which type of rock – gneiss, granite or limestone would provide the best backdrop? There were so many questions to be cleared up. In addition, the conditions had to be taken into account. One cliff that looked perfect on photos taken during summer was still covered in snow in March. Would it be free of snow in time for the Testevent in May? The project team also included a Swiss mountain guide with longstanding experience of conditions across the Alps. He was on hand to advise whether the project could be safely carried out at the chosen location. Mammut was going to put its dealers up on the face, so safety had to be the first priority.

As you can imagine, the team had to ditch several locations, once it became clear that they were unsuitable for assembling such a large number of people in such a short period of time without unreasonable effort and expense, no matter how grandiose a photo this would make. A four-member team investigated promising walls all over Switzerland. The mountain guide and a Mammut employee climbed each of these faces, positioning themselves as reference points while the photographer and a representative from the agency composed the possible shot. Is this the one we're looking for? We finally found the perfect location, in Osogna in Ticino, one of the sunniest parts of Switzerland. And we were just in time to carry out the preparations for the shooting.

Backpack workshops in an idyllic alpine setting

The perfect camp location was quickly located for the Testevent at Seelisberg in Central Switzerland. The tents were pitched on the grass surrounding a small lake. There were teepees to sleep in and a large circus tent for the backpack presentations and to provide a dry alternative venue for the outdoor kitchen, should the weather turn.

114 dealers from 14 different countries were invited to the Testevent. The aim was to present and test the new revamped Mammut backpack collection and organize a revolutionary photo shoot for the adversting compaign in summer 2010. Thanks to the sunny weather, the participants could enjoy relaxing in the outside whirlpool or swimming in the cooler lake. There was also time for a daily morning Qigong session overlooking the lake. The camp workshops provided dealers with an opportunity to get to grips with

the new technologies and innovative backpack systems and familiarize themselves with the fit adjustment options and designs. Designers, developers and product managers were all on hand to go through the details of the Alpine, Trekking, Hiking and Climbing packs. A range of fun activities including a slackline course provided plenty of opportunities to unwind.

Vertical photo shoot

The photo shoot was also focussed on the new packs. Dealers from all over the world were to become Mammut models and testers for a day. There was great excitement in the morning of the shoot during the one and a half hour steep walk to the top of the cliff face. Then it was finally time to get ready to rappel down. Helmet, harness, carabiner, sling and don't forget the pack! Once kitted out, each dealer was carefully checked by the Mammut Crew. After inspection the Testevent participants climbed down a short via ferrata to the rappel platform.

Here, harnesses and equipment were checked once again before the guests were handed over to the mountain guides, who had set up the unusual shooting location a few days previously. They then assisted each participant to rappel down the face to reach the designated position, providing encouragement where necessary. Not all of our budding top models looked completely at ease with a 100 meter drop beneath their feet. However, the guides soon had them safely secured at the prepared anchor points arranged in a circle. The view was spectacular and thanks to the friendly, collegial atmosphere among the dealers the international assembly of backpack experts was soon in place. It was time for the shooting; the red rucksacks were positioned for the photo. In no time at all, Röbi had the key campaign image in the can. And one more time, smile for the camera please – all the climbers turned to wave.

What then? Well, then each dealer had to rappel the remaining 30 meters down to the ground, laughing at their adventures. Daniel Meyer of Titlis Sport in Engelberg summed it up by saying, "The photo shoot on that vertical face was amazing. It's the sort of thing you only experience once in a lifetime. It's not easy to describe, but sharing an incredible moment like that with colleagues from all over the world makes it even more fun."

YEAH, MAN!

Giovanni Quirici | Gastlosen/Switzerland

The Gruyère region of Switzerland is the epitome of nature in harmony with human activity. Visitors are greeted by a scene of fairytale landscapes. Also known as "the little Dolomites" due to its pale limestone rock, Gastlosen is an imposing 400 meter high chain of cliffs that extends for 15 kilometers where the cantons of Berne, Freiburg and Waadt come together.

The story of the North Face of the Pfadflue starts in 1975. The first two ascents of the wall were climbed two years later using aid. Erhard Loretan, who later became the third person to climb all fourteen 8,000ers, was one of the first to arrive at the foot of this 300 meter high face. The plan of climbing the line up the face that would later be called "Yeah Man" originated in 1995. Three years later, this vision was realized by François Studenmann and Guy Scherrer with an extremely demanding route. It was not until the summer of 2004, however, that each pitch was climbed free by the Basque climber Josune Bereziartu with her partner Rikar Otegui. Despite many subsequent attempts, the free ascent of "Yeah Man" in one day remained a pipedream.

In September 2008 (already a bit late in the year), I accompanied Guy Scherrer onto the face. After the first four pitches (7a+, 7c, 7b+, 7c), progress became more difficult. I managed the very technical 8a+ section, which took a lot of stamina on the final hand traverse, on my first attempt. The next pitch, at 8a, proved more problematic. After several attempts, I opted for a more dynamic solution: by turning the tip of my left foot inwards slightly, I was able to reach a good hold. After the 6th pitch, we came to a ledge that was wide enough for us to sit and rest a bit. I threw a piece of bread out to a jackdaw, who caught it in a flash. The next pitch after the ledge, an overhanging 7c+ section, finished with a beautiful boulder problem sequence on bad footholds, with your right arm locked off. Then things got serious. The 8th pitch is 8b+, and is a 50 meter long endurance test 300 meters above the ground, with a top out onto pretty slick rock. After four attempts, I finally managed this last pitch. By that stage, it was unfortunately too cold to try to link all of the pitches.

In June 2009, shortly before the Mammut Teamtrip to Kyrgyzstan, I returned to Wandflue with my friend from Ticino, Pablo Moghini. Everything seemed to go really smoothly and I soon found myself 35 meters up the long 8th pitch. The dream of linking the whole route in one day was within my grasp but the most unpredictable section still lay ahead of me. My arms were starting to get pumped, success was in the balance. I was at my limit; I could feel my fingers uncurling. There was nothing I could do – I was suddenly hanging on the rope 10 meters lower down. Even though I had failed, I was happy; now I knew that it would go. Just a couple of days later, I was sitting on a train from Moscow to Bishkek with the Mammut Team.

In summer 2010, a musician friend explained to me that to be able to play a piece of music perfectly, you have to work through the whole thing, then take a break, let it settle, and when you go back to work on it again, something wonderful happens. It felt like every hold on this face had become a music note. If I was going to play this piece, composed of thousands of holds, without making a mistake, I would have to keep time and pay attention to the way the notes were arranged. Success depended on my ability to synchronize it. With the first seven pitches behind me, I threw myself into the 8b+ pitch. I was stuck to that big wave of rock, my entire consciousness focused on the tips of my toes exerting maximum pressure on the foot holds. Hanging from tiny dimples, my arms were directing the sequence of moves. With such small holds, there was only so long I could hold on. My entire focus was on keeping on going, there was no room for thought about what lay behind. I had to make use of the energy of the present moment. As always, the key to success is being able to pace yourself. Cautiously, I squeezed the two tiny holds above me. I was getting closer to the belay now. And would you believe it, it worked! I was so overjoyed that I forgot how strenuous it had been. I felt like crying and said a quiet thank you to everyone who had helped me. Just one more 7a pitch and I was on the top. As the sun set, fires were lit and a few fireworks crackled into the skies, reminding us that today was August 1st, Swiss National Day. Thank you, "Yeah Man"!

Giovanni Quirici was killed on August 12, 2011 on the Eiger route "Le chant du cygne". We will hold his cordial and cheerful character as well as his awesome ascents in fond remembrance.

OLTRE IS MORE THAN FINALE
Emil Zopfi | Oltre Finale/Italy

The grey cliffs shine in the morning sun; rough holds and glistening chromium steel bolts. We get warmed up and start on the easy routes. There are voices in the woods. A long procession of climbers is making its way up the hill. We can't help but notice the attractive women in their skin-tight outfits – blues, yellows, and violets. In a cheerful hubbub, rucksacks are dumped and unpacked; helmets are placed over dark, curly locks, shaven heads and grey manes. Then it all goes quiet again. Ropes stretch up the cliff, there are shouts of encouragement, helpful suggestions, and laughter echoes all around.

The sport climbing circus has come to town. Kids are yelling and dogs are barking; a Karelian bear dog splashes around in the pool at the foot of the face before rolling in the mud and then shaking itself dry over our rope bag. We smile patiently; the sun will dry everything in time. A lone melancholy voice asks: "What has happened to our sport?"

Yesterday at one of the overhanging walls, we could barely find space for all our gear amongst the toy cars and Barbie dolls strewn all over the place. At one point, we watched as twelve-year old Andrea from Zurich swung about on the ropes for a bit before waltzing up a 7a or 7b like it was a climbing tower at some kind of outdoor kindergarten.

Reinhold Messner is said to have coined the notion of "on-piste" or mass tourism mountaineering". We find ourselves in the thick of it. Oltre Finale is in, Finale is out. The classic climbing areas around Finale Ligure are now so well known that people know every route (in the guide book with three stars) and each polished hold by heart. New and uncharted territory was required, something "over and above" or as they say in Italy "oltre". The climbing in Albenga (just down the Ligurian coast from Finale Ligure) has little to do with its better known neighbor, but the area decided to market itself with the established brand. Word soon spread in the magazines, and the climbing community descended like a horde of locusts.

Dindo is one of the locals responsible for developing the area; we met him in a bar on a Saturday morning in Cisano sul Neva. He is a builder, a small but powerfully built man with brown skin and twinkling eyes. He bolts new routes on Saturdays and then climbs them on Sundays. He is responsible for something like 100 new routes a year, or so it says on the note hanging on the notice board, where he also points out that he does not receive a penny from the sale of Andrea Gallo's thick climbing guidebook for his efforts and his route descriptions. A collection box hangs next to the list; we throw in a couple of Euros. He and his friends are opening up cliff after cliff and are bringing a new source of income to the remote valley. Climbers come, need accommodation, buy provisions, go out for a meal or have a drink. Stones are being turned into bread. It's not big business by any means, maybe two or three jobs at most, or so we reckon.

Although, when measured according to the "Economics of Happiness", the results are very promising. Whatever Reinhold Messner might say, despite the boom in climbing tourism and the barking dogs, we're happy when we sit in our fine restaurants at the end of a hard day's climbing. There are also plenty of other happy faces in the bars, where people sit drinking their aperitif or sipping a cappuccino. The kids are happy, too, having swept up their Barbie dolls and their toy cars, and spending the day outdoors with their fit and motivated parents.

Of course, Messner is right. This is a form of mass tourism and it has little to do with mountaineering in the classic sense of the word, apart from the fact that it involves climbing on rock. It is a sport; it is something new, but the environmental impact is certainly less than that of the ski slopes.

One quirky aspect of Oltre Finale is the names given to the routes. As such a large number of new routes have been developed in such a short space of time people have started to run out of ideas and reached for the dictionary. There are routes named after plants, herbs, wines, Roman emperors, philosophers and even computer software – whole themes seemed to have been exhausted. Whereas the name of a route used to provide an indication of its character or even an insight into the cultural or political mindset of the person originally climbing it, in Oltre Finale this dimension is somewhat lacking. Only on routes such as "Bruto" is there occasionally a correlation between a route's name and its nature. My fall at the vicious crux came so suddenly that I had no time to utter those immortal words, "Et tu, Brute?" Unlike Julius Caesar, at least I was lucky enough to come out of it unscathed.

CLIMB UNTIL I DROP
Oswald Oelz | Around the world

I still live a pretty intense life and have no intention of dying any time soon. I plan to climb for at least another 20 years; in fact, I intend to climb until I drop. I have enough potential destinations to last me the next two hundred years. It's going to happen some day though; I've noticed that the obituaries in the papers are often about my generation. I have never been slow to grasp an opportunity, but at the end of the day, I'm going to have to leave a long list of unfinished projects behind.

Climbing the pocketed cliffs of Oman, snow bivouacs in Lunana in northwestern Bhutan and sheep-shearing and trekking in the Dolpa region of Nepal have all helped provide a real contrast to my career in medicine as the director of a hospital. For me, climbing has always been a complementary archaic lifestyle that has served to counterbalance the over-regulated plastic world that we live in. Life affords us comfort, a high standard of living, a more than doubled life expectancy, as well as allergies, cancer-inducing chemicals and obesity. We have destroyed the natural rhythms of the world, our nights are constantly illuminated, and we are not supposed to experience rain, cold or storms. There are no bears and no woolly mammoths left to threaten us. Food is now abundant and no longer has to be hunted or cultivated. Diesel and aviation gasoline save us from walking, layers of concrete, metal and other materials seal us off from the world outside. Electrical cables and radio networks transport billions of banalities across the globe on a daily basis. Everybody sends text messages, but only a few people seem to be actually able to talk.

All this is forced into an ever tighter corset of regulation; safety regulations have become the new terrorist networks. I am no longer supposed to consume the brains of my own lambs and in the near future, it will be illegal to leave offal to the foxes. Virtual worlds, safety standards, regulations and heteronomy make life more comfortable and also serve to fill the practices and pockets of the psychoindustry. The primeval world in which we developed was a very different sort of place. Like our ancestors, we were mainly occupied with finding food, keeping warm and fighting over women. If a bear spotted you, you had to either flee or turn and fight.

Climbing involves returning to the conditions experienced during the millions of years of human evolution. It is essential to find a safe place to bivouac, to build a fire to melt snow, to be able to cook potatoes with parmesan and to have sharp weapons (crampons). This is where the regenerative potential of wilderness experiences lies. Climbing in unknown regions makes flashmobs, the taxman or the size of your automobile irrelevant. Trekking in the high mountains of India recharges the batteries, leaving you better prepared for any challenge the urban jungles of New York, London, Paris or Berlin might throw at you.

This course of therapy is not entirely free of risk. I have lost more than 25 friends over the years. These are people with whom I have climbed on the same rope as, in whose company I've been privileged to appreciate that life is a beautiful gift. They have been buried by avalanches, have disappeared, fallen or died from high altitude cerebral edema. They have journeyed on ahead to another place. Whether all these things were a price worth paying remains a mystery to me.

The Grim Reaper has had me in his sights and only narrowly missed me on more than one occasion. Close shaves involving falling rocks, avalanches, and pulmonary edema or breaking bolts have made me appreciate my life in a more conscious manner. We climb to experience intensity, not because we have a death wish. "The secret for harvesting from existence the greatest fruitfulness and the greatest enjoyment is: to live dangerously! Build your cities on the slopes of Vesuvius!" said Friedrich Nietzsche, the German philosopher. In my opinion, mountaineering is a wonderful alternative.

The reason why we do these things is perhaps rather different than we would think. Take, for example, Diego Wellig's answer when asked why he wanted to climb 8,000 meter mountains. "Because

there are no 9,000 meter mountains." The same applies to George Leigh Mallory, who told a journalist in 1924 that he wanted to climb Everest "because it's there." Both of these answers express how futile and unanswerable the question is.

I continue to enjoy each day I get to climb; feeling for a hold, the sun beating down on the back of my neck, the rising thirst and the soaking snow. I feel that my own experiences on the Jabal Misht in Oman, the Cholatse in Khumbu, the Heiligkreuzkofel in South Tyrol and the Triemli Hospital in Zurich are best summed up by the Swiss playwright and novelist Max Frisch in his own inimitable manner in "An Answer from the Silence" (1937), where he writes: "Why don't we live when we know we're here just this one time, just one single, unrepeatable time in this unutterably magnificent world!"

"You don't climb a difficult and poorly protected route because you want to die; on the contrary, you do it because you want to live life more intensely."

88 **Oswald Oelz**

"IF I GO CLIMBING IN THE WENDEN, THEN I LEAVE MY CAMERA AT THE FOOT OF THE ROUTE"

89

Robert Bösch | Around the world

Robert Bösch, the alpine and outdoor photographer, needs no introduction. What is less well known about him is that in the 1980s, he put up a ninth grade new route in the Rätikon. Karin Steinbach Tarnutzer asked him about his second love, climbing.

What is more important to you, Röbi, climbing or photography?
That's difficult to answer. To begin with, it was certainly climbing. At university, I definitely spent more time in the mountains than studying. After that, I got my mountain guide ticket and worked as a mountain guide. But I made sure that I still had enough spare time to do my own climbing. In those days, there were no indoor climbing walls, we trained on boulders on the Uetliberg or at one of the few local crags around, and in winter, it was down to the gym. I was hooked on climbing, always doing it. Photography simply didn't feature.

When did you start to climb?
As a kid, I went up into the mountains with my parents. But I only started to climb properly at the age of 20, when I met someone who already had some experience using pitons and etriers. At the start of university, I worked as a night watchman, and the guy who introduced me to my rounds at the Lake Zurich site was a climber. We started to climb together and from then on that was all I was interested in.

So how did you get into photography?
While climbing, we naturally took photos, and occasionally I managed to sell one of them to a magazine. Then at the start of the 1980s, I started to focus more on photography. Even then, I thought it would be a great way to make a living. But deep down inside, I didn't really believe it would ever work out that way.

But it did. What is the difference when you go into the mountains to take photos rather than to climb?
They are usually two completely different things. When I am out on a shoot, then I am fully focused on the photography, and getting the best possible result. Any climbing ambitions have to take a back seat; I am only interested in the image. Questions arise like: Where are we going to go? Who is coming with us? Do we need the helicopter to work more effectively? Should we place fixed lines or should we climb the route? If I go climbing for myself, for example in the Wenden, then I leave my camera at the foot of the route. I like to concentrate on the climbing.

Is it not possible to climb and take photographs at the same time?
You can do it, but it requires a concerted effort and discipline; you have to force yourself to take the photos. On big routes, combining the two is the only way to get the images. They may not always be perfect but they are more authentic and therefore can often be more exciting than staged shots. That is why, for my book "Schweiz Alpin" (Alpine Switzerland), I made a conscious effort to climb as part of a team, taking turns to lead, and took photographs when the opportunity arose. On big expeditions, that is the only way you can work in any case. Being fit is also the key to taking successful photographs. With a planned shoot, it is completely different. Then I don't get into a climbing rhythm, quite apart from the fact that a camera like the one I use can be quite a handicap in itself. On shoots like that, I tend not to lead any of the route – and climbing is only truly exciting when you are on the lead. It is my deep-seated belief that I have only properly 'done' a route on the mountain when I have led it or have taken turns leading. I only truly experience it when I take full responsibility for it all, with all the risks attached. That is a deciding factor for me.

Is that because the experience is less intense otherwise?
Yes. I used to push my own limits much more than I do today. I often got into situations where I thought to myself: if I make it through this, I'll give up climbing. However, as soon as the situation was over, I was already thinking about the next difficult route I could do. That kind of intense experience in the face of danger was potentially addictive. Then there was the need for recognition and 'fame'. Since climbing was not as popular back then as it is today, it was the recognition of your peers that counted. Everyone knew what routes you had done.

So by doing the first ascent of "Hannibals Alptraum" (Hannibal's Nightmare) on the 4th Kirchlispitze in Rätikon, you were making a name for yourself?
That was not what we set out to do. Martin Scheel, who discovered the line, and I simply wanted to climb that route. It wasn't about sponsors or publicity in those days, just about accomplishing something that was challenging.

And you certainly succeeded in doing that. The 1986 route is in the guide as "one of the most fantastic neo-classical free climbing routes in the Alps" and "way ahead of its time". You have climbed some other demanding routes, too, though.
There were a few interesting things, including the second or third ascent of Martin's "Supertramp" on Bockmattli. There were certainly stronger climbers than me out there, but the route was viewed as psychologically testing. I was always interested in both aspects, rock climbing and mountaineering. I used to climb 8a, but then would also tackle big mixed routes like the ones on the Frêney Face on Mont Blanc. In the Bernina I soloed, amongst others, the three summits of Palü in 6 ½ hours of climbing. I also climbed a few Big Walls and did some big mountains in Peru, the Himalaya and the Karakorum.

Are there any mountains or routes you still dream of climbing one day?
I still like mountaineering but it isn't as important to me anymore. I love sport climbing in the Alps, or going abroad with a bunch of friends and doing a bit of relaxed climbing. But the willingness to suffer is nowhere near as great as it once was, nor do I have that determination to reach the summit. Having said that, I cannot imagine a life without mountains, without rock faces.

90

THE FIRST SKI SUMMITS –
FROM 1,000 TO 4,000 METERS
Daniel Anker | Alps/Switzerland

1,000 meters: Bachtel or Chasseral

There are two candidates for the proud title of first 1,000 meter peak in Switzerland to be reached on skis: the Chasseral (1,607 m), the highest mountain in the Bernese Jura and the Bachtel (1,115 m) in the Zürcher Oberland. The Norwegian Olaf Kjelsberg, who worked as an engineer at the Swiss Locomotive and Machine Works (SLM) in Winterthur, skied up the Bachtel in January 1890, although some documents state that this took place a year later, in 1891.

The situation is less clear in the case of the Chasseral. It is said that a teacher brought a pair of skis from Norway to Nods, a municipality at the foot of the Chasseral on its southern side. A local pastor, "Pfarrer Guiche", is then thought to have used them and subsequently ordered more pairs through the Norwegian Embassy in Berne. He then organized "ski trips on the Chasseron and Chasseral", as mentioned in the publication "Recollections of 50 years of Skiing" (Erinnerungen aus fünfzig Jahren Skisport). Was this third mountain the Chasseron (1,606 m) in the Jura Vaudois, a classic skiing mountain? It has been confirmed that Director L. Grosjean from Biel and Head Forester A. Morel from Corgémont climbed the Chasseral on skis in the second half of 1893. It is also certain that Guiche, Kjelsberg & Co. were just the forerunners. In January 1899, the skiing pioneer Wilhelm Krebs-Gygax from Thun took part in a Swiss Alpine Club (SAC) gathering on the Bachtel and made a speech praising the merits of skiing. However, most of the SAC members present were not interested: "Säb ischt dänn nüüt, wäge dene Ski. Das ischt nu so ne Mode, die chunt nie uf bi eus am Bachtel." ("Your skis are no good. It's just some new fashion. It will never become popular here at the Bachtel.")

2,000 meters: Schilt

In 1891, Christof Iselin from the canton of Glarus in central Switzerland had read Fridtjof Nansen's classic book on skiing "The First Crossing of Greenland" and made his own pair of primitive "snowshoes", as skis were often called. The first rather unsuccessful attempts took place at night or during snow storms (to avoid ridicule). The following year, he made the acquaintance of Kjelsberg, who brought genuine Christiania skis from Norway to Glarus and then taught him how to ski properly.

On January 8, 1893, Christof Iselin and his fellow countryman Jacques Jenny wanted to demonstrate how skis could be used in the mountains. They left Glarus (472 m) and climbed the Schilt (2,299 m) via Fronalp in five hours. This was the first two thousand meter mountain in Switzerland to be climbed on skis. Eduard Naef-Blumer from Winterthur, who was out on foot the same day, was astonished to see ski tracks in the snow only a few centimeters deep, whereas he sank up to his knees with each step. He observed though that the two skiers were forced to take off their skis on some of the steeper sections of the Schilt, as they were unable to make progress on the hard-packed snow (in those days, skis had no real edges). Christof Iselin wrote to Kjelsberg in February 1893: "I am convinced that the most difficult terrain, the steepest slopes and downhill sections can all be overcome using skis."

Olaf Kjelsberg

3,000 meters: Oberalpstock

On January 4, 1896 the Swiss mountaineer Victor de Beauclair and the German explorers and researchers Erwin Baur, Wilhelm Paulcke and Peter Steinweg left Amsteg (544 m) with heavy packs and followed the route of the "Gotthard railway" up through the Maderaner valley to the Hinterbalm hut (1,820 m). They took with them food for four days, a rope, warm clothes, skis and snow shoes as well as two cameras. They also were accompanied by a local man, Ambros Zgraggen, who carried the heaviest pack. It took them nine hours to reach the hut, only to find its kitchen full of drifted snow. "There was so little wood for cooking or heating that there was little danger of the melting snow causing a flood."

At 02:15 the following morning, they set out for "The ascent of the Oberalpstock (3,330 m) wearing Norwegian skis." This was also the title of a long report published by Wilhelm Paulcke on February 15, 1896 in the "Alpina" journal. Nowadays, I suppose he would have posted a blog on www.skitouren.ch the moment he had finished. The four of them then proceded to head up through the Brunnital. "At five in the morning, we strapped on the skis at Brunniboden, 2,047 m – and continued to make easy progress." At around half past two in the afternoon, they reached the foot of the cliffs at approximately 3,200 m. "We took the skis off, and strapped on the nailed sandals over our soft fur boots, then de Beauclair and I climbed up the rock and over the snow ridge to the summit. Our friends waited for us below."

Erwin Baur and Peter Steinweg also missed out on the panoramic view from the Oberalpstock. Wilhelm Paulcke described it in the following words: "Despite the bitter cold, we could hardly get enough of the shimmering splendor of our surroundings and shouted out a jubilant 'Ski Heil!' back down into the valley. We had completed the first ever ascent of a major summit using skis." But he was mistaken in this. The Oberalpstock was the first 3,000 meter mountain to be climbed using skis in Switzerland, but it was not the first in the Alps. In 1894, Wilhelm von Arlt climbed the glaciated heights of the Rauriser Sonnblick (3,105 m) in the Hohe Tauern, the highest range in the Alps, east of the Brenner Pass in Austria. It is said that he only took 35 minutes to ski from the summit down to the town of Kolm-Saigurn (1,596 m) in the valley – no wonder that the best skiers come from Austria...

4,000 meters: Dufourspitze

The first attempt to climb the Dufourspitze on skis, at 4,634 m the highest mountain in the Monte Rosa Massif and in Switzerland, failed on January 5, 1898. This was not due to the rather modest skiing abilities of the Swiss-born Robert Helbling (it was his first ever ski tour), but because of the sudden onset of a formidable headache, the first sign of altitude sickness. At 4,200 meters, just below the saddle, he and his partner Wilhelm Paulcke turned back and skied (or stumbled) their way down in two hours. It had taken them eleven hours to climb up.

In March 1898, a similarly mismatched pair spent the night in the Bétemps hut (2,795 m) – as the Monte Rosa hut was previously called. It was situated about 100 meters below where the futuristic new Monte Rosa hut was built in 2009. The German doctor Oscar Schuster was not very happy about the fact that his Zillertal mountain guide Heinrich Moser only demonstrated "a poor grasp" of the "noble art of skiing". On March 23, they left the hut at three in the morning. "With and without the skis, we reached the upper plateau. At 06:52, we put out the lamp and then used the skis all the way to the saddle of the Monte Rosa (up to approximately 4,250–4,300 m)," Oscar Schuster was quoted in the "Austrian Alpine Newspaper" in 1898. At 17:20, they stood on top of the first 4,000 meter summit in the Alps to be reached using skis. By 18:17, they had skied downhill to the ski depot and arrived at the Bétemps hut at 23:12. Heinrich Moser's lack of skiing ability had held them back (when it got dark they completed the final 900 meters of descent on foot with their skis tied to their packs). The German doctor summed up their expedition with the words, "it would have been impossible without skis."

A QUESTION OF LUCK
Jean-Yves Michellod | Verbier/Switzerland

Extreme skiing down steep slopes – that was my thing. As a passionate freerider, I especially liked to climb a peak and pick a line down it that looked totally impossible. I worked as a safety officer at the Verbier Xtreme Snowboard Race for three or four years, so I knew my way around pretty well. When the event organizer, Nicolas Hale-Woods, decided to open up the race to skiers in 2004, I asked if I could take part. He invited me to compete and I won the race first time out – I was 27 at the time. That was the beginning of my freeriding career. But I never wanted to be a professional sportsman, living off sponsorship entirely. I don't have enough of a business head for that. However, my profession as a mountain guide gave me enough spare time to hurl myself down steep slopes.

On March 12, 2006, everything changed. I was skiing down a 45 degree slope on Mont Fort, in Les 4 Vallées ski region, and set off an avalanche that took me with it for 300 meters and slammed me into the rocks. I broke all my ribs and fractured my back in several places; one of these was on my 12th vertebra. I was pretty much broken in two. They operated on me immediately and patched me together with metal plates. After a week in hospital, I was transferred to Sion for rehabilitation.

I had always said to myself that the worst thing that could ever happen would be to have an accident that left me paralyzed from the waist down. When my worst fear came true at the age of 29, I was in a bad mental state for a few days. But at the time, I had a 3-month old daughter, and as a father, your priorities are different. You cannot allow yourself to think of the end. What really helped was that, in spite of everything, I noticed that I was making a little bit of progress. The doctors started from the premise that it would be a great achievement if I was ever able to use crutches to get from my bed to the bathroom. I was incredibly fortunate that some of the

muscles in my thighs as well as some of the nerves could be revived because my spinal cord had not been severed, just squashed. After four or five months, I started to stand up and walk between two parallel handrails. Through constant training, I was also able to regain a sense of balance, so that today I am able to walk without crutches. Since I could not move my feet at all, they used splints to fix them to my ankles, which is why I walk with a slight stoop.

At the start of my rehabilitation, my goal was to be able to lift myself out of bed and into the wheelchair without any help. As I regained some mobility in my legs, the hope grew that one day I might be able to ski normally again. But it was such a struggle to walk that I realized it just wouldn't be possible. So I looked for a viable alternative and discovered that it was possible to ski in a seated position. I came across Dualski on the Internet, a French company that manufactures ski equipment for disabled people. They made me a kind of skibob, and in January 2007, eight months after my accident, I started to ski again.

Para-freeriding, as I call it, is very different to ordinary skiing. I sit on a carbon frame that is connected by a shock absorber to the substructure; this, in turn, is mounted on two skis so that you are more buoyant in powder. You can use any model of ski with the bob. I also have two small arm supports to help with balance. Apart from these aids, the skiing itself is pretty much the same, except that I can't snowplough to brake.

When you have skied your whole life and suddenly, from one day to the next, you cannot even stand, you feel like you are starting from scratch again, especially with the skibob. The toughest part was going back to where I always used to ski, where everyone knew me from before and felt sorry for me. But I got over that pretty quick too. It was not long before I was having fun again. I think that is the important thing when you have been in an accident; you have

to forget the past – not draw a line under it but move on to other things. In other words, free your mind and do what you can despite your disability.

The fact that I had skied so much before really helped. I was scared of course before my first ride on the skibob. To be able to turn the thing, I have to pick up some speed and slide through the turn. But I picked it up quickly and one day I actually skied down the pistes at Verbier again, without falling. Powder was a bit tricky with the skibob as it tends to sink in – especially for my friends who had to lift me out of it 30 times a day! There was only one way round the issue – go faster. Now I enjoy powder skiing just as much as I did before the accident. I am even quicker than the able-bodied skiers because I don't get thigh-burn like they do – you almost have to force me to stop. I enjoy the speed: it's like being on a kart track. I can even carve turns at full speed. Despite sitting in a seat, I feel totally free.

So I have ended up leading the life of a professional freerider after all. I have been lucky, all my partners have stuck by me, and because I continue to do film work I am almost more well-known these days than before. I get around a bit, too. I was in Chile and Russia, and I am on the panel of judges for the Freeride World Tour. I am no happier than before my accident, but I can still ski and travel. I think many people would gladly swap places with me – not my wheelchair, but my life.

I have always been passionate about skiing and it was skiing that gave me something to work towards. And to work up to – on May 7, 2009, with the active help of numerous friends, I managed a five hour ascent on crutches from the Vallot Hut to the summit of Mont Blanc. The snow conditions were perfect, so I became the first person to skibob down the North Face of Mont Blanc.

DEALING WITH THE LOCALS
Emil Zopfi I Galerie/Switzerland

Sport climbers generally fall into one of two categories. There are the locals and then there is everyone else. Take me, for example. I'm a typical local. Whether high summer, or the depths of winter, weekday or weekend, you'll find me at the "Galerie" above Weesen, in the canton of St. Gallen, Switzerland. Malicious gossip has it that I am actually the caretaker, and I admit that I have actually collected rubbish. This qualifies me as a typical local. Locals take more responsibility for their actions. They test bolts, chop paths through the undergrowth, ensure that restrictions are respected and generally keep an eye on things, including making sure that the beginners are belaying each other properly. There are no elections or committees to appoint you. Being a local is more a calling than an occupation. One might say that the cliffs simply call you, to use a rather worn phrase.

There are definite advantages to being a local. This is evident whenever locals run into one another, and this generally happens most days. You can tell by the handshakes, the kisses and the laughing that locals simply belong. When a local prepares to start climbing, other climbers make way, or at least apologize. Anyone who has had to travel to reach the crag will realize that here is a local about to set to work.

As everyone knows, locals are touchy; they expect to be treated with respect. This is a rule more rigid than the rules of redpointing, which any self-respecting local will rigorously adhere to. A local would never hang on a bolt in front of a stranger. It goes without saying that every local has his own perpetual project, one that he only attempts when everyone else has gone home. Should non-locals be at the crag, then he has more important duties to fulfill. These mainly involve making his (or her) presence felt. This helps to communicate a sense of order and security that is valued by all concerned. Locals know the score. If there is a query about a grading, a local always has the answer. Although when it comes to route grading local opinion should also be treated with caution. There is a general rule of thumb which goes like this: take the local opinion of a grade and add one. If he says 6a, it's at least a 6b. In all other respects, locals are to be trusted. They respond well to this.

And here we come to the million dollar question: how do you behave towards locals when you are at one of 'their' crags? The main rule is: modesty at all times! Nothing annoys the locals more than non-local climbers, who get out of the car, make a beeline for the hardest route and then climb it on-sight, although they naturally do it all wrong. The local of course knows every inch of the route, which he has spent years perfecting. If he should climb a route himself, which does occasionally happen, there is only one response you need to remember: brilliant!

At the City of Rocks in the United States, I once managed to pull off the perfect demonstration of how to deal with the locals. I warmed up carefully and then started way off to the left on the easiest routes, while the locals were torturing themselves on an overhang. I then modestly enquired if I might give it a go. With a low chuckle, one of the locals even placed his piece of carpet at the start of the route for me. By pure coincidence, the locals stopped for a break the moment I dared to pull on the first holds. When I reached the overhang, I became aware of the silence beneath me, the pressure of those expert gazes was nearly too much for me. However, I managed to compose myself and went on to complete the redpoint. Afterwards, we got to hear all the important information about the area and from then on, people actually started to greet us.

If you rub the locals up the wrong way, which is easily done, then things tend to get much more complicated. You might want to climb a route, but the locals on it just happen to be attempting the variation with the one-finger pull-up and are at it until it gets dark. This is because the one thing that the locals have that you don't is time. While non-locals might have to leave the next day, the locals will be back the day after and the day after that. Rather like the hare and the tortoise, they are always going to win in the end.

"Despite my detour over the mountains, I've come further than I would have done on the flat trails."

93 Reinhard Karl

NAKED HIKING BANNED
Adrian Huber | Alpstein/Switzerland

"The people of Appenzell have had enough of nude tourists," the Swiss papers reported on April 26, 2009. "Naked hiking is to be banned forthwith in Appenzell Innerrhoden. The Swiss canton passed the resolution with an absolute majority in what was an international first. Nude hiking, popular with naturists, is now illegal in the Alpstein and will be fined with 200 Swiss francs."

The vote was taken with a show of hands at Appenzell's annual rural council meeting, an open-air meeting of all registered voters held in the town square. No sooner had the anti-nudity legislation been passed than the online forums began to buzz with the debate. "Unbelievable!" wrote Aschi, who was apparently a supporter of more relaxed hiking dress codes. He went on to write, "Have these pen pushers got nothing better to do? Were they born wearing a tie? Thank God that the rest of the world is spared such puritanical local authorities. In my opinion, being naked outdoors is the most wonderful experience going!"

"Where would we be if everyone just made up laws as it suited them?" Siggi added, viewing the law as potentially destabilizing for the very fabric of life in Switzerland. "This is a real cheek, not to mention anti-democratic and a breach of human rights for people who just want to enjoy being out in nature without clothes." "People should be able to wear as much or as little as they like," he argued. "It's not as if the law can protect us from fully-clothed ugly people either," Brigitte added, banging the same drum, before asking, "or is this the next piece of legislation due to come out of Appenzell?"

Regula made what started out as a promisingly level-headed remark: "Nude hiking might give the libertines a bit of a kick. And make others choke with outrage." She then went on to suggest an image, which one would probably not wish to dwell on: "Who on earth wants to see people's sweaty dangly bits when they are out hiking?" Her contribution ended with a rather sweeping psychological generalization. "I'm sorry but these people really must be suffering from personality disorders!"

"We should all live according to the Bible," wrote Maria, "and according to Genesis." She proceeded to quote verse 25 from the first book of Moses, chapter 2: "And they were both naked, the man and his wife, and were not ashamed." Well, there you go then. Holger's contribution showed a pragmatic approach and logical thinking: "What's all the fuss about! We were born naked and will die naked." You have to admit that he's not wrong there.

Res, a mountain farmer, wrote that political, religious and philosophical opinions were making the debate too complicated. In an attempt to bring the bloggers back down to the realities of everyday life in the Alps, he suggested: "Why not dress the cows of Schwägalp in tangas and bras; after all, they also walk about with bare breasts and naked butts..." The analogy of the animal world was taken up by Reinhard, who suggested that it would be difficult to imagine a Yeti without his fur naked in the snow, and by Jasmin, who struck the vulnerable nudists below the belt, dismissing them as "filthy pigs".

Sandra, by contrast, demonstrated a keen, practical mind when she asked, "Where does the naked hiker put his penknife?" Britta also appeared concerned for similar reasons, as her rhetorical question showed: "And, where will they carry the money to pay the fine? Ah, yes of course!"

Julian from Juf, the highest village in Europe, had long ago recognized the benefits of warm, comfortable clothing for a life in the mountains. He argued vehemently that modern, functional outdoor apparel is lightweight, regulates body temperature and generally looks better than wandering round the hills in the buff. He went on to issue a challenge to naturist hikers: "If you really feel so restricted by your clothes, why don't you burn them and then come and visit me up here when it's minus 20? Then we'll see if you feel so much more liberated!" Tobias seemed less worried about weather conditions and more interested in aesthetical matters when he suggested, "How about imposing an upper age limit of say, 35, so as not to spoil the view?" Hermann showed more empathy, when he posted his concerned comment: "Did he really hike through the snow like that? It must have frozen his balls off!"

At Mammut, the creative marketing experts Andres Lietha and Christian Gisi felt that slowly but surely things were going a little too far below the belt and decided to inject a dose of humor and irony into the debate. They placed an ad in the Sunday papers, which had people chuckling all over Switzerland.

Dear Naked Hikers,
Please wear decent boots at least.

For further information on Mammut's new footwear collection, visit www.mammut.ch
For those who like to reveal a little less of themselves, our new summer
clothing range can also be found online!

MAMMUT
Absolute alpine.

SWISS TECHNOLOGY ⊛

"WE HELP EACH OTHER TO PUSH OUR LIMITS"
Anna Stöhr | Around the world

Karin Steinbach Tarnutzer spoke to two-time World Bouldering Champion and Mammut Athlete Anna Stöhr at the International Mountain Summit 2010 in Brixen about what drives her to compete.

What do you particularly love about climbing?
There is something for everyone, whether you like short, powerful boulder problems, sport climbing or multi-pitch Alpine routes with lots of fresh air beneath you. No two moves are the same. It is not like swimming, say, where movement is cyclical. It is never repetitive, it always presents a new challenge. And everyone has their own style of climbing.

And for you, at some stage it was bouldering?
Yes, it just seemed to evolve that way. In 2004, the European Championships were in Italy. I was 16 years old, and it was the first time that I was able to compete against the adults. But there were so many good Austrian women taking part in the leading comp that I would have been better off staying at home. But that was the last thing I wanted to do, so I took part in the bouldering comp. Straight away, I came second in the women's European Championships.

Fantastic!
I think bouldering also suits my physical makeup. You need to use maximum strength, you have to be a bit zippy, quick, dynamic, that suits me better.

Which do you prefer? Indoors or outdoors?
I need both somehow. Competitions are really exciting; gauging yourself against others, solving problems in the 4 minutes allotted time. Also, to see how I measure up internationally. But to be outside on the rock, bouldering with a bunch of friends on a beautiful day like today, that's just awesome. Both are really good fun.

Is it important to be in a group?
It plays an important role. Training on your own in some bouldering cellar, I could never do that. The climbing scene is so big in Innsbruck, I never have to train on my own, and that motivates you in a completely different way. We help each other to push our limits.

What got you into climbing?
Both of my parents climb and they always used to take me with them to the crag. When I was 8, I joined a climbing team in Innsbruck that was trained by Reinhard Scherer and Rupert Messner. There was a whole bunch of us little kids who went climbing together and trained together at the wall. David Lama was there, too.

Has climbing changed you?
I took part in junior competitions from an early age, also at European level, and so I met lots of different people. I think climbing taught me how to value doing things as a team. And, of course, you get to travel. When the World Cup was held in China, I was just 16 – you learn a lot on trips like that.

How long have you worked together with Mammut?
I have been on their international team for 5 years. Before that, they supported me with equipment as a member of the sponsored Innsbruck Team. Now, I have a budget for equipment every year, a fixed sum, and they pay me on top of that for any media presence. What is great about Mammut is that they really want to have long-term relationships with their athletes. In my case, they invested in me when I wasn't so well known and they believed in me.

Are there still differences between the sexes in climbing today?

The physical requirements are different, but even in terms of performance, the gap between men and women is shrinking all the time. Men have greater muscle mass and are therefore stronger, but we women can redress the balance by being more flexible. In terms of statistics, I would say that there are equal numbers of men and women at the climbing wall but as soon as you get outside, you come across more men, especially with bouldering and even more so on Alpine routes. A women only team is still an unusual sight.

How do you competition climbers deal with rivalry amongst yourselves?

We are pretty much like one big family of climbers. When we see each other at a competition – there might be 60 of us all at one comp – most of all, we are just happy to get together. Of course, when I am standing at the base of the wall, then everyone else is an opponent. But if I only saw them as 59 opponents all the time, then I would become bitter and twisted. It is best if I just keep to myself and try to do the best I can. If it doesn't work out, then it's just down to me and not anyone else. That means I don't have a problem congratulating others on their performance when it was better than mine.

Your boyfriend Kilian Fischhuber is also a top climber. Are you ever jealous of each other's success?

With Kilian it's just the same. I am totally happy for him when he does well, and I know it is exactly the same for him. You wouldn't believe how revved up I get when he is in some competition. I get more nervous when he climbs than when I do – my palms get really sweaty!

What has been your best win?

When I won the European Championships in Innsbruck in 2010. In 2007, I was World Champion but that came as more of a surprise. In 2010, however, I was the favorite and the pressure was immense, but then so was the challenge. I trained all summer for it, prepared thoroughly. The competition took place practically on my back doorstep. There were so many people – it was just great to be climbing there. A great atmosphere like that really spurs me on.

"THE JOY WAS GREATER THAN THE FEAR"

Yasushi Okada | Mount Logan/Canada

Japanese alpinist Yasushi Okada and his climbing partner Katsutake Yokoyama were awarded the Piolet d'Or Asia and the Golden Piton Award of the American magazine "Climbing" in 2010. In 2011 they both received the Piolet d'Or. Karin Steinbach Tarnutzer spoke with the Mammut athletes about the new route they put up on the hitherto unclimbed Southeast Face of Mount Logan.

A first ascent on the Southeast Face of Mount Logan ... Why?
Katsutake Yokoyama was given a picture of Mount Logan by a friend and showed it to me. We were captivated by this massive wall. It is 2,500 meters high and in a wild, natural setting. It's a very remote mountain – the nearest road is 150 kilometers away as the crow flies. It appealed to our sense of adventure, so we decided to go for it.

Where exactly is Mount Logan?
It is part of the Mount St. Elias chain, in the coastal range that stretches from Alaska down to Canada. It belongs to the Canadian Yukon Territory. At 5,959 meters, Mount Logan is the highest mountain in Canada and the second highest in North America. The area is so undeveloped we knew we would have to be completely self-reliant and rescue was out of the question. That made things pretty exciting.

Does that kind of vulnerability not scare you?
Unlike the Himalaya, we did not come across a single soul and it sometimes felt like we were on a deserted island. All we had with us was a satellite phone. It was unnerving but, at the same time, isolation like that meant I felt the power of nature more intensely. The joy of being in such amazing surroundings was greater than the fear.

You covered a lot of ground.
Initially, we were lucky with the weather and completed our ascent in just three days, from May 4 to 7, 2010. When you top out on the face, however, it's another 2 kilometers with 800 meters of height gain until you reach the summit. That part of the climb was very tiring and the weather was deteriorating. Because we hadn't been able to bank on stable weather conditions, we were carrying extra food and fuel with us, which made us slightly slower than usual – our packs were heavy! On the wall, whoever was in the lead still had to carry a pack, and the second had a 25 kilogram pack. Sometime during the first three days, it became clear we would not be able to reverse the route as we had originally planned. The wall turned out to have a complex structure, we found we had to make several traverses, and in places the rock was too loose to place secure protection.

How difficult was it?
We graded it ED+, WI 5, M6. The only possible descent was via the East Ridge and it was incredibly long – 30 kilometers! But it was a whole lot safer than reversing our ascent route. It just went on forever! At the end of five days, when we were back at the base of the mountain, we were exhausted but really happy with our adventure.

Will your next project be in warmer climes?
Right now, I'm keen on traditional crack climbing, the way they do it in England. I would like to visit climbing areas throughout the world with my wife, simply to enjoy the climbing. Ideas for new projects will just present themselves, I'm sure.

"I don't want to conquer mountains; I want to approach
them with gratitude and humility. Up in the stillness
of the high mountain ranges, I have learnt that goals
are reached through patience, restraint and enthusiasm.
In comparison to the mountains, I am only small
and fragile. However, every time I return from them
I return a far stronger person."

97 **Gerlinde Kaltenbrunner**

MAMMUT UP CLOSE
Gabriela Hodel | Alps/Switzerland

People still talk about that nice old lady who wanted to climb Everest with her dachshund. The 2006 Mammut campaign featuring Mary Woodbridge was a masterstroke of advertising. Correspondingly, expectations were high for the follow-up. The "Absolute alpine" campaign was conceived to highlight the functional and technical nature of Mammut products. After the fictitious Mary Woodbridge, a shift was needed back to authentic alpine experiences, but the innovation in communication needed to be retained. The advertising agency erdmannpeisker came up with a creative concept to meet these requirements. Inspired by the artist Spencer Tunick, they suggested using images of Mammut's seasonal highlight products worn by different target groups, for example employees, consumers, mountain guides, dealers and athletes. They were to be staged as creative formations in a natural alpine setting.

The first installation, on the theme of sleeping bags, was photographed with employees in the area of Corvatsch, Engadine. After the success of this first initiative, Mammut invited consumers to the "Underwear Test" in Grindelwald. Within weeks, there were 800 applicants from all over Europe. The opportunity to be personally involved in making an advert proved highly attractive. The volunteer Mammut models were also rewarded with a fun action weekend. On Saturday, participants were invited to either go climbing with Stephan Siegrist or improve their slackline skills, while in the evening, Ueli Gegenschatz and Evelyne Binsack both gave fascinating talks. The next day, it was off to the photo shoot on the Eiger Glacier where the 200 testers, wearing functional underwear, formed a serpentine along the glacier.

This marked the beginning of a series of successful Testevents. Next up was a photo shoot with mountain guides on the Kleines Kamel in the Furka region to launch Mammut's new range of moun-

tain boots. For the following winter theme, the "Safety Check" event, more than 3,000 consumers applied to freeride with Mammut in Melchsee-Frutt. This was followed up by 100 dealers who came to Osogna in Ticino to abseil down a vertical granite face for the "Packs Expert Circle". Mammut consumers came to ski the Julier Pass in the Alps of eastern Switzerland, Mammut professional climbers hung in a row from the Klausen Pass, and leading international mountaineers formed an "X" shape on the North Face of the Eiger for the Eiger Extreme alpine product line.

All these events captured the spirit of the times. In the era of Web 2.0 and social media, people want to share experiences with others, exchange photos, compare ideas and meet their heroes. The Internet provides no end of opportunities to do this. The idea to combine the existing website with live events and an advertising campaign fits the desire to communicate. People have been able to experience the Mammut brand up close, and a new community of Mammut fans has been established, who are ready to enter into a dialog with the company and spread the Mammut message.

In addition, the campaign was so successful because so many Mammut employees were involved. The Web 2.0 platform was designed by the web agency Unic, but it was the Mammut Marketing Communication team who planned the events and communicated with customers. The creative ideas for the key visuals were supplied by erdmannpeisker, but Mammut employees were actively involved right from the start, including the location scouting with photographer Röbi Bösch. Working together with mountain guides, the Mammut Crew members were also responsible for planning and implementation of the events as well as ensuring the health and safety of all participants. They put a lot of hard work and commitment into the Testevents and came back time and again to get involved in the shared experiences with Mammut customers.

GET TOGETHER FOR CLIMBING: TEAMTRIPS

Pascal Brönnimann I Around the world

The requirements for the Teamtrips are as clear-cut and direct as the routes at Rumney, the location of Mammut's first Teamtrip in the eastern state of New Hampshire, USA: authentic, credible, wide ranging, excellent quality, progressive . . . and efficient. It is a tool for turning marketing strategy into real activities.

On the first Teamtrip to Rumney in 2005, however, there was a brief spell of uncertainty as to whether the seven Pro Team athletes would even make it to the destination. They almost came unstuck with the immigration procedures at the Boston airport. Fingerprints had to be taken. Nina Caprez tried to explain: "We are climbers. Our skin is just too thin." The man at the immigration desk tried using grease – and failed. Daniel Schmid tried all of his fingers – it was no use. Finally, the officials had to settle for the explanation "we are climbers."

"Climb till your fingers bleed" was the motto over the next two weeks. The seven muscle-bound beasts ticked off practically all the hard routes in the area in next to no time. They left with a short film by Rob Frost, some stunning images and many exciting tales to tell.

Following that first trip to the East Coast of America, it was announced that the Andaman Sea off the East coast of Thailand was to be the destination for 2006. "Climbing above deep water" is how the Austrians unpretentiously described the latest craze on the climbing scene, Deep Water Soloing (DWS). "Using the ocean as the biggest ever bouldering mat" is how some of them raved about it. "You're about as free as you can be," said Klem Loskot, the pioneer of this revamped old school discipline, where you climb above the open sea without any ropes or protection. No bolts in the rock, no need to haul ropes around – DWS makes both ecological and economic sense. The pro's one and only tip: "Beware of the resident birds!"

The images captured were fantastic, as was the 15 minute film of spectacular dynos and equally impressive landings. The "Chuck Wao" route proved a special treat with its "spider traverse": the first one at ten meters, closely followed by a second and, at 18 meters, a double dyno. David Lama got as far as the dyno several times. After several falls and one particularly painful belly flop, he decided to climb around the killer dyno on tiny holds. He was the first to top out and the first guy ever to climb this variation of the route.

The next challenge was "in the name of his majesty, the Raja of Perlis". Just four hours' drive from Krabi, Reini Scherer and David Lama set about their 2007 Mammut Mission in Malaysia. They developed two completely new areas from scratch, putting up 91 routes in just 9 days, including what are now three of Asias's hardest routes. They were actively supported on their first ascents by Europe's climbing elite. Cédric Lachat and Christina Schmid traveled to Malaysia from Switzerland, Anna Stöhr and Katharina Saurwein came from Austria, and Juliane Wurm from Germany. It is to be hoped that investment in the area by climbers and local institutions will continue, so that climbers from all over the world can access these newly developed Malaysian climbing areas.

Summer 2008's highlight theme, urban climbing, was to be fueled by a classy road trip to Vienna – in a huge square surrounded by high-rises. There was some guy with dreads standing there, wearing shorts and rubber boots. In front of him was a chunk of granite at least 5 meters high and above him a young woman. The look on the guy's bearded face seemed to be saying "What's she doing up there? And how the hell did she get up there in any case?" "That's called 'buildering' or urban climbing," explained Rainer

Eder, the photographer, who has accompanied every Teamtrip since the first and taken some excellent photos, as well as adding a good measure of humor to the mix. Born in East Tyrol, Rainer has spent more than 20 years living in Zurich, photographing anything and everything, and was also selected for the Hall of Fame in the Red Bull Illume Contest.

"Make sure you don't step on the mat," he quickly added, as Barbara Bacher came flying down from 4 meters. Shoot locations like the Austriapark or the Flakturm formed the backdrops for the urban climbing film with its 007-styled sets. The man in charge was Christoph Frutiger, an unassuming yet exuberant Oberlander with a reputation as a sly old dog. He trained as a cameraman in New York, was Second Unit on two James Bond films as well as Steven Spielberg's "Band of Brothers", and has made advertising and documentary films. His expertise is internationally sought-after. Christoph Frutiger's skills are clearly of a creative nature, with breathtaking images showcased in perfectly orchestrated big screen productions.

It was exactly these qualities that were such a big help on the 2009 Teamtrip "In search of Lorenz Saladin" in Kyrgyzstan. Saladin, a Swiss mountaineer, made pioneering ascents of numerous peaks in the Karavshin region with the Abalakov brothers in 1935 and 1936. The Mammut Team's objective was the first redpoint ascent of an A3 aided classic on the 800 meter high West Face of Asan in the Kara-Su valley. David Lama, Stephan Siegrist, Giovanni Quirici and Nina Caprez not only discovered that it was made of bomber granite, but that it offered varied and challenging free climbing. This was especially true of the long, tricky slab sections on the Timofeev Route, which to date had only been aided. According to David, the route was "the real deal", with the hardest sections involving obligatory 7b climbing and Soviet-era 5 millimeter bolts providing "pretty exciting" protection. The team topped out on August 2.

A few days later, Siegrist, Caprez and Quirici repeated the 24 pitch "Perestroika Crack" (7b) on Pik Slesova, a.k.a. "Astroman of the East" on account of the beautiful climbing. Even back in 1936, Saladin called this place "a climber's Eldorado".

In 2010, the Pro Team, now on their sixth Teamtrip, visited another Eldorado, this time of the British variety. Lying between Manchester and Sheffield, the Peak District is well known for its moors, its extensive horizons, and for its jagged, weather-beaten gritstone crags that interrupt the gentle uplands, rising vertically from the valley sides, perfect for climbing. British climbing ethics forbid the use of bolts; only nuts and cams are allowed for protection. Gritstone is soft and heavily weathered, the holds are rough, the routes technically demanding and often quite run-out – "true grit" is certainly tough stuff!

Climbing on grit is not about strength; balance and a steady head are the keys to success. Anyone looking to master the Peak District grit would do well to heed the advice of gritstone legend Johnny Dawes. In the 1980s and 1990s, he set new standards in climbing and is still heralded today as "the last great hope of British climbing". The Mammut Team was fortunate enough to have him on board for their grit campaign and really profited from his advice. The moves became more precise from day to day, the fear of falling decreased and route after route was sent. By the end of the trip, legendary routes such as "Parthian Shot", "Master's Edge" and "Messiah" had been ticked off and properly documented with stunning pictures and film. Exciting new camera angles, achieved by using a model helicopter, added a special touch to the Teamtrip film, enhancing classic positions and creating previously unseen images.

Want to bet that the next Teamtrips will also be to interesting and promising locations? Let's wait and see...

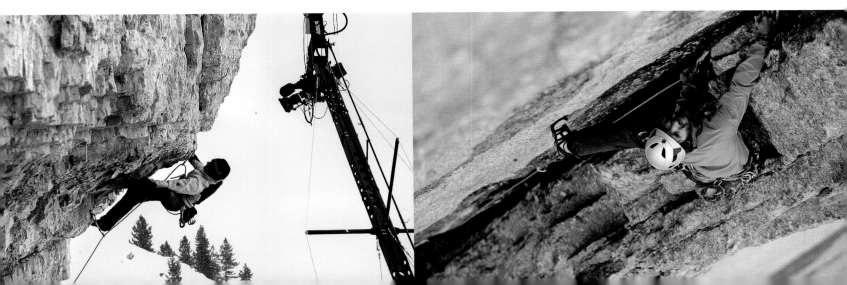

"WILLPOWER IS EVERYTHING"
Hirotaka Takeuchi | Himalaya

In February 2011, Karin Steinbach Tarnutzer spoke with Japanese high altitude mountaineer and Mammut Athlete Hirotaka Takeuchi, the first Japanese to attempt all fourteen 8,000 meter peaks.

To date, you have climbed twelve peaks above 8,000 meters. Hiro, which do you have left?
Cho Oyu and Dhaulagiri. In 1995, I summited my first 8,000er, Makalu, and in 2009, my twelfth, Lhotse. In 2010, on Cho Oyu, I unfortunately had to turn back at 7,700 meters because of avalanche risk. But I hope to get to the summit this fall.

What does it take to climb the highest mountains on the planet?
Aside from physical ability and technical competence, I think you have to have willpower. And you have to be able to suffer setbacks. I have been in two difficult situations so far. In 2005, I got bad altitude sickness on Everest – that time, I was rescued by the concerted efforts of Gerlinde Kaltenbrunner and Ralf Dujmovits. But I didn't let it get me down and one year later, I climbed Kangchenjunga with the two of them. In 2007, I was caught in an avalanche on Gasherbrum II and broke a vertebra in my spine and five ribs. I was lucky to get out alive and it took me a long time to recover. In spite of this, I went back to the Karakorum in 2008 and climbed both Gasherbrum II and Broad Peak.

I would say you are quite a rebounder. How do you train for 8,000 meter mountaineering?
My last 8,000er serves as training for the next one… I love climbing, not just at 8,000 meters; I love hiking or rock climbing just as much. Every mountain route is preparation for the next one.

Where does one go mountaineering in Japan?
There are lots of difficult and beautiful routes in Japan. Particularly through the cold months of the year, you can go winter climbing in the Japanese alps or ice climbing on Hokkaido. It can get really cold at home and we get a lot of snow.

Is mountaineering as popular in Japan as it is in the Alps?
In Japan, most people hike. Sport climbing has become very popular with young people over the last few years and lots of climbing walls have sprung up. But there are certainly fewer serious alpinists and Himalayan climbers than in the Alps.

Are Japanese climbers drawn to the outdoors in the same way that European ones are?
Of course! Japan has many beautiful rock climbing areas. They are varied in nature as well – limestone, granite and volcanic andesite. You should come and try it out!

MAN IS NOT MADE FOR HIGH ALTITUDE

Oswald Oelz | Aconcagua/Argentina

The story of Edward Fitzgerald is a classic example of how humans are not made for high altitudes. On January 14, 1897, the American, who had emigrated to England, led an expedition to attempt the first ascent of Aconcagua. With just 400 meters in vertical height gain between him and the prized summit, he was unable to continue. The sickness which had previously plagued him at high altitudes in the past had returned. His body simply refused to allow him to continue climbing. Bitterly disappointed, he sent his guide on alone to secure the success of the expedition. When he saw him nearing the 6,962 meter summit, he tried to continue. "I got up and tried to go on. I could only manage two or three steps before I was once again forced to stop and fight for breath. My gasping for breath was interspersed with overwhelming nausea. At points, I was forced to the ground and had difficulty getting back on my feet. I had black spots before my eyes and wandered around as if in a dream. I felt so dizzy and ill that the whole mountain seemed to spin around me." Fitzgerald abandoned his attempt and started to descend.

The memory of that descent remained with him for the rest of his life. "I was so weak that my legs threatened to give way with every step, I fell time and time again, cutting myself on the stones. [. . .] Finally, I reached a snowfield and just about managed to roll down it. The further I descended, the more my strength returned, but the terrible headaches remained. They were so bad that I could barely see properly." Fitzgerald was afflicted by Acute Mountain Sickness (AMS), also known as altitude sickness. Its main symptoms are functional disorders of the lungs and the brain. The severe headaches, dizziness, light headedness and affected vision indicate that in Fitzgerald's case there was already a swelling of the brain tissue, or High Altitude Cerebral Edema (HACE).

The increasing popularity of high-alpine walking, trekking tours and so-called expeditions now expose a growing number of tourists to the damaging effects of decreasing oxygen levels at higher altitudes. The symptoms or physical changes commonly occur from a few hours up to a few days after exceeding 2,500 meters or after continuing to ascend from an altitude level previously reached.

People susceptible to altitude sickness generally suffer from the following symptoms: headaches, fatigue, lack of appetite, dizziness or light-headedness, disturbed sleep, nausea, or vomiting. A swelling of the hands, feet, eyelids and face often occurs. High altitude cerebral edema (or HACE) is a severe (and frequently fatal) form of Acute Mountain Sickness (AMS). Patients with AMS have an increased risk of developing High Altitude Pulmonary Edema (HAPE). As a result of increased pulmonary arterial and capillary pressures (pulmonary hypertension), fluid accumulates in the soft tissue of the lungs and is then pressed into the air bubbles. This further restricts oxygen uptake, which leads to increasing shortage of breath, coughing and possibly coughing up blood. The patient may ultimately choke to death.

The most effective and prophylactic measure against altitude sickness is a "slow ascent", which allows the body to gradually acclimatize to the effects of altitude by adjusting to the decreasing oxygen levels at higher elevations. The general rule of thumb is that above 2,500 to 3,000 meters one should not increase the altitude at which one sleeps by more than 300–500 meters in any 24 hour period. A rest day is recommended every four days. There are other similar models, but all guidelines are problematic as there is a wide degree of variability in how individuals acclimatize to altitude. This means that above all common sense, an awareness of the symptoms and personal experience are important. Sometimes even perfectly fit mountaineers have to accept that they are suffering from altitude sickness. Should they show symptoms indicating AMS, HAPE or HACE, it cannot be emphasized strongly enough that they should not continue to ascend!

As well as the so-called "natural prophylaxis" by gradual ascent and altitude acclimatization, medical treatment is also available. This is recommended for use by rescue teams where natural acclimatization is not possible and for particularly susceptible individuals. It is also used for unreasonable ascent schedules, for example, as often practiced on Mount Kilimanjaro. As far as the medical treatment of patients already showing signs of altitude sickness is concerned, it is often difficult for expedition or trekking doctors (let alone people with no medical expertise) to determine which combination of symptoms is actually present in a given case. Descent is always the best form of therapy and recovery.

CLIMBING TILL MIDNIGHT
Magnus Midtbø | Norway

Norway is a large country with huge areas of pristine nature and un-touched rock. Most climbing areas close to the main cities of Oslo, Bergen, Trondheim and Stavanger have already been developed. We have a lot of different types of rock but on the whole it is very hard granite.

Around the capital Oslo, the climbing is largely vertical or slight-ly overhanging. On the west coast, however, there is some steeper stuff. Sometimes, the crags can be completely slick and featureless. We tend not to chip holds in Norway, so these faces will remain unclimbed in the hope that the next generation of climbers might be able to do them. As you carry on up the coast to the north, you come across excellent rock in the Trondheim area, which is yet to be developed. There is already a small bouldering scene but on the huge caves and overhanging faces, there are some hard lines just waiting for someone brave enough to forge them, in the middle of nowhere.

As far as climbing is concerned, Norway is definitely a land of limitless possibilities. For those seeking it, its hidden away areas offer real adventure. But climbing in Norway can also be relaxing and combined with sightseeing or a family holiday. Climbing guide-books are available at climbing gyms and sports shops. Around Norway's second largest city, Bergen, there are climbing areas to suit all levels. Some are approached by boat. And there is even potential for Deep Water Soloing in the area.

Getting around Norway can sometimes be a slow affair as the roads are often narrow. But the breathtaking landscape makes up for it – so make sure you drive during daylight hours. In the summer months, that should not prove difficult. It is the land of the midnight sun in the northern regions. The sun never sets, so you can climb at any time of the day or night. Even southern Norway gets lots of sunlight hours in the summer.

If you visit between April and September, the beaches are also recommended, and the warm Gulf Stream makes swimming toler-able. In the north, with a bit of luck, you can see whales or even killer whales. And if the climbing is not exciting enough, then you can always combine it with some surfing action.

THE MOST BEAUTIFUL GRANITE IN THE WORLD
Denis Burdet | Nameless Tower/Pakistan

Climbing the Trango Towers means climbing the most famous and classic big-wall routes in the world. The quality of the rock on the approx. 2,000 meter high faces is absolutely stunning! In summer 2003, I traveled to Pakistan with fellow Swiss climber Nicolas Zambetti and the Spaniard Tony Arbones. Our plan was to attempt to free the entire route of "Eternal Flame" on the Nameless Tower. The route was first climbed in 1989 by the Germans Kurt Albert, Wolfgang Güllich, Milan Sykora and Christoph Stiegler. They managed to do most of the route free, but were forced to use aid on four of the 22 pitches. They graded their first ascent, which involves hard climbing at over 6,000 m, VI, 7b+, A2. The route represented an important milestone in the history of freeclimbing.

We had four weeks and spent a total of 17 days on the wall – the ascent itself took four days. Unfortunately we didn't always get the weather we'd hoped for. Nevertheless, the climbing was absolutely amazing. The first six pitches follow a single crack which ranges from thin fingers to hand width. Moving up over this ocean of granite with the breathtaking backdrop of the Karakoram and the Gasherbrum massif was an almost dreamlike experience.

After their first ascent in 1989, the German team named each pitch after a line from the Bangles' song "Eternal Flame". This means that as you climb higher and higher, the full text of the song is gradually revealed until you reach the final pitch, which bears the same name as the route itself: "Eternal Flame". Then you exit via the final 150 meters of beautiful ice gullies that lead to the summit.

We were able to free climb the two crux pitches, pitch 15 ("A whole life so lonely", 7c/7c+) and pitch 16 ("Ease the pain", 7c), both of which are at an altitude of over 6,000 meters. This was no easy matter. The 16th pitch follows two parallel cracks that you either have to layback or bridge. The 15th pitch proved particularly difficult: sustained, strenuous and technical climbing up a thin crack. On our penultimate day on the wall, we started our final attempt. As we climbed the 500 meters of fixed rope we had left in place, the wind and gathering clouds looked ominous. I fell twice. It started to snow. In a mix of rage and desperation, I gave it everything I had and managed to finish it, albeit only on top rope – due to the impending storm, we had decided not to pull the rope. In spite of this "imperfection", we were happy with our success.

Two years later Eneko and Iker Pou climbed "Eternal Flame", finding a free variation to the right of the aided 10th pitch ("I believe it's meant to be") following advice from Kurt Albert. They managed to climb all the moves, but couldn't link the pitch in one go. In 2009, Alexander and Thomas Huber, Mario Walder and Franz Hinterbrandner freed this right-hand variation (also 7c+) and found a way of bypassing the pendulum on the second pitch (7a+). With these two new variations, the route was completely freed.

During our ascent in 2003, only a few of the cracks were partially iced up, e.g. the 7th pitch ("Do you feel the same?"), 8th pitch ("Am I only dreaming?") and the right-hand variation to the 10th pitch. On the summit day it was unusually cold and it took serious willpower to pull on our climbing shoes. However, in spite of the conditions, these are the most beautiful pitches I have ever climbed on granite. "Eternal Flame" is an amazing route of outstanding quality. My thanks go to the first ascentionists Wolfgang Güllich and Kurt Albert, who are both sadly no longer with us.

Eternal Flame
- Nameless Tower (6,251 m), Trango Towers, Karakoram
- 7c+, 16 pitches of sustained 7a
- 22 pitches in total, approximately 700 meters of climbing
- Start from the shoulder (5,400 m)
- Approach via the first 9 pitches of the Yugoslav Route (7a+, 400 m)
- Base camp on the Trango Glacier (4,000 m)

THE MAMMOTH
Harald Schreiber | Around the world

Throughout history, mammoths (German: Mammut) have taken on many different forms. These days, they are often red, black and white and found on the left arms of jackets, on hats and on the tongues of approach shoes and mountain boots. This is the mammoth which readers of this book are probably best acquainted with. But the mammoth has appeared in all manner of shapes and sizes. Take, for example, the legendary German "Mammut" motor bike made by Münch or the heavy transport "Mammut" military glider built by the German company Junkers. There was a "Mammut" German radar station and there are still mammoth trees growing in the Western United States. Italy's largest amusement park, "Gardaland" in Castelnuovo del Garda has a Mammoth steel roller coaster, while Germany boasts a traditional wooden "Mammut" roller coaster in Treffentrill. The mammoth has also made countless appearances on the big screen, running amok in an American feature film in 2006, travelling between New York and Thailand in 2009, and strolling through the Ice Age with a sloth. He gets around, this guy!

And here the wheel comes full circle. Given all these different mammoths, people often forget about the original species itself. They were huge creatures made of flesh and blood and, in the case of the woolly mammoth, meters and meters of hair. These giant pachyderms began to roam the prehistoric steppe over four million years ago and evolved into several different species. Always on the search for fresh pastures, the mammoths took their grazing

duties very seriously until they were forced to make way for better adapted successors at the end of the Ice Age. Apparently, a small population continued to live in East Siberia until as recently as 4,000 years ago.

Any animal capable of withstanding the rigors of a glacial climate must have been doing something right. The pachyderms were known for their strength, robustness and ability to function in all weathers. But in spite of all these characteristics, the climate change and spread of our own ancestors posed new challenges that even the mammoths were incapable of overcoming. However, the newspapers recently reported that a group of Japanese scientists are planning to turn back the Darwinian clock by extracting DNA from a mammoth found in a layer of permafrost in Russia in the hope of bringing it to life again. Which begs the question whether "Jurassic Park" and its ravenous cloned dinosaurs was only a box office hit in western countries. After millions of years of grazing and wandering, have these poor animals not earned their rest?

The original mammoths finally departed this world thousands of years ago. But their memory lives on in the most modern of manifestations. Their legendary strength, robustness and ability to cope with all weathers continue to this day.

"The secret of getting ahead is getting started."

Mark Twain

HOW I MET THE MAMMOTH
Betina Alexieva | Sofia/Bulgaria

My name is Betina. I am 15 years old and this is the story of how I met the mammoth. One day, when I was sitting on the tram on my way home from school, a guy sat down next to me. Something red on his shoulder caught my eye and so I turned to look at him. And guess what it was? A circle with a mammoth in the middle...

It seemed strange to me; I had no idea what it meant. So I started to do some research on the Internet, and after a while I found the answer – Mammut! I trawled through the website for at least an hour. It had the coolest stuff that I had ever seen! I then continued my search and found a shop in my city – Sofia in Bulgaria – that sold Mammut products. Of course, I went to the shop the very next day. There was a lot to see but what made the biggest impression on me were the Samurai climbing shoes. You may laugh but I had no idea what shoes like those were for. So I found a sales assistant and asked her. She looked at me like I had come from a different planet.

In some ways she was right, but she explained it all to me and I started to get interested in climbing. Over the following weeks, I visited the shop several times. The sales assistant, the same one that I had met the first time, realized how fascinated I was by the climbing gear and recommended a climbing center nearby. And that is how Mammut introduced me to climbing! I now train at the wall twice a week and also go climbing outside on the weekends. I started four months ago, but have already completed two courses and can now climb 6a; it will soon be 6b. I enjoy climbing, it is something I really love doing. Thank you Mammut – you have broadened my horizons!

CERRO TORRE IS A SPECIAL MOUNTAIN

David Lama | Cerro Torre/Patagonia

Hansjoerg Auer first put me on to the idea of free climbing the Compressor Route on Cerro Torre after a trip to Patagonia with him in 2008. I couldn't get the idea out of my head and was delighted when the financing was arranged as part of a film project and we got started in 2009/2010. Mammut came on board to supply the equipment and ropes for the camera team and their guides. I have been working with Mammut for a long time, from the days when I used to be the smallest climber on the Innsbruck team. Mammut supported the Innsbruck team and then, over ten years ago, I became a Mammut sponsored athlete when I joined the international Proteam. Like me, the guys at Mammut really value long-term partnerships. They have been very loyal and it's a lot of fun being involved with such a relaxed, easy-going company.

Some might say my first attempt on the Cerro Torre was a bit of a disappointment, but I didn't see it like that. I gained a lot of experience and came away from Patagonia completely fascinated by the place. Daniel Steuerer and I started up the route during a relatively long good weather window at the start of the expedition and climbed to the Col de la Paciencia where we set up the bivouac. We free climbed everything up to the bolt traverse. Then the weather took a turn for the worse and remained bad. According to the locals, it was the worst season in 15 years. We weren't able to see the Torre for weeks, and when the clouds finally cleared the mountain was sheathed in a thick armor of snow and ice, which meant free climbing was out of the question. We weren't even able to bring all our equipment back down off the mountain. We had to leave the bolts and fixed ropes used by the camera team and the gear we had stashed at the col.

We hired several Argentinean guides to go up and collect everything as soon as the weather allowed. That was done in the spring 2010; only one haulbag and the bolts were left behind. The Argentinean climber Rolando Garibotti removed some of the remaining bolts in fall 2010, and we took out the last of the bolts during our second expedition in 2011. In the meantime, a huge row had blown up in the climbing community about the bolts placed for the camera team. I dealt with all the accusations and decided together with my sponsors to climb the route the next time without placing any new bolts for the camera crew. If it was not going to be possible to guarantee their safety using removable protection then the nature of the film project would have to change.

In January 2011, I returned to Patagonia with Peter Ortner for a second attempt with a different approach. Unfortunately, the weather window was just not long enough to allow us to free climb the route. In February, at the end of our expedition, we took advantage of a day of good weather to make an aided ascent of the Compressor Route. We finally reached the summit at around 10.00 P.M. and rappelled back down in the dark. However, I was able to make out the crack systems, which would make it possible to free climb the route using removable protection.

This second expedition once again showed how intensely the activities on Cerro Torre are scrutinized. It is quite simply a special mountain, due to the myths surrounding its first ascent, its incredible shape, the exceptionally bad weather and the small number of ascents it's had. Once again, my plans were subject to further criticism from within the climbing community. My aim for 2011 was to reach the summit by aiding the route and then rap down from the top to find a way to free climb the head wall. The Trango Tower in the Karakoram was also recently climbed using the same technique. No one seemed to mind there, but in the case of Cerro Torre it seemed like the whole climbing world was shouting. I listened to what people were saying, took the criticism and decided to try and free the route ground up.

There's still so much to do next year – but once that's done I'd like to go back to Cerro Torre again. There are two sections that have never been freed: the bolt traverse half way up the face and the bolt ladder on the headwall. They both look difficult but not impossible. There are two or three sections that have really thin features. It will only be possible to see if they will go when I get there. I still feel really motivated about this project and look forward to my next attempt. I shall never forget the moment we reached the summit of Cerro Torre. The sun had already set below the Patagonian ice cap and everything was bathed in green light. It felt particularly intense because I thought at one stage I wasn't going to make it again – then suddenly I found myself standing on the summit.

ON HIS MAJESTY'S SERVICE

Pascal Brönnimann | Perlis/Malaysia For the Mammut 2007
Teamtrip, a new, unknown
and as far as possible untouched region was sought. The idea was
to take the Mammut Pro Team climbers to a location and document
the experience with a story and images to use in summer 2008. In
addition, a short film would be made to be included in the climbing
magazines and to be shown as part of the European Outdoor Film
Tour (EOFT). Given these objectives, there was no problem going for
a more exotic location to match the standards set by the previous
Teamtrips. There were also going to be no advance press releases.
Suggestions ranged from the Caribbean and South America to
Africa and Asia. It was no easy decision to take, but after several
checks it became clear that Malaysia was the ideal location to
cover all our requirements. On several occasions, it looked as if the
whole project was going to fall through, but after more than one
hundred emails, countless meetings and numerous telephone calls
we had everything pretty much organized. With the support of
Patrick Andrey from Camp 5, the largest climbing gym in Asia, a
smooth operation was guaranteed.

The bolting crew led by Reinhard Scherer and David Lama went
over two weeks in advance and put in sterling work to get everything ready. Together with Patrick and with local support from Zam,
Akmal and Man, they bolted nearly one hundred new routes from
scratch within just ten days in two new sectors. They were so enthusiastic by the cliffs of Ipoh that they ignored the scheduled rest
day to recover from the long haul flight and got out bolting straight
away, staying two days longer than planned. They had to deal
with swarms of stinging flies, various "souvenirs" left by obviously
talented monkeys (some on 6c terrain) and whole armies of ants.
Reini had to abandon one project after finding a hornets nest in a
large hole needed to complete the route. He was rewarded by finding the line and the photo on an overhanging wall.

The bolting crew then moved north to Keteri. By the time the remaining Pro Team members arrived (Anna Stöhr and Katharina
Saurwein from Austria, Christina Schmid and Cédric Lachat from
Switzerland and Juliane Wurm from Germany), they could have
gone out climbing straight away – in theory at least. First things first
though, they had to get smartened up. A reception had been or-

ganized with Raja Tuanku Syed Sirajuddin, the hereditary monarch
of Perlis, the smallest state in Malaysia. Mammut's investment in
the region, which had little tourist infrastructure, and the presence
of some of the best climbers in the world was met with enormous
engagement and overwhelming hospitality. Our official duties
proved none too onerous: two hours watching football, dinner with
the local tourist board and a karaoke evening. The crown prince
was so enthusiastic about what we were doing he even climbed one
of the new routes himself! Every day, streams of curious visitors
came to watch the climbing, and during the filming, which also featured the Raja's own helicopter that he had made freely available
to the team, there were crowds all the way down the street.

The trip's balance sheet speaks for itself: 10 articles in the Malaysian
press, 2 television interviews, 3 press conferences, 4,000 photos
and 20 hours of filming, 1,000 new bolts and a new retailer in Kuala
Lumpur. From a climbing point of view, the trip was a huge success
– in temperatures of 30° in the shade and over 12 days with not one
rest day. The hardest route in Malaysia and quite possibly in the
whole of Asia was sent by David Lama and Cédric Lachat in only
three days and graded 8c+. We hope that our investment in the area
will now be continued by local organisations so that climbers from
all over the world will come to this new climbing area, which has
routes from 4b to 8c+.

WHERE THE WILD DOGS ROAM
Walter Klier | Innsbruck/Austria

In Innsbruck, at the end of the 1950s, when the first climbing helmets started to emerge, Wastl Mariner, the ever lively hero of the 1930s, commented: "Now then, have the bikers arrived?" Everyone was getting soft, there was no stopping it. When my father took me climbing for the first time at the end of the 1960s, the family at least possessed one helmet. My father wore it, although he did let me borrow it once after he had inadvertently set off a rock slide as he led me up the infamously loose North Face of the Serles. When I suggested I might be willing to carry on this aspect of family tradition, I was duly given my own helmet.

The directives on clothing were strict (as they are today, just in a different way). One wore wool knee socks (red or grey, and scratchy), knickerbockers made from Loden (pale grey and very scratchy), a checked shirt and mum's lovingly knitted sweater (cable stitch). For the first summer at least, our feet were stuffed into what were soon given the derogatory nickname of "clod hoppers": stiff leather mountain boots that pinched when you walked, would quickly get wet through when in the snow, despite all efforts at proofing with highly specialized oils, and with hindsight, were completely unsuited to climbing. In those days, the ideal was an all-rounder, in other words someone who did not change their footwear. Changing anything (even shirts or such that were wet through) was a sign of weakness in any case.

We trained at the local crag to go climbing, not by going to the gym to get fit for the local crag. And climbing in the Calanques, which became the new trend, was only acceptable because for us in the Alps, as everyone knows, "everything is covered in snow until well into the summer months." But we still trained. The generation that preceded us, however, would have seen that as utter decadence. You either made it up the "Auckenthaler" route on Martinswand on the first go, or you were good for nothing but sitting at the bar. Special admiration was only reserved for those who, having just got back from the war or from prison camp, grabbed a little snack (that was all they would get in any case, given supply levels at the time), before quickly taking on some hair-raising route like the Bettelwurf North Face, descending back down to Hall that same night.

By the mid-1970s, sport climbing had already been discovered somewhere out there in the world and was soon headed our way, right into the heart of Europe – although, at heart, we were still mountain climbers in the classical sense. The sport climbing venues of today are simply what we used to call training crags. And the routes were not 'top-roped', 'on-sighted' or otherwise English, but were plain and simply secured from above – so that nothing could go wrong. If there was going to be an accident, then it was meant to take place up in the proper mountains.

Then came the 1980s, and everything changed. We bought 'slicks', we bought friends, we bought chalk, and holds that to date had been so greasy that even the world-class climbers amongst us found it impossible to gain any purchase on, could suddenly be

gripped with ease. Everything became easier, except for the routes; they got harder in incredibly short time. Grade 7 was established, then 8 and all the rest. And once you had mastered grade 6, placing you (theoretically at least) just behind the real climbing elite, then they, in turn, with the help of these new little numbers like 'French 6b+', would surge ahead, leaving you back where you started, plodding along in the midfield.

However, we were still able to rejoice when some notorious sport climber from the German speaking world would stray onto our beloved, yet somewhat crumbly, Kalkkögel limestone and take longer to climb the stomache traverse pitch on Fischer/Fohringer to the Alpenklubscharte, than for the rest of the route, including the approach and descent.

Nowadays, the Kalkkögel limestone is too crumbly for most of us as well.

BLACK SHEEP
Josh Wharton I Colorado/USA

The Black Canyon of the Gunnison in Southwestern Colorado has been my favorite climbing area for many years. It's a quiet place with big walls, and big adventure. The Canyon has a reputation for long routes (up to 700 meters) with poor rock and protection, yet some of its more difficult climbs are among the best big routes in the U.S. I especially like the Black's unique combination of relaxed camping and exciting climbing; you camp on the rim of the Canyon, and then descend via one of the many approach gullies, and hope to "escape" back to the campground by nightfall.

Like many climbers, I'm particularly fond of my own routes. The lines that required some creativity to discover, and a special personal effort to complete. For this reason, my route the "Black Sheep" (8a+) is my favorite route in the Canyon. Apart from having great climbing throughout its seven pitches, the devious crux pitch took me many attempts, spread over several days, which created a lasting impression.

Back in Switzerland, the home of Mammut, I know you have some excellent climbing areas with great routes on them – and how about those mountains! In April 2011, I spent a lot of time on the North Face of the Eiger, as I was acting as double for Jeff Lowe who was being filmed on the first ascent of "Metonia". While I was there, I soloed the classic route on both the Eiger and the Matterhorn North Face. Like I said, comparing things to routes like those is a tall order.

If you're planning a climbing trip to the States, don't miss the Black Canyon. You won't be disappointed!

111

AT THE FOOT OF MANASLU
Christine Kopp | Himalaya/Nepal

Bimthang, day 13. Lhagyelo! – the Gods have prevailed! – and helped us cross the Larkya La pass in glorious weather. Today is a rest day. A happy day, a day when you would gladly stop time, when you realize exactly why it is that we are drawn again and again to long, liberating treks in Nepal and elsewhere.

Our tented village is at the foot of Manaslu, bathed in sunlight below the moraine slope that I had scrambled up. The snow-covered peaks glisten in the sun, while below, the pretty little plateau with the stream flowing through it is flooded in light. In the distance, I can make out my companions: two of them reading, two sleeping, another writing and the last just sitting thinking. Our escorts are also enjoying themselves in their way. The Nepalis are playing cards, laughing, giggling, chatting and squealing with delight. Romance has blossomed in the last few days between the Head Sherpa, Takshi Pu, and the porter Bhim Maya – I discover them hiding out alone behind one of the tents.

In the background, the kerosene cooker is chugging away to itself in the kitchen tent. The freshly washed tin dishes are lying out to dry in the sun. The dog that has been faithfully following us for the past few days lies stretched out in the short grass sunning his matted coat. The porters gather dead wood for the evening's fire and the festivities we are planning. Obscene amounts of rakshi have already been purchased for the event. To give you an idea of the quantities involved, we filled an empty beer bottle 27 times with local schnapps – an acquired taste – and it cost just a handful of dollars, 555 Rupees for around 15 liters of schnapps!

And where is the sirdar, Kami Passang Sherpa, boss of the Nepalese crew? I spot him through the binoculars in the distance. He is having the few white hairs in his otherwise black head of hair plucked out again by a pretty local girl... "It itches," he says later, adding with a sheepish grin that he felt much younger after this weekly grooming ceremony.

The laundry is all done; a few pieces still hang from improvised washing lines strung between the tents but the bulk of it has already dried in the wind and the sun, been folded and put away. Pleasant everyday chores, on a day that is anything but ordinary, with none of the worries of everyday life.

Small caravans descend from the pass and continue on their way to their wintering grounds. The animals, the yaks and horses, will stay here in the valley and the people will walk back to Kathmandu. From the perspective of my perch, the caravans have an almost biblical air to them. "Peace," I think to myself; the scene I am looking at is the best illustration of that word I can think of.

But then, as if that perfect moment of timeless happiness could not last, a long column of Tibetans suddenly appears and walk past our tents. Their melancholy singing drifts up to where I am sitting. They are refugees who have left their homeland forever, and with just a bundle on their back, are heading into an uncertain future. I lie on my back, looking at the clouds, and think about the interconnectedness of it all.

BY SAILING BOAT TO GREENLAND
Jutta Römmelt | Greenland

In the summer of 2004, a ten-member team sailed from Reykjavik to Greenland. Passing giant icebergs en route, the crew sailed their boat "Daisy" into the longest fjord in the world, the "Scoresby Sund" (locally known as Kangertittivaq) on Greenland's eastern coast. The plan was to land the four climbers on the team so that they could cross the Greenland ice sheet before being picked up by the boat in a fjord on the other side. Having experienced Greenland's unique, solitary wilderness and experienced great, new adventures, the team would then sail back to Reykjavik.

Anchor's aweigh
The "Daisy" is still in Reykjavik, moored at the docks. Thank God. Our skipper Chris mercifully decided to spend an extra night in Reykjavik to give the gale-force storm that is currently raging over the North Sea the chance to blow over. Otherwise, it would certainly have been a real sailing baptism of fire for me, being the landlubber that I am. So as a novice sailor (climbers generally prefer to have something more solid underfoot), I make the most of the first night in my softly swaying bunk and the gentle introduction it gives me to a life on the ocean wave.

It is half past three. Uli, my husband, is fully dressed (rubber boots, oilskins, hood and woolly hat) and wakes me in our cabin. "It's your watch! Wrap up warm! It is wet and cold out there!" I jump up and call after Uli as he climbs up onto deck to ask if the boys from the bitter cold "middle watch" (0000 to 0400) want a hot drink or some soup. Swaying from side to side, I wobble my way into the galley and put the kettle on.

Apologetically, I wake my watch captains, Frank and Mo, who peel themselves grumbling and groaning out of their warm sleeping bags. Good morning! Up on deck, everything is shrouded in fog. Michi, Uli and Moritz perk up at the sight of the hot drinks. The diesel motor is quieter up here and with the help of a few sails, we're managing somewhere around 6 to 7 knots.

Two hours later, I hop from one foot to another in a vain attempt to bring some warmth back into my frozen feet. Frank Bleyer, the old sea dog, holds the wheel using his feet to give his hands a chance to warm up in his pockets. He and Moritz are talking shop, something to do with rigging and manoeuvring. It's all Greek to me.

I try to peer into the distance. But I can't see much through the fog. The sun is turning the mist bright orange. The dawn light is almost blinding. All you can make out is a single line – the horizon. My thoughts wander and I'm enjoying the salty wind blowing in my face. It's good to be out here, with the water and the wind. I try to shut out the fact that I am far from dry land in a small sailing boat in the middle of the freezing cold North Sea on my first ever sailing trip and that I have no idea how anything works. I enjoy the open space. It all feels so far away. I'm simply enjoying being here. I'm enjoying life.

Ashore
Shades of white and blue. Sky blue and snow white. These two colours dominate the view. This is hard work. I'm sweating like a pig. Puuhh! Somehow, I expected climbing in remote, icy Greenland to be different.

The view is magnificent. The horizon stretches as far as the eye can see in all directions. It is an amazing privilege to be able to experience all this.

I feel dwarfed by the vast, endless expanse. And alone? No, not exactly. The rope behind leads back to Uli, Michi and Moritz, who follow in my footsteps. Cutting steps in the soft snow is extremely

hard work. I sink in up to my knees with every step and heave my-self and my huge, heavy backpack out to plough on. My thighs are burning. Marching onwards I continue to pile fresh mounds on the snow's surface to help us hold course. I count my steps: 443 . . . 444 . . . 445 . . . I have decided to hand over the lead when I get to 600.

In the silence, I hear my pulse pounding in my ears.

A day later and we've left the glacial plateau behind us. We climb, crossing huge crevasses, in the direction of the fjord. The sun has been shining continuously for days and had a devastating effect on the glacier. Uli, tied into the long rope ahead of me, is care-fully feeling his way across a not very confidence-inspiring snow bridge over one of the many crevasses. For the umpteenth time, he sinks in up to the hips. The rope goes taut. He manoeuvres his heavy pack with difficulty and struggles back out of the hole. "I'm sick of this!" I put into words what the guys are already thinking. "I've had enough!"

We've been moving at only a snail's pace for days over the fragile, fissured glacier. In the last 2 hours, we've covered only 300 yards, zigzagging and mostly on all fours. Are we seriously risking life and limb just to end up at the bottom of some crevasse? We decide to stop and pitch the tents early, hoping for a cold night with temperatures below freezing, cold enough to improve conditions. Otherwise, it's going to be impossible to make progress through this slushy, sodden glacier. The way things stand at the moment, we can't go on and the way back is cut off, too.

Stuck in the middle, we wait.

I'm counting the minutes as they go by.

A cold front has been announced for Friday.

We have been stuck here since Tuesday.

Today is Thursday.

We still have some stock cubes, eight tea bags, a few grains of coffee and some fuel for the stove.

At least there is no shortage of water, as we can melt snow with Uli's fantastic melting machinery.

We're forced to sit and wait on the ice sheet. Despite the vast openness I can't travel more than 5 meters in any direction before I hit a huge crevasse. It's grotesque!

What am I doing here?

What have I let myself get into?

I was really excited about coming here. But I didn't expect to end up sitting around not being able to move!

I find myself thinking of people that I have not seen for years. How are they doing? What are they up to now? Probably not strand-ed on some "adventure" like me. Are they happier? More balanced? More satisfied?

But when I think about it I feel just fine.

I am out enjoying this incredible, natural world.

Uli is here beside me, sleeping in the tent.

Two good friends, Michi and Moritz, are in the tent next door.

Later that night, we are going to cook ourselves a thin soup.

What more could I want to make me happy?

A CLOSE CALL
Peter Mathis | Alaska/USA

The cheapest place to rent a car in Alaska turned out to be "Rent a Wreck". Tommy, Robby, Gerhard and I stood looking at the wheels we were given for the coming two weeks, a regular hatchback to accommodate four people plus skiing and boarding gear – the skis and board bags would have to go on the roof. The ferry left Juneau at 2 P.M., and after four hours sailing through the incredible Coast Mountains Fjords, we docked at our destination, Haines. Deep blue fjords, the wooded coastline, the snow-covered peaks of the Chilkat Range – the scenery and the weather were awesome.

After a big supermarket shop, we drove our totally overloaded rental car along the Haines River to our accommodation at Mosquito Lake. The weather forecast had warned of a huge low pressure system traveling our way from the Gulf of Alaska, set to bring huge downpours. It duly obliged, leaving us some time to kill by making fires, cooking, playing table football and other such pastimes. For the first three days it rained in the valley, but up where we were hanging out, playing games, it snowed non-stop. As we looked out the window on the fourth day, it was even white down in the valley. The wind was blowing clouds past us but the first rays of sunlight were just beginning to break through. Maybe we would be able to take our first flight that afternoon if the weather kept improving. But the wind got stronger throughout the morning so flying that afternoon was out of the question.

The following morning, there wasn't a cloud in the sky and the wind had also died down. We headed straight to the heli-base for the first flight up into the fantastic mountains of the Chilkat Range. When we got there, we were told that heavy windslab had built up

on the western slopes and we would only be able to fly into certain areas. Aside from us, there was one other film crew, so we opted for the same mountain – if something went wrong, at least we'd be able to help each other out. After the usual brief on safety in and around the helicopter, we were up and away, ready for the ultimate deep powder experience.

To the left and right, incredibly beautiful snowy peaks were the backdrop to our flight. We landed on a small summit area and got out. You could already see that a few avalanches had been triggered. Over one meter of fresh snow had fallen, so we chose a gentle slope for our first run. Our guide, an experienced heli-skier nicknamed "Fishbone", went first, skiing down 300 meters to a protruding ridgeline, where he waited for us in a safe spot. For the so-called "warm-up run", the photographer is allowed to follow straight after the guide because no shots are taken on the first run. A few intense minutes of powder billowing over my head later, and I had also made down it to the safe spot. When all of us had arrived at the ridge, it was big sweeping turns down to the base of the glacier and our pick-up point, where pilot Al – whose lengthy flying career started in war zones – picked us up.

While the second group filmed 800 meters above us, we loaded our equipment onto the helicopter, and one after another, climbed on board. My seat was by the window on the right-hand side, facing the down slope. Once Tommy, Gerhard and Robby were seated next to me and the sliding rear door was closed, we waited for Fishbone to stow my camera pack in the luggage store and take his seat next to the pilot. Suddenly, Al shouted: "Get in, get in!" Fishbone hurled himself onto the front seat, legs still hanging

out the open door, and Al tried to get the helicopter into the air. From where I was sitting, all I could see was a white cloud and I wondered whether it was a crevasse below us that had opened up. Al steered the helicopter upwards and in the wake of that white cloud, somehow managed to get us out of the danger zone at the very last moment – otherwise the avalanche would have hit us and buried the helicopter.

We flew in a big arc up to the safe spot on the ridge, where the film crew had set up their cameras to film their skiers. While we had been loading the kit down at the base of the glacier, one of their skiers had set off a 300 meter wide snow slab that headed straight for the helicopter. The film crew's guide had radioed Al to warn him and, tapping into his wealth of experience, he had just managed to save us. The skier who set off the avalanche was able to escape to a narrow rock outcrop in the middle of the face. It seemed we all had a guardian angel.

The next day, the heli-skiing base was closed. Since the weather was still perfect, we decided to charter a fixed-wing aircraft and fly over the Chilkat Mountains. A turboprop plane flew us across beautiful snowy landscapes and over what had to be the most stunning ski mountains in Alaska. We could also see there had been avalanches everywhere; in some cases, the crown line was up to two meters deep. The classic steeps like "Tomahawk" were no longer an option for our remaining seven days. But in the end, when the snow had settled and the risk of avalanche had diminished, we enjoyed a few great runs on more gentle terrain and still got the shots we were looking for.

BIG WALL CLIMBING WITH MRS. MÜLLER
Robert Steiner | Yosemite/USA

For the millennium, I traveled to Yosemite with a couple of climbers from British Columbia. It was winter. We were told that there might be avalanches and storms and that icicles could fall from high up on El Cap. There we were with our avalanche transceivers, down jackets, ice axes and screws – it was 25 degrees plus and the sun was blazing. We had estimated taking 3 liters of water per man per day. Given the conditions, we were probably losing a liter a day as our feet sweated – we were wearing alpine expedition boots. While climbing, we made every mistake you could possibly make. We were slow leading pitches and even slower seconding them. For food, we hauled 25 kg of cheap tinned food up with us, including ridiculous recipes such as chili con carne, which left you feeling thirsty for the rest of the day. We had also packed chocolate santas and chocolate eggs filled with rum. With these kinds of preparations, there was no way that we were going to make it. After eight pitches we abseiled back down. The boys from Vancouver drove back home. I decided to stay and started a mission on the "Nose".

I started out on January 2, 2000. The first pitches went pretty quickly. The wall was gigantic, the protection was good and the sack hauling was not as bad as expected. I was self-belaying the whole time. At around midday, I reached Sickle Ledge and then as night fell, I came to the huge pendulum traverse before the Stove-leg Cracks. It's an impressive move. You hang 15 meters below the fulcrum point and then have to run as far as you can to the left and then back to the right. In the middle is a scary crack, which you have to jump over each time. Doing it by the light of a headlamp was a strange experience. Finally, I managed to swing over to the far crack and jam my hand in. Unlucky for me, my headlamp stopped working and it was getting hard to hold on. My hand was getting weaker and weaker and I was about to swing back out again. At the last moment, in the dark night, I managed to find a cam, placed it in the even darker crack and clipped the rope in.

On the next pitches, everything went wrong. It was a case of Murphy's Law. I dropped several carabiners; one of them had five nuts on it. My haul rope snagged behind an old piton, which sat deep inside a crack. The more I pulled, the more it snagged. Finally, I was left with no choice but to climb back down and bang it out with a hammer. Back in those days, I had no sponsorship and my rope was so old that the sheath disintegrated during the climb. I cut it down to 35 meters. In the middle of the next pitch, my headlamp suddenly failed, even though I had put a new battery in it. It was pitch black. I placed all the gear I had in the crack and then rapped back down to my haulbag for a spare battery, which of course was right at the bottom. It was a complete fiasco. As I climbed back up, my rope got tangled up with the haulbag and I had to rappel back down again to free it. By now it was midnight and I was really tired. I tried sitting on the haulbag to rest and even tried to get some sleep. I couldn't sleep a wink, so I decided to carry on climbing. At around two in the morning, I reached the Dolt Tower. It was pretty desperate. Everything that could go wrong did. I was so exhausted that I thought about giving up.

As I fell asleep, I had terrible nightmares of stuck haulbags, never-ending cracks and useless headlamps. Finally, I had a dream that I had rappelled back down and gone back to Camp 4 with a bottle of Coca Cola, where I was bouldering surrounded by pretty girls. A perfect dream.

In reality, things looked rather different. My fingers were bruised and bloody. I could hardly do my shoes up. However, on the Dolt

Tower I found a faded, old 20 meter length of rope. This meant that I could extend my own rope to a more useful length. At midday, I reached El Cap Tower, which has a comfortable bivouac spot. It was really hot and the sweat was pouring off me. I took off my clothes and climbed the rest of the day in my boxer shorts – maybe this makes it the first winter ascent of El Cap in underpants. I carried on up over the Texas Flake. Between this flake and the face, there is a difficult chimney to climb. The shade was refreshingly cool and I was feeling pretty good. Unfortunately, I ripped my boxer shorts, though luckily only at the back.

My relationship with my haulbag continued to be a strained one. I had decided to call it "Mrs. Müller". I once rented a flat from a Mrs. Müller in Freiburg in Germany and she and my haulbag have a lot in common. Like the bag, she was also fat and of a nondescript color. Of course, I also swore at my haulbag, calling it "dirtbag", "pigbag" and "arsehole" just as other climbers do. But mainly, I called it "Mrs. Müller". At night, once I had found my food, drink and warm sleeping bag, I noticed that Mrs. Müller also had a good heart in spite of her bulk.

I spent the night at Boot Flake. It soon became apparent that my feet were hanging in the air. When I shifted along, my head hung in the air, which was definitely the worse of the two possibilities. In spite of everything, the night was glorious. Millions of stars lit up against the black sky. Once again, I found myself dreaming of cold beer, pretty girls and boulders.

The next day flew by, but Murphy and his proverbial law continued to dog me. On the pitch below the Great Roof, I dropped a cam. Soon afterwards, night fell and I struggled up the next two pitches up to Camp 5 in the dark. My headlamp – at that time there were only the old heavy ones with battery packs – had stopped working again. Whilst trying to pull it out of my haulbag, my jacket fell down the face, along with my tin opener and the route description. This was a real disaster, I got really annoyed with myself. It's probably just as well that I was on my own; had there been anyone else with me, I would probably have taken my anger out on him or her. I reached Camp 5 at 10 P.M. The last move is a mantle onto a ledge. In the middle of the move, I felt something catch, probably an etrier. I was stuck. I had my elbow on the ledge, and I knew that I couldn't reverse the move because I wouldn't be able to find the foothold in the dark. I was about to take a 20 meter fall when I finally found the foothold.

The next day, I was pretty wasted. Again, I lost another cam. This meant that I sometimes had to climb 10 or 15 meters without protection. Frau Müller was looking thinner, as I was starting to run out of water. She allowed herself to be pulled up without complaint. I had no more reason to hate her, apart from the fact that it had become a kind of ritual. It was 10 P.M. on my fourth day of climbing on the "Nose". A full moon shone over the Sierra Nevada. The final pitch is overhanging. I was tired; I was fed up of climbing, fed up of placing protection, clipping carabiners and hauling up my bag. I needed a wash. It was time to get off the wall.

I was amazed to see flat ground and trees. I scrambled on until I could stand up and then took off my harness and went to look for the nearest bush. I had bet the boys from Vancouver that I wouldn't use a poop tube because I only go to the john every four days when I'm climbing. So I had won the bet. What a relief. Beneath me in the light of the moon lay 34 pitches and one of my most bizarre adventures.

THE WAY INSIDE
Bernd Arnold | Saxony Sandstone/Germany

The sport of climbing encompasses an incredibly wide range of disciplines. It has also witnessed an explosion in growth over the last 40 years that is perhaps greater than in any other sport. Figuratively speaking, climbing is like a cupboard with numerous drawers, rather like the bureau that has served as my desk for so many years. The drawers represent the various sub-disciplines: trad, sport, bouldering etc. Throughout my life, I've filled each of these compartments with my experiences. And they are all united by one overriding emotion, embodied by the solid frame of the symbolic cupboard that surrounds them: the pleasure taken in their active performance.

Amidst all this diversity, one can often forget how it all began, about the original pioneers who paved the way. Everything has to start somewhere. I'm proud that free climbing started in the area where I was born, the Elbsandsteingebirge in south-eastern Germany. In 1874, O. E. Ufer and H. Frick made the first free ascent of the Mönchstein at Rathen via the *Ostweg* (III). The conscious decision to climb without recourse to any artificial aid, to concentrate on style, on climbing for climbing's sake, was pivotal. A similar development took place in England a few years later (in 1882 with Haskett Smith). However, there was still a way to go before the advent of real free climbing. The pioneering activities of Oscar Schuster and his fellow climbers (for example the Meurer Brothers) introduced a sporting element into free climbing from 1890. Their legacy includes classic routes such as the *Falkenstein Schusterweg* (III) and the *Meurerturm Südweg* (IV). During this pe-

riod, the Blossstock and Brosinnadel also witnessed first ascents. The final step in the development of Saxony rock climbing was provided by Rudolf Fehrmann from 1900. Building on the sporting ideas of Oscar Schuster, in 1913 he formulated the basic rules for climbing in Saxony, thereby creating the basis for a continued development and a means of measuring climbing performance. Unintentionally, Elbe Sandstone climbing remained at the vanguard of international climbing from the early days right up into the middle of the 1970s. However, there was also a certain amount of ballast in the overblown rule book, and rigid interpretation had an adverse effect on later developments.

Climbing on Elbe Sandstone might no longer be at the forefront of modern climbing in terms of difficulty. However, the physical and psychological challenges of climbing and the striking beauty of the natural surroundings still make it a unique experience. The demands are often similar to those of the classic routes in the Alps. This is where I acquired the skills that enabled me to climb all over the world.

A friend of mine described climbing in Saxony as a "challenge of the landscape," because for most visitors to the Elbe Sandstone region, the climbing and the natural environment are inseparable

and together form the complete experience. The area is named after the River Elbe, which carves a wide valley through this sandstone region. There are fabulous canyons and bizarre rock pillars and remote villages, surrounded by forests, nestled in the valleys. Given the particular appeal of the area, it's understandable that people ask if climbing somehow has romantic elements. Is climbing a form of romantic lifestyle? It's no coincidence that the Elbsandstein-gebirge were the inspiration for many artistic works during the Romantic Movement of the late 18th and early 19th centuries. Now-adays, most people generally understand the concept of Romanti-cism to be associated with quixotic infatuation (or kitsch), with purely emotional responses and a certain alienation from the world. This is neither the time nor the place for a detailed discussion of the connections between the Romantic era and climbing. However, I'd still like to leave you with a couple of thoughts and a single quote. "Nach innen geht der Weg" (The way leads inside) wrote Novalis, an author and philosopher of early German Romanticism in his *Blütenstaub* fragment #16. This notion sums up the main theme of romantic thinking.

To an outside observer, the physical and psychological effort involved in climbing might appear pointless. Unlike many other sports or even music, painting or writing, climbing generally requires no audience to recognize its achievements. Climbing is about being out in and interacting with nature. It often involves aes-thetic movements and intense interaction with a section of rock with all its different shapes and textures. It stimulates both the body and the mind. Climbing provides a unique perception of nature, by literally getting to grips with its very substance. It demands a prompt intellectual analysis of the impressions gained and a ration-al sequence of movements in response. Ideally, spirit and nature should become one. This is what enables climbers to experience such deep satisfaction; the way up actually proves to be a way in-side.

When preparing for a route (the physical and mental training), the climber experiences a borderline situation right from the start. If the challenge is overcome, the moment follows when this strain instantly dissolves into "the purest exultation". During climbing, and often as early as the target setting stage, the problems of everyday life are banished from the mind. The task at hand is com-pletely all-consuming. This experience is completed by the choice of partner, the walk-in, the influence of the surrounding nature and the act of overcoming the sporting challenge. The high point is not only to be found at the summit. Once a route is completed, a new goal is required. The longing for an elementary existence is ap-peased and rekindled simultaneously.

I WANT TO GET UP THERE!
Anke Hinrichs | Alps

I have been afflicted with cerebral palsy since birth. It manifests itself in the form of spasticity and disturbed coordination and balance. During the course of my life, I have often met with incomprehension from others when I have set out into the mountains to push my own limits. I climbed my first 2,000 meter summit in the Alps at the age of eighteen with my mother. People accused her of being reckless. "It's irresponsible to take this child on an alpine climb!" she was told. On one occasion, whilst skiing a black piste, after one of my (infrequent) falls some other skiers asked if I was drunk. When I explained that I was just physically handicapped, three men shook their heads and muttered that they were going to inform the piste patrol. "You should take off your skis immediately!" Why should I do that when I am more mobile on skis than on foot? Once at the *Deutsche Alpenverein* youth course, the leaders looked at me incredulously when I explained one morning that I intended to take part in the planned ski tour. And what a face they pulled when I actually made it to the summit on my own!

Physical challenges have accompanied me throughout my life. From an early age, I found it really motivating to set myself goals in the mountains. The various forms of therapy I had at home often seemed pointless, whereas alpine challenges had a very direct result: they enabled me to see the world from a different perspective. It was really important for me to achieve something exceptional in a physical sense. Completing that ski tour on a standard DAV youth course meant as much to me as passing my Abitur (high school exams). The ten courses I took part in provided me with a great opportunity to get involved in outdoor activities with other non-handicapped kids of the same age. Not only was I socially integrated and accepted in a way which I never experienced at school, I also had the chance to gradually push my own physical limits.

Looking back, it is now clear to me that these various physical challenges and experiences in the mountains enabled me to significantly improve my motor skills. My neurologist doesn't mind whether I go climbing, mountaineering or to physiotherapy. The youth courses allowed me to collect new alpine experiences. Of course, there were certain limitations. Due to my condition, I do need extra assistance or more time for classic outdoor activities. This wasn't always easy to admit in groups of non-disabled people.

I found exactly what I was looking for in Switzerland: a high-alpine camp for people with disabilities. With competent support, I climbed my first 3,000er, crossed glaciers and snow slopes as part of a roped party, abseiled into a crevasse, climbed out of the same crevasse using an ice axe and crampons and climbed a grade six pitch on a cliff. These were really important experiences for me – they made it clear what I was really capable of, in spite of my disabilities. I was also impressed by the fact that it was young Swiss Alpine Club (SAC) members who provided me with assistance as they also wanted new experiences and to see what was actually possible. They took no notice of my various physical disabilities; they supported me and remained open to what were often unusual solutions. For example, at one point, I abseiled over a steep snow slope on my knees, so as not to come down too quickly. They made it possible for a young woman like me with a muscle disease to go on a two-day trek to a SAC mountain hut at 3,000 meters by spontaneously building a functional and com-

fortable stretcher from four roof battens, two blankets and three ropes and carrying me up on that. The most difficult part of the two days was the return journey from the Simplon Pass to Brig and the train station – the local bus didn't have wheelchair access.

I shall never forget the two multi-day trips from hut to hut that Procap (formerly known as the *Schweizer Invalidenverband*), a Swiss self-help organization for people with disabilities, ran in co-operation with the Witzwil penal institution. It was open to wheelchair users and people with restricted mobility. The inmates carried us over obstacles and supported us in the mountain huts. I found this really helpful. By putting my trust in one of the inmates, who acted as personal "emergency brake" as it were, I was able to climb down over steep terrain. I shall never forget how I was able to travel from Fafleralp in the Valais and over the 3,000 meter Lötschen Pass to Leukerbad and then on to Kandersteg via Gem-

mi, all on my own two feet. Being able to directly experience this high-alpine environment and look over to the 4,000ers didn't just expand my own horizons; it put the worries and problems of every-day life in a completely different perceptive. My encounters with the prison inmates are also something I consider as an enriching experience.

I still feel that pushing one's limits is an important objective, but I now realize that limits are often relative and can be redefined, although I do admit that some limits simply have to be accepted as such. These days, I see both these factors as important. Finding a way between them is often something of a balancing act.

Established 150 years ago, Mammut is one of the oldest mountain equipment manufacturers in the world. However, sleeping bag manufacturer Ajungilak eclipses this monumental record by seven years – the Norwegian firm first saw the light of the great outdoors back in 1855. Ajungilak kept Fritjof Nansen warm on his Arctic expeditions, helped Amundsen reach the South Pole and has provided shelter for countless mountaineers on the highest peaks on the planet. When the first down sleeping bags appeared on the scene in 1920, the Norwegians were right there at the forefront, as they were with synthetic fills in 1950.

The company was named after its owner Fuglesand in 1869 and kept that name for four generations. The "Ajungilak" name was first adopted in 1932 during a Greenland expedition that was equipped with Fuglesand sleeping bags. The two explorers, Martin Mehren and Arne Hoygaard, had picked up the word "Ajungilak" when talking to the Inuit. Roughly translated, it means "warm" and "all is well". Upon their return to Norway, the new name was adopted, replacing the traditional family name.

Both in the past and now, whether down or synthetics, the name Ajungilak has always stood for innovative, high-tech sleeping bags. Since 2001, the Norwegian manufacturer has been part of the Mammut Sports Group. The name Ajungilak continues to be used as a technology label. Together, the brands can boast a total of over 300 years of outdoor experience!

ALL IS WELL, ALL IS WARM
Harald Schreiber | Norway and Switzerland

117

Om dagen föler De Dem vell i ......

Om natten sover De godt i

GUBBE!

10

1889: The first sleeping bags with a natural fiber fill – reindeer fur and kapok fibers – are one-off models, tailor-made for expeditions.

1920: The introduction of down fill reduces the weight of sleeping bags.

1936: The sleeping bag develops a broad appeal, resulting in innovative designs such as Ajungilak's "Gubbe".

1956: Ajungilak launches the "Igloo", the first sleeping bag with a pure polyester fiber fill and nylon fabrics.

2011: The synthetic fiber "Ajungilak Alpine" sleeping bag sets new standards in warmth-to-weight performance.

JUST MAKE SURE IT'S THE RIGHT LOGO...
Stephan Siegrist | Torre Egger/Patagonia

118

I think I probably speak for my fellow pro athletes when I say that it really is fantastic to work with great sponsors. We are all aware that we are only able to pursue our projects thanks to their support. And we're very grateful for this. However, occasionally, situations arise where the interests of mountaineers and sponsors don't exactly match 100 percent. Here are a couple of examples.

In 2008, I went to Patagonia with Alexander Huber to make an alpine-style ascent of Torre Egger. In order to be able to move fast, we set out with only small rucksacks and had very little bivouac equipment with us. Nevertheless, we were forced to stop and bivouac, belayed to a peg above us. It was pretty cold, so we huddled up to keep warm. Anyone who has ever slept on a train knows that when you fall asleep in a sitting position, your head always ends up slumped backwards, forwards or to one side. After a while, this gets really painful, so I had a think about how I could rig some kind of support. Alex lent me his headlamp, which was close by, and I gave him my warm Mammut jacket in return (he feels the cold more than me). I attached the headlamp to my helmet and then fixed the helmet to the peg above us. Then I put the helmet on (the wrong way round to increase stability). This ensured that my head was held upright and I was actually able to doze for a few hours. When we got back home I had to explain to Mammut why there was a photo of me wearing a headlamp from the wrong company...

I'm generally really happy when there is Internet access on expeditions, to get up to date information and for the weather forecasts. However, I'm not a big fan of blogs. I never blog while on expeditions because I don't want to get distracted; I like to concentrate fully on the project in hand. Mammut once invited me to take part in a Teamtrip. I was really pleased to accept the offer. The only catch was there had to be a blog about the trip, so that the Mammut Community could follow what was happening. I was pretty opposed to the idea, but in the end, I resigned myself to it. Rescue came in the form of the Kyrgyz locals. The gasoline they sold us was so bad that our generator gave up the ghost after only four days. No electricity = no blog. The world never did get to know which of us "sponsored heroes" wore what pajamas and other such vital information.

MOUNTAIN GUIDES FOR KYRGYZSTAN
Alexandra Steiner-Paholik | Pik Lenin/Kyrgyzstan

Base camp, Pik Lenin, August 2006. I crawl out of the tent. Everything has been plastered in a stiff white coat of snow after last night's storm. Three of our tents are ripped, two have broken poles – their inhabitants have fled for the warmth of the kitchen tent where they have been welcomed with hot tea. The others have spent the whole night shoveling snow from the entrances and the tent walls, cursing the wind as they worked. The radio crackles in the base camp manager's tent. "Base camp to camp one, base camp to camp one, base camp to camp one, are you receiving me, over . . ."

"Camp one to base camp. Everything is fine . . ." I feel a huge wave of relief. A group of Japanese climbers are up there with my good friend Serjoga, with whom I have reached many a summit. This is our second year working on Pik Lenin (7,134 m). Being a mountain guide means more than just walking and climbing. It also means pitching tents, carrying luggage, preparing meals, attending to injuries and above all ensuring the safety of your clients. Serjoga and I enjoy what we do – we have found our calling in life.

The issue of whether we need mountain guides and training for mountain guides in Kyrgyzstan arose at the start of the 1990s when the first Western mountaineers started to travel here and asked if there were local guides. Exactly what a mountain guide is and what he or she is supposed to do was something that we only had a vague idea of in Kyrgyzstan back then. Some climbers began to work as mountain guides. It wasn't long before the first problems started, in particular with regards to safety and conduct. The way our guides
acted had little in common with how a good, qualified guide should behave. (Vladimir Kommissarov, coordinator of training for mountain guides in Kyrgyzstan)

Base camp is starting to wake up. I can hear cheerful voices in the kitchen. People are queuing outside a tent for replacement parts: new tent poles or material to patch up their flysheets. I hurry over to help out the camp manager and end up being occupied until lunch. Then it's time for radio contact and I'm able to communicate with Serjoga. They are on their way back down. And none too early. In an hour's time, the sun will have softened the snow to such an extent there will be a real danger of avalanches.

What is the difference between a mountain guide and a normal mountaineer or instructor? A mountaineer chooses when he or she wants to go up into the mountains, they are only responsible for themselves. An instructor goes up into the mountains to teach others about mountaineering techniques and tactics. A guide does many things for his clients that neither the mountaineer nor the instructor would think of. He selects the route, looks after the clients, cooks and carries their loads and generally helps them. Their aim is not to reach the summit themselves, but to do everything in their power to ensure that their clients reach it safely. Being a mountain guide is about more than passion: it's a profession.

The weather is good, but that is no reason to go racing off up the mountain. A lot of snow has fallen and the warm weather brings with it an increased risk of avalanches. It will take two days for the snow to settle. This is why Serjoga is bringing the Japanese group back down.

A few hours later and we're all together in the dinner tent. We sit drinking tea. Serjoga's clients are a young woman and three powerfully-built men. They look like mountaineers, I say to Serjoga – their sort will always be welcome here. Serjoga's eyes flash mischievously. An old lady comes to join us at our table. She also belongs to the group. I'm lost for words, while Serjoga grins from ear to ear and pours tea into the 72 year old lady's glass.

Since 2007, Mammut Sports Group AG has been pursuing its commitment to training mountain guides in Kyrgyzstan in accordance with international standards. The project is run in cooperation with the International Federation of Mountain Guides Associations (IFMGA), the British Association of Mountain Guides, the Swiss Mountain Guides' Association and the expert mountain guides Adolf Schlunegger (Switzerland) and Terry Ralphs (United Kingdom). The local partner is the Kyrgyz Mountain Guides Association (KMGA). The second phase of the project started in 2010 to train aspirant guides and expert guides in accordance with IFMGA standards.

A few days later, Chiro, the leader of the Japanese group, suggests that I join them as a second guide on the Pik Lenin. I'm well acclimatized and I enjoy leading. The clients also seem to like the idea.

We set off the next day. I ask the young Japanese woman if this is her first mountain. As she lists the various 8,000 meter peaks she has climbed, I can feel my self-confidence sinking. I'm worried about my reputation – I had neither the money nor the opportunity to go on such expeditions – and turn instead to the old lady. It gets worse. She was on Cho Oyu earlier this year, her name is in the Guinness Book of Records. I'm shocked – Serjoga grins quietly to himself.

It all changed in 2007. A group of mountain guides took matters into their own hands and founded the Kyrgyz Mountain Guides Association (KMGA). In the same year, Mammut Sports Group launched the Kyrgyzstan Mountain Project and appointed Corina Zanetti and Alexandra Steiner-Paholik as project leaders and Adolf Schlunegger as expert mountain guide and partner for mountain guide training. In the first phase of the project (2007–2009), training for mountain guides was initiated in Kyrgyzstan in accordance with the standards of the International Federation of Mountain Guides Associations (IFMGA) and the profession of mountain guide received official recognition. Project initiatives also helped to improve infrastructure in the mountains and environmental protection.

We set off for camp 2 early. The weather couldn't be better. The air is dry, the sun is scorching, so you have to keep drinking all the time. We cross a lot of crevasses on the way. A short, steep 40-degree slope is secured with ropes, which the guides put in place. Then it's on up the north flank. Fortunately, the snow has settled,

everything is going well. In the middle of the stage, the 72 year old stops, pulls a can of beer out of her rucksack and drinks it down as we stare in astonishment. She moves slowly, almost ten times as slow as the others, but she never stops and we even manage to overtake other climbers. Serjoga leads the group on; I accompany the old woman. After 7 hours, we get to camp 2. I had expected it to take a whole day and half the night . . .

Chiro asks Serjoga and me to go on ahead to set up the camp, while he leads the group. Just as we reach the camp, I become aware of Serjoga shouting behind us. "Quick, get back to the group!" We run so fast, I hardly have time to collect my thoughts. Four members of the group are lying on the snow; the rope between them is taut. And the fifth member? Where he should have been there is a black hole in the snow down which the taut rope disappears. We are able to pull him out of the crevasse. He is unhurt. The rescue is successful!

The second phase of the project (2010–2011) is already well underway. The focus is on expanding and consolidating the training of mountain guides. The first cohort of guides has its final assessment in October 2011. Three of these ten Kyrgyz mountain guides want to go on to obtain expert status, which would allow them to train other guides from 2012. The second cohort has already started.

Unfortunately, a huge storm puts an end to our expedition. We are forced to descend. The most important thing for Serjoga and me is that we all get back down safely and in good spirits. If the weather had been better, we would have made it. The summit can wait – it will still be there next year.

THE BLAME GAME
Ernst Kohler | Alps/Switzerland

Breathtaking, daredevil jumps over cliff edges, white snow and blue skies, pumping music in the background. There are plenty of videos on YouTube showing what is possible on a steep mountain slope. A third of the way down, the skier doing the filming accidentally sets off a snow slab avalanche, falls, is swept head over heels and then miraculously lands the right way up. A few minutes later, he's shown still out of breath, talking about his radical ride. It's not clear to the viewer whether the young man is under shock because he had a narrow escape or whether he views what has just happened as an amazing, crazy adrenaline-fuelled stunt.

People are quick to condemn young off-piste skiers, or roped parties who don't make it to the summit in time and get into difficulties in bad weather: seeking publicity, drastic overestimation of their own skills, flawed analysis of subjective and objective dangers, insufficient preparation or equipment. The criticism comes flying in thick and fast. Irresponsible mountaineers put their fellow alpinists' lives at risk, not to mention those of the rescue services. The most common public reaction seems to be: who actually foots the bill for the rescue operations? All these reactions are perfectly understandable and yet they fall prey to crass generalization.

Nobody disputes the fact that, in today's leisure society, certain individuals expose themselves to senseless, inexplicable risks. But are reckless mountaineers or freeriders the only ones to blame? Does not today's society relentlessly demand new records in all disciplines? News of a successful ascent is sent directly from the summit via mobile phone and Internet; the world is immediately informed of the victory or failure. Equipment manufacturers promote ubiquitous competition: "Accept no limits," one paragliding company exults. The user is called upon to push his limits further and further and maybe to even go beyond them. Of course, we are all responsible for our own actions. Respecting your own limits and being able to say no when challenged requires great strength of character, especially for younger people. Melchior Anderegg (1828–1914), the first ever Swiss mountain guide, who was first to stand on many of the main summits of the Western Alps used to say: "One could go, but I Melchior Anderegg, will not go." When it comes to risk management we would do well to follow his example.

Current trends and marketing only echo emotions that are present within us. Anyone who is honest with himself knows that a life lived in total safety, where every element of risk is minimized, would be bleak and joyless. In the search for the intensive experiences, for the next big kick, we sometimes go too far in suppressing our fears, take too great a risk and only realize it when it is too late.

Society today expects to have an immediate solution to every problem; every mountain casualty expects an immediate rescue. The emergency services, the doctors, mountain rescue teams and paramedics are now asking whether their efficient response is actually encouraging people to take even greater risks. Rega (Swiss Air-Rescue) is often criticized for its constant readiness to provide emergency medical assistance to even the most remote crevasse, or for its use of the most modern technology night and day. It is said that mountaineers rely too heavily on these factors when

Ernst Kohler, born 1963, is a qualified mountain guide and a former mountain rescue expert and Luftwaffe Group Captain. From 1999 to 2005, he was a Member of the Board of the Rega (Swiss Air-Rescue) and a member of the Rega Finance Committee. Since 2006, he has been Chairman of the Executive Board of Rega, Board Member of the Alpine Rettung Schweiz (ARS/Swiss Mountain Rescue Service) and Board Member of the European HEMS & Air Ambulance Committee (EHAC).

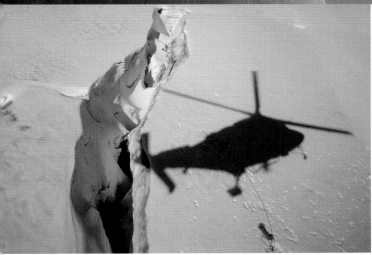

considering the risk levels of a proposed climb or ski tour. Critics say that individual responsibility decreases as the fear threshold increases.

If it were the case that rescue teams and the emergency services have a counter-productive effect and actually encourage greater risk-taking, this would indeed be undesirable. But let us take a look at the other side of the argument. Does this mean that we should have less efficient rescue services, stop providing such a high level of training for our paramedics and stop helicopter rescue missions at night? Would this help reduce the false sense of security and risk taking? Clearly, this would get us nowhere. No one in

their right mind would suggest that we do away with seat belts, ABS or Airbags in an effort to make people drive more carefully. In the same respect, it would also be naive to condemn sports equipment manufacturers for doing too much to increase safety standards by investing in measures to educate their customers and taking preventative measures wherever possible.

Instead, it is the ongoing duty of all responsible parties to continually remind mountaineers and skiers that rescue systems, medical expertise and technical achievements cannot guarantee 100 percent safety. All off-piste skiers should be made aware of the fact that 20 percent of all avalanche victims are dead by the time the avalanche has subsided and that a further 40 percent die within 30 minutes of being buried. It has to be made clear in our leisure-orientated society that the best form of rescue is to avoid having to resort to a rescue in the first place and that most outdoor sports have no pause or delete button. Risk planning for outdoor activities should not rely on mountain rescue or the emergency services – and should recognize that the forces of nature are always stronger than the best efforts of mankind.

Maybe there is one current trend that provides grounds for optimism. Survivors often provide details of their experiences on the Internet and openly acknowledge their errors of judgment. This is often discussed in the online forums. As a society, we are getting better at admitting our mistakes and talking about them as opposed to treating them as taboos. There is hope for the future.

SALBITISSIMA!
Hans Berger | Salbit hut/Switzerland

I will never forget that moment in February 1984 in Davos when the phone rang and the Swiss Alpine Club (SAC) Lindenberg section hut manager called to say that I had been selected as warden of the Salbit Mountain Hut. As young climbers, we had climbed all the classic routes on the Salbitschijen, a mountain in the Urner Alps overlooking Göschenen in the canton of Uri. Among other things, we were the first to climb the West Ridge without a bivouac. It might come as a surprise to certain people that a mountain guide from Berne with plenty of experience on the classic North Faces (including leading parties) should choose to become a hut warden in the heart of Switzerland.

Back in those days, it was mainly only climbers who stayed there. They often brought their own food with them and ordered only soup. The previous warden got fed up and left, despite the fact that his family had run the hut since 1931. The area definitely needed some improvements, for example marking the trails for hikers. The first hiking trail was the ascent to the Bandlückli, Gross and Chli Lake with the descent back down to Wassen.

The West Ridge of the Salbitschijen could be reached from the hut by a grade four climb with some sections of abseiling; this meant that it was rarely done. I put a 200 meter chain in place which could be used with a harness and slings so that guests could climb the West Ridge in a day without having to bivouac. More and more parties came to climb the ridge every year – I have climbed it 52 times myself. The crags near the hut were the ideal spot to establish some short climbs, and with the help of friends and my assistant Vreni, we got to work.

The first routes were protected with bolts and nuts. The first new route was the Parallel East Ridge. My nine-year old daughter and I made the first ascent using only slings over spikes and nuts for protection. In those days, bolts still had to be drilled by hand; the development of more efficient batteries speeded up the process and made things much easier. During my second summer at the Salbit Hut, I spied a fantastic line up through the huge cliff above the grass and scree fields known as the "Gemsplanggen". During the first ascent, which I did with Mario Verin and other friends, it became clear that it offered particularly beautiful climbing. We had no idea that it would turn out to be even more popular than the South Ridge. The route was christened the Gemsplanggenstock and today, it has been joined by 14 other new routes. In 1991, many of them were re-bolted and the lines improved.

The era of "convenience" climbing had arrived. I didn't find it easy to accept at first, but then I saw which way the wind was blowing. New climbing areas were being developed all over the region and suddenly the summit was no longer the main focus; instead, the prime objective was the cliff itself, the structure or the route grade. In 1994, together with Jürg von Känel, I produced a climbing guide to the Salbit region ("Salbit erleben"). It is now in its third edition. The maintenance work paid off. Originally, there were approximately 1,000 visitors each summer and soon we reached the 2,000 mark. New routes by the Remy brothers helped sustain interest and, in addition to my work guiding groups, I was also able to put up some new routes myself. To date, this includes 24 multi-pitch routes. "Genesis" (6b+, 17 pitches) und "Salbittissima" (6b+, 16 pitches) are now regarded as must-do routes for experienced climbers.

Following two years of intensive planning, we completely renovated the hut in 1998. The outside latrine went, as did having to clean your teeth outside. Thanks to the SAC section's many volunteers, we were able to finish all the work in the course of one summer. One of our long-term aims was to be able to serve up fresh food for visiting climbers. The hut's home-made bread still proves extremely popular, and it has been serving beer for 24 years.

SAC huts have become increasingly popular with families and hikers. The possibilities for Salbit were a constant topic of discussion. I was determined to establish a trail linking the Salbit Hut to the Voralp Hut. A hunter from Uri put me onto the idea of installing a hanging bridge to cross the deep Tobel Valley, like the ones used in Nepal. After overcoming several obstacles, we were able to build the bridge in the summer of 2009 and the connecting paths were finished. This now forms part of the "Urner Alpenkranz", a wonderful hiking route with 38 joined up sections through the Urner Alps. Worries that there would be no room left at the hut for climbers have proved unfounded. At the end of the day, you will often see a mixed bag of visitors sitting in front of the hut swopping stories and enthusing about their adventures.

CLIMBING UNDER LONDON'S WESTWAY
Emil Zopfi | London/England

Mettmen can be found under London's Westway, where the alpenglow is reflected in the windows of the neighboring tower blocks and you hear the muffled roar of the traffic rushing past overhead. This doesn't bother Alan and me much. Our goal is the upper edge of the overhanging concrete wall in front of us, a meter below the grey capping roof of the dual carriageway bridge. The planners had a good idea when they decide to use this rather bizarre space underneath a West London highway junction to build a sports center. Sport is probably no bad thing for the local kids in an area which Alan says he wouldn't walk around in at night – and that's coming from someone who lived in New York for four years. Outside there are cars with smashed windows and a Volvo with missing wheels. However, the sports center makes a favorable impression. It has indoor tennis courts, football pitches and outside, concrete blocks to climb on. One of them is shaped rather like the Matterhorn, just right for a cool evening.

Back in Switzerland, Mettmen would be looking beautiful; this is the time of year when my thoughts always wander back home. I long for the huge mounds of prehistoric rock strewn around the foot of the Gandstock, as if hurled there by some mighty giant. Above the Mettmenalp, the brown slopes would now be showing the first signs of green. The remaining snows cling on the shadowy slopes, warm sun on rock, the Glärnisch towering over the valleys with its rock bands, gullies and glaciers. When we were kids, Mum and Dad would bring us to Mettmen to collect the bilberries. Each spring, the feeling returns – a subconscious longing for a childhood that was still intact. Sleeping under wool blankets, cow bells, sweat, bread, cheese and hot, sweet tea sat on the rocks. Mettmen has no sig-

nificant climbing crags worth mentioning and yet as pathetic as it may sound, they are a place I call home. My father and mother are long dead, both buried somewhere abroad. The stones have remained with me. Some day, my ashes will be scattered at the cliffs of Mettmen.

When the sun sets in West London, it turns the dull, grey concrete slightly red transforming this bleak urban world; I often find myself thinking of Mettmen and all those happy times.

"If you come to Switzerland one day," I say to Alan, "I know a wonderful place where we can go climbing together."

He looks sadly into the evening, but doesn't reply.

I turn to watch the younger climbers. One of them has a shaved head and lip and ear piercings. He's not a bad climber, maybe he'll go on to climb on real rock one day – maybe he'll even have his own Mettmen. Or maybe it's enough that he is able to feel his strength and develop a feeling for his own body. He's out of mischief and at least here he's not out breaking into cars, messing with knives or throwing beer bottles around with the other hooligans. The sports center under the highway must have cost only a fraction of the bridge itself but probably has a far more socially useful impact. Alan and I, two old men in early retirement, also make good use of it. We sit on the cool stones at the foot of the wall and silently watch the other climbers brave enough to attempt its bulges and roofs. Our muscles hurt; we're getting tired.

"You have to come to Switzerland," I say to Alan. "I know a place up in the mountains which is really beautiful; it has cliffs like this wall, only they're real."

He nods. Alan, I know that you will never come.

"In delving into bouldering, I found that it wasn't much help to me to watch the way other climbers solved a problem. Being small, with my own unique physical characteristics, I found that I often climbed completely differently from the men who surrounded me. To get up a boulder problem, I had to explore all the options and touch all the holds myself."

Lynn Hill

DOES CLIMBING
MAKE YOU BEAUTIFUL?
**Christine Kopp | Magnet,
Berne/Switzerland**

124

So you started climbing for aesthetic reasons? A "beauty through sport" kind of thing? You had the image of a climber in your head, with sculpted muscles, slim legs, a tanned face and a look in the eye that hinted at freedom and adventure? No, ladies and gentlemen, this is not the case. Climbing definitely does not make you beautiful. A brief wander around the climbing wall will suffice to demonstrate this.

The typical male sport climber has a few unmistakable physical traits. He is light, sometimes even underweight (which for women in particular is not necessarily a good thing), his legs are like dried twigs and he has the waistline of a wasp. Not attractive. Then there are the shoulders: expansive in shape, their impressive muscles continue down onto their backs. However, this kind of top-heavy musculature has a negative effect on the posture of the sport climber, who tends to walk into the gym leaning forwards – as if his eagerness to train was literally weighing him down. To be honest, he reminds us distinctly of the kind of animal from which Man is descended.

If, as in the case of some climbers, he then enters the chalk and sweat laden atmosphere of the climbing wall (it seems that the majority of climbers have not yet embraced the concept of deodorant), and reveals his naked torso, this is only ever a marginal improvement in terms of looks. And if he then ties his thinning hair into a pitiful ponytail or shakes his full mane on every dynamic move, he is walking the knife edge between looking athletic and looking ridiculous.

But even the female representatives of this sport do not get any more beautiful through intensive climbing antics. Over time, their knuckles start to bulge so much that they struggle to get their rings off before training. At some point, their wedding ring will no longer fit in any case, so it is best to keep it permanently attached to their earlobe or (very trendy amongst climbers) hang it on a chain around their neck. Women who build up too much muscle sooner or later end up looking masculine. Others, who hug the wall in fear, will end up having to banish short skirts from their wardrobes forever because of all the bruises and grazes on their knees.

Which brings us, finally, to the ultimate low point in the aesthetics of climbing physiques. Wearing tightly fitting climbing shoes for long periods is never a good thing for either men's or women's feet. Unfortunately, however, it seems that it is also fashionable for the wearers of said shoes not to look after their enslaved feet. Brittle toenails that are blue and yellow with damage and the calloused skin on their horribly stinking feet are paraded without embarrassment between routes or held under their friends' noses. Hands do not fare much better, either. Forget about manicures, girls – climbing gives you, let's call it, "crunchy" nails, rather than French nails. Susceptible cuticles are also weakened by the chalk, and one of the favorite pastimes for climbers is to then spend the evening chewing these off in front of the TV. Avoid at all costs placing your hands on the table at an elegant dinner party – it will only attract quizzical looks.

Looking like a Neanderthal, with scruffy hands and feet, thickened joints and with bruises and grazes all over? If you want to do something to enhance your physique, then go swimming in the sea, play golf or go cross-country skiing – but do not, for heaven's sake, start climbing!

THE SECRET LANGUAGE OF GRADES
Fritz Schäfer | Around the world

"Exceptional difficulties. A level of difficulty only achieved through intensive training and improved equipment. Even the best climbers need specific training on this type of rock in order to climb at this standard, which is right at the fall limit. In addition to acrobatic climbing skills, full knowledge of sophisticated protection techniques is essential." This is how, in 1979, the new UIAA grade 7 was described – at a time when it was mostly Alpine faces being climbed and sport climbing had not yet emerged. Improved training facilities at climbing walls, modern climbing gear and increased safety with bolted crags means that, today, virtually any ambitious climber can master grade 7. The world elite now operate at levels that were unimaginable 30 years ago.

The German climbing pioneer, Wolfgang Güllich, made a significant contribution to pushing the grades. Güllich put up the world's first 10+, the first 11– and, in 1991, the first full grade 11 route in the Frankenjura, "Action Directe". It was another ten years before the bar was raised again when Chris Sharma climbed "Realization" in 2001 in Céüse, France, the first 11+ (arguably Alexander Huber had already climbed at this grade in 1996 with "Open Air", if Adam Ondra's 9a+ rating is confirmed). The American is also responsible for the current highest grade of 11+/12– with his 2008 route "Jumbo Love". With current performance standards, the next step up to 12– or 12 seems a real possibility in the near future.

The grades comparison table gives an overview of the most commonly used grading systems. These days, the French grading system is used for pure sport climbing. All these systems originate from the varied climbing traditions that exist throughout the world. The American grades, for example, come from the Californian climbing Mecca of Yosemite. The prefix of 5 indicates that it is free climbing with the use of ropes and protection. The British system uses the letter 'E' to denote the serious nature of the route, followed by a number to indicate the technical difficulty of the climbing. It comes from the predominantly traditional climbing style of the Brits, where the protection is placed by the climber on the lead. The higher the E-grade, the more dangerous the route. E6 6c is the equivalent of UIAA 9, but with difficult and spaced protection, and therefore substantially bolder than a bolted grade 9 route.

Free Climbing						Bouldering	
UIAA	Saxony Sandstone	France	USA	British Trad		France	USA
1–3	I–III	1–3	5.0-5.2			Fb 1–2	
4	IV	4	5.3	VD		Fb 3	Vb–
4+			5.4	HVD			
5–	V	4+	5.5	MS			
5	VI	5a	5.6	S	4a	Fb 4a	Vb
5+	VIIa		5.7	VS	4b		
6–	VIIb	5b	5.8		4c		
6		5c	5.9	HVS	5a	Fb 4b	V0–
6+	VIIc	6a	5.10a	E1			
7–	VIIIa	6a+	5.10b		5b		
7	VIIIb	6b	5.10c	E2			
		6b+	5.10d		5c	Fb 4c	V0
7+	VIIIc	6c	5.11a	E3		Fb 5a	V1
8–	IXa	6c+	5.11b		6a	Fb 5b	V2
			5.11c			Fb 5c	V3
8	IXb	7a	5.11d	E4	6b	Fb 6a	V4
8+	IXc	7a+	5.12a			Fb 6b	
		7b					
9–	Xa	7b+	5.12b	E5		Fb 6c	V5
9	Xb	7c	5.12c		6c	Fb 7a	V6
9+	Xc	7c+	5.12d	E6		Fb 7a+	V7
		8a	5.13a			Fb 7b	V8
10–	XIa	8a+	5.13b	E7	7a	Fb 7c	V9
10	XIb	8b	5.13c	E8		Fb 7c+	V10
			5.13d			Fb 8a	V11
10+	XIc	8b+	5.14a	E9	7b	Fb 8a+	V12
		8c	5.14b			Fb 8b	V13
11–	XIIa	8c+	5.14c	E10		Fb 8b+	V14
11		9a	5.14d			Fb 8c	V15
11+		9a+	5.15a			Fb 8c+	V16
12–		9b	5.15b				

A GREENHORN IN THE MOUNTAINS
Christoph Frutiger | Around the world

"I can't climb, I am scared of heights and besides, I can't cope with the cold." That was what I thought, until one day, almost 20 years ago, Stephan Siegrist took me to Staubbach Falls as a cameraman on a film shoot. As a complete beginner, I did not have the rope between my legs whilst jumaring; instead, I struggled to haul myself up sideways. And it was only that evening that I realized that in all the excitement I had put my helmet on backwards and had worn it that way all day long. I truly was a 'greenhorn in the mountains'.

Yet, I could not get that experience out of my head. I knew for sure that I wanted to do more work on the cliffs and so one contract followed another, not only in Switzerland but in mountains all over the world. Traveling, often miles away from civilization, forges firm bonds of friendship. As soon as the cell phone signal disappears, everyone is more relaxed and peaceful, you can concentrate on your work, and suddenly, different things become important. Many friendships have resulted from years of working with Mammut athletes, friendships that have lasted to the present day.

Thanks to the expeditions and Teamtrips with Mammut, I have traveled a lot in the world and experienced other cultures and living conditions. In India, en route to the Arwa Tower, we had an amusing time at the local barber shop. In Kyrgyzstan, we learnt why the same bottle of Vodka reappeared every night, full, at base camp, and how to get heavily laden donkeys back up on their feet and moving again. At Cerro Torre base camp, Stef and I tried to develop an effective method of getting rid of the mice that were nibbling away at our supplies.

On all of these trips, I learnt a great deal. Once, many years ago, I had to wait for 24 hours at Moscow customs with my camera; I was not allowed to take it with me, because apparently, I was miss-

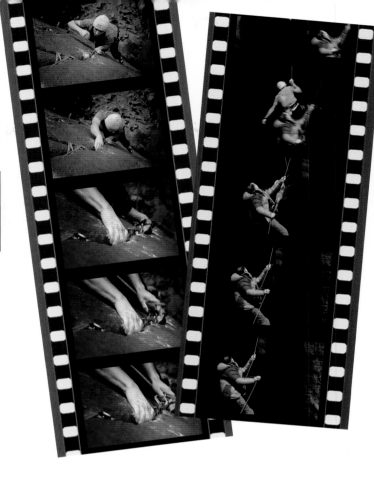

ing a stamp. When I was finally given the film equipment, it was dark and we were only able to take a couple of shots in the dark before having to fly back home. On the following occasion, I came armed with friends' addresses that were fluent in Russian and with $100 notes for bribes. But that time, nobody even looked at my passport! I made up for it soon after at the customs check on the Kyrgyzstan border, however, when I sacrificed one of David Lama's Red Bull boxes, thus ensuring that the customs official 'overlooked' the camera batteries in my luggage.

The older I get, the more I doubt whether I can still keep up in the mountains. So it gave me even greater pleasure to accompany David to the Dolomites in the summer of 2010 and film his ascent of "Bellavista" from the Cima Ovest, and to attend the Testevent shoot on the Eiger as location cameraman.

And yes, I still can't climb, not really. I have a go on straightforward routes, but only when my daughters have pre-clipped the bolts for me. My respect for the achievements of these athletes has become much greater. Meanwhile, I have honed the skill of jumaring to perfection.

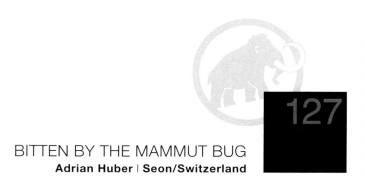

BITTEN BY THE MAMMUT BUG
Adrian Huber | Seon/Switzerland

"Never at a standstill, always on the move, climbing steeply up to the summit, new challenges around every corner." That is how Peter, Shipping and Distribution Manager at Memmingen, describes our corporate culture. John, in American Customer Services, sees it in much the same way: "There is one thing you can always count on, and it is that things will always change." In fact, Mammut's dizzying growth rate leads one to assume that, each day, there are many highly motivated people working diligently to make sure that the once lethargic beast now lives up to its dynamic reputation. Passion and motivation are endemic; work-rates are soaring, as is commitment. "If you don't pedal like a maniac, you will never win the Tour de France," says Team Leader Fabrics Apparel Daniela, with a wink of the eye.

It's a good job we are not a bicycle company and so can forget about pedaling. We are alpinists, climbing is what we do. And despite the workload, we still find time to climb. Not everybody at Mammut climbs anymore, but from warehouse workers to Team Leaders, most of us are into sports. Even during the lunch break. In the summer, jogging with colleagues in the nearby woods or playing beach volleyball at the open-air swimming pool are popular activities. Indoor sports include the legendary table tennis and table football tournaments, or yoga and 'spinning' in the multi-gym – and yes there are static bikes there, too, so we do pedal. The true Mammutees, however, spend their lunchtimes bouldering. Iris, our Product Manager Climbing Apparel, likes it best when everyone meets up on the deck chairs and bouldering mats in front of the bouldering room, where they sit in the sun, have a barbecue, listen to music and chat about sports, their private lives or even work-related topics.

Welcome to the career/hobby melting pot! Many work colleagues at Mammut have become firm friends. Even international sales meetings, where the whole Mammut family gathers twice a year, are popular events, not just to philosophize on the latest collections but also as an opportunity to get to know each other better. Bernd, our Head of Sales Germany, still raves about his first sales meeting in Berchtesgaden in 1989. Unforgettable are the many joint ski, climbing and high mountain tours with people from many different markets: like climbing partnerships that bridge national and cultural divides.

We cultivate a casual, sporty and open ethos here, the "flip-flops, baseball caps and shorts culture" as Logistics Specialist Beat likes to call it. We are forward thinking and do not practice antiquated rituals. Nobody wears a suit and tie round here. "Addressing people with the familiar German 'du' creates a relaxed working environment," says Sabrina, a Trainee in Sales Administration. Of course, we are not on first-name terms with the CEO from day one, as Pierre, our Head of Product Design found out when he was the new kid on the block. He mischievously remembers the following encounter: "In my very first week at Mammut, there was a sales meeting. It was a good opportunity to get to know the products and the people. I had met a couple of people during my interviews but most of them were new to me. In the sports trade, people tend to address each other using the familiar 'du', and this was working fine to start with. But then, in a fit of enthusiasm, I asked this one guy: 'So what do you ("du") do here at Mammut?' and the short reply was: 'C-E-O.' I stalled, and after a lengthy pause, came up

Mammut's corporate culture is based on the following:

We require a corporate culture that
1. makes us exceptional,
2. allows us to cross boundaries,
3. is characterized by openness and an interest in and understanding for our stakeholders,
4. enables us to attract the best employees,
5. accepts that mistakes happen,
6. fosters 'out-of-the-box' thinking and allows 'awkward' or bold employees to have their say,
7. sets clear guidelines,
8. has fun,
9. leads by example.

with the reply: 'A-h-a'. I had to look away and a colleague said to me: 'You're meant to address him with "Sie"!'

But whether it is the formal "Sie" or the informal "du", the team spirit is about much more than how people address each other. It is all about big communal offices, where a "can do" attitude prevails. "Anyone who wants to move things forward is encouraged. We like to step on the gas!" says Sem, Head of Innovation and Process Development. He has embraced the precept of our management that authority is not given to you, you have to go out and get it – and we'll holler you back if needs be! The same is true for Developer Apparel Sandra, who feels there are no strict boundaries in your job at Mammut, it is results that count.

This kind of attitude creates an atmosphere that is motivating. The tolerance of errors is high for those employees who get off to a roaring start and then crash-land shortly afterwards. Management also takes an innovative approach in such circumstances: mistakes are acceptable; we just have to learn from them! The CEO tells a little anecdote, which proves that this statement is true. Thirteen years ago, the "Urban Trek" messenger bags proved a complete flop. But the decision was made and he stands by it. "Mistakes can and should happen, because if you don't risk making mistakes, you will never succeed."

And we are in it to win, that is an important driving force in the workplace. "We are a team of winners. We are committed and proud to work for Mammut," says Chief Marketing Officer Michael. Every one of us wants to get things moving, and tries their best to do so. The company's success is shared equally amongst all employees. "A lot is expected from every one of us. But we reap the rewards," says Susanne, Head of Business Unit Apparel. Some of the long-standing employees look back ten years and feel that expectations were lower then. There is no doubt about it, times have changed. Things are more complex, everyone agrees. As to how to deal with such a complex business, that is where opinions differ. To start with, we thought we should reduce the complexity and consolidate things, and then we realized that it was just unrealistic. Today, we are happy with the responsible way we handle our complex business model. Nobody believes we should trim down anymore, there are too many different projects running alongside each other, the outdoor trade is too dynamic and is growing so fast. Sabine – she manages the IT applications and is greatly affected by the complexities – puts the term "complexity reduction" down as the worst expression of the year. Frank, in his role as a Purchasing Manager Apparel and Fabrics, also one of the 'affected', describes the complexity trap in the following terms: "Somehow, we are caught between performance on the one hand and crazy amounts of paperwork on the other. Our size, the range of products we offer and our demanding supply chain sometimes seem to slow us down and make us less flexible."

The place to raise matters such as these is at the "GL Brunch", a communal breakfast meeting, where the management team takes time to listen to the concerns and views of their employees. Issues are discussed like those that concern Mischa, Head of Planning and Process Development. In his view, there is more of a culture of harmony rather than of lively debate. He thinks a bit more courage to dispute things would get us further in some cases. When it comes to praise, we are not world champions either, in the opinion of another brunch attendee. We often indulge in too much self-criticism. "We do not praise our performance and achievements enough. When it does happen, however, it is of all the more value," qualifies Corina, who is in charge of Sustainability. In fact, we all have good reason to pat ourselves on the back. Mammut has an excellent image. Many of our friends and colleagues are envious of where we work and of our employers. We are deeply committed to our work, and we identify with the brand and the products. Admittedly, it is easier to feel that way than it would be if we were out selling insurance policies.

It is often difficult for all of us to fully grasp the nature of our corporate culture, particularly as it has many roots whose influences are not explicit or immediately obvious. Over the years, it has grown and become a – somewhat underrated – factor in our success, and something that is also unique. Our corporate culture is characterized by the example set by our management crew and underpinned by dedicated employees, who are proud to be part of a successful team and are prepared to go all out to achieve new heights. The employees feel like they are a part of Mammut – or as Reiner, Product and Quality Manager Mammut Alpine School, aptly puts it: "Everyone is in some way bitten by the Mammut bug."

A DANGEROUS MISSION FOR MAMMUT
Daniel Corabian | Cheile Turzii/Romania

One sunny autumn morning, we decided to go hiking in a wonderful place that is well known for its climbing, adventure sports and tourism: Cheile Turzii, the Turda Gorge. We packed our backpacks and drove to the start point. At a cross-roads, I failed to give way to another driver, who then proceeded to give chase. 30 kilometers later, we arrived at the entrance to Cheile Turzii, parked the car, and the driver who had been following us, parked up right next to us. He got out of his car fuming and immediately started to shout at me. "Who do you think you are, pulling out at a cross-roads like that? You really think you are something special, with your mammoth sticker on your car and lettering on your windscreen, don't you?"

While I apologized to him for what I had done, he looked at me and realized that I was wearing only Mammut clothing. He started to laugh and asked: "So that is what the mammoth means? A clothing label?" Here in Romania there was a campaign called "Traffic Buffalos"; the aim was to identify careless drivers. The campaign logo was similar to the Mammut one, so the driver thought that the Mammut logo was from another such campaign.

As he looked at everything I was wearing, he started to ask me what kind of equipment it was, where the factory was, etc. I had to explain what Mammut was all about and which shops stocked Mammut products. He wanted to know all about double-layer fabrics, soft shells, hard shells, ski equipment, ropes, helmets and backpacks. I told him so much about Mammut that he would not believe that I was not a Mammut dealer.

In the end, he was glad that he had followed me, decided he was going to buy a Mammut jacket at the very least and spent the whole day with us in Cheile Turzii.

The original ancestor of the Smart was the Antz belay device, developed by Wolfgang Antz in 1985. It was the first half-automatic belay device on the market and functioned well. However, its complicated handling and heavy weight meant that it could only be used by experts/specialists.

Walter Britschgi, creative maverick from the Zurich climbing wall "Gaswerk", was quick to recognize the potential of the device and built his own prototype in 2000. As evidenced by the marks and scratching, he subjected it to rigorous testing.

The Mammut research & development team took up the baton from Walter Britschgi and refined the design in 2004 and 2005 during a series of design stages. This also involved extensive testing on the drop tower and in practice.

The first version was ready in 2007 and was being prepared for release when tests showed that its shape could lead to it being used incorrectly. Mammut decided to revise the design again.

Not everything has to be high-tech. An early prototype (2007) of the present form showed that with this shape the pontential for incorrect use can be reduced to a minimum.

The Smart was launched in 2009 and received a Red Dot Design Award and the OutDoor Industry Award (Silver). It was successfully introduced onto the market and has established itself in the growing climbing community.

THE SMART HAS COME A LONG WAY
Andres Lietha | Seon/Schweiz

In Summer 2009, Mammut launched the Smart – a new type of belay device: with no moving parts, it offers considerable braking support to the point of completely blocking the rope at the least exertion by the protector. Its potential for misuse is minimal, as it is designed to respond to human reflex actions. It took years of development until its exact geometry was determined in a series of tests. The Smart has come a long way . . .

129
@

'KRAN'

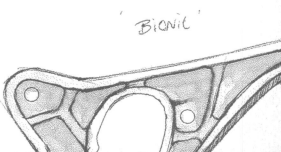

'BIONIC'

HOW NOT TO CONDUCT A GEAR TEST
Peter Habeler | Zillertal/Austria

I passed my exams to become a mountain guide in 1965 and was very active in the mountains over the years that followed, guiding in the Zillertal in Tyrol, Austria and all over the Alps. I had taken the training together with Horst Fankhauser, a friend from the neighboring village who was slightly younger than me. We pretty much grew up together; he was one of my first climbing partners on rock as well as ice. We also worked together for several years at the same ski school in Mayrhofen, Austria. From time to time, we would lead larger groups together and continued to climb lots together in our spare time, especially on more extreme routes, for example in the Laliderer Wände. We enjoyed each other's company and complemented each other well. Horst later moved to the Stubai Alps in South Tyrol, where he met Klara, the woman who was later to become his wife. Together they took over management of the Franz Senn Mountain Hut. We have remained close friends to this day and continue to share the same passion for climbing. In 2006, we climbed the Micheluzzi Route on the Piz Ciavazes in the Sella massif in the Dolomites of Northern Italy.

On one occasion, I nearly battered him to death. We were sitting in the kitchen of the Berliner Mountain Hut, the oldest and largest hut in the Zillertal Alps. It is a listed building and the start-ing point for numerous high alpine treks and mountaineering expeditions. It was late and it is quite possible that we were not completely sober. I had recently become the proud owner of a new climbing helmet. It was one of the first generation of plastic helmets and was white with black edging. I had gone by train especially to Munich, just to buy it. And I had already tested it by placing it on a piece of concrete and then hitting it with my climbing hammer. It would fly off into the air, but I never managed to break it. This was all rather very reassuring. However, I particularly enjoyed showing off my helmet to my fellow guides and asking them if they thought they could break it. Not one of them could.

That evening in the Berlin Hut, I challenged Horst. He couldn't break it either, despite placing it on the stone floor in the kitchen and hitting it as hard as he could with the hammer. Then I had an idea. I would get Horst to wear the helmet while I hit it. I wouldn't hit it too hard and he would see that it could take the shock. No sooner said than done. The hut warden came back with a pipe wrench; Horst kneeled down in front of me, as if I was going to behead him. I raised the wrench and brought it crashing down on the helmet – the helmet broke into two pieces. Horst lay sprawled on the floor and didn't move – my God, I thought, I hope I haven't killed him! Luckily, he did recover quickly, albeit with a bloody gash on his head. Fortunately, it was only a shallow wound. I decided to forego this particular type of test with my next helmet.

Until the mid-1950s, the only ropes that were available were (non-standardized) hemp ropes. As a result, climbers were understandably keen to avoid taking a fall. Things changed with the arrival of Perlon/Nylon ropes from the USA. At that point, there was no safety certification for ropes, although safety norms were being worked on in Europe. The first safety standard was introduced in 1963. It was based on the UIAA (Union Internationale des Associations d'Alpinisme/International Mountaineering and Climbing Federation, founded 1932) rope conformance requirements, which specified that a rope should be capable of withstanding two standard falls. The second fall test was required statistically to verify the result of the first!

In 1969, the UIAA introduced a safety standard for carabiners. The initial value for the breaking strength was too high and had to be subsequently lowered. Nevertheless, we now had certification standards for the two most important items of equipment. There were no harnesses at that point, helmets were available but they were not subject to conformance standards.

As the equipment improved, the UIAA standards also had to be modified accordingly. Ropes that could withstand five standard falls became available. Certification standards were increased to at least three standard falls and then five, although by this point, the ropes could withstand nine standard falls. This criterion still applies to single and double ropes today. The safety standard for twin ropes was introduced at a later point.

At length, the *Deutsches Institut für Normung* (German Institute for Standardization) decided that mountaineering equipment should also be subject to certified German safety standards. The DIN emphasized their requirements in rather drastic terms: "It is essential that mountaineering equipment is standardized. If the experts are not interested then this should be overseen by the maritime authorities in Hamburg." This threat was irritating to all parties involved: the manufacturers, the German Alpine Club and the German Technical Inspection Association, as we felt strongly that we should carry out DIN certification of mountaineering equipment ourselves.

In the meantime, new UIAA standards had been drawn up and these were then followed by the first DIN standards. The difference between them is that UIAA standards are not compulsory (they act as a recommendation for manufacturers), whereas DIN standards were compulsory in Germany. German manufacturers were obliged to comply with them; otherwise they would not be allowed to release a product onto the market.

In the mid-1990s, Euro Norms for standardized products arrived. The German DIN standards were then brought into line with the norms of the other European countries. A product rated as safe in France could not be classed as unsafe in Germany and vice versa. There were only four national standards organizations at the time: Austria, (Ö Norms), France (AFNOR Norms), England (BS Norms) and Germany (DIN Norms). Their standards were consolidated and the European EN Norm was created – on the basis of the UIAA standards. Today, EN Norms apply to all products made in Europe, and other non-European manufacturers often adhere to them, too. In fact, the EU is recognized as the international leader for safety standards and certification.

This may all sound rather confusing, but it was the only way to make the different safety standard systems uniform. Nowadays, it is impossible to think of mountaineering equipment without rigorous international safety standards. There are now a total of 19 EN Norms and 20 UIAA standards: the UIAA has one more because there is currently no EN Norm for "Dead Man" snow anchors. As the EN Norms are legally binding, the UIAA standards text refers to the EN Norms and only specifies those points that go beyond the EN Norms. This is the only way to maintain an overview. It might sound complicated – but it works!

EXPERIENCE MOUNTAIN SPORTS – EXPERIENCE MAMMUT
Dean Polic | Alps

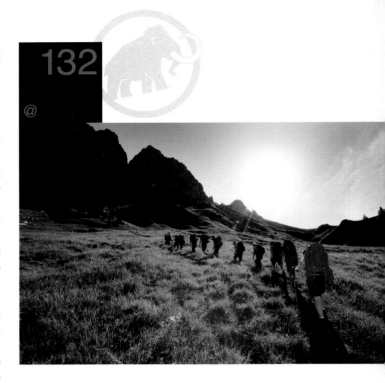

"How can we convince people that Mammut really is 'Absolute alpine', that we really mean it?" This is the question the Mammut team constantly asks itself. They live and breathe their brand philosophy; it is not just empty words. Mammut defines itself first and foremost as outfitters for adventures above the 1,000 meter mark. Naturally, the products are in keeping with this brand statement. But Mammut is also about spreading the love of mountain sports, inspiring others to get out and experience their passion. But, how do you make the qualities that are of utmost priority to Mammut – safety, innovation, reliability and commitment – tangible to the consumer? Therein lies the challenge! Strong image-led advertising campaigns, proper on-line discussions with customers, and long-term sponsoring of top athletes – these are all excellent measures. But how can Joe Public, the "normal" climber, experience the Mammut brand for himself?

The most truthful way to find out whether a mountain sports brand really means what it says, whether its products are up to the job, is quite simple – test the equipment for yourself, in the company of or with the guidance of a professional – a mountain guide. And in the environment it is made for – the mountains. Who better than a state approved mountain guide to give you an honest and comprehensive explanation of how a piece of mountain kit should work? They train long and hard, and only those who really have what it takes pass the exams. A mountain guide also knows what makes a good mountain sports product – and can pass on this knowledge to his protégés in a way that is credible and jargon-free.

Rather than kitting out an existing alpine school, Mammut opted for a different approach. In 2008, they founded the Mammut Alpine School at the headquarters of Mammut Germany in Memmingen, Allgau. And so, an idea that was born one late evening in the corner of the Gimpelhaus hut up at 1,659 meters in the Tannheimer Mountains became Mammut's own experience platform. Amongst others, it was Reiner Taglinger, Senior Product Manager at the Mammut Alpine School, himself not only an experienced mountain guide but also a mountain guide instructor, who set the wheels in motion. And they sure are turning! Just three years on and the Mammut Alpine School has already exceeded all expectations. In Austria as well as Germany, and in Mammut's home country of Switzerland, it is becoming the 'go-to' place for mountain sports enthusiasts and Mammut fans. No small feat. Many established alpine schools could view it as potential competition. Mammut's

intention, however, is much more about connecting with new target groups, to inspire more people to go out and enjoy the mountains and all that they offer. In the end, this will also benefit other alpine schools.

Safety is key at the Mammut Alpine School. Safety breeds trust – trust in the equipment as well as in one's own abilities. It is also true to say that trust is good but control is better. That is why the Mammut Alpine School undergoes a yearly safety examination carried out by an independent foundation for the safety of outdoor and mountain sports providers. The blue "S" stands for "Safety in adventures", and is a seal of quality and safety.

The programming is clear: mountain sports for all tastes, abilities and all ages – with Mammut equipment. There is something for everyone here – the competent alpinist, the climbing 'newbie' or the occasional ski tourer. The program ranges from classics like sport climbing or avalanche safety courses to breathtaking high alpine tours and mountaineering experiences and also includes a special program of family camps and pro-led photography courses. And it runs throughout the year; there is no 'bad' season for mountain sports.

Every pioneer has a vision. Reiner Taglinger's is as follows: "I hope that the Mammut Alpine School will be viewed neither as a traditional alpine school nor as a Mammut publicity stunt, but rather as an exceptional, authentic mountain sports platform that sets new standards in safety and service – throughout the world." Well, mountain guides are known for their modesty.

THE MAMMUT GERMANY EXPEDITION
Moritz Becher I Memmingen/Germany

To climb new peaks in undiscovered regions – a "first ascent" in mountaineering jargon – is the dream of every ambitious mountaineer. Venturing into uncharted territory is a fascinating challenge. The success of such an expedition depends on two key factors: perfect organization and the desire to succeed, regardless of the hardship or discomfort involved. However, the extreme alpinists making these ascents are not the only ones worthy of praise. Behind the scenes, there are often unsung heroes, who work to ensure the success of expeditions of a rather different nature. They also have to demonstrate not only amazing organizational talents, but also the endurance and willpower to see their mission right through to the end. You won't see their names in the summit logs and they don't get a mention in the mountaineering yearbooks. And yet, companies like Mammut owe much of their success to these tireless backstage heroes.

Ernst Schweble is one of these heroes. He is the first and to date the only general manager of Mammut Germany. When Mammut celebrates its 150th anniversary in 2012, he will celebrate 25 years with the company. He has been leading the Mammut expedition to Germany for all this time. The development of Mammut's first in-ternational subsidiary in Germany is inextricably linked with this colorful and charismatic character.

As a born and bred Bavarian and self-confessed fan of Munich's Schwabing district, he started his career, as you might expect, in a Munich Biergarten – the legendary "Waldwirtschaft", which he leased and ran together with a friend. It was here that another friend, Gerd Pfeffer, convinced him that he had a real talent for selling mountain equipment and clothing. Ernst Schweble started working in Gerd Pfeffer's "Kletter- und Hochtourenecke", a specialist retailer selling a selected range of high-end alpine equipment. After all, he had been up in the mountains from an early age, as his father would take him and his five brothers and sisters climbing every weekend. He was to start making a living from what he enjoyed doing most. Seven years later, in 1987, Mammut became aware of his abilities and invited him to build the brand in Germany.

Stories from the early days tell of his adventures in uncharted territory in East Germany, accompanied by his trusty Opel Omega, which served as delivery van and camper all in one. Hotels were generally the exception to the rule; the Omega doubled as base camp. Crammed full of mountaineering equipment and clothing, the East German campaign was conducted from the back of his Opel. The first coffee of the day was normally an East German "Muckefuck", a coffee substitute made from barley malt, shared on the rear bumper with a retailer. This formed an important part of his sales ritual. He arranged his appointments using the first generation of analog cellular mobile phones, a (6 kg) "C-Netz" device, a far cry from the (137 g) iPhone 4 he uses today.

Rather like a first ascent, his route to success was only possible thanks to discipline, passion and (sales) skill. Problems and setbacks only served to drive and inspire the next attempt. Today, Ernst Schweble's Opel Omega the "Omnimobile" can still be seen at Mammut Germany's headquarters in Memmingen. It serves as a reminder of the core values behind Ernst Schweble's efforts in establishing Mammut Germany: continuity, sustainability, responsibility for oneself and others, credibility, sincerity, honesty and having fun with the products.

If you've met Ernst Schweble, you can't help but like him. In the meantime, his expedition team has grown from 5 employees in 1987 to nearly 130 in 2011. Mammut Germany's success is thanks to all of them.

HOT ICE
Dani Arnold | Alps/Switzerland

We were off to Kandersteg, and not for the first time. Today's objective was to hit "Mach 3" on the Breitwangflue – a modern five pitch mixed route graded M9 and with water ice up to WI 6. On the approach, the temperature was a bit of a worry, minus 10 degrees. When it is too cold the ice becomes brittle, and climbing it all the more difficult. But we figured we would still have a crack at it.

The first pitch was short, but there was so little ice on it that I was happy to make it to the first belay. The second pitch is where it really gets going and at M8+ it is the second hardest pitch on the route. The first 15 to 20 meters were only rock, then there were a few meters on a big icicle before pure ice led to the second belay.

For me, the main difficulty with mixed climbing is summoning up the necessary levels of patience. To make sure the ice tools are secure, I find I really have to concentrate on my placements. If I've already climbed a lot of routes in a winter, I can feel exactly if my axe placement is good or bad, whether I can only weight one side

of the tool, or how to position my crampons so that they don't skate off the rock. As any climber will tell you, you have to look carefully and have patience. But another factor to consider is that the more patience you have, the more energy you need. I have to be able to support my weight on the ice tools for a good amount of time.

The higher I got, the thicker the ice was and the tension eased a little. The next two pitches were all ice. That is when I noticed just how cold it was. Experience is key: where is it best to place my tools, what is the safest line to opt for, where are the best places to get protection?

The exit was a big overhanging icicle – the crux pitch. We stood right below the overhang, and it was clear to me that I had to keep control of my nerves. That was the only way that I was going to pull it off. The tension was palpable, but I stayed calm and kept climbing, one move after another. In a situation like that, it is vital to have a reliable belayer – then and only then am I able to concentrate on the job at hand. I was getting closer and closer to the big icicle. I made it onto it alright, but just before the top, I had to be careful again. You cannot use any ice screws on a free hanging icicle, because you risk breaking the whole thing off. So I was having to climb many meters above the last piece of protection.

Above the icicle, I came across a little recess where I could rig a good belay. The feeling of joy was immense. I was the first to onsight that pitch, without knowing where the hooks were, and I had just climbed the big overhang on "Mach 3" with no falls! That kind of success does not happen every day and it would remain etched in my memory for a long time.

I have always been fascinated by the winter. I love the cold months and the snowy landscape, especially when it gets really cold. As soon as the days become shorter, I look forward to mixed climbing, which to me is one of the best sports ever. Although it was all-ice routes that first attracted me, now it is routes where you come across a bit of rock here and there, or have to negotiate a thin veneer of ice. For me, the trend of climbing rock with ice tools is just the natural progression of things. Alpinism is sure to keep evolving in this vein, because it is just not possible to climb difficult, big mountains with a pair of climbing shoes and no gloves.

135

SKIING IN THIN AIR
Mike Marolt | Around the world

When you grow up in a place like Aspen with a father who skied at the Olympic Games, you tend to appreciate the culture of skiing. For my twin brother Steve and I, being identical twins also gave us the added benefit of never having to look for people to ski with. We also had the advantage of always having a coach, someone to push each other. We competed with each other, but we also encouraged and shared each other's accomplishments.

As we grew older, our father introduced us to the thrill of skiing the high peaks around Aspen, but more importantly, he drove home the importance of respecting nature, and the magnitude, power, and extreme beauty of being in the high peaks. He stressed that being humble and paying your dues, was key in longevity which was important because skiing is something that by example he showed you could do at many levels, but more importantly, you could do your whole life, and later on, share with your family. Our bond of being twin brothers only enhanced these concepts, and along with encouragement, we both realized we had a responsibility to take care of each other, to help each other avoid the potential dangers that we knew existed in the mountains.

Together and with a handful of life-long friends, we slowly progressed the sport of our skiing to the high peaks of the world to an ultimate level. In this journey, we have spent over 20 years traveling to the world's greatest ranges. Along the way, we have learned about how many different cultures in the world live, and we have climbed and skied remote peaks where few people have thought about skiing. We have seen the incredible beauty of the natural world. To share these experiences together has been a driving force in the natural progression that has led to skiing in our favorite mountains, the 6,000, 7,000, and 8,000 meter peaks in the Andes and Himalayan ranges.

High altitude skiing forces you to rely on your partners in all aspects as it forces you to do an activity in an environment where survival in and of itself is the main objective. To climb and ski at these altitudes in the pure style we choose, without any medical aides or supplemental oxygen is daunting and difficult work. It is often nerve-racking and scary. But in the process of working as individuals in a team, and accomplishing our goals, the nature of surviving and pushing is extremely satisfying, and has created a quality of life that exists around our passion, skiing.

Tuesday, June 15, 2010: Midday departure from St. Gallen. I felt somewhat ridiculous going to the train station with backpack and skis at a time of year when most people are thinking of going swimming. Caroline was waiting for me on the platform in Zurich. We talked about the weather over and over on our long train journey to Chamonix. Most of the forecasts predicted cloud cover for the next couple of days and snow up high, but one of them said there would be a window of high pressure on the Friday morning. We put our faith in that one.

We got to the 'Office de Haute Montagne' in Chamonix just before it closed. The outlook here was also gloomy. Plus we were wearing jackets that were too fashionable for us to be taken as serious alpinists. In any case, the friendly gentleman seemed to think our plan of climbing Mont Blanc and skiing down on Friday morning was completely unrealistic. We hoped he would be proved wrong.

Wednesday, June 16, 2010: We took the first cable car up to the Aiguille du Midi. There were not many people due to the weather. We had to ditch our plans of skinning across the glacier to acclimatize because of the visibility – or lack thereof. Nevertheless, we still spent 8 hours up at 3,800 meters and even climbed up to the viewing terrace, where we could not see a thing but were photographed by a bunch of enthusiastic Japanese tourists. At least someone thought we were alpinists . . .

We went to the middle station in the afternoon and booted up to the Plan de l'Aiguille Refuge. We were the only guests and were given an amazing dinner with raspberry tart for dessert, only to be woken up by a crack of lightening in the night. There was no electricity in the morning – we had to wee sparingly, as the water pump for the toilet was out of action.

Thursday, June 17, 2010: We met Thomas, the hut warden, and joined him for the climb up to the Grands Mulets hut. He had come down earlier in the week because there were no guests. "Are you sure you want to go up there?" he asked us, given how wet snow was now falling. Yes, we were sure. We whiled away the laborious scramble across the moraine by talking about the football World Cup; after all, Switzerland had just beaten Spain the previous day!

ABOVE US ONLY SKY
Karin Steinbach Tarnutzer | Mont Blanc/France

Nobody talked any more as we crossed the maze of crevasses on the Bossons Glacier. We were glad when we finally made it up the rock face secured with chains and arrived at the hut. That afternoon Dani and Thomas emerged from the dense cloud and our group was complete. But the weather was still looking bad, making it hard to believe in that window of high pressure.

Friday, June 18, 2010: Rising at 1 A.M., it was black outside. I was on auto-pilot, not thinking, like a machine. We set off. By 2 A.M., we were back at the glacier. And then suddenly, two bright spots appeared in the sky. A little while later, there were ten of them, then more and more appeared until the sky above us was a twinkling blanket of stars. The clouds now lay below us, diffusing the lights from Chamonix town. We zigzagged our way up the north ridge of the Dôme du Goûter, which was so steep in some places that we had to take off our skis and use crampons. As dawn broke, we were already higher than many of the summits, with their peaks poking through the clouds.

We took a break and deposited our skis at the Vallot hut, then tramped the last 450 meters up the Bosses Ridge. At 11 A.M., Dani and I were standing on top of the highest mountain in the Alps, tired but happy. So that is what it feels like to be on top of the world! And it was all the more beautiful because for a while it had looked like we weren't going to make it! As we got back to Chamonix, exhausted after a long ski down, a tiring traverse to the middle station and a ride back down in the cable car, we felt the first little drops of rain.

ON LOCATION WITH THEODOR WUNDT ON THE KLEINE ZINNE, IN 1893
Jeanne Immink | Dolomites/Italy

Thank God, it is nighttime! Helios has finally moved on with his chariot of sun and that fearful object had lost some of its strength. You'll be surprised when I tell you that, yes, I am actually referring to my traveling companion's infernal photographic apparatus. I had stupidly agreed to place myself in his hands and climb a mountain with him. And what did it turn out to be? Twelve hours of uninterrupted photography! My limbs are still absolutely worn out from all the dreadful positions I had to hold. What are the Alps to him, even the world for that matter, other than one big photographic studio, an experimental workshop, where patience levels are tested, right to their limits? And all those affectations! "Right, now smile for the camera," when you are hanging there on the rock like a bird on the wing. And again "Nice smile!"

It was my first route of the year. I had already climbed the Kleine Zinne once before, but it was no walk in the park. We had a leisurely stroll to the big ledge with Wundt trailing slowly behind. Up to that point he had been quite sensible. He had not struck me as unusual in any way. But suddenly, he was afflicted with a peculiar kind of agitation. He could no longer contain himself and stormed ahead without a word. What was he planning to do? Nothing reckless I hoped. This was not the place for messing around.

Then, just as I was negotiating a narrow section, the most treacherous so far, where the rock bulged out above me and fell away abruptly into the void below, I heard him shout "stop!". What was this all about? There he was, pressed up against the vertical wall, wanting to take a photograph. My God, you should have seen it! The ledge on which he stood was barely a foot's width, and although he was not in a much better position himself, the good man Giovanni was giving his all to keep tight hold of him. But that did not seem to bother Wundt. In an instant, he had set up his tripod and flung a black cloth over his head. "A little higher with your left hand please. A bit more, ok – and put your left foot forward a touch, good." All of this in a commandeering tone, as if I was able to move any way I wanted on terrain as steep and rocky as this.

Oh, the twists and turns he performed so as not to shake his camera or – heaven forbid – let it drop! High above on a block of rock hung his satchel containing the plates, here on the small ledge stood the camera with Wundt behind it – I have no idea how he made himself so thin – and good old Giovanni trying to make a bit of space for himself as well. It was so dangerous; an accident waiting to happen. But instead, Wundt started saying, "Pay attention! Now, please, look happily at the drop below!" Yes, he made me do that, too. I actually laughed out loud, it was so ridiculous. But at least he had now finished and had even survived the process. I was free once again.

My celebrations were a little premature, however, for no sooner had I taken a few more steps than I heard his "stop!" coming from above again and once more I was forced to pose in the most God-awful positions: hand further up, foot further back and "keep smiling". And so it continued, without a break.

When we finally made it to the top of the tower, Wundt left us and descended to the southern summit with Mansueto Barbaria, while the rest of us carried on up to the alcove. Just watching him scramble about in daredevil fashion to get the right shot was painful in itself. Huge chunks broke away from the brittle rock, tumbling ominously into the abyss. Mansueto was close to despair, but he was now more than a hundred yards away so at least we were out of his reach, or so we thought. How wrong we were. He was only just getting started.

Several more photographs followed in the alcove, but when we tried to negotiate the chimney to get to the summit, that merciless "stop!" sounded yet again. It was not the right time apparently. The light was all wrong. So we climbed up and then down, and there he was again – like an insatiable beast! I almost came a cropper at one stage. Precisely at the most difficult spot, I was told I was getting it all wrong. My right foot had to be further sideways on, further, further. Suddenly, the entire block I was standing on just broke away and crashed down into the void. I was airborne. I came to a stop with a sharp jolt, as Pietro grabbed tight hold of the rope . . . and the photography could begin again. Then he came over towards the alcove, stopping to place his camera here and there, up, down, left, right, in the most impossible positions!

But I am becoming a bore. The process continued in this way, all day long. He took 26 pictures in total. Never again will I have my picture taken – ever!

TEACHING PICTURES TO FLY
Dionys Frei | Peak District/England

April 2010. Six Mammut Pro Team athletes came to Sheffield to climb on British gritstone and the Dedicam went with them. Christoph Frutiger wanted to bring a new perspective to the film of the team's trip and invited Davide and me to come and take shots with our "flying camera". This came as a welcome opportunity for us to expand the scope of our Dedicam and proved a learning experience and, above all, an inspiring cooperation.

The Dedicam was born in 2003 as a rather vague notion. I wondered whether it was possible to attach a camera to a model helicopter to take aerial photographs. I got straight down to business. I went out and came back with a large cardboard box that said "T-Rex 450" and had a nice photo of a helicopter on it.

The instructions said that this is exactly what my model would look like after 60 minutes of putting it together. And so it did, although I admit this was only several hours later... A beautiful model helicopter was now sitting on my desk! All I had to do was learn how to fly it.

Shortly afterwards, I stood clutching my T-Rex 450 on an area of open ground. I had no idea how to fly it, but was confident that my enthusiasm would be more than enough to overcome any problems. Maybe I was just a touch over-hasty. They say that "what goes up must come down" ... my helicopter certainly did and was soon lying sprawled at my feet with its individual parts scattered all over the ground. It took me a while to become a reasonable pilot. With practise, I gradually learned how to keep the little devil in the air and with each flight hour my skills improved.

The weeks flew by. Alongside my work running a cinema, I studied the theory and technique of model helicopter flying. I also be-

came more and more fascinated by the idea of aerial photography. Two years later, in 2005, I finally plucked up the courage (quite possibly after one or two beers too many) to attach my camera to the helicopter. It actually worked!

The first shots were a rather wobbly aerial view of a field and weren't particularly clear. Nevertheless, it still counted as aerial photography and was the direct result of a lot of enthusiasm and commitment. This really fired my enthusiasm and made me even more motivated. I spent weekend after weekend and countless evenings perfecting my technique. Flying became easier, the helicopters got bigger and the quality of the pictures improved. My first small projects had me almost bursting with pride.

February 2009, a few years down the line, several projects and a couple more grey hairs later, it was time for a new challenge. The location: Sörenberg, Switzerland. The project: a ski and snowboard film. During shooting, cameraman Davide Tiraboschi came by

somewhat wide-eyed and fell promptly in love with my helicopter and the idea of aerial photography. Up until that point, I had been a one-man business without even a company name. Things were about to change.

A week later found me back on the practice field. This time though, I had a new friend and double enthusiasm, double ambition and double drive. There was also a new camera suspension frame, designed by Davide. The first shots we took that day were pretty good. The next ones were even better. We spent long evenings editing – there was always something to improve – and many hours practicing. We came up with new ideas, tested them out, went back and improved them and then took on more and more assignments. Davide and I now both dedicate 120 percent of our working life to aerial photography. We are both equally passionate about getting the perfect aerial shot.

The Mammut Teamtrip to the Peak District presented us with a new challenge: the helicopter needed to fly slowly enough to film the climbers moving. A drone has many advantages over a camera crane. Cranes can generally only film up to about 15 meters off the ground, whereas a drone can fly much higher, has natural movement and can fly over rough terrain.

We've tested our drones at up to 4,000 m on the Jungfraujoch. The pilot is able to control the drone within a circular range of 150 meters. It takes two people to operate the whole system: the pilot flies the radio-controlled helicopter and the cameraman controls the steadicam – the pictures are transmitted directly to his video glasses.

Using this technique, we were able to get fantastic, authentic footage of climbing on gritstone. Our dreams of being able to teach pictures to fly have come true.

THE HAUTE ROUTE – IN THE HEART OF THE ALPS
Caroline Fink | Valais/Switzerland

It was 5 A.M. in the Valais village of Bourg-St-Pierre. We trotted past the closed village store, past street lamps that were still glowing in the pale morning light. Our poles scratched along the asphalt, our touring skis swayed on our backpacks. It was drizzling and there was a dreary atmosphere hanging over the Val d'Entremont. Of this we were blissfully unaware, however, because we were on a mission to fulfill a dream: the Haute Route. This, the king of ski tours, would take us five days to complete. It runs straight through the mountains of Valais, right in the heart of the main Alpine chain, where shimmering blue ice fields flow over the mountain slopes, where the storms of the central Alps brew.

The fact that this part of the Alps is less predictable than other areas was demonstrated to us on our first night at the Valsorey hut. According to the weather forecast, there should have been stars twinkling in the skies above us. Instead, thick swirls of cloud engulfed the hut like cotton wool – not the kind of weather for setting off the following morning and heading up the steep crux section of the tour to reach the Plateau du Couloir. We sat in the wood paneled room drinking verbena tea, looking out the window – and waited. Waiting with us were ski mountaineers from all over the world, who also shared our dream. English, Americans, Japanese.

The winter traverse of the Alps on touring skis has captured the imagination of alpinists since 1903. It was already referred to as the "Haute Route" back then, and it was the French doctor Michel Pay-

ot, together with several mountain guides, who accomplished the first ski traverse from Chamonix to Zermatt, although bad weather meant that it was done in stages. In the years that followed, various alternative routes were opened up. It was several years before the route currently regarded as the most spectacular, the 'classic' route was established. It was only in January 1911 that the Neuchâtel ski touring pioneer Marcel Kurz and the historian François Frédéric Roget from Geneva, together with four guides, successfully completed the "Haute Route" via the steep passage up to the Plateau du Couloir and then over the Col du Sonadon to the Chanrion hut.

One hundred years on, and we were following in the footsteps of Kurz and Roget. Fastening our crampons securely and strapping our touring skis to our backpacks, we had that same white slope above us that the pioneers had faced back in 1911: the steep crux section, at the upper end of which lay the Plateau du Couloir. Step by step, we climbed higher, and with every step, more space opened up below us. Increasingly focused, we hammered our ice axes into the snow, hundreds of times, thousands of times, until we finally burrowed our way through a cornice and stood on the plateau, laughing, patting each other on the back, the crux of the route now behind us.

Barely an hour later, the wind was whipping ice crystals through the air, hammering at our cheeks and erasing our footsteps in the snow. The Col du Sonadon disappeared in the whiteout, vanishing in one of those infamous storms that can suddenly occur in the cen-

tral chain of the Alps, thundering up and over the peaks as if the Earth had just been formed yesterday. Up on the pass, the storm tugged at our jackets, carried our words away, tried to rip the skins out of our hands. And as we skied down the Mont Durand glacier, the mighty séracs lay hidden next to us like sleeping dragons in the white inferno. We felt small and fragile, like snowflakes in the wind. The first time we realized we were not alone in the world was when we suddenly came out from under the clouds, leaving the storm hanging above us like a grey cloak. On the other side of the valley, we could see a grey dot, the Chanrion hut, and not far in front of us, the English and Japanese. We waved with our poles. They waved back.

The following day, the Otemma Glacier lay peacefully ahead of us; a sea of powder snow, wide and white, as if a row of mountains had gone missing. Its tongue is 8 kilometers long, and we let our touring skis glide straight ahead – no kick turns, no downhill sections, not even a change in direction, just the hissing zip-zip of the skins gripping uphill in the powder snow. Hours went by. Here and there, we would look at the sea of white in front of us. Zip-zip. Then we would look at the summits that bordered it. Zip-zip. "Rösti with a fried egg would be nice," said one of our group of four. Zip-zip. "Are those the tracks of the Japanese over there?" asked another. Zip-zip. "Maybe it's the English," replied the third. The inner alpine Otemma Glacier is beautiful. But we only really appreciated it once

we had arrived at the Vignettes hut at 3 P.M., and, having toasted the English and Japanese seated at the next table, placed an order for four röstis with a fried egg on top.

On the last day, there were 1,300 meters of height difference, 33 kilometers and three glacier passes between us and our final goal, Zermatt. This is known as the "King's Stage" in the guide book. And soon we could see why. Every now and then, the 4,000 meter high pyramids of the Dent Blanche and Dent d'Hérens would appear in between the clouds as we glided past glistening white snow peaks and rock towers, turned through the powder snow in wide basins and discovered hanging glaciers like blue glass perched above us in the rock. It was as if we were gliding through an ocean, where rocky ridges rose up above waves made of snow and ice, as far as the eye could see. And suddenly we felt as if we were a part of the Haute Route, a part of the pioneering spirit of those first ski tourers, a part of the Alps, a part of their soul that is made of rock and ice, wind and snow.

Shortly after midday, all of us – the Japanese, Americans, English and us – were standing on the 3,557 meter high Col de Valpelline. Zermatt lay below us, the Matterhorn within striking distance. Once again, there were lots of pats on the back and "congratulations!" and we all posed for the obligatory summit shots on the pass. Then it was time to snap shut our touring bindings one last time on the Haute Route and weave our way down to the valley.

THE DARK SIDE OF THE MOUNTAINS
Robert Steiner | Grandes Jorasses/France

The German writer and alpinist Robert Steiner fell during an attempt on the Colton/McIntyre Route on the North Face of the Grandes Jorasses in January 1997 just below the summit. He was badly injured. He remained alone on the face, while his three friends climbed on to raise the alarm. He spent two days hanging from a rope with several broken bones, suffering from frostbite. His life hung in the balance until he was rescued. He has started climbing again and says that he is now making the most of his second life.

Sunday, January 26, 1997
"Suddenly the thought shot through my mind. Damn. The belay. There is no gear between me and the belay. I'm going to die. We are all going to die. I fall backwards into the void. The heavens are filled with our screams."

"As the glow from our emergency distress flare fades, it goes quiet once again. None of us speaks."

"I watch the moonlight for a long time and the pain seems to have faded. Then I pull my balaclava up over my nose, my hat down over my eyes and press my face against the inside of the sleeping bag once again. Time seems to be frozen. Time. The minute hand on my watch seems to move like sap oozing from a tree; as if pain and desperation were staunching the flow of time."

Monday, January 27, 1997
"The morning sky is filled with white cirrus clouds that hang over me like a pale white shroud. The sight of it makes my spirits sink; it used to fill me with a sense of freedom and infiniteness."

"In the twilight, I peer out of my bivouac sack again. I'm here on my own. Trussed up like a corpse. The mountain is dark and ugly. The Whymper Spur falls away hideously into an icy defile. I can feel the bile rising in my throat. All I can see is rock and snow, snow and rock, rock and snow ... What is this mountain? How could I possibly have considered it to be beautiful?"

Tuesday, January 28, 1997
"Tuesday morning. The pale sky is filled with silent, dancing snowflakes."

"Will I be able to hang on? Am I going to die?"

"Nothing but the wind, the mist and the falling snow; and then there is a noise, a thudding and throbbing accompanied by a high pitched whine, which could only come from a helicopter."

June 1998
"I see the mountains differently these days. I no longer project my dreams upon them in the way that I used to. I used to hold them up as the pure, untouched realm, the home of the last great adventures on this planet. They were dignified and majestic. I saw mountaineers as a superior group of people, whose experience of nature made them finer and more genuine. I saw mountaineering as a catharsis for the dull and brooding entanglements of everyday life with its deception and blows of fate that ambush you and cannot be escaped. I now see everything differently. The mountains are beautiful, but they are also just heaps of rubble. They can be unfair, brutal and ugly. They can suddenly cut you short in the prime of your life."

" Living for the moment, for nothing but the present, brings with it an unexpected bonus. It seems to me that if you can escape from the need to know the future (...) then you achieve absolute freedom. **"**

141 Joe Simpson

By the 1980s, Mammut had an established international reputation for the pioneering innovation and outstanding quality of its climbing ropes. However, it had no clothing of its own and instead distributed products by other brands such as Salewa, Millet or Anoralp. This changed in 1984, when Mammut introduced a small range of "Mammut Clothing" including fleece jackets and pants for climbing and ski-touring. As the mountain sports department only consisted of my boss, myself as product manager, two sales representatives and two administrative staff, the development of functional clothing for the mountains had to be a step-by-step process.

The breakthrough came in 1987 with the launch of a new type of alpine pants. Up until then, most pants were either knickerbockers or full-length pants made of heavy wool. Climbers, who wanted trousers that enabled greater freedom of movement, preferred so-called 'Manchester pants' made of corduroy. During the rise of sport climbing, white, baggy-cut painters' pants were worn by the new generation of young climbers. They had the drawbacks of being rather stiff, not particularly durable, and once wet, they took a long time to dry.

As is so often the case, the development of a new type of more functional climbing trousers was the result of team work. As with a mosaic, when all the parties involved have added enough pieces, the end result starts to take shape. In our case, it all started with a young and innovative man from Martigny, who ran a sports shop and had a small company that made its own clothing. He approached us to ask if we would be interested in distributing his full-stretch pants. We recognized the potential in the idea and developed it further. In my youth, I was a passionate climber and mountaineer – known for his modest attire and tendency towards perfectionism (basically, I was always adapting my clothes to im-

Albert Wenk

prove them). Before I joined Mammut, my mother-in-law had reworked a pair of stretch ski trousers to make me a pair of knickerbockers. They were so comfortable and practical that I immediately decided to begin working on the idea myself.

We looked for a fabric that would meet the requirements of both climbers and mountaineers. It needed to be light, comfortable to wear, stretchy, fast-drying, robust, windproof and, above all, it had to be breathable. During tests, we discovered that only one manufacturer was capable of making such a fabric and that was Schoeller. I had some interesting experiences while testing other fabrics. In one case, after a day's climbing, my pants were ten centimeters longer than when I had started – the fabric didn't contain enough Lycra. Other fabrics tended to pilling. Our pants were successful because they were full-length and had a simple, functional fit. For example, the leg cuff was made with one sewn-in elasticated band, so that the trousers could easily be shortened if required. This solution elegantly bypassed the various discussions circulating at the time regarding optimal pant length.

We started out with three models: "Calanques" for climbers, simple full-length pants with elasticated cuffs, our "Chamonix" pants for mountaineers, where we used the same design but reinforced the seat and knee sections, and knee-length pants with suspenders. One year later, we followed these up with the "Silvretta" ski touring pants, which were made using a sandwich construction that combined the same face fabric as the "Chamonix" with an additional layer of insulating lining. The face fabric was partly given a special coating, but it proved to be too warm – our "Chamonix" pants combined with long thermal leggings from our underwear range proved a more functional solution. The knee-length model was less successful; the full-length designs were more practical and also more fashionable.

In the Mammut catalogue, we described our "free climbing pants" as "highly functional sportswear" and praised their robustness. "These pants will last longer than at least three pairs of tracksuit bottoms worn for the same purpose." Traditionalists sniffed at the idea of fully-synthetic pants. However, we in product development had done our homework and were convinced that our pants would sell. Wearers' experiences using our pants confirmed our approach and helped win over the critics.

Our detailed understanding of market demands and consistently meeting these requirements led to the breakthrough of Soft Shell pants. The Mammut brand name in conjunction with widespread recognition of the outstanding quality of Mammut ropes was undoubtedly an important contributory factor. A no-name manufacturer with the same product would probably not have been as successful. Nowadays, Soft Shell pants are one of the essential items of outdoor equipment. Most mountaineers prefer them. Over the last twenty-five years, there has been intensive investment in their continuing development. "Coldblack" is a good example of this. On early mornings up in the mountains, you are generally glad that the sun warms up your legs. By midday though, the heat starts to become unwelcome. Thanks to "coldblack" technology, the sun's rays are reflected so that the pants only heat up to around 40 degrees, instead of 80 to 90 degrees as was the case with earlier fabrics. This guarantees that mountaineers are provided with maximum wear comfort throughout an entire day in the Alps without getting heatstroke. We've come a long way since the humble knickerbocker.

I see huge chunks tumbling towards me.
There is a crackle and rumble.
An avalanche!!
I bunch up into a tiny ball, so that I am at least more compact and
the avalanche will not tear me apart when it hits me.
I whimper and cry bitter tears for fear.
I am so alone.
So alone.
So long, everyone!

I am shaken
By a strong blast of wind,
A large, man-sized chunk is coming towards me,
I am hit a heavy blow
At incredible speed.
It hurls me up into the air.
Everything is spinning.
I can't stay compact any more.
I am being torn apart.
It feels like I am being cut into pieces.
My arms and legs and my head seem so far away from each other.
The sound of ripping is all around.
I can hear it cracking, tearing, bursting, thundering.

Help, no, I do not want to die,
No. Not in this way!
No! No! No!
Everything is spinning out of control.
It is dark.
And suddenly I feel nothing.

What is splashing like that?
Am I under a waterfall?
Oh, I get it; I am in the thermal spa with my head under the jet.
But it's a bit fierce now. I think I'll go out for a bit.
But I can't.
Where am I?
Where was I?
Am I dreaming?
I have a think.
Have I not just been caught in an avalanche?
Me in an avalanche?
And that stuff that is pouring down on me so hard is the avalan-
che?
Am I now buried under an avalanche?
This is extremely serious.
I have to take action now!
I scream: help, help, help!!!
I cannot hear my own voice, the avalanche is so loud.

I AM UNDER HERE
Monika Leuthold I Oberalppass/Switzerland

143

On March 16, 2006, Monika Leuthold was hit by an avalanche while ski touring in the Oberalp region. Since she was not wearing an avalanche transceiver, the chances of rescuing her were very slim. The fact that she was dug out alive after almost one and a half hours is down to two lucky occurrences: one of her ski poles was deposited on top of the avalanche debris, and nearby one of the rescue team happened to find her ski boot as he was poking around in the snow. After a long period of convalescence, she resumed her life and is now thankful for her near-death experience in the avalanche, which took away her fear of dying.

OK, first I have to make space around my head, so that I have air to breath and do not suffocate. I want to use my arms and hands but I cannot move them. Where are my arms? I do not have the faintest idea where they are. So, first the right arm. I cannot feel it. The left arm. Again, nothing. Are my arms still attached to my body? I want to raise hands to my face. I cannot feel them. I do not even know whether I still have gloves on or not. I do not know whether my poles are still attached or not. It is as if I was in cement.

Am I still alive?
I want to open my eyes but there is not enough space for that. I manage to open my right eye a tiny bit but then cannot close it. It is black all around me.
Can I move my legs? My feet? – No.
I would like to move in some way. Nothing happens.
It is like I am cemented in.
I get terribly scared.
I am going to be buried alive.
I am dying.
It gets tighter and tighter.

I exhale loudly. Or rather, I am being forced to exhale. Something is pushing the air out of my lungs. There is not much air to come out but little by little it comes. I can feel immense pressure on my chest; it is as if I were being wrung out in a mechanical press.
I have to save oxygen and breathe lightly, otherwise I will suffocate.

All of a sudden, I am reminded of Jesus on the cross. I sob:
oh, God . . .
oh, God . . .
oh, God . . .
Why have you forsaken me?

I scream. I am so lonely.
I scream uncontrollably, just like I did in birthing.
So, I am dying.
For once I do not care that I have no control of myself and my feelings.
I am so incredibly lonely.
And forsaken.
It is getting tighter and tighter.
I am being suffocated.
I know for sure I am going to suffocate.

I am losing air.
I am losing strength.
I cannot fight any more.
I am lost.
This is the end for me.
This is my death.

A LIFE OF BALANCE
Heinz Zak | Yosemite/USA

Our house in Scharnitz is decorated with slacklines. There's a "homeline" in the living room, another one in the garden strung between two wooden posts and two that lead from the roof of the house into the woods. Not a day goes by without me walking one of them. As I step up onto the line, it is a special time, a time just for me. Slacklining has many aspects to it: I can simply switch off from the day's chores and clear my head, it can be all about fun and games with friends, a challenge and a goal, conquering fear and pushing the limits, a lifestyle statement and a philosophy. Each line provides unimaginable variety. Everyone can discover their own particular preference and learn to love it. For me, the one constant with slacklines is the feeling of having done something that is good for me. I feel relaxed, happy, at peace; sometimes I also feel physically tired, and my head is empty – it is all good!

Ever since I can remember, I have been fascinated by figuring out and playing with balance. As a small boy, I used to balance on fences and railings – it was just exciting to see how far I could get on skinny wooden planks or metal edges. In 1979, when I went on my first climbing trip to the USA and saw people "chain walking" in Yosemite, it was like a gift for me. The chain gave the balancing act a concrete structure and a real purpose as training for climbing.

I am sure that balancing on ropes is as old a practice as the very first rope itself! Thousands of years ago, it was developed into an art form of sorts. In Roman times, there was even a precise distinction between the "funamboli" (those who balanced on static ropes) and the "neurobatae", who balanced on thin catgut strings and were therefore amongst the many forefathers of today's slackliners. In the 19th century, tightrope walkers came on the scene. In 1859,

Jean-François Gravelet (stage name: "Blondin") crossed the Niagara Falls on a tightrope. Many years later, Philippe Petit attracted a lot of attention with his illegal balancing act on a 60 meter steel cable strung between the twin towers of the World Trade Center on August 7, 1974.

By definition, however, a slackline has nothing to do with a tightrope. Slacklining, as we know it, started out in the climbing scene of Yosemite, California in the 1980s. Renowned valley climber, Chuck Pratt, had already experimented with balancing and juggling on a chain in the early 1970s. Local climbers then adopted chain walking as part of their training routine. Rockstar Ron Kauk explained: "You had to do your 100 pull-ups a day, and you also had to balance on the flat chain." The chain he refers to was around 6 meters long and set up at the training camp on the edge of Camp IV. Many climbers became infected by the balance virus and have balanced on chains or ropes ever since. From fall 1979, I even had a chain rigged in my garden and would try my hand at balancing on climbing ropes.

Climber Adam Grosowsky had watched Ron Kauk on the chain. When he got home, he tried it on a climbing rope but it kept spinning him off. He happened to have a few meters of 'Supertape' handy and tried doing it on that. And thus slacklining was born! Grosowsky and his friend Jeff Ellington called their line a "slackwire" (like those of the circus artists) and introduced it to Yosemite. In 1983, Jeff Ellington tried walking a highline on the Lost Arrow Spire. When one of the rotten bolts ripped out on one of his first attempts, he had enough. Chuck Tucker, aka "Chongo", developed

an incredibly smooth and flowing style on the line. Meanwhile, Scott Balcom and Chris Carpenter pursued the idea of a highline. By fall 1983, together with Rob Slater, they rigged up a practice highline on a bridge in Pasadena, near Los Angeles.

On July 13, Scott Balcom pulled off the first walk of the still legendary Lost Arrow Spire highline. In 1995, Darrin Carter was the first to make a solo repeat of the highline. In the mid-1990s, a charismatic climber appeared on the Yosemite scene, who was also an incredible slackliner and spread the slacklining word – Dean Potter. He also inspired me. Slacklining moved quickly from being a totally marginal sport to the fun focus of rest days and chilled-out post-climb evenings.

In 1999, I was on Lost Arrow with Dean Potter to photograph him on his first walk. I slipped across the line and looked down. I shuddered to think about it – no way. But I could not get the idea of highlining out of my head. In 2001, I rigged my first spans above Zirl in the Karwendel Mountains. In 2002, I rigged and walked the first lines in the Dolomites, and in 2003, I returned to the Lost Arrow Spire with Dean Potter. Dean walked the line, unleashed. After battling the fear and thanks largely to encouragement from Dean, who sat next to me and really fired me up, I sent it and became the first European to walk the line across that terror-inducing drop.

The slackline parties at Camp IV got bigger and bigger and evermore talented people would turn up. Inspired by the positive energy, I decided to organize the first international slacklining event in my home town of Scharnitz, Tyrol, in the summer of 2006. I made sure that slacklining icon Chongo got his first passport and hauled him over to Europe for three months – he was living in Sacramento under a bridge at the time. Over 250 enthusiastic slackliners from all over Europe attended the event. Sascha, the Russian, enthralled people with his dance-like performance, Chongo was Chongo and everyone experienced what will eternally be seen as the Woodstock of slacklining, endless slacklining in a relaxed, party atmosphere, without any competitiveness. A unique kind of magic pervaded the event, and it heralded a new beginning. In terms of performance, it also provided a big impetus and the chance to share ideas and techniques. Many attempted their first somersault, and I managed to walk the first ever 100 meter longline.

In my opinion, two factors contributed to the boom in slacklining that followed. Bernhard Friedrich from Graz launched the first slacklining Internet forum, slackline.at, which gave our slacklining community a place to exchange ideas and make social contacts. The second reason slacklining took off was that Tom Strobl, in collaboration with the Jürgen Peter ropeworks and me, produced the first commercially available slackline set. Suddenly, our sport was accessible to a broad sector of the population. The media were eager to get the scoop on this unusual and spectacular sport and, in next to no time, there was an incredible development in slacklining styles and a real explosion in performance. Just as Damian Cooksey's front somersault at the 2007 event in Scharnitz was world-class, jumplining today, with Andy Lewis as the driving force, is experiencing an incredible surge in popularity. For the young jumplining generation, performing a somersault is virtually the norm, and Tyrolean Michi Aschaber has now pulled off the first front and back somersault combo.

PEPPERMINTS AND OTHER ESSENTIAL ALPINE EQUIPMENT
Martin Achrainer | Alps

In 1699, Johann Jakob Scheuchzer, a Zurich doctor and naturalist asked, "what kind of equipment would make it easier for the inhabitants of the Alps to travel over the rocks and mountains?" In 2007, the historian and ethnologist Martin Scharfe took up the question in his book "Berg-Sucht" and provided an answer for the period up to the middle of the 19th century. This was also when the oldest alpine associations were formed, including the (British) Alpine Club (1857/58), the Austrian Alpine Club (1862), the Swiss Alpine Club (1863) and the German Alpine Club (1869). Scharfe wrote: "He who is familiar, if only from a distance, with everyday life in the pre-industrial setting of the Alps, and, in particular, with the world of work, will recognize immediately that none of these items of equipment, which have been deployed from the earliest days of mountaineering on the most daring of ascents, needed to be invented or adapted for the bourgeois tourist and his new objectives. They already existed as part of the cultural heritage of the Alps – like a treasure chest waiting to be opened."

Most mountaineers were members of alpine associations, which led to increasing professionalism. They exchanged tips and suggestions and equipment was invented and improved to make climbing easier and safer. In 1863, during the first year of its existence, the Austrian Alpine Club published an article in its journal entitled "Zur Equipirung auf Alpenreisen" (Equipment for journeys in the Alps). "Due to the diverse nature of individual habits and requirements, it is not feasible to give general recommendations regarding equipment. However, we are of the opinion that we do all

travelers a service by issuing the following advice." The author recommended "woolen (flannel) shirts as worn almost exclusively by English tourists" as "prophylactic protection against the cold." For footwear, he recommended the "laced boots made by London shoemakers for members of the Alpine Club", which were also available in Vienna. They were the "most elegant and robust type of boot available." Shoemakers in the Alps did make "excellent mountain boots for woodcutters and hunters," however they were not suitable for "the more delicate feet of lowlanders and townsfolk." As well as advice on the correct choice of socks, the author recommended cold tea, Dover's powder (a traditional medicine against cold and fever), glycerin oil against sunburn and smoked glass goggles to protect the eyes.

No mention was made of ropes, ice axes or other equipment, as these remained the responsibility of the mountain guide and were not matters that the "gentleman tourist" needed to consider. As Martin Scharfe points out, they would not have been of much use to the "tourists", since it was the guides' "expertise gained from years of practice and tough training from an early age, which saw visitors safely to the summit and back." However, as tourists started to travel without guides – a fiercely debated topic in the alpine associations until the turn of the century – their packing lists started to get longer and more elaborate. Nineteenth century equipment lists strongly reflect the bourgeois needs and desires of the time, as well as mountaineering requirements. The journals of the various alpine associations were full of discussions, recommendations for individual products and general advice.

In 1844, the German and Austrian Alpine Club, which was disbanded in 1938, published the following list of essential equipment for high-alpine tours. Among its 63 items, mountaineers are recommended to carry a revolver and acquire a rucksack with "as many pockets as possible." This was probably good advice, as the list was a long one:

Barometer	Gloves (robust)	Revolver	Shoe wax (solid)
Buttons (spare)	Handkerchiefs (2)	Rope	Snow goggles
Candles	Knife	Rucksack with as many	Socks and stockings (spares)
Cigars	Lantern	pockets as possible	String
Clothes brush	Log book	Sackcloth	Sugar
Coffee spoons	Magnifying glass	Safety pins	Tea
Compass	Maps	Salicylic Vaseline (against lupus)	Thermometer
Crampons	Matches	Salt	Thread
Cup	Neck scarves	Scissors	Tinder stick
Elastic bands	Notepad	Scribe-compass	Tobacco
First-aid kit	Passport	Sewing needles	Tobacco tamper
Flask	Pepper	Sherbert powder	Travel guide
Food bag	Peppermints	Shirt buttons (spares)	Veils
Foot ointment	Pins	Shirt collars	Waistcoat (knitted)
Gaiters	Pipe	Shirts, woolen	Walking stick or ice axe
Gloves (light)	Raincoat	Shoe laces (spares)	Washing kit

The modern reader will be amused and maybe even amazed at some of these "essential" items. However, mountaineers in the year 2250 will probably be equally amused to find an antique iPhone with a Mammut Packing List App from 2011, which apparently allowed their ancestors to prepare and coordinate group equipment lists back in the old days.

A FIRST TIME FOR EVERYTHING
Thomas Senf | Kyzyl Asker/Kyrgyzstan

You are bound to fail at some point. I have been pretty lucky on most of my expeditions and have nearly always been able to summit. In 2004, together with Stephan Siegrist, I climbed Thalay Sagar in the Garhwal Himalaya. In 2007, again with Stef, I climbed the Arwa Tower and in 2010, I completed the first winter ascent of Torre Egger in Patagonia with Stef and Dani Arnold. However, in the fall of 2010, I traveled with Ines Papert to climb the Kyzyl Asker in Kyrgyzstan. We planned to establish a new ice line, but were forced to turn back just 200 meters from the summit, as the weather deteriorated. I was really disappointed, but I guess it's to be expected with this kind of expedition, where the chances of reaching the summit are pretty slim.

Once we had landed in Bishkek and the formalities had been dispensed with, we headed for the Kyrgyz Steppe. I felt rather uneasy about our transport, as I'd already been involved in one crash in a similar MI-8 helicopter on Elbrus. A pilot error led to us falling the final 20–30 meters before landing and I was really lucky to escape uninjured. The interior setup of Russian helicopters differs somewhat to standard flight safety regulations. Most of the space is taken up by luggage. Any passengers are squeezed in somewhere in between and the cockpit is accessible to anyone wishing to admire the wonders of Soviet technology in action.

We landed, without any problems, near the Kamarova Glacier, where we set up base camp. The weather was amazing but both Ines and Wolfgang Russegger had colds and we had to get acclimatized, as base camp was at 3,900 meters. It took two weeks before everyone was completely fit and we started climbing in ideal conditions. During a bivouac on the face, it started to snow, and following a rather uncomfortable night, where we got to savor the unpleasant sensation of snow in our sleeping bags and jackets, we decided to turn back. We were forced to wait another two weeks in the tent for it to stop snowing. Towards the end of the expedition, the weather improved and we set out again. We made good progress, but again it started to snow during the night and the next morning, the conditions were so appalling that we had no choice but to rap back down. We had run out of time. So we waited for our helicopter to arrive to take us back to Bishkek.

At the designated rendezvous, there was no sign of the helicopter, despite the clear blue skies and ideal flying conditions. The following day, there was still no helicopter. We were running out of gas and food and it was pretty cold so there was no meltwater. Reasons enough to start to see about how we would get back. Via satellite telephone, we were able to contact the travel agency, who got in touch with the German embassy. It turned out that there had been elections in Kyrgyzstan and that the newly-appointed defense minister had banned the renting of army helicopters. I have no idea where the German embassy managed to find another helicopter, but we were very glad to see it and were really grateful for their assistance. As we landed in Bishkek, smoke billowed out of the turbine, but the pilot assured us that this was normal. On expedition, even the transport can be an adventure.

"What you see as the summit
is just a step."

147   **Seneca**

WHERE THE CONDOR SOARS
Dorothée Fierz | Cordillera Blanca/Peru

Back in July 2000, I was sitting on a mountain pass at nearly 5,000 meters above sea level, gazing into the distance at the huge, white Peruvian Cordilleras and beyond to the dark blue lagoons. The direct sunlight was warming; the cold shade behind me insidious. Hidalgo, our local guide, looked up into the deep blue sky silently and expectantly. He was on the look-out for condors, the "King of the Andes". Silently and respectfully, he hummed a song in Quechua, the language of the Incas. He later confessed he was praying to the gods of the Andes to protect us on this long trek.

A few hours later – night had fallen – we were sitting in the mess tent, huddled together on rather uncomfortable camping stools. Hidalgo joined us. The cook served our dinner and the two donkey drivers, or 'arrieros' as they are known here, also pushed their way in under the tarp. Their faces were tanned by the sun and the wind, and in their big dark eyes, I could see the anticipation that tonight they would again be transported into a world they only knew of from stories, a world that seemed impossibly far away to them.

They wanted to know more about Napoleon, the rules that govern Switzerland's direct democracy and to hear about the culture and history of European countries. And that was coming from the sons of simple and mostly very poor 'campesinos'. Bit by bit,

they also started to talk about themselves, about their lack of prospects, the lack of options for professional training and further education, and their wish to exchange their knowledge and experience with guides from other countries. Cross border initiatives that have worked in the Alpine countries of Europe for decades are still just a pipedream in Peru. The huge distances and lack of financial means seem to be insurmountable obstacles. The fear of missing out on tourism developments and being overtaken one day by other mountain countries is palpable.

We pushed on through the sublime scenery of the Cordillera Blanca, day after day, like nomads, without talking, lost in our thoughts for hours at a time. The situation of the Peruvian mountain and trekking guides upset me but my hands were tied. After 18 days, our trek came to an end and I returned home to my other world, the world of politics in Switzerland.

It was May 2006 and something nobody expected suddenly happened: after 28 years in politics, I resigned overnight from my post as member of the Zurich Government Council. My diary was suddenly completely free. The initial shock was big but, luckily, I saw the impending emptiness as not so much intimidating but more as an opportunity to start something new, something com-

pletely different. Time and again, my thoughts went back to the Peruvian mountain and trekking guides and the image of those expectant, hopeful brown eyes would not leave me.

And that is how the "Cooperación Alpinista Suiza–Perú" project was founded in 2007. The Peruvian embassy in Switzerland, Swisscontact and the International Federation of Mountain Guides Associations were quick to become the founding partners of the project. Within a short time, we managed to combine forces and build new, viable links between Switzerland and Peru. Peruvian guides attended a training course in Switzerland, European instructors taught their guide colleagues in Peru and a new friendship between the two mountainous countries created completely new perspectives. The only thing missing was a major company to support the project. I made tentative enquiries at Mammut and amazingly they agreed. Suddenly, the door was opened. I now had an innovative company on board, a team that liked our project philosophy and wanted to make Peru its second partner country – after Kirghizstan. What luck!

There is no doubt that Mammut's involvement in the project, the generosity and innovative drive of such a global concern is what gave the project the push that it needed. What had previously seemed virtually impossible now seemed within reach. The Peruvian guides could believe in their future once again and were inspired by their prospects. Words were unnecessary; you could feel their gratitude. Their animated eyes said it all and reminded me of our evening mess tent talks, now 10 years ago. My commitments these days are entirely different. No more intrusive journalists, who are only interested in filling columns in their sensationalized papers, no more endless parliamentary debates about absurd political issues. I am a long way from the red carpets, black limos, high-ranking officials and lavish dinners at white clad tables. My attention is now wholly focused on the sustainable development of tourism in Peru's Cordillera Blanca.

Their anniversary celebration year sees Mammut increasing their work with the International Federation of Mountain Guides Associations (IFMGA) with a long-term project called "Roped together in solidarity" supporting Peru's official mountain and trekking guides. Unlike Kyrgyzstan, where Mammut has helped fund the training of mountain guides since 2007, the main focus in Peru is on kitting out guides with modern mountain sports equipment.

IN THE MOUNTAINS FOR MAMMUT

Karin Hörhager | **Seon/Switzerland**

Like most sports clothing and equipment brands, Mammut sponsors a team of professional athletes from different mountain sports disciplines. Stephan Siegrist, Anna Stöhr, Josh Wharton and their Pro Team colleagues are more than just ambassadors for Mammut in competitions and expeditions; they are world-class athletes, leaders and specialists in their own field, whose contributions are invaluable in developing innovative new products that capture the zeitgeist in terms of technology and trends.

Mammut's sponsorship concept is based on several different elements. There are the Teamtrips, where a selection of Mammut athletes set off together to check out new or famous climbing destinations. And then there are the Testevents, where Mammut Pros are on hand to provide help and advice to consumers. In addition, Pro Team athletes test Mammut products in the most extreme conditions and provide important feedback for their further development and improvement.

Mammut sees its athletes first and foremost as partners and expects them to behave as such. New sponsorship deals are not primarily based on good results in competitions or on media profile – athlete and sponsoring partner have to be a good character match. Of course, Mammut doesn't simply dole out sponsorship contracts because it happens to like a particular climber or mountaineer; a sponsorship decision is a business decision and requires exceptional achievements from an athlete. Yes, there is pressure to perform, but not at any cost. This is probably the best way to describe Mammut's sponsorship philosophy. It's only by making mistakes or by knowing when to turn back from the summit that we learn to develop and grow. Mammut's company philosophy is also reflected in the way it deals with its athletes. Three recent examples show that we mean what we say.

In 2008, Stephan Siegrist was planning to climb the North Face of Gasherbrum East with his friend Ueli Steck. Due to the high risk of avalanches and a bad feeling about the climb on the day of the planned summit attempt, Siegrist and five other members of the exhibition decided to turn back. Ueli Steck and two fellow climbers decided to risk it and reached the summit. It was no easy decision to abort the expedition. The Swiss journalist Röbi Koller wrote in his biography of Stephan Siegrist: "He does have a duty toward his sponsors, who provide him with financial support and equipment. They require success stories to ensure that their athlete, who is under contract to them, and their products continue to get media exposure." The fact that not all members of the expedition turned back made Siegrist's decision particularly difficult. Despite his friendship with Ueli Steck, the two mountaineers were described in the media as competitors. Siegrist immediately informed Mammut CEO Rolf Schmid of the aborted expedition and explained that he would understand if this meant that his sponsorship agreement was over. Schmid promptly reassured the athlete and told him that he should not see turning back as a failure. When Siegrist returned to Switzerland, Schmid spoke to his athlete and listened to his account of the Gasherbrum East expedition. The people at Mammut felt that Siegrist's openness, honesty and courage to be able to turn back so near to the summit spoke for themselves and turned the supposed failure into a success story for both sides of the partnership. Stephan Siegrist is still a

Josh Wharton

Anna Stöhr

Stephan Siegrist

Mammut Pro Team member. His close partnership with the company is symbolic of the relationship that Mammut maintains with its athletes.

In mid-August 2010, Mammut announced the apparently amazing success of "Skyrunner" Christian Stangl: a new record time for the ascent of K2. Several weeks later, the Austrian held a press conference to announce that he never reached the summit and that the supposed summit photo was taken 1,000 meters from the top. Mammut was quick to condemn his actions and pointed out that this kind of deception contradicts the basic principles of mountaineering. Stangl said of his actions: "Achievement and success were and are the determining factors in my sport. I think that I tried to suppress my personal failure after three summers and altogether seven attempts at this mountain." He went on to say that "fear of death is bad enough, but the fear of failure in an achievement-oriented society is worse." Despite his obvious wrongdoings, Mammut stood by the athlete. A mountaineer's previous achievements are not wiped out by one incident. Stangl was also praised for having the courage to own up to his mistakes. The future of the partnership now depends on Christian's future plans and his conduct in the mountains. "Everyone deserves a second chance," said CEO Rolf Schmid.

In March 2006, freerider and extreme skier Jean-Yves Michellod's life changed forever. The Xtreme Verbier 2004 winner was hit by an avalanche and carried 300 meters down the side of a mountain. He broke his back and has been paralyzed from the waist down ever since. It looked like his career was over. He spent nine months in rehabilitation, fighting to recover the use of his legs. He made a partial recovery, but he had to get used to the fact that he would never be able to ski normally again – both his driving pas-sion and his career were at stake. Such serious accidents naturally force sponsors to question the future of a partnership. Having said that, no sponsor would walk away from an athlete in such a situation. However, in the medium or long term, the question is a legitimate one. In Jean-Yves Michellod's case, the issue never had to be faced; being the fighter that he is, he went out and reinvented himself. He discovered skibobs and became a "parafreerider" – a freerider in a skibob. His handicap has not stopped him climbing either. In May 2009, he climbed Mont Blanc on crutches and made the first ever skibob descent of its North Face. Mammut was main sponsor to Jean-Yves Michellod for six years. Supporting an athlete through a difficult time in their life goes without saying at Mammut. "I am very thankful to Mammut for their fantastic support at a time which was not easy for me either personally or as an athlete," Michellod said in hindsight.

An athlete might turn back from the summit, make a regrettable mistake or be caught in an accident, but that doesn't mean they simply get dropped by Mammut. A company that allows its athletes and employees to make mistakes or to turn back, and that provides support at difficult times will be rewarded by greater motivation and commitment – a win-win situation for both sides. Mammut respects "being different" and supports individual solutions. Mammut believes in fairness, modesty, credibility, accountability, partnership and honesty. If there is one thing that Rolf Schmid asks for from his employees and athletes, then it is these values. As he says, "we always honor our promises."

"WE TRUST ONE ANOTHER AND SHARE A COMMON GOAL"
Röbi Koller | Bernese Oberland/Switzerland

Jacob Schmidheiny and Rolf Schmid have known each other for 15 years. During that time, they have also had a professional connection. Schmidheiny is Chairman of Conzzeta and Schmid is CEO of Mammut. TV presenter Röbi Koller wanted to find out about their work together, their views on the development of the outdoor industry and what Mammut means to them. The interview took place in January 2011, in glorious sunshine on the Niederhorn, above Beatenberg.

You are out walking together today. Do you often do that?
Rolf Schmid: No, this is a first for us.
Jacob Schmidheiny: Sadly, that's right. Although any psychologist will tell you that your best ideas come when your are out for a walk, we managers tend to operate differently. We hold meetings in darkened boardrooms and gaze at incredibly strategic looking slides projected onto the wall. (He laughs.) That is why it is great for us to be able to get out for a walk together in these kinds of surroundings for a change.

Figuratively speaking, could you compare your relationship to a climbing partnership?
Schmid: Maybe. Trust is a very important ingredient in any climbing team. That is the feeling that I got from Mr. Schmidheiny from the very beginning. Trust has to be earned, but once you have, then it is there. And you don't have to demonstrate brilliant results from the get go. When I arrived on the scene, Mammut was making heavy losses. But Mr. Schmidheiny gave me time to settle in and implement a new course of action. He spoke in terms of two, three years. That kind of attitude permeates the whole company culture.
Schmidheiny: Personally, I am not all that interested in results, rather...

...I find that hard to believe.
Schmidheiny: No, let me explain. Of course I want a successful, healthy business, one that's still going well 20 years from now. But quarterly and end of year figures are simply interim targets. It is important to keep investing. At Mammut, the emphasis is on people and development. Developing a new line of products or breaking into a new market count as running costs and affect the bottom line. In short, you get better results from doing nothing than you do by investing. But getting back to the climbing partnership, the term is unfortunately often missused. If you mean that one guy pulls the other

one up and in return looks for a reward, then that's not the kind of partnership we have. We trust one another and share a common goal. And after achieving our goal, we want to celebrate and share a meal in the mountain hut. All of these things are what make a good partnership.
Schmid: It also depends if you are on a short rope or a long one.

Does Mr. Schmidheiny give you plenty of slack?
Schmid: He does. The rope is extremely long and he very rarely pulls on it at all. I see Conzzeta as a partner standing up above, holding the rope when necessary. With that, I am referring to the financial security which makes many things possible for us. As far as selecting the route is concerned, we enjoy complete freedom. As long as we stay within the boundaries of our agreed strategy, we're left to get on with it. I feel much less restricted than many of my counterparts, whose banks are breathing down their necks all the time.
Schmidheiny: I am glad to hear you say that. He is not always that positive...

Mr. Schmid, Mammut was struggling when you came on board. Did you hesitate before embarking on such an adventure with an uncertain outcome?
Schmid: I knew there were problems. But looking in from the outside, I did not really see them. In any case, I have never been afraid of a challenge. If I had realized the scale of the problems, however, then I might have had second thoughts.
Schmidheiny: We weren't really aware of it then, either.
Schmid: That's right, it wasn't generally known. Above all, there was a lack of vision back then. But that meant there was a chance. Taking something apart and building it up again from scratch is great.

Nowadays, Mammut is more successful than ever. It has been on the up for years, to such an extent that you do have to wonder whether the market will soon be saturated and a limit will be reached. What are your views on the current situation?
Schmid: I think the outdoor movement, which has been going strong for the past 15–20 years, is only now really taking off. The outdoors helps to balance out the hectic lifestyles that people lead today, where brains are fried in meetings that are held indoors. I am convinced that, in the future, lots of people out there will want to switch off, detach themselves from their computerized, technical world and get out into nature, to think about something different and experience

a feeling of wellbeing. That is why the market is growing. Also, this is only really the case in the so-called developed markets – Europe, USA, Japan. In the next 5 to 10 years, customers in the emerging markets will be looking for the same things. So there is still huge potential for us. I am certain that the outdoor industry will experience a boom in the next 10 or 20 years.

How do you bridge the gap between your original core business – ropes and specialist climbing equipment – and your trendy outdoor products? Do they still sit well together?

Schmid: Certain trends have helped us out there. In the past, mountain sports were synonymous with red socks and wacky colored jackets.
Schmidheiny: And these days? (He points to Schmid's bright orange jacket.)
Schmid: These days we also have wacky colors, just different.
Schmidheiny: I am more of a muted colors man. I was given a selection to choose from for today's interview. I was meant to wear some ultra-bright blue jacket – what is the color called again?
Schmid: Cyan, probably.
Schmidheiny: Exactly. But I said, "No, I am not wearing that."

Back to the question. Are you not concerned that the market is getting watered down?

Schmid: No. But it is a balancing act. Distribution channels are a crucial factor. If we were to concentrate too much on cheap distribution channels and popular sports, the brand would suffer. The second important point is communication, which is how a brand comes to life. It is not simply jackets and pants that we are selling. We are selling dreams.
Schmidheiny: Most of all, we have to be believable. All the marketing in the world is of no use if nobody believes it. The quality has to be there.

Conzzeta specialises mostly in machinery. How does the Mammut sport and leisure range fit in with the holding company's portfolio?

Schmidheiny: The holding company is a real mixed bag. That is why we don't have central management – although in certain matters, we do make the most of synergies: pension funds, insurance and the like. We have individual companies that run alongside each other, but they all have to adhere to strict financial and legal rules. Each individual business deals with its own operational and strategic issues.

Over the last few years, Mammut has acquired a few brands: Ajungilak, Toko, Raichle. What is the plan in this respect?

Schmid: It is not like we have some big shopping list. I think we have a broad selection, but we now need to sell more of our current products. We would like to make use of the economy of scale; in other words to reduce costs through greater volumes. If we bought any more brands, it would result in more dispersion. In fact, we have even split with Toko to reduce complexities and to focus on a single brand and the outdoor sector.

You launched the new Eiger Extreme collection this year. Is that a nod to your roots, to alpinism and your original core business?

Schmid: 15 years ago, when we had our breakthrough, the Extreme line was very successful. But more recently, some of the top alpinists thought we were not innovative enough. The pros could not bear to look at those colors any more. We had to make the line more technical and functional. And I think that the Eiger Extreme line is just that. We also decided to offer it as a line that is very selectively distributed and not available to everyone. We have focused on just 200 shops worldwide.
Schmidheiny: I didn't know that. I am learning some amazing new things in this interview today. However, that is just our management style. I don't go spying on all the businesses to find out every detail of what they have planned.

But you do have to pay attention. People of Mr. Schmidheiny's generation are not extreme climbers, but they have a lot of money – it is a costumer segment that is constantly growing.

Schmid: That is true, but his age group does not want to look like they are already past it.
Schmidheiny: I have to say, I really like this jacket. Just like I enjoy anything that is new. Look, a big proportion of our clientele are probably right in the thick of their professional careers, and they may be quite successful, too. People like that expect us to keep trying something new. With the risk of a possible flop.

Only catering to extreme mountaineers like Stephan Siegrist would not generate enough business either, though.

Schmid: This segment gives us lots of good input, and the athletes are great image bearers. But they are too few that we could live off them alone. What is important is that these pros approve of our products and enjoy wearing them.

Schmidheiny: Let us imagine somebody is on the Eiger with a mountain guide, a down-home, reliable kind of guy. If this mountain guide has Mammut equipment and clothing then it looks really good for the brand. The same goes for piste bashers or cable car employees. They are all credible brand ambassadors.

Mammut claims that it guarantees fair production conditions and that it places great importance on environmental concerns. Is that just PR-speak or is it a real commitment?
Schmid: We have employed two people to ensure that fair wages are paid in East Asia, that no child labor is used and that the workers are free to set up unions. These two people do nothing else than address those concerns. It costs us a lot of money. As Swiss, we also enjoy a measure of credibility. By nature, the Swiss are not the type of people who exploit others, and that is how we are perceived.

Your products have to be incredibly tough and durable. At the same time, you also want your customers to buy new gear from time to time, a new jacket, for example. This conflicts with Mammut's eco commitment.
Schmid: Correct. Our materials are to a large extent made from crude oil. The biodegradable jacket has not been invented yet! It would have relatively limited use, however. Imagine if I was on Everest and my equipment started to decompose on the way up. I doubt I would be very pleased. Butt naked on the summit, just imagine that! Functionality is our number one priority.

Mammut employs disabled people. Is that also part of your social responsibility policy?
Schmidheiny: I welcome it. What I admire about Mr. Schmid and his team is that they will say "Why not?" and try something out, instead of saying we won't do this or we won't do that. We should remind ourselves more often that it is a privilege to be fit, healthy and successful.

How important is it that Mammut is based in Switzerland?
Schmid: It gives the brand great credibility. The birth of mountain sports happened here. That is an important factor. But also the many attributes that are assigned to Switzerland – quality, reliability, safety, only promising what we can deliver and not more, modesty over arrogance – all these qualities, to a large extent, represent the brand as well, and make us likeable and believable. We cannot say it is "Made in Switzerland" but we can push home our 'Swissness'. We design and develop everything in Switzerland.

On to your anniversary. The firm is celebrating its 150th anniversary. You have owned Mammut for the last 30 of those 150 years. Which were the toughest years, the biggest challenges?
Schmidheiny: I tend not to dwell on the challenges of the past but on those that lie ahead of us. The biggest challenge we face is in breaking into new markets, places where alpine sports are practised, but perhaps in a different way than they are here. We will have to be very careful if we want to establish ourselves as a big name. How should we break away from our Alpine idyll and into Asia or South America? How do we bridge the cultural divide?

Have there been any products that have flopped in recent years? Ones you had high hopes for but later realized you were on the wrong track?
Schmid: About 13 years ago, we came up with an idea of making courier bags – Messenger Bags. We called it the "Urban Trek", and I was convinced that it was the perfect addition to our range. I was in Asia at the time and had to decide how many of these bags to manufacture. I was so optimistic that I said we would order 15,000 of them. But I was completely wrong. We finally sold the last of these bags about two years ago. It was a complete flop.
Schmidheiny: I am glad we have setbacks like that. We learn the most from them. We have also decided to temporarily withdraw from making climbing shoes because we could not maintain the level of quality that we desired.

But you still make ropes, your original core product?
Schmidheiny: That is one of Mammut's attributes, the fact that we are not just focused on textiles. The ropes are part of our hardware selection – and they are not simply bought in, we make them ourselves. I clearly remember when I was considering purchasing Mammut. My father, a passionate mountain man, was on the Conzzeta board of directors at the time. There was a real twinkle in his eye when the ropes were mentioned. It did not take me long to convince him to agree to buying the business. And Mammut has been with us ever since.

Schmid: Ropes are our core product because there is no room for error in terms of quality. A rope cannot be 95% or even 99% secure; it has to be 100% secure, otherwise it will result in certain death. This is the standard that we all live by. Everything that we produce and offer for sale has to be of similar quality to our ropes.

Mr. Schmid has been at Mammut now for 15 years, which is a very long time for a CEO. Some might say it is time to replace him. But when I listen to you talk, it sounds like he will be busy until he retires.

Schmidheiny: I am hoping that they will discover gene replacement therapy in Basel so we can try it out on Mr. Schmid. (He laughs.)

In other words, you are happy with him and would like to keep on working together?

Schmidheiny: Yes, we still have a lot to achieve.

If I turn the question round, Mr. Schmid, you are now 52. Now would actually be your last opportunity to change jobs – before it gets too late.

Schmid: That is right. Everyone has thoughts like that at some stage. And there are other lucrative offers out there...

Did you hear that Mr. Schmidheiny?

Schmidheiny: Of course. I imagine he said that for my benefit.

Schmid: But the most important argument against a change is how I feel. I have to be comfortable in my job. In the last 15 years, I have managed to create an environment that I am able to mould to my liking. If I were to change jobs, it would be doubtful if the same would apply. Then there is also the fact that I strongly identify with the brand. I think of myself as Mr. Mammut.

Mr. Schmid, do you get out in the mountains?

Schmid: No. When they employed me, they were looking for a mountaineer climber, ideally a mountain guide, who had at least 20 years experience in the sports sector. Then they took me on "by mistake". Up until then, I had worked in various fields: chemicals, watches, the travel industry. But ultimately, the fact I was not a climber was good. That way, I was able to ask ignorant questions without any comeback in a company which, apart from me, only employed top alpinists. Thanks to my outsider's perspective, we were able to prevent Mammut from chasing its own tail.

Mr. Schmidheiny, back then you were on the lookout for a climber but ended up choosing someone with a background in clocks and travel. Why?

Schmidheiny: Because of the person he is. I remember our discussions clearly. In the end, the selection procedure came down to two final candidates. One was a mountain guide and would also have been a good choice. The other was Rolf Schmid, a man with no mountain experience. It was a tough choice to make because both of them were good. What I liked was his previous experience in the watch industry. I thought: this man knows about marketing and branding. We needed someone who was going to get a consumer product out there to the customer. And I had to laugh to myself because, back then, he had never made it up any mountain higher than 2,000 meters under his own steam.

Mr. Schmid, we have heard rumors that you have recently been on one or two mountains. On the Mönch, for instance?

Schmid: It is not like I despise the whole thing. Quite the opposite: the older I get, the more I enjoy it. I even like getting cold these days.

I beg your pardon? You like freezing?

Schmid: No, I like to be out in cold weather – warmly dressed. I went cross-country skiing with my son in Finland and it was minus 39 degrees. We really got to appreciate the benefits of our products.

And what was it like on the Mönch?

Schmid: Well, I didn't really want to do it. It was all planned but I realized the night before we set off, when we were in the hut, that we would be roped up in teams of three and four. I am not totally comfortable with heights and had hoped I would have a mountain guide to myself. So I said I would give it a miss. But the guides would hear nothing of it. Early the next morning, one of them woke me up and said, "Get dressed, I will be your guide, we leave shortly." So I couldn't really say no. It was ideal. The decision had been made for me and I just resigned myself to my fate. (He laughs.) And it was worth it, it was wonderful.

A 150-YEAR SUCCESS STORY

1860: The Swiss canton of Aargau removes the legal obligation to be a member of a trade guild.

1862: After having completed his three-year apprenticeship as a rope-maker in Wohlen and spending a few years as a journeyman, mainly in Germany, Kaspar Tanner starts making his own ropes in Dintikon.

1897: Oscar Tanner takes over the ropemakers from his father Kaspar.

1899: Tanner builds a roof over the ropewalk, making production independent of the weather.

1952: "Mammut Argenta" is the first ever glacier rope by Mammut to be made of nylon yarn.

1958: The "Mammut Everest", the first ever braided Mammut mountaineering rope with a kernmantel construction, celebrates its market launch.

1924: Oscar Tanner leaves the company.

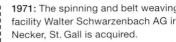

1971: The spinning and belt weaving facility Walter Schwarzenbach AG in Necker, St. Gall is acquired.

1974: A new brand is launched. "Mammut Ropes" becomes "Mammut Guarantee".

1978: Mammut presents its first Gore-Tex jackets and trousers, the "Altitude" range.

1860 · 1870 · 1880 · 1890 · 1900 · 1910 · 1920 · 1930 · 1940 · 1950 · 1960 · 1970 · 198

1874: The new Swiss Federal Constitution guarantees freedom of trade and industry.

1878: Kaspar Tanner moves to Lenzburg. He is permitted to use the public way next to his flat as a ropewalk to braid and coil his ropes.

1911: Oscar Tanner registers his rope braiding machinery as Swiss patent no. 59645.

1918: Tanner modernizes the company, invests in new machinery and oversees the construction of a new multi-storey factory.

1919: The ropemakers becomes a stock corporation. The new *Seilerwarenfabrik AG Lenzburg* now belongs to the *Schweizerische Bindfadenfabrik*.

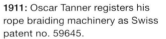

1964: "Mammut Dynamic" is the first ever single rope to be certified by the international federation representing mountaineering and climbing, the UIAA.

1968: The Heberlein Group takes over the *Seilerwarenfabrik* and renames it Arova Lenzburg AG.

1943: The Mammut brand is introduced to sell Mammut ropes. The Mammut is chosen to symbolize power and strength. *Seilerwarenfabrik AG Lenzburg* intends to set itself apart from the competition with the new brand.

1984: The company is renamed Arova-Mammut AG.

1984: In a burst of innovation, Mammut launches new soft-shell trousers, fleece jackets, thermal underwear, the A. F. harness and a new range of carabiners.

1989: Mammut acquires the rucksack specialist Fürst AG.

2000: Rolf G. Schmid becomes Mammut CEO.

2000: Mammut AG is formed and the rope and hoisting technology division is spun off as mamutec AG in 2008 to the *Seilfabrik Ullmann Group*, based in St. Gallen.

2000: Mammut purchases the North American mountain sports and outdoor specialists Climb High in order to consolidate its market position in the USA. Climb High is the largest distributor of European climbing and mountaineering equipment in the USA.

1993: Conzzeta takes over Toko AG. Production of ski wax and care products is integrated into the Mammut Group.

1987: Mammut takes over the German company *Gebrüder Kesel GmbH & Co.* in Kempten and establishes *Elite-Mammut Sportartikel GmbH* in 1988 to distribute Mammut products in Germany.

1996: Rolf G. Schmid joins Arova-Mammut AG and heads up the Sport division.

`1981` `1982` `1983` `1984` `1985` `1986` `1987` `1988` `1989` `1990` `1991` `1992` `1993` `1994` `1995` `1996` `1997` `1998` `1999` `2000`

1982: The *Zürcher Ziegeleien* (now Conzzeta) takes over Arova Lenzburg AG.

conzzeta

1999: A range of ski- and snowboarding clothing is launched.

1997: The Mammut outdoor collection is released.

1992: Mammut moves from its premises in Lenzburg to new buildings in Seon.

1992: Mammut purchases the ropemakers and braid factory Bürki AG in Oberbipp, Switzerland. *Bürki Verpackungstechnik AG* is sold off (without the ropemakers).

1981: A «Mammut collection» with clothing and sleeping bags is launched.

1994: The Mammut logo and lettering, still in use today, is launched.

1995: The "Mammut Extreme" clothing collection and the first ever range of Mammut rucksacks is introduced.

2007: Mammut Sports Group Japan Inc. takes over the distribution of Mammut products in Japan.

2007: Mammut acquires Lucido, the headlamp and torch manufacturer.

2007: The first Mammut stores are opened in Basel, Switzerland and Kempten, Germany.

2010: Toko AG is sold to the Norwegian company Swix Sport AG so that Mammut Sports Group AG can further focus on the outdoor sports market and its main brand Mammut.

2001: Mammut acquires Norwegian sleeping bag specialists Ajungilak. Two years later, Mammut relies on Ajungilak technology to present jackets and gilets with down and synthetic fiber fills as part of its collection.

2002: Mammut AG and Toko AG combine their sales and logistics activities.

2011: Mammut announces its largest investment since the company was founded. A new central warehouse is built in Germany, to be opened in 2012.

2011: Mammut becomes a bluesign member. The bluesign standard guarantees that textile products are manufactured with respect for people and the environment.

| 2001 | 2002 | 2003 | 2004 | 2005 | 2006 | 2007 | 2008 | 2009 | 2010 | 2011 | 2012 |

2003: The footwear brand Raichle is taken over from the Austrian group Kneissl & Friends. This brings the renowned Swiss mountain and trekking shoe brand back to Switzerland.

2003: Mammut AG changes its name to Mammut Sports Group AG, to which the brands Mammut, Ajungilak, Toko and Raichle belong.

2003: Mammut Sports Group Austria GmbH distributes Mammut products in Austria.

2008: Mammut founds its own mountain school, the Mammut Alpine School.

2008: Mammut UK Limited is founded to manage distribution of Mammut products in the United Kingdom.

2008: The first Mammut store in Japan opens in Tokyo.

2008: Mammut makes a commitment to social labor conditions by joining the Fair Wear Foundation. Mammut ropes are now climate neutral.

2012: Mammut Sports Group AG celebrates its 150th anniversary with the Biggest Peak Project in History.

2012: The Ride Airbag Rucksack, with the Removable Airbag System R.A.S., celebrates its market launch.

2009: Raichle is incorporated into Mammut, but lives on as an official Mammut technology label.

2006: Mammut launches the PULSE Barryvox® avalanche rescue device (LVS) with its innovative technology and user-friendly, easy operation.

2006: Mammut Sports Group Benelux BV is formed to concentrate on the Benelux countries Belgium, Luxemburg and the Netherlands.

GLOSSARY

Accessory cord: Thin, static rope made of polyamide.

AFNOR standards: Technical standards certified by the French national organization for standardization, Association française de normalisation (AFNOR).

Ascender: A mechanical device with a unidirectional blocking system, used to ascend a rope.

Avalanche cord: A historical avalanche rescue device. A long attached length of cord that was supposed to make it easier to find a person buried in an avalanche.

Belay ledge: A ledge on or at the end of a climb where a belay can be set up. Also known as a stance.

Big wall: A large cliff, which most parties will not normally be able to climb in a single day and will therefore require a bivouac.

Bolt: A point of protection permanently installed in a hole drilled into the rock.

Bolting: Setting up a new climbing route with bolts.

Bolting team: A team that bolts new routes.

Boulder out: Working out a complex sequence of moves on a climb.

Bouldering: Rope-free climbing on large boulders. Typically, this is close to the ground and protection takes the form of crash pads.

BS standards: British Standards for products.

Canyoning: Descending canyons using a variety of techniques.

Chalk: A compound used to improve grip when climbing by absorbing sweat, usually gymnastics chalk (magnesium carbonate).

Coldblack®: A new finish for textiles from Schoeller® that reduces the absorption of heat from the sun, particularly by darker colors, and produces a noticeably cooler feel.

Crash pad: A thick mat used to soften landings in the event of a fall when bouldering. Also known as a bouldering mat.

Deadman: A metal plate buried into compact snow to serve as an anchor.

Deep Water Soloing (DWS): Rope-free climbing above deep water.

Dry-tooling: Using ice tools and crampons to climb predominantly on rock.

Dyno: A dynamic move when climbing to grab a hold that would otherwise be out of reach.

E grades: A component of the British grading system, which evaluates the difficulty of climbs with leader-placed protection.

EN standards: EN technical standards certified by one of the three European Standards Organizations.

Fixed rope: A rope with a fixed attachment point, to provide protection on a steep section of ice or rock.

Free solo: Rope-free climbing without aid or protection.

Freeriding: Off-piste skiing or snowboarding.

Friends: A special mobile, spring-loaded camming device used to protect rock routes.

Haul bag: A large bag which is hauled up a cliff from stance to stance on big wall routes.

Highlining: Slacklining high above the ground.

Homeline: A slackline used at home.

Ice tools: Special ice axes used for climbing steep ice.

ISPO: International trade fair for sports and sports fashion in Munich.

Jumar: Ascending a fixed rope using two mechanical ascenders ("jumars").

Jumplining: Doing jumps on a slackline.

Lead: Climbing with rope protection from below.

Lead climber: The climber who leads the route.

Longlining: Balancing on a very long slackline.

Mantle: A climbing technique, which involves pulling on and then pushing down on a hold and then reaching up for the next one.

Micro search strips: A systematic search strategy when using an avalanche transceiver for situations involving multiple buried victims. It dramatically improves the probability of location and survival.

Mixed route: A route on rock and ice generally climbed using ice tools and crampons.

Mixed terrain: Combined sections of climbing on rock and ice.

Nut: A metal wedge threaded onto a wire, used for protection by wedging it into a crack in the rock.

On-sight: Climbing a route the first time without prior inspection or any other form of information about the route and its moves.

Pilling: The small balls of fiber or "bobbles" that form on a piece of fabric, caused by wear.

Piton: A flat or angled metal blade of steel hammered into a thin crack in the rock for protection or aid.

Prusik sling: A sling with a special Prusik knot, used for ascending a rope.

PULSE Barryvox: A type of avalanche receiver.

Quickdraw: A protection device consisting of two carabiners connected by a sewn loop of tape. Used to attach the rope to a bolt or other piece of protection. Also known as a "draw".

Rope length: The distance of a climb between the ground and the belay point or two belay points. Also known as a pitch.

Runout: An unusually long distance between two points of protection, which could lead to a potentially greater fall.

Second: The second man on the rope; following a climb when belayed by the leader.

Sérac: A large ice tower.

Seven Summits: The highest mountains of each of the seven continents.

Shit bag: A bag to contain the inevitable detritus produced during big wall ascents.

Skijöring: A winter sport from Scandinavia where a person on skis is pulled by a horse.

Skyhook: A metal hook rather like a grappling hook, used in aid climbing and for marginal protection on free climbs.

Skyrunning: Fast climbing in the high mountains.

Slacklining: A balance sport, similar to tightrope walking on nylon webbing stretched tight between two anchor points.

Slackwire: The wire used by circus artists.

Sling: Webbing tape, sewn or tied into a loop, which can be placed over a spike of rock for protection.

Sloper: A sloping hold requiring good friction and open-handed strength.

Solo: Climbing without a partner, protected or unprotected.

Speed ascent: Climbing a route in the fastest time possible.

Speleo guide: Potholing or caving guide.

The Nose: The best-known route on El Capitan in the Yosemite Valley, California.

Top rope: Climbing a route with the rope protecting from above.

Tricouni nails: Historical nailing system used for mountain boots (now replaced by crampons).

UIAA: Union Internationale des Associations d'Alpinisme (International Mountaineering and Climbing Federation).

AUTHORS AND CONTRIBUTORS

The numbers in parentheses refer to their respective contributions.

Martin Achrainer, born 1968, responsible for the Austrian Alpine Club archives in Innsbruck and co-author of a history of the German and Austrian Alpine Clubs from 1918 to 1945. (145)

Beat Aerni, born 1976, a business economist who works in marketing international companies in the medical technology sector. (44)

Betina Alexieva, a member of the Mammut Community, born 1995, lives in Sofia, Bulgaria and started climbing thanks to Mammut. She is fascinated by the fact that with Mammut, you always have to expect the unexpected. (106)

Aljaž Anderle, born 1973, member of the Mammut Pro Team Alpin and ice-climbing specialist (www.anderle.info). The Slovenian alpinist and mountain guide can be found either up in the mountains or playing with his young daughter Ajda. (54)

Esther Angst, born 1970, trained as a cartoonist and works as freelance illustrator (www.estherangst.ch). Her pictures are sold in exhibitions and she creates commissioned work. She is currently working on an illustrated book about mountaineering. (22)

Daniel Anker, born 1954 and resident in Berne, Switzerland. He is a historian, travel writer and mountaineering journalist for numerous publications. He is also employed as a critic by the Swiss library service. He has written numerous skiing, hiking and biking guides as well a large number of monographs on the largest mountains in Switzerland. (7, 17, 35, 59, 90)

Mo Anthoine (1939–1989) lived and climbed in Wales, where he set up and ran his own company Snowdon Mouldings, which manufactured climbing helmets and other equipment. In the 1970s and 1980s, he was involved in a number of expeditions, including the now legendary 1977 first ascent of the Ogre with Doug Scott, who broke both ankles on the mountain. (3)

Bernd Arnold, born 1947, lives in Hohnstein in the Elbe Sandstone Mountains of Saxony in southeastern Germany, where he has been a huge influence on the development of climbing for over 25 years (www.bergsport-arnold.de). A pioneering climber, prior to German reunification, he was responsible for numerous new routes in Eastern Germany. After reunification, he traveled to Karakoram, Patagonia, Venezuela, Madagascar, Mali, Algeria, Jordan and Yemen. He was often accompanied by his friend and companion, Kurt Albert. (115)

Dani Arnold, born 1984, a qualified polymechanic and Mammut Pro Team Alpin member. He works as a professional alpinist and mountain guide in Bürglen, Switzerland (www.daniarnold.ch). He made a name for himself through his on-sight ascents of difficult mixed routes, including the first winter ascent of the Torre Egger with Stephan Siegrist and speed ascents of the West Ridge of the Salbit and the North Face of the Eiger. (134)

Moritz Becher, born 1977, is a freelance journalist who has made a career out of his passion for mountaineering and outdoor sports. (133)

Hans Berger, born 1948, qualified first as a carpenter then as a mountain guide. He has led clients on demanding expeditions all around the world. He has been the custodian of the SAC Salbit Hut every summer for 28 years (www.salbit.ch). He lives with his family in Andermatt and Olten. (121)

Hermann Biner, born 1952, has been a mountain guide in Zermatt since 1974 and spent 18 years in mountain guide training (www.hermannbiner.ch). He is currently President of the International Federation of Mountain Guide Associations. (19)

Evelyne Binsack, born 1967, is a qualified mountain guide, explorer, motivational speaker and author (www.binsack.ch). In 2001, she was the first Swiss woman to reach the summit of Mount Everest and in 2008, she completed a 484-day expedition to the South Pole. (8, 31)

Robert Bösch, born 1954, geographer and mountain guide. He has been a freelance photographer for more than 20 years, specializing in outdoor and action sports (www.robertboesch.ch). He has visited all four continents as a climber and mountaineer, climbed Mount Everest for one project and has also documented many of Ueli Steck's extreme routes. His work was honored in 2009 with the Eiger Special Award. (76, 89)

Pascal Brönnimann, born 1976, has been in charge of sponsoring at Mammut for six years. He is responsible for all international sponsoring activities. (99, 108)

Denis Burdet, born 1971, engineer, mountain guide and Mammut Pro Team Alpin member. He is particularly interested in long routes and the adventurous aspects of expeditions (www.denisburdet.ch). He's driven by an insatiable desire to climb new routes on mountains around the world and discover (and climb in) new countries. (103)

Tim Carruthers, born 1958, has been a climber since the age of 14. He has travelled and climbed extensively in Europe, the USA and South America and has a number of hard first ascents to his name. He worked as a teacher and lecturer in modern foreign languages until 1999, when he resigned his full time teaching post to move to the mountains. Tim has translated over a dozen books, including works by Hermann Buhl, Heinrich Harrer, Anderl Heckmair and Reinhold Messner. (www.timcarruthers.com)

Daniel Corabian from the Mammut Community, born 1972, works as a network administrator in Cluj Napoca, Romania. He values the design and quality of Mammut clothing for hiking, walking and skiing. (128)

Steph Davis, born 1972, is one of America's most outstanding female climbers (www.highinfatuation.com). She was the first woman to reach the summit of Torre Egger and made the first female free ascent of the *Salathé Wall* on El Capitan. Her interests also include base jumping and free soloing, which she describes in her book "High Infatuation" (The Mountaineers Books, Seattle 2007). We would like to thank the publishers for their permission to translate and print her contribution. (78)

Johnny Dawes, born 1964, made a decisive contribution to British climbing in the 1980s and pioneered the first ascents of many E8 and E9 routes (www.johnnydawes.com). When he is not leading climbing courses or workshops, he is working on his autobiography. (12)

Tanja Delfs, born 1973, has been working for 12 years as a teacher of children with special needs in the city of St. Gall. She is active in the mountains the whole year round. (2)

Catherine Destivelle, born 1960, started climbing in Fontainebleau and became an experienced mountaineer in Chamonix. After winning several competitions in the 1980s, she went on to become one of the first ever professional female climbers (www.destivelle.com). She is particularly well-known for her solo winter ascents of the North Faces of the Eiger, Grandes Jorasses and Matterhorn. (75)

Ralf Dujmovits, born 1961, has led numerous expeditions to the Himalayas, Alaska and the Antarctic, both as a guide and as a commercial tour operator (www.amical.de). He was the first German to climb all fourteen 8,000 m peaks, some of them with his wife Gerlinde Kaltenbrunner. (31)

"Erbse", Eberhard Köpf, born in 1968, combined his passion for climbing with his love of drawing and became the comic strip artist of the German sport climbing scene. He lives with his family on a farm near Heidelberg and works as a freelance illustrator, cartoonist and cabaret artist (www.klettercomics.de). (130)

Dorothée Fierz, born 1947, was member of the governing council of the canton of Zurich until 2006. She is a passionate outdoor enthusiast who among other things runs the project "Cooperación Alpinista Suiza–Perú". (148)

Caroline Fink, born 1977, studied sociology and worked as an economics editor. She is a freelance journalist, specializing in travel and mountaineering (www.caroline-fink.ch). Her texts and images capture the things she loves most: mountain climbing and the rugged landscapes and people who inspire her. (12, 61, 139)

Dionys Frei, born 1976, is co-founder of Dedicam GmbH (www.dedicam.tv). He pilots the Dedicam radio-controlled drones and is responsible for technology, research and development at the company. (138)

Christoph Frutiger, born 1965, is a freelance cameraman with more than 20 years experience of international film projects (www.christophfrutiger.ch). (126)

Ralf Gantzhorn, born 1964, is a freelance photographer, author and geographer based in Hamburg (www.ralf-gantzhorn.de). After spending a year cycling through South America in 1985, he became fascinated by Patagonia. He has spent over three years there and climbed numerous summits, including Fitz Roy in 2007. (38)

Manuel Genswein, born 1974, has been involved in the development of avalanche receivers and avalanche search and rescue strategies for over 17 years. He has delivered training courses in over 25 countries (www.genswein.com). (51)

Hansruedi Gertsch, born 1966, is a Swiss mountain guide who lives in Grindelwald. In 1999, he was involved in the 'Eiger live' project. At this point, he had already climbed the North Face of the Eiger in both summer and winter. In particular, he has climbed the Heckmair Route more than ten times and has given up counting the number of times he has stood on the summit. (31)

Susi Good, born 1966, grew up in Mels in the canton of St. Gall. She was one of Switzerland's first female competition climbers. She lives with her husband and four children in Gams. (37)

Uwe Gottschalk, born 1973, graduated in sports science and economics and has held the post of Senior Product Manager Ropes & Electronics at Mammut since 2009. He is an active climber and mountaineer. (6)

Stephanie Grunder, born 1973, has worked as a graphic designer at Mammut since 2006. Her responsibilities include corporate design and branding. She was the project manger for this book.

Wolfgang Güllich (1961–1992) was, together with Kurt Albert, one of the driving forces behind sport climbing in the 1980s. His *Action Directe* in the Frankenjura was one of the world's first grade 11 (F9a) routes. He later put his extreme free-climbing skills to good use in the Alps and the high peaks of the Karakoram. He was also a stunt double for Sylvester Stallone in the movie "Cliffhanger". (67)

Peter Habeler, born 1942 in Mayrhofen, Austria, was considered one of Austria's best climbers even before his legendary first ascent of Mount Everest without bottled oxygen together with Reinhold Messner. For many years, he was responsible for the training of mountain guides and ski instructors in Austria and was awarded the title of Honorary Professor for his services to alpine safety (www.habeler.com). (130)

Sem Hedinger, born 1978, has worked at Mammut since 2005 in Innovation & Technology Management and Design & Development. (69)

James Heath, born 1972, works as a freelance copywriter and translator in Hamburg and the English Peak District. He specializes in mountaineering, climbing and outdoor sports. He worked on the translations for this book.

Lynn Hill, born 1961, was the first person to free climb *The Nose* on El Capitan in 1993, which shook up the rather masculine world of climbing at the time. The world's best female climber went back a year later to become the first person to free climb the entire route in 24 hours. She lives with her son and his father in Boulder (Colorado), where she runs climbing courses. She is currently working on an instructional video (www.lynnhillclimbing.com). (123)

Anke Hinrichs, born 1974, is a certified educator, has a Masters in Social Management, and works as a freelance educationalist (www.hinrichs-erlebnispaedagogik.de). She spends her free time skiing, mountaineering, climbing and traveling. (116)

Gabriela Hodel, born 1972, was Head of Marketing Communication at Mammut from 2007 to 2011. As such, she was responsible for the hugely successful Testevent campaigns, and took part in them all. (98)

Karin Hörhager, born 1976, is a geographer and communications specialist. She has been in charge of the "150 years of Mammut" project at Mammut since 2010. (48, 149)

Adrian Huber, born 1972, has worked in textiles and marketing for over 20 years. He joined Mammut in 2002. He was originally in charge of Apparel, but has since gone on to become Head of Brand and Product Development. (14, 23, 60, 65, 94, 127)

Eugen E. Hüsler, born 1944 in Zurich, has lived for more than 25 years in Upper Bavaria. A mountaineer with unlimited energy, he has also produced more than 70 travel and hiking guides and had countless articles printed in various publications. He is a via ferrata expert. (43)

Manuela Imboden from the Mammut Community, born 1973, she has a son, works in the family business and runs mountain and ultra marathons in her spare time. She is passionate about endurance sports and plans to complete the Ironman. (73)

Jeanne Immink (1853–1929) climbed grade four at the end of the 19th century. Together with her guides she made numerous first ascents in the Dolomites, climbed 4,000ers in the Valais, Switzerland, and lived an unconventional life as a single mother (www.jeanne-immink.at). The Dutch journalist and author Harry Muré has produced a fitting literary tribute to this extraordinary woman with his book "Jeanne Immink" (Tyrolia, Innsbruck 2010, available in German only). We would like to thank the publishers for their permission to reprint (and translate) an extract. (137)

Alex Johnson, born 1989, is one of the few women to climb the American boulder grade V12. She has won numerous American bouldering competitions and took first place at the 2008 World Cup in Vail. She lives in Hudson, Wisconsin. (74)

Gerlinde Kaltenbrunner, born 1970 in Austria, qualified as a nurse before going on to become one of the world's most successful female mountaineers. Between 1998 and 2010, she climbed thirteen 8,000ers (www.gerlinde-kaltenbrunner.at). She now lives with her husband Ralf Dujmovits in Bühl, in the Black Forest, Germany. (97)

Miss Kamikaze, was born in the year of the horse and has been a rock gymnast for 18 years. She is known for her unconventional antics. (40)

Reinhard Karl (1946–1982) was a great all-round alpinist and the first German mountaineer to reach the summit of Everest. As an author and photographer, he has documented his generation of climbers and others. We would like to thank his widow, Eva Altmeier for her permission to reprint (and translate) these extracts from his work. (77, 93)

Andy Kirkpatrick, born 1971, British extreme mountaineer, became famous for his second ascent of the Lafaille Route in the West Face of Aiguille du Dru, which he relates in the award-winning film "Cold Haul" (www.andy-kirkpatrick.com). In his book "Psychovertical" (Hutchinson: London 2008) he describes how he grew up in disadvantaged circumstances to become a winter mountaineering specialist and a solo climber known for his technical ascents. Reprinted by permission of The Random House Group Ltd. (63, 79)

Walter Klier, born 1955, works as a writer and painter in Innsbruck. He is an author of climbing and walking guidebooks who regularly contributes to alpine publications. He was also editor of Austrian Alpine Club Yearbook from 1995 to 2001 (www.walterklier.at). He has written a novel "Leutnant Pepi zieht in den Krieg" (Limbus, Hohenems 2008) and the anthology "Wo die wilden Hunde wohnen. Klettergeschichten aus Tirol" (Tyrolia, Innsbruck 2009). (109)

Kari Kobler, born 1955, grew up in the Rhine Valley and qualified as a mountain guide in 1985. He gained his first experiences as expedition leader at the University in Berne and has since climbed seven 8,000ers. In 2001, he founded the company Kobler & Partner, together with Ruedi Kellerhals, where he now plans and leads expeditions (www.kobler-partner.ch). (9)

Ernst Kohler, born 1963, is a qualified mountain guide and a former mountain rescue expert and Luftwaffe Group Captain. From 1999 to 2005, he was a Member of the Board of the Rega (Swiss Air-Rescue) and a member of the Rega Finance Committee. Since 2006, he has been Chairman of the Executive Board of Rega, Board Member of the *Alpine Rettung Schweiz* (ARS/Swiss Mountain Rescue Service) and Board Member of the European HEMS & Air Ambulance Committee (EHAC). (120)

Röbi Koller, born 1957, is a journalist and television presenter. He is well-known in Switzerland for his television programs "Club" and "Happy Day" (www.gespraechspartner.ch). He has published a biography of the Swiss alpinist Stephan Siegrist, "Balance zwischen Berg und Alltag" (AS Verlag, Zurich 2007). (150)

Christine Kopp, born 1967, is a freelance translator, journalist and author who lives in Berne and at Lake Como. She was editor of the mountaineering section of the "Neue Zürcher Zeitung" from 1994 to 2007 and has translated twelve books on mountaineering – including works by Erhard Loretan, Walter Bonatti and Riccardo Cassin – and produced three films. (27, 29, 111, 124)

Cédric Lachat, born 1984 and member of the Mammut Pro Team Climbing, is currently the most successful Swiss competition climber (www.cedric-lachat.com). In 2010, he won the European Championship combination ranking and became European Boulder Champion. He is based with his partner Nina Caprez in France, from where they both regularly set out to climb the hardest and most attractive routes in the world. (66)

Claudia Laggai from the Mammut Community, born 1962, works in Ottobrunn near Munich as an industrial business management assistant and enjoys walking, hiking and skiing in her spare time. She is also a passionate mountain biker and had her dreams come true in 2006 when she rode the Trans-Himalayan Route through Tibet. (10)

David Lama, born 1990, is a member of the Mammut Pro Team Climbing. As a young boy, he trained with Reinhold Scherer's junior climbing group with the Austrian Alpine Club (OeAV) in Innsbruck. When he was ten years old, he climbed his first F8a route and he climbed 8c at the age of thirteen (www.david-lama.com). Following a very successful ten-year career in competition climbing, he now concentrates on multi-pitch alpine routes, first ascents and expeditions. (71, 107)

Monika Leuthold, born 1954, was rescued after being buried in an avalanche. She wrote about her experiences in her book "Die Lawine. Ich bin drunterdrindraussen" (Verlag Claudia Wartmann Natürlich, Oberengstringen 2008). We would like to thank the publishers for their permission to reprint (and translate) a section of her work. (143)

Andres Lietha, born 1965, spent 13 years working as a mountain guide before she joined Mammut ten years ago. She now heads the Hardware division. (129)

Josef Lingg, born 1959, has worked for the Mammut Sports Group since 1993 and is a member of the Executive Board. He is the Chief Supply Chain Officer responsible for Purchasing, Logistics, Planning and Production. (36)

Kathrin Malzach, born 1980, has been a member of the Mammut Anniversary Celebrations Team since 2010. She has been working on the biggest peak project in history. (41)

Mike Marolt, born 1964, and his twin brother Steve Marolt are the only Americans to have skied down several 8,000ers (Everest, Shisha Pangma, Cho Oyu). Along with Hans Kammerlander they are also the only mountaineers to have skied down six 7,000ers. They have been on expedition to more than 40 of the highest mountains in the world. (135)

Peter Mathis, born 1961, has worked for more than 25 years as a professional photographer specializing in sport, landscapes and portraits (www.mathis-photographs.com). (113)

Nives Meroi, born 1961 in Italy, climbed more than eleven 8,000ers between 1998 and 2008. She has always climbed in small teams without bottled oxygen (www.nivesmeroi.it). Her fellow countryman and author Erri de Luca accompanied her on one of her expeditions. As a result he wrote the book "Sulla traccia di Nives" (first published by Arnoldo Mondadori Editore S.p.A., Milano 2005). Published by arrangement with Susanna Zevi Agenzia Letteraria. (47)

Reinhold Messner, born 1944 in South Tyrol, climbed countless new routes, was the first to climb all fourteen 8,000ers and has crossed sand and ice deserts on foot. He lives according to his personal philosophy that we should expose ourselves to nature without changing it (www.reinhold-messner.de). The author, speaker, mountain farmer and former Member of the European Parliament is also the founder of the Messner Mountain Museum. (18, 24, 62)

Veronika Meyer, born 1951, was the first woman from the German-speaking countries to climb the Seven Summits. Moreover, she is the only person with an artificial valve in their heart to have completed this challenge. She is a qualified chemist with a passion for the mountains, which she describes in her book "Gaias Gipfel" (Appenzeller Verlag, Herisau 2011). She lives and works in St. Gall, Switzerland. (46)

Jean-Yves Michellod, born 1976, is a mountain guide and passionate freerider. He won the Xtreme Verbier ski race and worked with Mammut for over six years. He was paralyzed from the waist down after a ski accident and is now a skibob parafreerider (www.jym-guide.com). (91)

Magnus Midtbø, born 1988 in Norway, is a member of the Mammut Pro Team Climbing and one of the most successful climbers in the world (www.magnusmidtboe.com). He has won several competitions and is one of the few climbers in the world to climb F9b on rock. (102)

Claudio Miozzari, born 1977, is a historian and works as a project leader at the Swiss Sports Museum. (58)

Sandra Monse from the Mammut Community, born 1979, comes from Hamburg and spent a long time in Africa before moving to Switzerland, where she soon became interested in the mountains and outdoor sports. She has ten years' experience working as a producer and production manager in the film industry – including mountaineering projects – and lives in Zurich. (72)

Max Niedermann, born 1927, climbed 40 new routes in the Swiss Alps in the 1950s, 1960s and 1970s. His routes are considered to be classics, for their lines and the quality of the rock. On some of his crux sections, he was climbing grade 7 (in the 1950s!). (57)

Oswald Oelz, born 1943 in Vorarlberg, Austria has taken part in numerous expeditions. He was the third person to complete the Seven Summits and has a proclivity for climbing routes in foreign countries (www.oswald-oelz.ch). As an expedition doctor, expert in high-altitude medicine and Chief Medical Director, his second passion in life is internal medicine. His latest book was published in May 2011, "Orte, die ich lebte, bevor ich starb" (AS Verlag). (28, 87, 88, 101)

Yasushi Okada, born 1973, is a mountain guide who is passionate about all forms of mountaineering (www.okadablue.ecnet.jp). He has climbed the North East Face of Teng Kangpoche (Nepal) and the East Face of Meru (India). Together with Katsutaka Yokohama, he was awarded the Golden Piton Award, the Piolet d'Or Asia and the Piolet d'Or for the first ascent of "I TO" on Mount Logan. (96)

Torbjørn C. Pedersen from the Mammut Community, born 1978, runs a logistics company from Denmark that specializes in supply and procurement in difficult environments. He has visited over 40 countries on five continents. (45)

Benedikt Pfister, born 1978, is a historian and works as a project leader at the Swiss Sports Museum. (1, 13)

Dean Polic, born 1972, is a qualified sports scientist and ambitious mountaineer. He has been responsible for Marketing at Mammut Germany for over ten years. (132)

Giovanni Quirici (1978–2011), was a member of the Mammut Pro Team Alpin, was happiest when exploring new climbing opportunities in the largest cliffs in the world (www.arium.ch). He was a qualified biologist, known to occasionally take part in scientific expeditions. In 2010, he published a philosophical novel, "Le Penseur sans pensées". In August 2011 he was killed in a tragic accident on the Eiger North Face. (85)

Claude Remy, born 1953, is an alpine historian who forms one half of the unstoppable climbing team with his brother **Yves Remy**. Since 1970, he has made more than 2,000 first ascents, many of which are now regarded as absolute classics. (26, 80, 81)

Jutta Römmelt, born 1970, has been team leader for Multimedia in the Marketing Communication department at Mammut for three years. She is interested in skiing, mountaineering, climbing and mountain biking. (84, 112)

Reto Rüegger, born 1963 in Switzerland, is a qualified gymnastics and sports instructor who has been active in the outdoor trade for over 25 years. He is Senior Product Manager Footwear at Mammut. (4, 56)

Bernhard Russi, born 1948, was one of the world's best downhill skiers in the 1970s (www.bernhardrussi.ch). He won Olympic Gold and Silver, was world champion twice and won the Downhill World Cup Overall Classification. (39)

Katharina Saurwein, born 1987, studied Health & Performance Sport in Innsbruck. 'Katha' is an accomplished international climber and boulderer who won the 2008 Rockmaster competition (www.katharina-saurwein.com). She is a member of the Innsbruck Team, which is sponsored by Mammut. She was a member of the Mammut Pro Team from 2004 to 2010. (25)

Fritz Schäfer, born 1981, is since 2 years Product Manager Climbing Equipment at Mammut. (125)

Martin Scheel, born 1960, was one of the leading pioneers of alpine sport climbing. He went on to become a paragliding instructor and coached the Swiss National Paraglider Team. Since 1998, he has run a marketing agency in Chur, Switzerland. For more information, visit www.azoom.ch. (33)

Rolf Schmid, born 1959, is Chief Executive Officer of the Mammut Sports Group. He is an economist who joined Mammut in 1995, with no specific mountaineering experience, from the watch making and travel industry. Today, he is known as "Mister Mammut". (150)

Thomas Schmid, born 1987, has been a member of the Mammut Pro Team Climbing since 2005. He is currently also completing a business management internship at Mammut (www.schmid-climbing.ch). (66)

Jacob Schmidheiny, born 1943, is Chairman of the Board of Directors of the Mammut Sports Group and President of the Board of Directors of the Conzzeta AG, the Swiss holding company that owns Mammut. He purchased the company Arova-Mammut over 30 years ago. (150)

Harald Schreiber, born 1983, is responsible for Public Relations at Mammut and gets onto rock and snow as often as possible. (11, 30, 104, 117)

Pit Schubert, born 1935 in Breslau, studied mechanical engineering. In 1968, as an active climber and mountaineer, he helped found the DAV Safety Commission, which he led until 2000. He was particularly involved in accident research, evaluation, prevention and the testing and standardization of climbing and mountaineering equipment. He has written numerous books on this topic. (131)

The **Swiss Foundation for Alpine Research (SSAF)** was set up in 1939 in Zurich by members of the SAC to collect information on mountain areas and alpine expeditions, conduct scientific research and publish topographic maps (www.alpine-research.ch). It organized the 1956 expedition responsible for the first ascent of the Lhotse and the second and third ascents of Mount Everest. We would like to thank Adelheid Warring for her friendly support and the foundation for its permission to reproduce original documents. (82)

Lucius Annaeus Seneca (approx. 4 BCE – 65 CE), known as Seneca the Younger, was a Roman statesman, naturalist and philosopher, who along with Cicero was one of the most important Roman poets. His tragedies and dialogues are concerned with proper conduct and behavior and teaching people how to live the free and contented life of the wise man. (147)

Thomas Senf, born 1981, grew up in Leipzig and studied mechanical engineering in Dresden. During a successful internship at Mammut, he became a passionate mountaineer. In 2002, he moved to Switzerland to become a mountain guide. Apart from climbing big mountain faces of the world, he is also a professional photographer who specializes in alpine photography (www.thomassenf.ch). He continues to work with Mammut as well as for the outdoor photo agency Visual Impact. (146)

Nadja Sharman, born in Canada in 1973 to an Austrian mother and English father, works as a translator for the outdoor and mountain sports trade from her home in the English Lake District. She worked on the translations for this book.

Stephan Siegrist, born 1972, has worked with Mammut for over 15 years and is a member of the Mammut Pro Team Alpin. He is a talented all-round climber whose major achievements include three new routes on the North Face of the Eiger, the first winter ascent of Cerro Torre and Torre Egger in Patagonia and the first ascent of Thalay Sagar and the North Face of the Arwa Tower in the Himalayas (www.stephan-siegrist.ch). He is a professional climber and an enthusiastic highliner and base jumper. He lives with his family in Ringgenberg, Switzerland. (31, 70, 83, 118)

Joe Simpson, born 1960, studied English and Philosophy before devoting himself to the mountains and writing. "Touching the Void", his dramatic portrayal of his ordeal on the Siula Grande, is one of the most successful mountaineering books of all time. He lives and works near Sheffield and in Ireland (www.noordinaryjoe.co.uk). (141)

Karin Steinbach Tarnutzer, born 1966, grew up in Munich and was out in the mountains from an early age. As a literary and communications expert, she has worked together with numerous alpinists at publishing houses in Munich and Zurich. She now lives and works as freelance journalist, author and lector in St. Gall, Switzerland. (15, 20, 22, 37, 46, 49, 57, 68, 74, 82, 89, 95, 96, 100, 136, 146)

Robert Steiner, born 1976, received widespread acclaim for his first novel "Selig, wer in Träumen stirbt" (Panico Alpinverlag, Köngen 2009), where he describes his serious accident on the North Face of the Grandes Jorasses. A passionate mountaineer and author of numerous books, he also teaches German and Geography at a high school in Memmingen, Germany. (32, 83, 114, 140)

Alexandra Steiner-Paholik, born 1981, comes from Kirgistan and has been involved in the Kyrgyzstan Mountain Project since 2007. (50, 119)

Anna Stöhr, born 1988, studied Health & Performance Sport at the University of Innsbruck. She is an athlete with the Austrian army and a member of the Mammut Pro Team Climbing (www.anna-stoehr.at). Anna is a successful competition boulderer, who won the Rockmaster competition in Arco on two occasions. She was the overall World Cup winner in 2008 and 2011, European Champion in 2010 and World Champion in 2007 and 2011. (95)

Hirotaka Takeuchi, born 1971, is Japan's most successful mountaineer. He has already climbed twelve of the fourteen 8,000ers and plans to complete the two remaining summits (weblog.hochi.co.jp/takeuchi). He lives with his wife and two children in Tokyo. (100)

Mark Twain (1835–1919), whose real name was Samuel Langhorne Clemens, was the American writer famous in particular for his books about the adventures of Tom Sawyer and Huckleberry Finn. He also wrote several humorous and ironic reports about his travels in Europe including "A Tramp Abroad". (105)

Thomas Ulrich, born 1967, mountain guide, photographer and cameraman, has made a name for himself working with extreme sportsmen and women (www.thomasulrich.com). He specializes in adventure, marketing and action photography. His recent projects have taken him from the highest mountains of the world to the ice deserts of the Artic. (55)

Marco Volken, born 1965, lives in Zurich. He is a freelance photographer and author of several illustrated books, non-fictional works and guidebooks (www.marcovolken.ch). He works for various publications and takes on commercial and marketing commissions. (42, 52)

Albert Wenk, born 1944, held various positions during the 36 years he has worked at Mammut. He also served 10 years as the SAC delegate to the UIAA Safety Commission in a voluntary capacity. (5, 142)

Josh Wharton, born 1979, is one of the most versatile rock and ice climbers in America. He has worked with Mammut since 2004. He made the first ascent of the "The Flame" and the South Ridge of the Great Trango Tower in Pakistan and has been successful in Patagonia and Alaska. He also won the 2009 Ouray Mixed Climbing Competition. When not climbing or on an expedition, he lives in Estes Park in Colorado. (110)

Stefan Winiger, born in 1969, is a gourmet chef who dedicates his time to delighting the palate and the eye. He enjoys being able to pamper people with his cuisine on a daily basis. (www.kulinariker.ch)

Pesche Wüthrich, born 1964, is a trained civil engineering draughtsman who has spent the last 13 years in Ticino in Switzerland. He has the Rockshop climbing shop in Ponte Brolla and his own climbing school (www.bigwall.ch) where he runs training courses for Mammut. He is as passionate as ever about climbing new routes. (64)

Monica Wyss-Läubli, born 1962, is a qualified kindergarten teacher, adventure instructor, ornithologist and enthusiastic campfire and kitchen cook. She values the physical and spiritual aspects of being out in nature (www.mond-feuer.ch, www.feueressen.ch). (53)

Heinz Zak, born 1958 in Austria, is a climbing photographer who has documented many of Alexander Huber's extreme routes and often climbs extreme routes himself. In 2005, he became the second person, after Wolfgang Güllich, to free solo the roof crack "Separate Reality" in the Yosemite Valley. He is also credited with bringing slacklining from America to Europe (www.heinzzak.com). (144)

Emil Zopfi, born 1943, is a passionate mountaineer and sport climber, who lives as a freelance writer in Zurich (www.zopfi.ch). He has received numerous awards for his children's books, radio plays, novels, short stories, mountain monographs and detective novels, including the King Albert I Mountain Award. (16, 21, 34, 86, 92, 122)

PICTURE CREDITS

In cases where it has proved impossible to ascertain or contact the copyright holder, the publisher requests that the holder provides this information. The numbers refer to their respective contributions.

Abbreviations: **t** top, **m** middle, **b** bottom, **l** left, **r** right

Alpenverein-Museum des Oesterreichischen Alpenvereins, Foto: WEST Fotostudio Wörgl (Tyrol): 145
Esther Angst, Mitlödi: 22
Ski archives Daniel Anker, Berne: (4x)
Daniel Anker/Marco Volken, Bietschhorn – Erbe der Alpinisten, AS Verlag, Zurich: 35 l
Daniel Anker/Marco Volken, Monte Rosa – Königin der Alpen, AS Verlag, Zurich: 29 l
Toni Arbones, Siurana: 103 r
Archives Bernd Arnold, Hohnstein: 115 (2x)
Ruedi Baumann: 148 (5x)
Hans Berger, Andermatt und Olten: 121 l
Robert Bösch, Oberägeri: Cover, 7, 19 r, 31 (3x), 33, 35 (Panorama), 39, 42 l, 53 (2x), 64, 76 (2x), 84 mt, mb, 86, 87, 89 (3x), 98 (4x), 121 r, 134 (3x), 149 r
Denis Burdet, Neuchâtel: 103 l
Archives Evelyne Binsack, Innertkirchen: 8
Daniel Corabian, Romania: 128 r
Hermann Biner, Zermatt: 19 l
Laurent de Senarclens, Blonay: 102
Jolanda Flubacher Derungs, Sebastian Derungs, Zurich: 14 (5x)
Archiv des Deutschen Alpenvereins, Munich: 137 r
Rainer Eder, Baar: 3, 12 (3x), 34, 58 rt (2x), 75, 83 (2x), 95 rb, 99 (4x), 108 (4x), 126 b, 128 l, 138 r (2x)

Erbse, Eberhard Köpf, Helmstadt-Bargen: 130
Reinhard Fichtinger, Innsbruck: 25 (2x), 124, 149 m
Caroline Fink, Zurich: 61 m, r, 136 r, 139 (9x)
Hermann Froidl, Munich: 133
Rob Frost, USA: 71
Christoph Frutiger, Interlaken: 126 t, 138 l
Ralf Gantzhorn, Hamburg: 38 (3x)
Urban Golob, Ljubljana: 20, 54
Chris Goplerud, Colorado: 110 (2x)
A. Greppin, Schweizerisches Alpines Museum, Berne: 61 lt, rt
Jansci Hadik, Verbier: 91 l, mb
Archives Anke Hinrichs: 116 (5x)
Kazuya Hiraide, Japan: 100 l
Ruedi Homberger, Arosa: 26 rb
Karl-Heinz Hug, Barberêche: 21 m
Eugen E. Hüsler, Dietramszell: 43 (2x)
Miss Kamikaze: 40
Archives Reinhard Karl, Heidelberg: 77 (4x)
Kurt Keinrath: 56
Brian Kimball: 78
Archives Andy Kirkpatrick: 63 (4x)
Archives Walter Klier, Innsbruck: 109 (3x)
Kari Kobler, Berne: 9
Vladimir Komissarov, Bishkek: 50 (2x)
Christine Kopp, Muri und Pasturo: 28, 111 (2x)
Klaus Kranebitter, Aldrans: 95 rt
Oliver Lang, Lenzburg: 36
Archives Mammut, Seon: 1 (3x), 13 (2x), 30, 37, 48, 58 l, rb, 65 (4x), 69 (11x), 73, 94, 104, 117, 119, 129, 142
Christoph Margot, Choëx: 91 mt
Steve Marolt, Colorado: 135 (2x)
Peter Mathis, Hohenems: 6, 51 (2x), 113, 143
Archives Messner Mountain Museum, Bozen: 18
Kenro Nakajima, Japan: 100 r
Archives Max Niedermann, Hagenbuch: 57
Jiří Novák, Kladno: 35 r
Archives Oswald Oelz, Wernetshausen: 101

Archives Torbjørn C. Pedersen, Denmark: 45
Albert Precht, Bischofshofen: 88
Christophe Racat, Les Diablerets: 5 m
Archives Rega: 120
Kurt Reichenbach, RDB, SI: 21 r
Archives Remy: 5 rb, 80
Claude Remy, Vers-l'Eglise: 5 l, rm
Yves Remy, Vevey: 5 rt
Claude & Yves Remy, Gastlosen, Charlet, Lausanne: 26 rm
Corey Rich, South Lake Tahoe: 107 (3x)
Patrick Rohner, Zurich: 4 (2x)
Jutta Römmelt, Unterentfelden: 112 (3x)
Stefan Schlumpf, Felsberg: 2, 10 (8x), 67, 72 (2x), 84 l, lm, r, 95 lt, lb, 125, 127 (6x), 150 (6x)
Bernd Schmid, haricot-vert, Pfronten: 132
Schweizerische Stiftung für Alpine Forschung, Zurich: 82 (8x)
Thomas Senf, Ringgenberg: 24, 29 r, 47, 60 (2x), 70 (2x), 131, 146, 147
Simon Starkl, Zurich: 6 lt, lb
Archives Stephan Siegrist, Ringgenberg: 118
Karin Steinbach Tarnutzer, St. Gall: 15, 16, 49 (5x), 68 (6x), 136 l
Archives Robert Steiner, Aitrach: 32 (3x), 114 (2x), 140 (2x)
Thomas Ulrich, Interlaken: 55 (3x), 149 l
Ignacio Vidal, Spain: 21 m
Marco Volken, Zurich: 52 (3x), 92 (2x)
Marco Volken, Badile – Kathedrale aus Granit, AS Verlag, Zurich: 26 lb, lm, 42 m, r
Webguerillas GmbH, Munich: 41
Erhard Wendenbaum, Séchilienne: 85
Werke Theodor Wundt: 137 l
Edward Whymper, Matterhorn – Der lange Weg auf den Gipfel, AS Verlag, Zurich: 17 (3x)
Katsutaka Yokoyama, Japan: 96, 97
Heinz Zak, Scharnitz: 144 (2x)

ACHIM WEGST · ADRIAN HUBER · ADRIAN RUHSTALLER · ADRIAN SCHMID · AGNES HACKI · ALBERT GASSER · ALBERT
WENK · ALCIDA ROMAN · ALESSANDRO ACCOGLI · ALEXANDER MÜLLER · ALEXANDER WYSS · ALEXANDRA STEINER
PAHOLIK · ALEXANDRE JACQUOD · ALFONS PFENNINGER · ALINA LYTVYNENKO · ALMUT WEISSBRICH · AMELI RÅSTRÖ
ANAÏS KELLER · ANDREA ECKERT · ANDREA MEERHOLZ · ANDREA MÜLLER-HOFSTETTER · ANDREA BRUN · ANDRE
ORTELLI · ANDREAS ALLEMANN · ANDREAS FISCHER · ANDREAS SAXER · ANDRES LIETHA · ANDREW HOLT · ANDY
RODRIGUEZ HERRERA · ANGELIKA STAAB · ANGELO CHIEFFO · ANGELO DE NISCO · ANITA ANDRESEN · ANITA KOPP-DUN
ANJA EGGERIKSEN · ANTONELLA ESPOSITO · ANTONIO CAMBEIRO · ARIJANA HIDIC · ARNE TSCHUGG · ARNO WÜR
ATSUSHI SAITO · AUGUSTIN HÖRLER · AYHAN KÖSEOGLU · AYSE ÖZKAN · BARBARA BIECHTELER · BARBARA EBERHAR
BARBARA GALATI · BARBARA GLOOR · BARBARA GRAF · BARBARA HÄUPTLI-GERBER · BARBARA STREBE
BARBARA WEGMANN · BEA RENGGLI · BEAT BRUN · BEAT KOHLER · BEAT ZENTNER · BENDICHT LIECHTI · BENN
REICHARD · BERND HEFELE · BERND SCHATULL · BERND WODARZ · BERNHARD BOLLIGER · BERNY ACKERMAN
BETTINA DAMBACH · BETTINA SCHNEIDER · BETTINA STÄHLI · BETTINA WEBER-STEINER · BIANCA STEINER · BIRG
FÜLLGRAFF · BIRGIT SCHIELE · BRIAN LAROCQUE · BRIGITTE BRUNNER-KELLER · BRUNO HUGENTOBLER · CANS
KÖSEOGLU · CARMEN HAFNER · CARMEN LEDERLE-KÖHLER · CAROLINE SEPP · CAROLINE STEGER-SCHLÜSSE
CARSTEN VAN BIRCKHAHN · CATHERINE HEGNAUER · CHRISTIAN BINDER · CHRISTIAN BOMAN · CHRISTIAN BRA
CHRISTIAN GISI · CHRISTIAN HALLER · CHRISTIAN HÄRIG · CHRISTIAN KELLER · CHRISTIAN LOCHER · CHRISTIA
PRANG · CHRISTIAN ROHR · CHRISTIAN STALDER · CHRISTINE SOHM · CHRISTOPHER ROBERTS · CLAUDIA GESE
CLAUDIA HÄCHLER · CLAUDIA REHBEIN · CLAUDIA ROOS · CLAUDINE HOFER · CLAUDIO RÜEDI · CLAUDIO STALLON
CORDELIA MÜLLER · CORINA FISCHBACHER · CORINA ZANETTI · CORNELIA EBERT · DALE RANDALL · DANI
HAGEL · DANIEL RÖLLI · DANIEL SEYMOUR · DANIEL SIEGENTHALER · DANIEL STEINER · DANIELA ARBTE
DANIELA HUG · DANIELA SCHÜRMANN · DANILA MAZZEI · DAVE ESCOTT · DAVID FURMAN · DAVID HILFIKE
DAVID KOCH · DEAN POLIC · DECIO VIVOLO · DENISE FANKHAUSER · DENISE KÖFLER-GOUMAZ · DIEGO TROXLE
DIETMAR KEUSCHNIG · DIMITRI ISLER · DIRK HELLWIG · DOMENIC BUSCHOR · DOMINIK RYSER · DORIS EN
HOLENSTEIN · DRAGAN MARJANOVIC · EDGAR FALLER · EDITH CADENA-MICHEL · EDWARD SMITH · ERIC NICHO
ERIC SIEFER · ERIKA WELTI · ERNST LÜTHI · ERNST SCHWEBLE · ESTHER DOPPMANN · EVELYNE BLASER · EVELYN
DUMONT · FABIAN BAUMLI · FABIAN HÜRZELER · FABIO PANNOFINO · FADILA KERANOVIC · FELICE GARRAFFO · FEL
HEMUND · FELIX KÜNDIG · FLAVIANO MEDICI · FLORENCE CHRISTINAT · FLORIAN LENZ · FRANCO GALATI · FRAN
HÖPTNER · FRANK PEDERSEN · FRANK STEINHAUSER · FRANK TROMMER · FRANZ SIGL · FRANZ WIDMER · FRANZISK
BITTERLI · FRANZISKA GEHRIG-KNEUSS · FRANZISKA RÜNZI · FRANZISKA STINER · FRITZ SCHÄFER · FUATA HERZO
GABI GRATWOHL-GUERINI · GABRIELA HODEL · GEIR ARNE HJELVIK · GESA WILMS · GILLES CANDEL · GIUSEPP
CHIORAZZO · GREG CONNOR · GREGOR HIRNER · GRIBBIN LORING · GÜLSÜM CEKER-KARA · HAKI BEDZETI · HANN
WEBER · HANS AMBÜHL · HARALD SCHREIBER · HARRY SONDEREGGER · HARUMI NISHIO · HEDWIG RAUBER-JOH
HEIDI DAL CERE · HEIDI TRUNZ · HEIKE GEWEHR · HEINRICH WEBER · HEINZ GESKE · HEINZ KOLLY · HEINZ WEBE
HELENA DIGLIO · HELENE FLORIO · HELMUT GAWLIK · HELMUT WINKLER · HERBERT WIBLISHAUSER · HERT
SCHREINER · IBRAIM MUSTAFI · IGNAZ BRUNNER · INGRID HURTER · INGRID STAHL · INGVILL BEATE PETTERSE
IRFAN TÜRKEKUL · IRIS STAUDECKER · ISABELL HÜBNER · ITALO SORICELLI · JACQUELINE MÜLLER-SEEHOLZE
JANA PEINELT · JANICK TIREZ · JANINE ZEMP · JASMINE DUCRET · JASMINE STAUB · JASON BRISSON · JEANET
BREGENZER · JEANETTE STRUB · JEANNETTE SANDMEIER · JESSICA WIELAND · JO FLOSBACH · JOAKIM OPSA
JOANNA TOMASINO · JOCHEN WEBER · JODI SNELLING · JOHANN RITTER · JOHN HONG · JOHN DAG GRIMSEN · JO
FORRER · JOSÉ ANTONIO LOURENCO · JOSEF LINGG · JUDITH GLÜCK · JUDITH KOHLER-SETZ · JUDITH SCHM
JULIA EBENHOCH · JULIA LÖFFLER · JUMPEI MOCHIZUKI · JÜRG WEBER · JÜRGEN LEGUTTKY · JÜRGEN SCHÜT
JUTTA RÖMMELT · KARIN ANDRASCHKO · KARIN ECKE · KARIN HÖRHAGER · KARIN LASANCE · KARIN SOLAN
KARINA DIMMELER · KARINA WALZ · KATALIN DOZSA · KATHARINA HAAS · KATHARINA HABERMANN · KATHARIN
SCHERER · KATHARINA WALZ · KATHRIN MALZACH · KATRIN FREY · KAZUYUKI KITAJIMA · KEITH SYKES · KERST
GUBLER-IMHOF · KEVIN THOMPSON · KEVIN WEY · KIM OLIVER GAYK · KOUROSH BARGHI · LADISLAV MAŠEK · L
GITTERMANN · LARS PASCHEK · LAURA FRIESENEGGER · LAURA TERESA WELLIGE · LEO CARREZ · LORENZA EGLOF